D1297722

History of Bigotry in the United States

HISTORY
OF
BIGOTRY
IN THE
UNITED
STATES

BY GUSTAVUS MYERS

Edited and Revised by

HENRY M. CHRISTMAN

CAPRICORN BOOKS · NEW YORK

TABLE OF CONTENTS

iii

vi

PREFACE TO THE ORIGINAL EDITION

This work was conceived in 1925 but, as is evident, many years were to elapse before I was enabled finally to proceed to its completion.[1] In first proposing it, my effort was to enlist the support of a committee of religious leaders or of a nonsectarian committee under the auspices of which such a book, in view of its special nature, would reflect opposition to all kinds of bigotry as well as attest absence of any partisan aim.

In the case of all of my books the sole point animating me was the need, as I saw it, of writing them, whatever their immediate or ultimate fate. Judged by mounting interest, time has borne me out. Year after year I continued my research and adherence to the work, hoping that somehow I eventually would be able to present the published book.

This, as is here obvious, is not one of those academic issues of tolerance and intolerance, but a realistic narrative of the origins and course of bigotry in the United States. When this book was originally planned and for some years later, no doubt many opposed to bigotry looked upon it as spasmodic, having its occasional flashes and then seeming to subside, and in nowise significant or affrighting. But this sanguine attitude has been shattered by fearfully tragic events in great parts of Europe and elsewhere, with repercussions here, and the subject has become of instructive timeliness.

Committees composed of broadminded men of all faiths have been formed to combat bigotry. This can be done most effectively by a full knowledge of the facts. To understand the phenomena of the present, it is vital to grasp the past with which there is the closest interrelation. Precedents in forming inherited notions, legends and prejudices are, as unfortunately seen herein, the precursors of terrific outbreaks or bigotry. Cloaked over as this may appear at times, it is none the less a fateful undercurrent. A period may come when it is used with powerful and ghastly effect, as in Hitlerized

---

[1] Gustavus Myers died on December 7, 1942, three months after he had completed the manuscript of *History of Bigotry in the United States.*—Ed.

Germany and subjugated countries, not only against the people of one religion, but the spirit of persecution has there been extended to all religions and to religion itself.

With its Constitutional guarantees of full religious freedom and the right of anybody to believe or not as his convictions dictate, this Republic of the United States of America is the last place, it may be thought, where bigotry should have recurred as formidable movements. Yet here are the authentic facts. Over and under fixed organic principles bigotry has persisted, and each movement has left its sinister traces. The impetus often goes back to Colonial years, and was only a reflex of conditions in Europe. Of course, far beyond that time bigotry had its sway in the ancient world, references to which are made in the following chapters. Unhappily bigotry remains constant, its victims varying from time to time, but in essence continuing the same. There came intermissions which are only deceptive, for thus far the facts show the smoldering distorted views of a mass of people blindly ready to follow a leader as often as the propitious occasion presents itself.

By means of a grant of Fellowship (in the year 1941 and again in 1942) the John Simon Guggenheim Memorial Foundation provided me with the necessary means to write this book. Consistent with the standards of the founders of this organization, it was done without any question being asked as to contents or treatment, or any restriction whatever upon the fullest freedom of expression. In establishing the Foundation, in 1925, Senator Simon Guggenheim, announced that he and Mrs. Guggenheim desired through such a medium to add to the country's educational, literary and scientific achievements. This manifestly could only be done by according to writers absolute liberty in their work, and such, I am glad to add my tribute, has been the steadfast policy of the Board of Trustees, the Committee of Selection and of Henry Allen Moe, Secretary-General of the John Simon Guggenheim Memorial Foundation.

Gustavus Myers

New York
September, 1942

EDITOR'S PREFACE TO THE REVISED EDITION

The late Gustavus Myers (1872-1942) devoted his life to the intensive study and analysis of American life. In addition to this volume, his works include *The History of the Great American Fortunes, The History of Tammany Hall,* and nine other books.

The general outline of *The History of Bigotry in the United States* was first conceived by Mr. Myers in 1925, but it was not until 1942 that he was able to complete the manuscript. Of all his books, *The History of Bigotry in the United States* received the most enthusiastic reception; the original edition went through four printings shortly after publication. Tragically, Mr. Myers did not live to see this; he died but three months after delivering the manuscript to the publisher.

My responsibility has been both to amplify and to condense—the former by the addition of three new chapters which cover the years from 1942 to 1960, and thus bring the book up to date; and the latter by the deletion of four early chapters dealing chiefly with European history in a very general sense. My intention throughout has been to adapt this classic work for the contemporary reader.

A word of caution to the reader: this book requires careful reading. Just because an individual is mentioned does not imply that he is adjudged a bigot. There are some persons prominently mentioned who were for a time guilty of poor judgment, but who certainly were not bigots. Henry Ford and Charles A. Lindbergh fall into this category.

Finally, I might say that this book shows the pattern and interrelationship of the various kinds of bigotry in the United States; and that is its only purpose. It is not presented to praise or to discredit any group, any area or any individual. As Gustavus Myers defined his outlook: "In the case of all of my books the sole point animating me was the need, as I saw it, of writing them, whatever their immediate or ultimate fate." In bringing the book into print in a new and revised edition, I have been guided by the same precept.

New York   *Henry M. Christman*
August, 1960

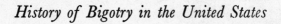

History of Bigotry in the United States

CHAPTER I

THE INFUSION BEGINS

FROM era to era political, social and economic institutions may be altered or undergo great transformations. The pace of invention may and does effect vast changes in the social structure. Deceived by these things, fresh generations are tempted to pride themselves on living in an order radically removed from what has gone before. Nevertheless, side by side with all of the progress in other directions, some very ancient attributes persist. One of the most tenacious is bigotry, often having its roots of prejudice far in the past, and, with malignant longevity, able to renew itself from generation to generation. In this particular sphere the past is, not always but too frequently, the present. While seemingly unrelated to prior times, successive outbreaks of bigotry in America have been, in a large sense, the results of inheritance of ideas and courses originating long ago. To elucidate this most important fact, it is requisite to begin with the past, particularly the influences acting upon America in early days, and thence, by regular process, to the surges of bigotry manifested in later and modern times.

Settlers of America came into a new domain, but they brought with them Old World ideas of proscription by force of which the established religion or creed aimed to enforce its code of doctrines and assure its supremacy. Prejudices are one of those human frailties prevalent in all ages, evil enough even when confined to individual and private habit, in causing misunderstandings and misjudgments. But breaking loose in mass movements they may and do lead to sinister if not dire results. When, as a further step, they are taken over by the mighty arm of government and put into punitive law, they become instrumentalities of systematic persecution intensifying its course by calumny of its victims. Religious controversies, commotions and conflicts rife in the epoch wit-

3

nessing settlement of America generated the fiercest passions and prejudices. These were translated to the New World which, in this respect, was infected by the frenzy of the Old. In the period of America's original settlement much of its territory, needless to say, was both a cultural and political dependency of England, and what was not, such as New Netherland, soon became so. Dominant English methods in legislating on religious matters were authoritative, and if some colonies, according to which creed controlled, differed from others in application, the general spirit was that prevalent in England. That spirit was one of rampant persecution.

In view of this potent fact a report made in 1666, by a set of functionaries entitled the King's Commissioners, was a strange document. They had been sent from London to investigate Massachusetts and other colonies. The most marked feature of their report to the Lords of Council for Trade and Plantations was its condemnation of Puritans. More than ever these were hated by the English governing, ecclesiastical and aristocratic classes, often interconnected. The Puritan claim of representing purity in orthodox religion—hence their name—and their disdain for the state religion in operation drew upon them vituperation and persecution. Puritans denounced the pomp of church edifices and ceremonials and the sumptuous mode of prelates, some of whom lived in almost regal style. For Puritans, as well as other non-conformists, to hold in matters of faith a doctrine of their own was in itself a crime. Following the lines of previous religions in power in various ages, the whole weight of law after the establishment of the Church of England by Henry VIII was to compel uniformity of belief and church ritual; not the slightest deviation from the ordained doctrine was permitted.

The controlling classes in England had special grudges against the Puritans at this time. Monarchy, under Charles II, had been restored; Puritans were additionally in obloquy as adherers of the Cromwell regime, and those in Massachusetts still persisted in terming their land a Commonwealth. Finally, the Massachusetts Puritans were accused of seizing upon every occasion to pronounce their independence, at least in local affairs, of English interference.

Obviously, therefore, the King's Commissioners' report had not a single good word to say of the Puritans. Among other inimical findings the report characterized the Puritan way of worship as "rude," and related how, in the zeal for their faith, they "persecute all other forms." The report construed persecution as a product typical of fanatical Puritans and exclusive to them. "Puritans," the report complained, "have put many Quakers to death, of other Provinces . . . First, they banished them as Quakers upon pain of death, and then executed them for returning. They have beaten some to jelly and been (in other ways) exceedingly cruel to others . . ." And now to fix hypocrisy upon the Puritans the report added the innuendo: "They yet pray constantly for their brethren in England . . ."[1]

But, of course, the King's Commissioners could not have been unaware of the fact that Quakers were proscribed and persecuted in other American colonies which only copied procedure in England itself. The Pilgrims of Plymouth Colony had enacted an anti-Quaker law in 1658: "No Quaker Rantor or any other such corrupt person shall be admitted to be a freeman of this Corporation," and likewise "all manifest opposers of the true worship of God."[2] In thus stigmatizing Quakers as corrupt, pecuniary corruption was not meant. To such excesses was religious contention carried in that age, and on such fine shades and often fantastic points, that anyone holding a different opinion was sequentially corrupt in doctrine. And this kind of ascribed corruption was regarded with far more seriousness than financial or even moral corruption. This did not engender animosity and violence as did doctrinal disputes.

For an example of a bitter anti-Quaker colony not in the remotest degree subject to Puritan influence Virginia will serve. There the Church of England, under the sway of the distant Bishop of London, was the ruling power and party, and, for a long time, no other creed was tolerated. The terrors of a drastic law "for suppressing them" confronted Quakers either fleeing from England or consigned by the courts to transportation. For each Quaker brought into Virginia a vessel's captain was amenable to a penalty of £100. All Quakers contriving to enter were imprisoned without

---

[1] *Documents Relating to the Colonial History of the State of New York,* *London Documents,* Vol. 3, p. 111.

[2] *Records of Plymouth Colony: Laws, 1623-1682,* Vol. 5, p. 177. However, by a law of July 7, 1681, Quakers who were old inhabitants of Sandwich were allowed some voting and other rights "so long as they carry civilly and not abuse their liberty." Ibid., Vol. 6, p. 71.

bail until some responsible person gave surety for their quitting the colony. If they returned they were to be proceeded against as contemners of the law and the magistracy. Should they come back a third time, they were to be prosecuted as felons. Under the penalty of £100 sterling, all persons were prohibited from housing them, or permitting Quaker assemblies in or near their houses. And no person was permitted to dispose of or publish any books or pamphlets containing the tenets of the Quaker religion.[3] This outlawing of Quakers was only a prelude to a time when, in Virginia, Baptists were proscribed and sometimes beaten.

For years London officials kept prodding Puritans regarding persecution of Quakers for their religion. The pretence herein made was that in England nobody was proceeded against for religion's sake but for violations of the laws. When, on October 2, 1678, the General Court or Legislature of Massachusetts replied, it accordingly retorted in kind. When Quakers first arrived, the report set forth, they were "insolent and contemptuous toward authority." They "publicly disseminated and insinuated their damnable opinions and heterodoxies." Above all, they "transgressed Puritan laws and some were put to death." And now came a reminder to the English Government of the fate in England of "Jesuits and seminary priests put to death in the time of Queen Elizabeth and King James." The General Court could not assume that those men were executed for religion; they "suffered death justly for their breach and contempt of his majesty's laws."[4]

This device of justification was of ancient heritage. Instead of avowing the real cause, that of difference of religious outlook, violation of laws made to prohibit and punish differences was declared the explicit and valid ground for inflicting penalties. In the infancy of Christianity, Emperors of Rome, expressing their own antagonism as well as that of the pagan priestcraft and their following, used this as their pretext for virulent persecutions. Refusal to accept mythological gods made Christians appear a peculiar, obstinate and dangerous sect. From this it was but a step to inhibiting

[3] William Waller Hening's legal treatise in Preface to his compilation *Collection of the Laws of Virginia*, written in 1809 and published in 1823.
[4] *The Records of the Colony of Massachusetts Bay in New England*, Vol. 5, pp. 198-199.

in law their meetings as conspiracies fraught with peril to the State, and then, in the name of laws disregarded, putting Christians to torture or death. And when well after the middle of the second century A.D., Christians had grown in strength and influence and were viewed by the Roman rulers as both a political and religious problem, the same laws were invoked during the reign of even the great philosopher-Emperor Marcus Aurelius to sanction a particularly cruel persecution of the Christians.

The English code of laws converting religious beliefs diverging from the established creed into crimes only followed and accompanied decrees and laws in various other European countries. Physical plagues came and went, yet this kind of contagion was widespread, continuous and lasting. But it is with conditions in England that we are concerned, since those formed the background of the American colonists in general. Nominally or altruistically it may be supposed that those who have suffered the pangs of persecution would naturally wish to spare others the experience of the same calamity. But when persecution is persistent, overlapping many generations, it becomes to accustomed peoples the expected and normal thing and settles into a commonplace. Inasmuch as for centuries the course of the English governmental action was a series of proscriptives and persecutions, populations grew up under these familiar processes. They accepted them all the more because the clergy told them that it was the will of God to exterminate creatures of the Devil. Each new group of dissenters knew what they had to encounter, but this knowledge neither disconcerted nor deterred them. They expected full measure of reprisals from the ruling powers comprising the established Church, united in interest and purpose with the State. Continually the body of laws was expanded to include every kind of manifestation of lack of conformity with the Church in control, and this was true of the Catholic Church as well as the subsequently introduced Church of England. Thus was built up in law a formidable list of offences, all held crimes of the first magnitude.

Heresy was the affrighting term long made to cover any kind of nonconformity to doctrine or ritual. While this charge was rigorously applied at the behest of ecclesiasticism, it was no less a convenient political tool of the State machine

to rid itself of opponents by an easy stroke, and it was also
a handy weapon of personal malice. Among the English Parliament's earliest statutes were laws dealing with heresy; under a long surviving law, enacted in the year 1400, heretics
were to be imprisoned by the Diocesan—under the authority
of the bishop—and on relapse to be burned at the stake.[5] This
was a customary mode of execution for certain other crimes
as well as for heresy, and ordered for women as well as for
men. The burning of women alive was derived from Norman
practice which quartered—disemboweled and cut into four
pieces—men and (for reasons of delicacy!) burned women.[6]
Joan of Arc, as we well know, was burned at the stake for
heresy.

After Henry VIII established the Church of England, laws
against heresy were still being passed and also in Queen Elizabeth's reign. William Tyndale, an English reformer, had
committed the grievous, unpardonable crime of making his
own translation of the Bible. At the instance of Henry VIII
he was arrested, strangled and his body burned at the stake.
Some men who had the hardihood to sell his Bible were likewise put to death. Among victims of the heresy accusation
was a number of Anabaptists burned at the stake in London
and outlying places in 1535 and in later years. In six years
alone at this time twenty-three persons were burned for
heresy, and some more under Henry's successor.

The conventional idea of a mob is that of a rabble. But the
street mobs which hooted at heretics and pelted them were
no different in spirit from the bigoted aristocratic and clerical
mobs that looked upon a burning at the stake as an edifying
spectacle either to be relished or not missed. A description
of the burning in 1539 of one Forest, an Observant Friar,
was written by a contemporary. At the place of execution in
Smithfield there was "a great scaffold on which sat the nobles
of the realm and the king's majesty's most honorable coun-

---

[5] *The Statutes at Large, Great Britain's Parliament* (2 Henry IV cap. 15)
Vol. 1, p. 404.
[6] The formal sentence passed upon a woman thus doomed was that she
was "to be drawn upon a hurdle to the place of execution and there to be
burnt with fire till she is dead." As late as 1790 this judgment of burning was
still given in courts, but no English sheriff, although liable under an old law
to prosecution for failure, would enforce it. See *The Parliamentary History
of England*, Vol. 28, pp. 782-783, motion, May 10, 1790, to repeal the ancient
law.

cil. . . . There was also prepared a pulpit, where a Right Reverend Father in God, and a renowned and famous clerk, the Bishop of Winchester, called Hugh Latimer, declared to him [Forest] his errors but such was his frowardness that he would neither hear nor speak." Forest was hanged by the middle of his body and armpits in chains and upon the gallows were set ribald verses. When the fire was lit under the gallows the mob, commoners and betters, jeered at a fellow human being writhing in torture.[7]

A century later burnings at the stake were still in malignant operation. There had come into being the Unitarians, a new religious denomination. They believed in one God, the Father, and could not and would not accede to the orthodox doctrine of a Trinity of Father, Son and the Holy Spirit. They accepted Christ as a divinely appointed teacher to be followed, not worshipped. Their advent caused the greatest excitement among the ecclesiastical set; to them, treason itself was not a greater crime than to deny the sacredness of their tenets and teachings. Were this to be countenanced the stability of true religion would be undermined. Peebles, founder of the Unitarians, was long and viciously persecuted, and at various times before the year 1641, four persons professing Unitarianism were burned at the stake.

From the time the denomination was founded in England, in 1646, by George Fox, the mild, humane, pacific Quakers or Society of Friends had undergone persecution. In the list of their convictions was objection to taking or administering oaths, and opposition to war in all its forms. Such beliefs were viewed by entrenched officialdom, clericalism and public sentiment as those of deranged extremists. In derision, the name Quaker was applied because of their quaking motions and tremulous mode of delivery. Fox was frequently imprisoned and his followers put under the stigma of severe laws.

In the austerity of their life, their adverse, somber attitude toward self-indulgent pleasures and diversions, Puritans and Quakers had much in common. Puritans in Massachusetts felt that they had reasons for proceeding against

[7] This account was reproduced in Luke Owen Pike, M.A.'s *A History of Crime in England,* London, 1873, Vol. 2, pp. 53-54. Pike made an exhaustive research into crimes of all kinds as defined by law in past centuries and he included the imputed crime of heresy and the outcome.

Quakers. With difficulty Puritans had settled a wilderness to be able to follow their own faith without interference or intrusion. To bar other faiths was the regulative measure of the age. The habit of Quaker zealots in taking every opportunity to urge the authorities to tremble before the Lord was a provoking personal circumstance, giving Puritans plausible ground for accusing Quakers of insolence and ranting. Quaker opposition to war grated upon Puritans who were frequently at war with Indians. From this came a peculiar grievance against Quakers but of a kind by no means unfamiliar in human history. Often persecutors have sought self-extenuation and the beclouding of their deeds by accusing the persecuted of responsibility for existing evils. Among the causes of God's having "commissioned the barbarous heathen"—the Indians—to rise against Puritans, the General Court of Massachusetts gave this as reason No. 5: "For suffering the Quakers to dwell among them and to set up their thresholds by God's thresholds, contrary to their old laws and resolutions." [8] At this time there were but few tolerated Quakers in Massachusetts and their tenure was highly precarious.

The one aim of English officialdom in its accounts of the American colonies at this period was to discredit the Puritan Colony of Massachusetts as the prime perpetrator of bigotry. While it was doing this, it was continuing in England the persecutions of Quakers and other dissenters, and loading them with discriminations. The grant of territory in America to William Penn—Pennsylvania was named after him—by Charles II, in 1681, did not signify any abatement of persecution. Penn, in 1668, had become a Quaker preacher. Following the publication of an essay by him, he was imprisoned in the Tower of London for seven months. Despairing of any cessation of raging persecution, he sought a haven for Quakers in the New World. He had inherited from his father a claim for $80,000 against the Government which, in settlement, gave him the grant.

[8] Edward Randolph's *Report to the Council of Trade*, 1676. See *Documents Relative to the Colonial History of the State of New York, London Documents*, Vol. 3, p. 243. Randolph did not take the sanctimonious reasons given by the Puritans seriously. He pointed out that notwithstanding an old law imposing a fine of £10 for every gun, and £5 for every pound of powder sold to Indians, the Massachusetts Government, in 1657, allowed licensed fur traders to sell them to Indians.

Only a few years after the King's Commissioners had reported on the persecution of Quakers by Puritans, a rigorous law against Quakers was passed by Parliament. Laws of a general scope already existed to invoke against dissenters. But this act (13 and 14 Charles II, Cap. 1 Clause 2) was specific to Quakers. It prohibited them from assembling under "pretence of religious worship"; it heavily penalized them for refusing to take an oath; and for the third offence they had to "abjure the realm"—leave England—or be transported. Many were thus ruthlessly shipped off to America, where they were faced with repressions already noted. Not until almost the advent of the eighteenth century, during the reign of William and Mary, was toleration accorded to Quakers, but it was the merest sufferance. At about the very time when this boasted toleration was extended, Parliament passed several acts against Quakers. They were not allowed to vote for members of Parliament, nor to give evidence in criminal cases, serve on juries or hold offices of profit. Until 1739 they could not be admitted as attorneys.

These English laws and the hostility underlying them were more or less duplicated in some of the American colonies. Although in the southern part of New Jersey there was a settlement of Quakers, the majority creed there disfranchised them, and only after hard agitation did Quakers in that colony secure, in 1713, the right to vote. Even after they obtained the same right in New York, in 1735, discriminations in law against them remained. There they were fined £10 for each act of solemnizing marriage according to their own rites. This led them, on July 4, 1760, to petition for the removal of a penalty which cast reflection upon their faith and was so humiliating to their religious principles.[9]

[9] *The Documentary History of the State of New York,* by E. B. O'Callaghan, Vol. 3, pp. 605-606.

Chapter II

THE STRIFE OF CREEDS

ENGAGED in contention among themselves, the various Protestant sects in American colonies sought in common the suppression of Catholics; and Protestant and Catholics alike desired the elimination of Freethinkers.

The characteristic of that long-drawn age was the effort of religious authority to stifle iconoclastic thought. Arrogating to itself all rightness, each creed condemned other creeds as wrong. None could prove that it was the sole repository of truth, yet each maintained that position. And to make it inviolate, the force of law was stretched to its utmost against anyone voicing skepticism or challenge of the cardinal tenets of the established creed. With all the execration implicit in it, the hard epithet "blasphemer" was applied. Often blasphemy was made synonymous with atheism. This is not supposition. Embedded in laws of the time we find the attitude and atmosphere, and dry as such search may seem, it yields results which do not stand upon the slippery ground of assumption or inference. If a particular law was transient, soon to be wiped out, it would now convey no special significance. But when we find a series of laws, all to the same end and extending over large stretches of time, then we can accept them as a sure depiction of the processes of that time.

However they might be deprived of it, every one of the creeds insisted upon its full right to differ from the others, but none allowed the same right to the disbeliever. Unbelief need not go to the length of denying God. It might object to the special interpretation of God. Or it might do little more than balk at accepting the claims made in the name of God, the forms with which religion invested itself, and the utter restraint on all criticism. All of this was branded as the crime of blasphemy. In the era of America's settlement

12

the impetus was already given by the mother-country's stern laws against blasphemy, and the settlers took over that course as a necessity of upholding ordained religion and the sanctity of its dogmas. After the induction of the Church of England, legislation in England fixed blasphemy as denial of the Trinity, denial of the truth of the Christian religion, or denial of the Divine source of the Scriptures. To the convicted offender severe punishment was meted.

In American Colonies laws pertaining to blasphemy were framed consonant to the beliefs of the dominant creed. Usually creed and government were interfused. This was duplicating the condition in European countries with their union of Church and State. But in such a place as Massachusetts the announced aim was not so much that of material policy as it was the utilization of the whole power of government to usher in a heavenly state on earth. This proclamation by the General Court went forth on May 6, 1646: "The right form of church government being a good part of the kingdom of Christ upon earth, the settling and establishment thereof by the joint and public agreement and consent of churches and by the sanction of civil authority, must needs greatly conduce to the honor and glory of our Lord Jesus Christ." [1] In these appalling times when great parts of the world are under subjugation by dictators and racked by war's desolations, we are unavoidably tempted to look back with either wonderment or envy at the leaders of a people who could entertain such a dream. But this observation is departing from the point at issue. To question any essential of the instituted religion was considered equally an attack upon government itself.

The terrors of a Massachusetts Colony law of November, 1646, were speedily decreed. Among the species of vanity we have never been disposed to include that of devout worship. But the phraseology of this law seems to signify somewhat as much an aim to enforce reverence to elect worshippers as design to shield the props of religion itself. Not only was any person of Christian upbringing and age of discretion who denied the Scriptures to be the word of God declared a blasphemer; anyone who refused to acknowledge its wor-

[1] *The Records of the Colony of Massachusetts Bay in New England*, Vol. 3, p. 711.

ship by "illuminated Christians" was also pronounced the same. And in both cases, if there was obstinacy after conviction, death was to be the punishment.[2]

In the preamble of their law of May 27, 1652, Puritan legislators seem to have found reason to declare: "The Holy Scriptures of the Old and New Testament being written by the prophets, apostles and holy men of God, inspired by the Holy Ghost, containing in them the infallible and whole will of God which he purposed to make known to mankind," therefore penalties for refusal to assent to the same were ordered. Any person more than sixteen years old, professing the Christian religion, who by word or writing denied any of the books of the Old or New Testament "to be the written and infallible word of God" should be arrested. Then he was to be committed, without bail, to prison, and held for trial. Unless he publicly recanted after conviction, he was to pay a fine not exceeding £50 or "be openly and severely whipt by the executioner, not more than forty strokes." And if, after recantation, he persisted in "maintaining his wicked opinion" he was to be banished or put to death, as the court should judge.[3]

Presently, in Massachusetts, came another stroke to fetter expression. A law forbade any publication except upon approval by two censors. That opposition manifested itself is indicated by the law's repeal in the next year. But, with enlargements, the law was restored to the statutes, on October 19, 1664. The fact that only in the town of Cambridge, the seat of Harvard College, was any printing press now allowed perhaps tends to show the source of the previous objection. A succession of ministers filled the post of censors, and with punctilious rigor did they discharge their duties. For instance, the Rev. Thomas Thatcher and Rev. Increase Mather officiated as censors in 1674, and at a later time Rev. James Alin was appointed a censor after the death of Rev. John Oxenbridge.[4] No word which in the slightest degree reflected upon church, creed or government was allowed to creep into print. Yet, at the same time, these ministers made great professions of concern for liberty of conscience which did not go beyond the kind *they* wanted. Thus, in 1687, Increase Mather, now President of Harvard College, was delegated by the New England ministers to convey a vote of thanks to James II for his declaration of liberty of conscience.

Legislators in Massachusetts as elsewhere seemed confirmed in the simple belief that a law once made had miraculous power to bring about a change in human behavior. And each time that law failed to do so they emitted great surprise. So, on October 15, 1679, came a wail from the Assembly of Massachusetts. Conditions tending to "irreligion and atheism," it deplored, existed. The remedy now adopted was to confer magisterial powers upon titheingmen—functionaries who collected a tithe or levy for church support. They were ordered "diligently" to inspect the course or practice of any suspected person, and had power to punish by fine or imprisonment.[5] In the view of this law inattention to "religious duties" was irreligion, the breeder of atheism. This law had an eighteen years' trial, and then came another law. Therein, blasphemy was definitely termed atheism when the Divine authority of both Old and New Testament was denied. At the judge's discretion the offender could be variously punished. He could be put in the pillory, set upon the gallows with a rope around his neck, whipped, his tongue bored with a red-hot iron, or he could be imprisoned for six months.[6]

The early Maryland blasphemy law, enacted by Catholics, was on a par with the Puritan. Founded by the Catholic Lord Baltimore as a refuge for persecuted English Catholics, Maryland nevertheless soon sheltered a population three-fourths of which were Presbyterians, Anabaptists and Quakers. For the reason that such and other different sects were allowed, the Maryland of that time has long been extolled for its religious tolerance. Judged by conditions in many other places, there was considerable, but by no means complete, tolerance. Unitarians and Jews were banned. The scope of a Maryland act of 1649 throws edifying light upon the multifarious wrangling sects, to stop the recriminations of which was the purpose of this law. It ordered fining, whipping or imprison-

[5] Ibid., Vol. 5, pp. 240-241.
[6] *The Acts and Resolves, Public and Private, of the Province of Massachusetts,* Vol. 1, p. 297.

ment or the alternative of the public supplication of forgiveness to "persons reproaching any other within the province by the name or denomination of Heretic, Schismatic, Idolator, Puritan, Independent, Presbyterian, Popish priest, Lutheran, Calvinist, Anabaptist, Brownist, Antinomian, Round-Head, Separatist, or by any other name or term, in a reproachful manner relating to the subject of religion."

But toward Freethinkers or Protestant critics of Catholic tenets there was no tolerance whatever. The Maryland blasphemy act of 1649 was sweeping. For anyone denying "our Savior Jesus Christ to be the sonne of God," the penalty was death or confiscation of property to inure to the Lord Proprietary—Baltimore—or his heirs. And "anyone using or uttering reproachful words or speeches concerning the blessed Virgin Mary, the Mother of our Savior, or the Holy Apostles or Evangelists" was, for the first offence, to forfeit £5 sterling to the Lord Proprietary or his heirs.

With Cromwell's coming into power in England, "Popish Councillors" in Maryland were ousted, and a Protestant Assembly disqualified Catholics. The Province was later restored to Lord Baltimore and a proclamation against Quakers was issued. In 1685 James II commanded that all offices in Maryland be put in the hands of Protestants. Now came a studied endeavor to make the Catholic priesthood in Maryland odious as responsible for prevailing licentiousness. To deepen the opprobrium, the Catholic clergy was accused of fastening such evils for a particular invidious design. In a report, on May 27, 1697, to the Board of Trade at London, Governor Francis Nicholson of Maryland set forth how men and women there freely indulged in bigamy and other crimes "too much practiced and seldom punished." He went on: "I suppose the Jesuits and Priests were willing to have a very loose Government, both in Church and State, that they might bring the people to be Atheists, in order to make them Papists." [7]

Came now the familiar tactics of the religious party in power effacing legislation decreed by its expelled predecessor. What had been a crime now became a virtue. No longer did anyone expose himself to punishment by remarks of any kind

---

[7] *Maryland Archives*, Vol. 23, p. 81. After Lord Baltimore's return to London, Nicholson noted, fines were seldom collected.

regarding the Virgin Mary and other Catholic fundamentals. Rather he proved himself in good standing as a worthy Protestant. We could pause to moralize on the follies of shifting law, at one time condemning as criminal things which at another time were viewed differently. But not musing upon that subject, the matter at hand is Protestant Maryland law of 1699. This prescribed blasphemy as denial of Christ to be the son of God, or denial of the Holy Trinity. Heavy and cruel were the penalties provided. Boring through the tongue and a fine of £20 sterling for the first offence. If unable to pay, or having no goods, lands or dwellings upon which to levy, the offender was to be kept in prison for six months. For the second offence the letter B was to be branded in the man's or woman's forehead, and the alternative of £40 sterling fine or a year's imprisonment. Conviction for the third offence was punishable by death and confiscation of property.[8] Whether mutilation or execution was actually consummated in Maryland or elsewhere is not determinable from accessible documentary records.

The civil disqualifications of such a law as Virginia's, enacted in April, 1699, were of a nature to arouse the apprehensive self-interest of the upper classes. In the case of laws involving criminal penalties, judges, if so disposed, could select the lesser punishment. But there was no such latitude where law specifically ordered civil disabilities. If the verdict was that of conviction they had to be applied. In substance, Virginia's law was patterned after the English blasphemy law of 1668. This, amplifying previous laws, extended the provisions to the civil realm. A convicted person was divested of all right to hold any office whatever. Upon a second conviction he was debarred from suing, pleading, serving as a guardian, executor or administrator, nor could he receive any legacy or gift, or hold any office, civil or military.[9]

[8] Ibid., Vol. 15, p. 154.
[9] *The Statutes at Large, Great Britain's Parliament*, Vol. 3, p. 689. As for British laws ordering criminal proceedings for blasphemy, statutes remained well into the twentieth century. In the nineteenth century, prosecutions, although intermittent, still went on. This led *The Spectator* of London, on April 28, 1883, to comment upon the anomaly. The last prosecution was in 1917, 1920 and 1921 against a man named Gott who was thrice imprisoned. When, in 1930, the matter of the repeal of the blasphemy laws came before the House of Commons, those laws were denounced as archaic, and so far behind modern thought as to provoke contempt. A Laborite member pointed out that such skilful writers as H. G. Wells, Bertrand Russell, Aldous Huxley

Remonstrating that laws hitherto made had not checked persons "who avow their horrid and atheistic principles, greatly tending to the dishonor of Almighty God," the Virginia law made the provisions applicable to any person brought up in the Christian religion who expressed: Denial of the being of a god or the Holy Trinity; asserted there were more gods than one; declined to recognize the truth of the Christian religion; and refused to acknowledge the Divine authority of the Old and New Testaments. For his first offence, the culprit was disqualified from holding any office, ecclesiastical, civil or military. If he did hold an office he was to be removed. Repetition of the offence brought barring from the right to bring any suit, and he was not allowed to be a guardian or an executor, or to take any gift or legacy. Finally he was to be imprisoned for three years. In the hands of opponents or enemies, making real or trumped-up charges, these provisions could be invoked to make much trouble. However, the same law obligingly proffered a way of escape. If, within six months, the convicted person renounced his opinions, he was to be relieved of all penalties.[10]

The tenor of the Pennsylvania law of November 27, 1700, was precautionary. Entitled "Law Concerning Liberty of Conscience," this act allowed enjoyment of religious freedom to all who believed in God. But "to the end that looseness, irreligion and atheism may not creep in under pretence of conscience," Bible reading or devotional worship on Sunday were, as stated in a previous chapter, made compulsory.[11]

We shall now relevantly turn to consideration of the privileged and powerful ministerial groups which long and systematically extended their pressure toward molding thought, law and custom. Side by side with their benign professions of piety, many in these groups had a large and commanding share in fostering and inflaming bigotry.

could have their say about the Christian religion, but a poor man expressing the same points of view more bluntly and candidly was liable to fine and imprisonment.
[10] Hening's *Collection of Laws of Virginia*, Vol. 3, pp. 168-169.
[11] *The Statutes at Large of Pennsylvania, 1682 to 1801*, Vol. 2, pp. 3 and 4.

CHAPTER III

THEOCRACY COMES OVER

FOR a considerable time Massachusetts and Connecticut were dominated by a theocracy, and where this was absent in other colonies, there was a strong theocratic trend. In no sense was it a pure theocracy or system whereby the organization of government was held to be under God's direct rulership and full authority exercised by the clergy in His name. Nevertheless it was as nearly a theocracy, or in other colonies, a quasi-theocracy, as circumstances allowed. Over the colonies was rule by the royal government and its appointed officials, but in matters of local legislation the ministerial forces controlled. Often ministers themselves would occupy important public offices, but much more frequently these were filled variously by church wardens, elders or vestrymen who took their orders from ministers, or at any rate made law and its administration conform to the established creed.

Theocracy was an institution which flourished in many an ancient country. Venerating, as they did, the Old Testament equally with the New, the Puritans could find in the books of Moses and the Prophets ample warrant, as they believed, for instituting theocratic sway. But they, as well as some other sects, had before them recent examples in the doctrines and projects of John Calvin and John Knox, both austere religious zealots, and both of whom sought to implant, the one in Geneva, the other in Scotland, their idea of a theocratic Christianity. Whether a short-lived chartered company like the Virginia Company, first settling Virginia, was essentially mercantile, or fervently religious like the Puritan New England Company, the declared aim was that of concern in propagating the Gospel. As a matter of fact, this was, then and later, the favorite claim made to give a religious character to settlement enterprises, whether in the wilds of North or

South America or of Africa. Ordinarily the minister's and priest's place was one of high importance. But it was then made doubly so as a carrier of the Gospel in new countries; and in New England especially, where the scheme was to create a celestial condition, ministers were exalted as supreme. In one, they were chosen spokesmen for God, regulators of the religious, moral and social life of the settlers, and missionaries among the Indians.

This, at least, was the view expressed by the Governor and associates of the New England Company, in their first General Letter sent from Gravesend, April 17, 1629. "We have been careful to make plentiful provision of godly ministers, by whose faithful preaching, godly conversation and exemplary life, we trust, not only those of our own nation will be built up in the knowledge of God, but also the Indians in God's appointed time to be reduced to the obedience of the Gospel of Christ." Ministers were instructed to bend all effort in having their persons reverenced; otherwise their doctrines would not be well valued. By setting a leading example and by "commanding" all others to do likewise, "due honor" would be bestowed upon the ministers.[1]

The theocracy, however, soon encountered an outspoken uncompromising opponent in Roger Williams. A Puritan by conversion, he was pastor in Salem when he announced his radical tenets. Churches, he propounded, should exclude magistrates from membership; he denied the right of magistrates to punish anybody for Sabbath breaking and for alleged heretical opinions; and he disapproved of other assumed powers and required practices. Above all, his proposition of complete separation of Church and State, leaving to the individual conscience voluntary choice of religion, was considered abominably subversive by the theocratic rulers who, on October 19, 1635, issued a decree of banishment. He left and founded Rhode Island, but meanwhile another objector came forward to denounce many of the doctrines held as immutable truths. Mrs. Anne Hutchinson's opposition was not against the structure of the institutions; she attacked the ideas underlying dogmas and law. The law, or the preaching of it, she contended, was of no use at all to drive a man

[1] *The Records of the Colony of Massachusetts Bay in New England,* Vol. 1, p. 386.

to Christ; no Christian must be pressed to duties of holiness; a man was united to Christ only by the work of the Spirit upon him. Many more were the points in her thesis which the ministerial body condemned as a vicious assault upon divinely ordained precepts. The retaliation visited upon her was to make her life exasperatingly uncomfortable, and then banish her.

The ministry proceeded to encase their persons, livings and callings in a series of protective laws. But, be it remarked, Puritans were not the first in America to do this. More than twenty years before Puritan action, Virginia had passed a law, that of 1623-1624, substantially repeated in 1632, making disparagement of any minister a crime if done "without sufficient proof of justification." Why this proviso? According to Henry Hammond, an English clergyman and voluminous writer of that time, "Virginia savoring not handsomely in England, very few good gospel ministers of good conversation would adventure thither . . . yet many came as wore black coats, and could babble in a pulpit, roar in a tavern, exact from their parishioners, and rather by their dissoluteness destroy than feed their flocks." [2] Such statements could be taken with extreme reserve, were they not confirmed by the fact that Virginia, facing scandalous conditions, found it necessary, in February, 1631, to pass a law beginning: "Ministers shall not give themselves to excess in drinking, or riot, spending their time idly by day or night, playing at dice, cards or any other unlawful game, but at all times convenient they shall hear or read somewhat of the Holy Scriptures," and more to the like effect. Poor settlers were more discreet in their remarks about the parsons than the landed gentry who often openly expressed ridicule. Preachers continuously had to refrain from saying anything against the vices of the rich and important vestrymen who had power of displacing any minister and taking away his livelihood. Instances of such action, without a charge made or even a reason assigned, were numerous. [3] However, the Virginia ministry, as a whole, proved itself well able to get laws to shield and entrench itself. It was not easy to get witnesses to appear against a min-

[2] *Leah and Rachel,* published in London, in 1656 and cited in Force's *Historical Tracts.*
[3] Francis L. Hawks' *Contributions to the Ecclesiastical History of the United States of America,* 1836, Vol. 1, p. 91.

ister, and with formal proof lacking, the disparager was liable to a fine of 500 pounds of tobacco and to ask the minister "so wronged" forgiveness in the congregation.[4]

To make the slightest criticism, whether of doctrine, deportment or in any other way was, by the Massachusetts colony law of 1646, a disparagement of the minister's "holy office." For the first offence the miscreant was to be reproved publicly by the magistrate and bound to good behavior; the like "contemptuous carriages" a second time brought a £5 fine or standing exposed on a block with a paper, "A Wanton Gospeller," fixed on his breast.[5] These and other silencing laws operated to make people close-mouthed and, if some did choose to drop a few critical remarks, wary of informers. Yet despite pressure of laws, there were some daring spirits refusing to be affrighted and gagged, and taking delight in coming forth boldly. We find record, in 1646, of heavy fines imposed upon Dr. Robert Child and sundry others for utterances construed as "slandering the people of God."[6] Turning to Plymouth Colony we find a number of convictions, but not many from 1652 to 1685. For meeting at William Allen's house at Sandwich and "inveighing against ministers and magistrates to the dishonor of God and contempt of Government," Nicholas Upsiall, in 1657, was ordered out of the colony, and other participants were imprisoned until their fines were paid.[7] At various times subsequently Josiah Palmer was convicted and fined for speaking contemptuously of the ministry; Christopher Gifford for doing the same against "the dispensers of the word of God"; Elizabeth Snow for using "railing expressions to the Rev. Samuel Treat."[8]

The inflexible endeavor of ministers to exact reverence for themselves went on in a number of other colonies and long continued. Previous to referring to a typical case in New York, the fact bears mentioning here that, in September, 1693, Governor Fletcher of that Province urged the Assembly to give him a monopoly of appointing ministers. But his purpose was not the ostensible one of "the settling of an able

[4] Hening's *Collection of Laws of Virginia*, Vol. 1, pp. 123-124.
[5] *The Records of the Colony of Massachusetts Bay in New England*, Vol. 1, p. 386.
[6] Ibid., p. 179.
[7] *Plymouth Colony Records: Court Orders*, Vol. 3, pp. 111-130.
[8] Ibid., Vol. 6, pp. 81, 94, 153.

ministry that the worship of God may be observed amongst us." He would have sold appointments just as he corruptly gave away huge land grants—transactions exposed by his successor, Captain-General the Earl of Bellomont—and in selling clerical appointments he would have followed the practice in England.[9] The Assembly refused to accede to Fletcher, whereupon he angrily denounced them, warned them to keep their places, and then dissolved the Assembly.[10] Bellomont reported to the Lords of Trade at London, on April 13, 1696, that he could prove by credible witnesses several immoralities including drunkenness, on the part of Mr. Delius, minister of the Dutch Reformed Church at Albany, New York. Delius threatened to excommunicate the Mayor of Albany and others because they forsook his church. Since Delius' church was the only one in Albany, Bellomont persuaded the Mayor to get an intermediary to seek a reconciliation from Delius, "but" Bellomont added, "Delius sent word . . . 'twas vain to seek a reconciliation with him, and so refused absolutely." [11]

A more notable recorded instance of ministerial arrogance or presumption was that of the Rev. George Whitefield, an English clergyman and one of the founders of Methodism. He frequently visited America. When in Savannah, in January, 1740, he took it upon himself to appear before the Court and Grand Jury and lecture them on the prevailing "bare-faced wickedness." That there was plenty of lawbreaking was true enough, as General Oglethorpe, founder of Georgia, had previously charged, with particular application to the liquor law. People who broke it, Oglethorpe complained, "were acquitted by juries in spite of evidence.[12] Whitefield inveighed before the Court and Grand Jury against "persons living the most scandalous lives with their

[9] Judge William Smith's *History of New York*, Vol. 1, pp. 132-133.
[10] This was a festering scandal. Finally came the act of 1713 in Queen Anne's reign. "Whereas, some of the clergy have procured preferments for themselves by buying Ecclesiastical Livings, and others have thereby been discouraged," therefore enacted that "anybody who gave money, reward, gift or other things in his own name or that of others in such a matter should be deemed to have made a corrupt contract which was to be declared void and adjudged as simony." *The Statutes at Large, Great Britain's Parliament*, Vol. 4, p. 619.
[11] *Documents Relative to the Colonial History of the State of New York, London Documents*, Vol. 4, p. 489.
[12] *The Colonial Records of Georgia*, Vol. 22, Part II, pp. 160-161.

whores and went impure in open defiance of all Laws both divine and human." His tirade was a long one. But although many of the Grand Jurymen agreed in principle with his urgings, yet, so wrote Colonel William Stephens, Secretary to the Georgia Trustees, they "seemed not well pleased at his taking upon him to harangue the Grand Jury with what more properly would have come from the pulpit, and I myself feared it would have a diffe :nt effect upon the Grand Jury than what was hoped and expected." And it did. In its presentment the Grand Jury "told only of ordinary matters." [13]

Ministerial supersensitiveness to criticism extended to their sermons. Often these went beyond religious exposition into the domain of political meddling and sectarian controversy. The prodigious energy and acrimony then manifested in squabbling over such moot points as eternal election, original sin, grace in conversion, justification by faith and preservations of saints awaken the sardonic wonderment of later times. The Rev. Gilbert Tennent, of Boston, was an extreme Presbyterian. One of his sermons largely contributed to division in the Presbyterian Church. The Moravians were a vigorous missionary sect of German emigrants who believed in the Scriptures as the only rule of faith and practice and who maintained among other doctrines the total depravity of human nature. Tennent savagely denounced the Moravians. He was only one of a number of examples of this kind of pulpiteering.

Then and much subsequently, even well into the dawn of the nineteenth century, the delivery of prayers would sometimes take forty minutes, and that of sermons anywhere from an hour to two hours and occasionally not less than three hours.[14] Some ministers were not satisfied with quitting at having performed that feat. There is record of Pastor Hasselius' Swedish church in Philadelphia, where the entire congregation was catechized and examined in the contents of the sermon.[15] Rev. Joshua Moody, Trinitarian Congregational

---

[13] Ibid., Stephens' *Journal, 1737-1740*, Vol. 4, pp. 495-496.
[14] See Sprague's *Annals of the American Pulpit*, Vol. I, pp. 57 and 516.
[15] Scharf and Westcott's *History of Philadelphia*, Vol. 1, p. 139. This minister's arbitrariness—and far from being exclusive to him—was shown in his forbidding people to sing, if they were calling their cows, and persons with harsh voices were ordered to "sing softly" or stand mute. Ibid.

minister at Portsmouth N. H., took enormous pride, at the close of his life before 1697, in his having delivered 4,070 sermons.[16] How did congregations endure long-winded sermons? The younger members didn't. They "would escape from the church for awhile, and after a brief recreation in the neighborhood return to their places in time for the conclusion of the services." [17] Doubtless these protracted sermons were responsible for impelling the current flow of jeering songs and writings. But the ministers saw in these only the depravity of the godless. So, in Massachusetts came forth the law of March 19, 1712. Anyone who in song or print reflected upon or mimicked a minister's way of preaching was, upon conviction, to be fined not exceeding £20, or put in the pillory with an inscription in capital letters "of his crime" affixed over his head.[18] Connecticut's laws did not fulfill their aim of securing reverence for ministers. An act of 1715, listing many subsisting practices, accounted evils, included calumniation of ecclesiastical and civil authority and contempt for it. The cause was complacently assigned as the "want of Bibles" and the remedy prescribed the still sterner enforcement of laws.[19]

It is not necessary to raise the question of what benefits, on the whole, redounded to communities because of the presence and ministering of the clergymen. The fact was that they stood out not only as a highly privileged class, but, so far as mandate of law went, as a well-nigh sacred caste. In nearly all the Colonies—later Provinces—ministers and churches of the ruling established creed were supported by public taxation. In some places even uttered opposition to such laws was a crime. Arraigned in court in Plymouth Colony, on October 6, 1658, for saying that the law compelling public maintenance of ministers was "a wicked and devilish law," Lieutenant Matthew Fuller was fined fifty shillings and censured.[20] Not to pay taxes for support of ministers was a criminal offence. Those refusing to do so were

[16] Sprague's *Annals of the American Pulpit*, Vol. 1, p. 161.
[17] Ibid., which gave a characteristic example relating to the Rev. Jonas Clark's church at Lexington, Mass.
[18] *Province Laws. The Acts and Resolves, Public and Private of the Province of Massachusetts*, Vol. 1, p. 682.
[19] *The Public Records of Connecticut*, Vol. 5, p. 529.
[20] *Records of Plymouth Colony: Court Orders*, Vol. 3, p. 150.

haled to court and heavy fines inflicted.[21] Usually the form of taxation in these Colonies was a direct requisition of money. In New England, towns were required to pay over the allotted sums to ministers; a Massachusetts law provided that if towns were destitute or did not support their ministers, then the support of these were to be defrayed from specific sums collected for the public treasury.[22] Other colonies paid ministers from the general public treasury but the method of collecting varied. In Maryland and Virginia the taxpayer had to hand over a stated yearly amount in tobacco payments;[23] South Carolina raised funds for support of its Church of England ministers by a tax on furs and skins.[24]

At the same time, in most Colonies, ministers of the dominant creed had an assured monopoly which yielded them fees and perquisites in officiating at baptisms, marriage and death ceremonies and in other ways. Maryland was but one instance in which the Church of England was the only legalized ecclesiastical institution. If any minister not connected with it, or any priest, married a couple, he was, under the Maryland law, liable to a fine of 5,000 pounds of tobacco, and persons so married were also subject to the same penalty.[25] On the other hand, ministers widely and progressively secured complete exemption from all taxation of their estates and other property. Generally they were supplied at public expense with a house and appendages and a glebe—or area of land, often stocked with cattle—adjoining the parish house. Sometimes, too, ministers would marry well-to-do or rich women and thus acquire extensive estates either represented in land or commerce or cash. These were free of all taxation. Not content with such personal immunity from taxation, ministers in New England and elsewhere obtained exemption from taxation for their widows and families, and in Massachusetts later for church elders.[26]

[21] Ibid., Vol. 4, pp. 28, 31, 38, 40, 98.
[22] *Province Laws, The Acts and Resolves, Public and Private, of the Province of Massachusetts*, Vol. 1, pp. 597-598.
[23] Thus in Maryland each taxable person had to pay forty pounds of tobacco annually for support of church and ministry. *Maryland Archives*, Vol. 24, p. 91.
[24] Cooper's *Statutes of South Carolina*, Vol. 2, p. 247.
[25] *Maryland Archives*, Vol. 24, p. 91.
[26] Acts of 1671, 1695, 1696, 1702 and 1704, *The Records of the Colony of Massachusetts Bay in New England*, Vol. 4, Part 2, pp. 214 and 486; *Province Laws, The Acts and Resolves, Public and Private, of the Province of Massa-*

This grasping policy was a leading cause of the reform movement, miscalled a rebellion, led by Nathaniel Bacon, a lawyer, in Virginia, in 1676. One of the series of laws passed by his regime was the repeal of a taxation law which had become odious to many Virginians. Among other provisions this law had exempted both ministers and their families from payment of tax levies. Bacon's law still allowed exemption of taxation to ministers, but compelled other persons in the family to pay levies. But Bacon's government was soon overthrown by Governor Berkeley's forces, and he was proclaimed a traitor. His acquittal upon trial, however, showed the popular support of his · efforts to relieve oppressive taxation, modify church tyranny[27] and reform abuses in the courts. Firmly restored to power, the Church of England ministers waited for a more propitious occasion. In 1696 the Virginia Assembly enacted a law "whereby the glory of God may be advanced, the church propagated and the people edified." Besides making allowance for perquisites, this law fixed ministers' salaries at 16,000 pounds of tobacco a year, and this remained so until the American Revolution,[28] although —in 1755 and 1757—when the tobacco crop failed, laws were speedily passed compelling payment of the equivalent in money. All inhabitants, whether or not members of the established church, were assessed to pay these salaries.

Only New York and Pennsylvania did not erect any State ecclesiastical establishment. But in New York the absence of this did not prevent flares of bigotry, jarring of sects, and an attempt later by the Episcopalian clergy to institute theirs as the State-supported religion. Succeeding the Earl of Bellomont as Governor of New York, in 1702, Lord Cornbury, an Anglican religious fanatic and, above all, a hater of Presbyterians, caused in January, 1707, the arrest of two Presbyterian ministers. They were mainly charged with having unlawfully preached without the Governor's license, and were

chusetts, Vol. 1, pp. 167, 214, etc., and The Public Records of Connecticut, Vol. 5, Act of October, 1706.

[27] One of the many laws conserving this was an act of 1662. Every person who refused to have his child baptized by a Church of England minister was to be "amerced" (mulcted) 200 pounds of tobacco, half to go to the parish, half to the informer. And to punish other deviations, called offences, every county court was required to set up near the court house, a pillory, a pair of stocks, a whipping post and a ducking stool. Bacon struck also at the law allowing vestrymen to perpetuate themselves in office.

[28] Hening's Collection of Laws of Virginia, Vol. 3, pp. 151-153.

held in jail for more than six weeks. Cornbury had a Grand
Jury picked and packed for the purpose of indicting them.
As, however, one of them, Hampton, had not preached at all,
the Grand Jury was left with no alternative but to discharge
him. The other, McKennie, who had preached, was indicted.
At the trial the Chief Justice strenuously sought to bring
about his conviction, but the arguments of McKennie's counsel that Cornbury's instructions were not law induced the
jury to acquit him. Nevertheless, Cornbury's rancor persisted.
His subservient court would not allow McKennie to go free
until it had illegally extorted all the costs of his prosecution.
Together with his expenses, these amounted to more than
£83, a large and onerous sum at that time.[29]

There were only a few Jews in New York, but because
some had voted for Adolphus Philipse, his opponents contested the election on the ground that it was questionable
whether Jews were qualified as electors. The matter coming,
in 1737, before the Assembly for determination, Philipse's
counsel fell back upon the scope and authority of the election
law. This, he pointed out, allowed the vote to certain classes
of land owners, and among the exceptions Jews were not
specifically barred. The opposition spokesman did not dwell
at all upon the merits of the case. First, he worked upon the
emotions, prejudices and bigotry of the legislature's members. He "artfully appealed to his hearers by describing the
bloody tragedy on Calvary." Then he urged them "for the
honor of Christianity and the preservation of the Constitution" to deny Jews any rights of citizenship. And finally he
held up the specter of a mob massacre of Jews, a danger, he
represented, that his party had thus far prevented. The Assembly pronounced Jews disqualified from voting.[30]

Presently came an episode causing bitter feeling on the
part of various Christian sects. The contributions of all sects,
through public lotteries, had provided funds for the founding
of a college in New York City. By a legislative act, of November, 1751, these funds were put in the hands of a board of
trustees. Although the Episcopalians did not constitute one-
tenth of New York's population, they were intrenched in im-

[29] Judge William Smith's *History of the Province of New York*, published
in 1757, later published as *History of New York*, Vol. 1, 186-190. Smith became Chief Justice of the Province of New York in 1763.
[30] Ibid., Vol. 2, p. 48.

portant official positions, and, with Trinity Church's large real-estate holdings, had foremost economic power. When now an Episcopalian minister was installed as president of the new institution, churches of other denominations were alarmed at the prospect of Episcopal control of college and funds. Newspapers stormed against the obvious high-handed grab whereby funds raised by all sects for a common purpose would be under the dominion of one sect.

These fears turned out to be well founded. Soon came the avowed purpose of excluding from the Presidency of the college anyone who was not in communion with the Church of England and who also did not favor that church's common prayer book for the college's religious exercises. Against this action formal protests were made to the Governor.[31] The matter kept rankling. Finally, in 1784, when the New York Legislature changed the name from King's to Columbia College, it inserted special provisions in the act. "To the end that the intention of the donor and benefactors of the said aforementioned college be not defeated," this law ordered that, notwithstanding any of the college by-laws or customs, no professor should have to take any religious oath, nor could he be declared ineligible because of any religious tenets which he held.[32] Such was the origin of what in modern times became Columbia University.

About this time ministers sought a grab in another direction. Under New York's laws a rather wide latitude was allowed in the performance of marriage ceremonies. By the Governor's license, ministers of most Protestant sects had permission, and even when justices of the peace united couples, courts held such marriages legal. It was during the administration of George Clinton, Governor of New York for some years up to 1751, that Episcopalian ministers petitioned him to vest in them a monopoly of the privilege of solemnizing all marriages. The historian of the time succinctly related: "A great clamor ensued and the attempt was abortive."[33]

Not in the least dismayed by this setback and haughtily

[31] Ibid., Vol. 2, pp. 233-234.
[32] *Laws of New York, 1777 to 1784*, (Cap. 51, Laws of 1784) p. 688.
[33] Ibid., Vol. 1, p. 349. The George Clinton here referred to was the second son of the Earl of Lincoln. He is not to be confused with the Governor George Clinton of a later time.

scornful of all opposition the Episcopal clergy now tried the bolder stroke of agitating for the instituting in law of the Church of England as the ecclesiastical establishment of New York. This effort aroused the indignation of Presbyterians, Congregationalists, Anabaptists, Quakers, Independents and other dissenting sects. That the laws of England were obligatory upon every new colony was the Episcopalians' main argument. This was denounced as both untenable doctrine and an absurd plea; if such a plan were consummated it would compel all other sects to shoulder the "iniquitous and unreasonable burden" of paying taxes for the support of a church alien to their religious views. The Episcopalians were unsuccessful.[34]

The embroilments long arising from clash of sects may be gleaned from the significant preamble of an act passed by the South Carolina Assembly in May, 1704. Here we get an official statement of just what were the effects and extent to which they went. ". . . It hath been found by experience that the admitting of persons of different religious persuasions hath often caused great contentions and animosities in this Province and hath very much obstructed the public business." This had been ascribed as the reason why, at the same time, the Church of England had been made the State Church.[35]

Ministers of the ascendant creed surrounded themselves with an ostentatious yield of reverence. A custom, especially in the smaller towns of some localities, required the congregation to wait before the pastor's house, until, when service was to begin, he came forth in prim posture. Under one arm he carried Bible and manuscript of sermon. Leaning on his other arm, his wife, attended by servants, Negro or other. Behind the ministerial couple trooped all of the other members of the family, ranged in order of precedence by age and rank. As soon as this procession appeared, the congregation moved quickly toward the church to take their places before the arrival of pastor and retinue. When these entered, the congregation rose and did not seat itself until he was in the

---

[34] *Arguments in Support of an Ecclesiastical Establishment in this Province, Impartially Considered and Refuted.* Published in September, 1753, under the title of *The Independent Reflector.* Quoted in Chapter IV of Appendix in Smith's *History of New York.*

[35] Cooper's *Statutes of South Carolina*, Vol. 2, pp. 232, 236.

pulpit and his family in its pew. After service was finished, the congregation rose and continued standing until he and his family had left the church. The procedure in the forenoon was repeated at afternoon service.

Superficially, this tribute might have seemed to attest a voluntary deference of pious regard for pastor and occasion. But much of it was due to weight of law which, from demanding church attendance, was stretched to include auxiliary ceremonials. Nor, as clearly evinced by various proofs of the times, did the common people relish their subordination in church or elsewhere to the status of underlings. In church as outside of it people were stratified on class lines according to rank and calling. In various colonies law after law had been passed forbidding "men and women of mean condition, educations and callings" or persons of "low estate" from wearing any but the plainest clothes. And where law did not specifically decree this, inexorable custom did down to and somewhat beyond the period of the American Revolution.

Such laws in America were substantially correspondences of English laws enacted under successive sovereigns from the reign of Edward IV to that of Henry VIII. Those English laws, altered from time to time, prescribed what clothes men of every estate and degree might wear and what they might not.[36] A Massachusetts law prohibited anyone whose property holdings did not exceed £200 from wearing gold or silver lace, gold or silver buttons, ruffles, expensive lace, or silk hoods, scarfs, ribbons and other fineries which were declared "intolerable" when worn by the menial orders.[37] In several respects the original Massachusetts and Connecticut laws were identically phrased. Penalizing "excess in apparel," both sides did so on the ground of its "unbecoming a wilderness condition and the profession of the Gospel whereby the rising generation are in danger to be corrupted and effeminated which practices are witnessed against by the laws of God." [38]

[36] For example, the various statutes of Henry VIII in *The Statutes at Large, Great Britain's Parliament*, Vol. 2, pp. 101, 111, 168, *et seq.*
[37] This law was but one of a series all to the same purport. *The Records of the Colony of Massachusetts Bay in New England*, Vol. 1, pp. 126, 183, Vol. 3, pp. 243-244, Vol. 5, pp. 59-60.
[38] Comparison of the Connecticut law of May 11, 1676, with the Massachusetts law of May 7, 1662, shows this sameness. As to the Connecticut law see *The Public Records of Connecticut*, Vol. 2, p. 283. For repeated violations of the Massachusetts law fines were progressively increased up to forty shillings.

But, as we have already textually noted, the purview and purport of these laws did not extend to the rich. Equally in Virginia where law discriminated in favor of "persons of quality," and in New York, Pennsylvania and other places, each social layer was denoted by its distinctive garments. While the upper class could resplendently bedeck itself as much as it pleased, the tradesman, artisan, laborer, farmer and servant, each was restricted to special and sober clothing unerringly proclaiming his station. In every function people were graded by position in life; the fixed rule at Harvard College was to catalogue and allot students in the order of their social rank, and even after the actual practice was dropped at the time of the American Revolution, the spirit long persisted.

Although addicted to the system, it was galling to many of the common people consigned to the rear in churches and otherwise humiliated. Added to the onus of laws and the stigma of custom were the preachments of many ministers instructing these people to be content with the station in which God had placed them. This counsel was most irritating to men and women who had seen church officers plucking wealth because of their connections. Again and again had this church influence been effective in getting from the allied civil authorities the dispensing of land grants or the award of business contracts. If the church itself owned a great area of land, church officers would be able to manipulate the direct granting of concessions to themselves.[39]

If we are to accept newspaper criticisms of the time as criteria of considerable public sentiment, churchmanship and religiosity were often targets for derision. While having attained a degree of freedom by their own audacity, newspapers, particularly in Massachusetts, had somewhat of a precarious time in maintaining outspokenness. The editorial policy was not that of overt attack upon ministers but the oblique one of assailing in general terms the characters

In Connecticut the fine was ten shillings for persons wearing clothes "beyond the degree of their calling or station."

[39] One of a long line of instances was that of Anthony Lispenard, a vestryman of Trinity Church. In 1779 he secured a lease from that church of eighty-one lots for a term of eighty-three years at a total annual rental of $177.50. As New York City later grew phenomenally in population and real-estate values, that lease brought his family a millionaire's fortune. *Doc. No. 130, New York Assembly Documents, 1854*, pp. 22-23.

around them. In a blast against certain men "full of pious pretensions" *The New England Courant* of Boston, on January 14, 1722, went on in this hot fashion: "But yet, these very men are found to be the greatest cheats imaginable; they will dissemble and lie, sniffle and whiffle; and if possible, they will overreach and defraud all who deal with them. Indeed all their fine pretences to religion are only to qualify them to act their villainy the more securely. For when once they have gained a great reputation for *piety,* and are cried up by their neighbors for eminent saints, everyone will be ready to trust to their honesty in any affair whatsoever; though they seldom fail to trick and bite them, as a reward for their credulity and good opinion. . . . It is far worse dealing with such *religious hypocrites* than with the most arrant knave in the world; and if a man is *nicked* by a notorious rogue, it does not vex him half so much as to be cheated under pretense of religion. . . ." [40]

It was twelve years after this assailment that John Wesley came to Savannah, where the first rudiments of Methodism in America were developed. As a social reformer Wesley was much in advance of his time, and against the dry formalism of existing churches he believed in appealing to the plain people who to him were brothers, not rabble. All of the canting or supercilious bigotry of the orthodox ministers and their satellites was vented against this new faith, its methods and its evangelists. Ignoring indoor church ceremonials, these held their revival meetings in the streets, welcoming all comers, and exhorting them on terms of complete equality before God. Foremost in this work was the impetuous and fiery enthusiast, the Rev. George Whitefield who, in 1736, had come under Methodism's influence. With amazement the regular clerics considered the spectacle of people flocking *voluntarily* to hear him, and many responding spontaneously to his stirring exhortations. From the Court House Gallery, in Philadelphia, in November, 1739, on successive

---

[40] The autocratic ministerial stand against any discussion in the press of churches or religious matters drew this editorial comment from the *Boston Evening Post,* in December, 1742: "We are credibly informed that an eminent minister of this town has lately warned his people against reading of pamphlets and newspapers, wherein are contained religious controversies. This seems a bold stroke and a considerable step (if the advice should be regarded) toward that state of ignorance in which, it seems, some folk would willingly see the body of the people enveloped. . . ."

nights and at a time when laborers and housewives were
freed from the day's toil, he addressed audiences estimated
each time as thousands, and on one night as 6,000. The
Boston Gazette, on November 29, 1739, reported that, in
New York City, Whitefield "preached twice a day for three
days to a vast concourse of all sorts of people . . . Some
judge that there was not less than two or three thousand
people each time. The like concourse, on such an occasion
was never known here before." In his own *Journal* Whitefield wrote that in New Brunswick, N. J., on April 27, 1740,
he "preached morning and evening to near 7,000 or 8,000
people."

While the advent of this new faith injected a fresh religious
spirit into the times, it only added one more element to the
variegated sects united in the fiercest hostility to Catholics.

CHAPTER IV

EPIDEMIC OF PLOTS

MAKING its transit to America, the charge of Jesuit subtlety in plotting trouble was exploited in the one way in which it could be used in the new country. The main activity of such Jesuits as adventured into the wilderness was as missionaries among the Indians. Hence, was the Protestant conclusion, they could be there for no other purpose than to follow their reputed course of inciting turbulence and warfare. The next quick step on the part of the bigoted royal officials and many colonists was to make the conclusion seem a reality. Apart from their fostered beliefs in Jesuit intrigue, the emphasis on this incitement became the fashion of the times, preeminently in England—the country to which they looked for direction. Consequently, to lay to Jesuit culpability results for which they themselves were responsible was a convenient and plausible pretext.

During King Philip's war—that between the New England colonists and the confederated Indians under the lead of Philip, an Indian chief—the reason advanced by settlers as explaining the fusion of tribes were the maneuvers of "vagrant and Jesuitical priests." These had "made it their business and design, for some years past, to go from Sachem to Sachem to exasperate the Indians against the English." In reporting this expression of colonial opinion to the Council of Trade, at London, in 1676, Edward Randolph gave other aspects of the war's causes. One was that the colonists, under pretence that he and his tribe had injured their stock of cattle, had stolen a valuable tract of land from Sachem Philip. Another aspect was the intense resentment of Indians against "intolerable white man's laws." In Canada Indians could get plenty of liquor, but when they returned drunk to Massachusetts they either had to pay ten shillings fine or be lashed on the back. Massachusetts magistrates, tired of inflicting a profitless whipping, changed the punishment into a sentence of ten days' work "which did highly incense the Indians." [1]

But in explaining to the British Government why Indians had been on the warpath, the Commissioners of the United Colonies, at Boston, put the entire accountability upon the Jesuits. Writing, on August 25, 1679, to the Earl of Sunderland, Secretary of State, at London, the Commissioners affirmed as to the war: "We have cause to fear that these malicious designers, the Jesuits (those grand enemies to his Majesty's crown, as well as to the Protestant religion professed) have had their influence in the contrivement thereof; and of the certainty hereof we have been credibly informed by both Indians and English, at home and abroad." [2]

As to the Onondagas, Cayugas, Mohawks and other Indian tribes comprising the Five Nations in New York, Randolph, by 1689, seems to have veered to accepting altogether the notion of Jesuit artifices. On July 3rd of that year he reported to the Lords of the Committee for Trade and Plantations charging Jesuits with strangely alluring members of the Five Nations to Canada, and also by means "of their beads, crucifixes and like painted images, gaining many converts." [3] At the same time, in an address to the Five Nations, Governor Henry Sloughter, of New York, enjoined them not to treat with the common enemy, the French. This course he asked them to observe all the more "because the Jesuits are too subtle for you, and always endeavor to deceive you as they have lately done to some of our Indians which they have drawn over to their own religion and country." [4] The king's instructions to Sloughter were to permit liberty of conscience to all persons except "Papists." [5]

The extravagant lengths to which bigoted credulity could go was shown by the Earl of Bellomont's transmitting in July, 1700, to the Lords of Trade in London, a detailed and weird story of how Jesuits bewitched and poisoned. This story,

[1] *Documents Relating to the Colonial History of the State of New York, London Documents,* Vol. 3, pp. 241-243.
[2] *The Records of the Colony of Plymouth in New England,* Vol. 2, p. 407.
[3] *Documents Relative to the Colonial History of the State of New York, London Documents,* Vol. 3, p. 580.
[4] Ibid.
[5] Ibid., p. 689.

which he had heard at Albany, Bellomont wrote, "I think worth relating to your Lordships." As Bellomont told it the tale ran:

Decannisore, one of the Sachems of the Onondagas, married one of the praying Indians in Canada (by 'praying Indians' is meant such as are instructed by the Jesuits); this woman was taught to poison as well as to pray. The Jesuits had furnished her with so subtle a poison, and taught her a legerdemain in using it; so that whenever she had a mind to poison, she would drink to 'em a cup of water, and let drop the poison from under her nails (which are always very long, for the Indians never pare them) into the cup. This woman was so true a disciple to the Jesuits, that she has poisoned a multitude of our Five Nations that were best affected to us; she lately coming from Canada in company of some of our Indians who went to visit their relations in that country who have taken sides with the French, and there being among others a Protestant Mohawk (a proper goodly young man) him this woman poisoned so that he died two days' journey short of Albany, and the Magistrates of that town sent for his body and gave it a Christian burial. The woman comes to Albany, where some of the Mohawks happened to be, and among 'em a young man nearly related to the man that had been poisoned, who, espying the woman, cries out with great horror that there was that beastly woman who had poisoned so many of their friends, and 'twas not fit that she should live any longer in the world to do more mischief; and so made up to her and with a club beat out her brains.[6]

A little later Bellomont further pleased clerical and official sentiment in England by writing to the Lords of Trade that although it was the Jesuit custom to purchase proselytes by bribes and rewards, it was not the Protestant method.[7] But he soon found himself in a position where he had to admit the mental superiority of the Jesuit missionaries. Confronted by the conversion of Indians to Catholicism, he urged the Lords of Trade to send over two ministers "or we shall hazard the loss of Indians." Of the requested ministers he wrote: "They ought to be young men or they will never be able to learn the Indian tongue. They must be men of sober and

[6] Ibid., Vol. 4, p. 689.
[7] Ibid., p. 734.

exemplary lives and good scholars, or they will not be fit to instruct the Indians and encounter the Jesuits in point of argument." [8]

It was in this same year—August 9, 1700—that the Province of New York enacted a law the preamble of which began: "Whereas, divers Jesuit priests and Popish missionaries have of late and for some time have had their residence in the remote parts of this Province and others of his majesty's adjacent colonies, who by their wicked and subtle insinuations industriously labor to debauch, seduce and withdraw the Indians from their due obedience to his most sacred majesty and to excite and stir them to sedition, rebellion and open hostility toward his majesty's government, therefore for protection whereof . . ." All Jesuits, priests or any other ecclesiastic ordained by the Pope had to leave the Province of New York before November 1, 1700. He who remained after that date teaching Catholic doctrines or using its rites or granting absolutions "shall be deemed and accounted an incendiary and disturber of the public peace and safety and an enemy to the true Christian religion and shall be adjudged to suffer perpetual imprisonment." Any such Jesuit or other retaken after escape from prison was to be put to death. Every person convicted of knowingly harboring any Jesuit or other priest "of the Romish clergy" was made liable to a fine of £200. Justices of the Peace were empowered to cause the arrest of any person suspected of being a Jesuit or priest, and if the accused did not give a satisfactory account of himself, he could be committed to prison and held for trial. The only exceptions made were those of Jesuits shipwrecked or otherwise driven into New York by adversity, but in such emergencies they immediately had to depart. [9]

Tagged as the Jesuits thus were with malignancy, it was a facile course to hold them responsible for every possible untoward happening. To the loss of New York traders, the Indians had taken much of their fur gatherings to French traders in Canada. A memorial on the causes of this deflection was submitted on November 10, 1724, by Cadwallader Colden to Governor Burnet of New York. Pertaining to the Jesuits he gave many credit for having "spent their lives

[8] Ibid., p. 717.
[9] Laws of the Colony of New York, Vol. I, pp. 428-430.

under the greatest hardship in endeavoring to gain the Indians to their religion." Chief among French explorers into the wilderness were Jesuits, and grouping them under the general term of the French he gave tribute to them for having been "indefatigable in making discoveries and carrying on their commerce with nations whom the English know nothing about except what they see in French maps and books." Then Colden proceeded to depict the consequences of the small salary paid to the Governor of Canada and the insignificant stipend paid to the priests. Both the one and the other had to depend upon perquisites, and both combined religion and business. Colden represented the religious missions, mainly those of the Jesuits, as utilized for prevailing upon many of the Indian tribes to settle in Canada whither they went "with their beads and crucifixes," and pursued their chase for furs, bartering them in Montreal.[10]

These are but some of the facts showing how Old World distortions and fixed ideas concerning Jesuits were transported not only to settlers in America but also used by French officials in Canada when it suited their purpose.[11] No set of men are so far above criticism as to warrant grant of exculpation, yet this was clearly one more recurring example of the habit of people to accept a label attached and lastingly seek to make it adhere.

Attention to the plot scare coming from England is now in order. There were not many Catholics in New York in 1689, yet the mere presence of a few there as in other places was considered legitimate reason to believe in their hatching some infernal plot. Jacob Leisler, who had come from Holland as a soldier in the Dutch West India Company's service, had taken the oath of allegiance to the English and now headed the militia in New York City. Coarse, vulgar and uneducated he nevertheless had the power of successful demagoguery. He had many enemies, the foremost of whom was Sir Francis

[10] *Documents Relative to the Colonial History of the State of New York, London Documents*, Vol. 5, pp. 727-728.

[11] Count Frontenac, serving two terms, nineteen years in all, as Governor of Canada, was noted for his irascibility and jealousy. In a report to Colbert, Minister of Finance under Louis XIV, he attacked the Jesuits as having "ever-active ambition" and as avaricious in seeking to profit from traffic in beaver furs. In the following year Duchesnau, then appointed to a high office in Canada, accused Frontenac of extorting bribes of packages of beaver furs of large value which he had henchmen dispose of for him. Ibid., *Paris Documents*, Vol. 9, p. 120.

Nicholson, royal Lieutenant-Governor of New York under Sir Edmond Andros having jurisdiction over all colonies. Nicholson professed adherence to the Anglican Church, yet because he had knelt at a "popish" mass in the presence of King James, his sincerity was questioned. An angry remark made by Nicholson was magnified by rumor into a threat of firing the city and massacring the people. Backed by troops and mob, Leisler gained control of the city and usurped Nicholson's place.[12]

In defense of his action Leisler wrote to King William and Queen Mary that he had been successful in thwarting a "popish powder plot." This frustration, he set forth, had been effected on June 22, 1689, "when we had a miraculous deliverance of a fire which had been kindled in several places upon the turret of the church; in the fort, 6,000 pounds of powder being next under the same roof and suspected to be done by one papist who had been there before and was discovered by one neger; and fort, city and people were [by] true God's mercy miraculously saved of that hellish design . . ."[13] But in Andros' view Leisler was nothing more than an open rebel, and to put him down as such, companies of English troops were sent to New York City. Leisler spread the report that these soldiers were "papists." With 400 men he was beseiged in the fort and finally had to surrender. He and a chief aide were put in prison. Governor Sloughter wished to hold back their being hanged, but the merchants and large land owners from whom he had extorted illegal taxes demanded and obtained execution of the sentence.

Making representations of a "popish plot" threatening not only New York City but inland areas as well, Leisler had sent emissaries to Maryland and Virginia for assistance. The effect in Maryland was especially pronounced. At once responsive to the plot notion, Maryland Protestants believed the conveyed intelligence that, incited by French Catholics, Indians "had destroyed Schenectady and had committed great and

[12] Brodhead's *History of the State of New York*, Vol. 2, p. 557. An address of Leisler's Militia to William and Mary denounced Nicholson as "a pretended Protestant" who had "countenanced the Popish party, refusing to exclude Papist officers in the custom house and soldiers in the fort." *Documents Relating to the Colonial History of the State of New York, London Documents*, Vol. 3, p. 584.

[13] *Documents Relating to the Colonial History of the State of New York, London Documents*, Vol. 3, pp. 614-615.

barbarous massacre there upon the Protestants," and had also made an attempt upon New England Protestants. About one in eight of Maryland's population was Catholic. Yet by their having control of the Provincial Government, fear was expressed for the safety of Maryland Protestants. So John Coode informed the Secretary of State.[14] Sinking their differences in what they considered a direful exigency, Protestants of all shades joined in an "Association in Arms for the Defense of the Protestant Religion," and now chose Coode as their leader. Catholics denounced the alarms thus spread as the product of senseless fear fomented by the artifice of ill-disposed persons. But Catholic disclaimers had no effect upon minds already anchored in belief, from repeated experiences in England, of the reality of plots. Mustering a force of nearly a thousand men, the coalesced Protestants marched to the seat of Maryland's Provincial Council and installed their own government subject to William and Mary.

The longevity of the influence of the imputed Catholic plot in burning London was shown by the repetition of that charge when, in 1741, parts of New York City were destroyed by fire. At first, reporting to the Lords of Trade, Lieutenant-Governor Clarke of New York wrote that he could not discover "whether the hand of popery has been in this hellish conspiracy," but he suspected it. Reporting, however, two months later—on August 24, 1741—Clarke avowed his conviction that "papists" had caused the fire. How this began nobody knew, but charging it to "papists" gave the event an air of momentous State importance and fitted in with engendered Protestant preconceptions. The trial proceedings were not put in the records. John Ury, said to be a "Romish" priest, was, Clarke reported, the head of the conspirators. These, Clarke even went to the point of asserting, had hopes of getting help from the Spaniards.[15] By the time Clarke last reported, three white men and twenty-one Negroes had been executed, and eighty-eight Negroes transported.

The disarming of Catholics in England also communicated itself to America. On June 10, 1696, Governor-General Fletcher of New York transmitted to the Lords of Trade a

[14] *Maryland Archives*, Vol. 8, pp. 177-178.
[15] *Documents Relative to the Colonial History of the State of New York, London Documents*, Vol. 6, p. 196.

list of Catholics and reputed "papists" who had been disarmed and obliged to give bond with surety for their good behavior or be confined in prison.[16] There was similar action in some other colonies, but Pennsylvania did not get to the stage of taking action until more than a half century later. In the meantime—on July 25, 1734—Governor Thomas Penn had complained of a house in Walnut Street commonly called "the Romish Chapel" in which mass was said by a priest. "Under no small concern about the matter," Thomas Penn regarded "the public exercise of the Roman Catholic religion to be contrary to the laws of England some of which . . . were extended to all of the dominions."[17]

The number of Catholics then in Pennsylvania was shown as the result of an inquiry ordered by Governor William Denny, in 1757. Robert Harding, a Catholic priest, supplied the information. Of Pennsylvania's supposed population of 200,000 not more than 2,000 were Catholics, with 139 in Philadelphia. In the whole of Pennsylvania there were 1,365 Catholics twelve years of age or more.[18]

After the defeat of General Braddock, caught in an ambush by French and Indians ten miles from Fort Duquesne, a letter from Henry Harvey and four other justices in Berks County had been sent to Governor Morris of Pennsylvania, on July, 23, 1755. Protestants in that county, the letter declared, were very uneasy at the behavior of Catholics "who show joy at news coming of the defeat of our army with the Indians." The letter beseeched the Governor for some legal authority "to disarm or otherwise disable the papists from doing any injury to other people who are not of their vile principles . . . It is a great unhappiness at this time to other people of this Province that the papists should keep arms in their houses, against which the Protestants are not prepared, who, therefore, are subject to a massacre, whenever the papists are ready."[19]

Merely for being of Catholic birth men were suspected of plotting with the French and Indians. One Colonel Johnson gave John Lidius, a trader, "the character of a very dangerous person in any province, as he was certain of his being a Ro-

[16] Ibid., Vol. 4, p. 160.
[17] *Colonial Records of Pennsylvania*, Vol. 3, p. 589.
[18] Ibid., Vol. 7, p. 448, and *Pennsylvania Archives, First Series*, Vol. 3, p. 145.
[19] *Colonial Records of Pennsylvania*, Vol. 6, p. 503.

man Catholic." [20] George Crogan, another trader, having great influence with the Indians, had served as a captain of them in Braddock's army. Yet he was under scrutiny by three Governors of as many provinces, solely because he was a Catholic. One of these Governors, Charles Hardy of New York, wrote to Governor Morris that treasonable correspondence charged to Crogan "must have been carried on by some Roman Catholics." Hardy added: "I have heard you have an ingenious Jesuit in Philadelphia." [21] Governor Dinwiddie of Virginia was not one of the three Governors in question but he had his plaint to make to Governor Morris. This was of "the dangers we are in from German Catholics." [22]

Pennsylvania's law, passed in 1757, required the taking over within a month of all arms and ammunition owned by any "papist," or one reputed to be such. Any concealment of arms was to be punished by three months in prison. And to keep Catholics out of the army, this law exempted all "papists" or suspected "papists" from military duty, but each in lieu thereof, had to pay a military fine of twenty shillings.[23]

A case in Pennsylvania's records indicates the particular discrimination against prisoners of war taken during the American Revolution if they happened to be Catholics. Patrick Keane was a lieutenant in—so it was described—the Roman Catholic Regiment of Volunteers in the British service. After his interrogation Colonel Nichols was ordered to "observe closely" Keane's conduct.[24]

[20] *Pennsylvania Archives, First Series*, Vol. 2, p. 176.
[21] Ibid., Vol. 2, p. 694.
[22] Ibid., Vol. 2, p. 423.
[23] Ibid., Vol. 3, p. 132.
[24] *Colonial Records of Pennsylvania*, Vol. 12, p. 177.

CHAPTER V

PARTIAL OBLITERATION

THE period of the American Revolution ushered in some notable changes, one of which was to sunder the power of the theocratic elements, the other to diminish the spirit of bigotry cohering in previous codes of laws. Although theocracy was not then entirely effaced, it suffered heavy blows, and although, too, bigotry still notoriously remained fixed in the Constitutions of many States, the steps taken were an improvement over the pre-existent conditions, and in time led the way to further modifications.

At the outset of the Revolution in 1776, three States took measures to bar ministers from holding public office, and two other States followed in the next year. The long persistent evil of pastors occupying a dual position as expounders of the gospel and makers of legislation was so manifest that four of these States took the ground that no explanation of their action was necessary. Section 16 of the Bill of Rights in the Virginia Constitution was concise; all ministers of the gospel, of every denomination, were declared incapable of being elected members of the House of Assembly or of the Privy Council.[1] "No clergyman or preacher of the gospel, of any denomination," ran Article XXXI of the North Carolina Constitution of 1776, "shall be capable of being a member of either the Senate, House of Commons [Assembly] or Council of the State while he continues in the exercise of the pastoral function."[2] Inasmuch as North Carolina did not adopt and ratify another Constitution until 1868, this barrier, at least in Constitutional mandate, was clearly no short-lived one.

---

[1] *Federal and State Constitutions,* Compiled and Edited by Francis Newton Thorpe, Ph.D., LL.D., "Doc. No. 357," 59th Congress, 2nd Session, Published in 1909, Vol. 7, p. 3814. This document, comprising many volumes, gives the text of all the Constitutions verbatim.
[2] Ibid., Vol. 5, p. 2793.

Delaware's Article XXIX of its Constitution of 1776 was along the same lines; it was repeated in its Constitution of 1792 and 1813,[3] which latter Constitution remained in force until its Constitution of 1897. The clause in the Georgia Constitution of 1777, prohibiting any clergyman of any denomination being allowed a seat in the Legislature, was reaffirmed in its Constitution of 1789.[4] Article XXXIX of the New York Constitution of 1777 did set out to proffer an explanation but considerately took care not to incorporate the current resentment against ministers intermingling in politics. New York's provision put the case on this ground: "And whereas the ministers of the gospel are, by their profession, dedicated to the service of God and the care of souls, and ought not to be diverted from the great duties of their function; therefore no minister of the gospel or priest of any denomination whatever, shall, at any time hereafter, be eligible to, or capable of holding, any civil or military office or place within this State." This provision was repeated in New York's Constitution of 1821.[5]

The accompanying and second thrust at the theocratic hold was in the general elimination of all tithes and taxes for the support of ministers and churches and the cessation of compulsory church attendance. Church and State were severed except in Connecticut, where the Congregational Church remained as the State institution until the adoption, supplanting the old charter, of a Constitution, in 1818. Of a temporizing nature, Maryland's Constitution of 1776 relieved all persons from the obligation to frequent or maintain any

---

[3] Ibid., Vol. 1, pp. 567-568, 579.

[4] Georgia Laws, edit. of 1802, p. 13.

[5] Federal and State Constitutions, Vol. 5, pp. 2637 and 2648. Why, it may be asked, were successive Constitutional Conventions of States concerned to retain such laws? Because, kept out of seats of political vantage, many ministers redoubled efforts to influence public opinion by means of political sermons. During the Revolution that part of the clergy which refused to espouse the American cause had been in popular disfavor, and after the Revolution's pressure upon speech had gone, those who remained, abetted by others of their calling, opposed the incoming of democracy. The many political sermons arguing against the election of Thomas Jefferson as President, in 1800, left such a vivid impression upon Martin Van Buren, that in his memoirs entitled, *Inquiry into the Origin and Course of Parties in the United States*, published in 1867, he related that living witnesses still remembered the ministerial tirades. Jefferson's election, these declared, would mean the burning of Bibles, the prostration of religion and the substitution of some Goddess of Reason. As late as 1815 Jefferson was pointing out the gross impropriety of political sermons.

particular church or involuntarily supporting any minister, "yet," Article XXXIII further provided, "the Legislature may, in their discretion, lay a general and equal tax for the support of the Christian religion . . ." [6] Under this authorization Jews and non-believers could, if the Legislature ordered, be forced to pay taxes for the upkeep of Christian churches as a whole.

"Why," wrote Thomas Jefferson, presumably in 1776, "have Christians been distinguished above all people who have ever lived for persecutions? Is it because it is the genius of their religion? No, its genius is the reverse. It is the refusing *toleration* to those of a different opinion which has produced all the bustles and wars on account of religion." In the Virginia Bill of Rights, drawn under his inspiration, all men, according to their reason and conviction, were declared equally entitled to the free exercise of religion, and people were exhorted "to practice Christian forbearance, love and charity toward each other." [7] Pennsylvania's Constitution of 1776 and 1790 made no discriminations in respect to creed; the only religious test required of any office holder was a belief in one God, and in a future state of rewards and punishments. [8] Georgia's Constitutions of 1777 and 1798 contained no distinctions; all persons were guaranteed the free exercise of their religion provided "it be not repugnant to the peace and safety of the State." [9] New York's Constitution of 1777 in assuring the undiscriminating right to free religious profession and worship gave as a reason the need of guarding "against that spiritual oppression and intolerance wherewith the bigotry and ambition of weak and wicked priests and princes have scourged mankind." [10] At the same time, for the express purpose of excluding Catholics from public office, New York State applied a test oath calling for abjuration of all foreign allegiance, "ecclesiastical as well as civil."

The Massachusetts Constitution of 1780 professed to give every denomination of Christians equal protection under the law, but prescribed for those taking office a test oath which no

[6] *Federal and State Constitutions*, Vol. 3, p. 1689.
[7] Ibid., Vol. 7, p. 3814.
[8] Ibid., Vol. 5, pp. 3085 and 3100.
[9] *Georgia Laws*, edit. of 1802, pp. 13 and 30.
[10] *Federal and State Constitutions*, Vol. 5, pp. 2637 and 2648.

devout Catholic could conscientiously take. Whether the office was appointive or elective, the person before incumbency had to swear renunciation and abjuration of allegiance to any foreign power. Further that "no foreign prince, person, prelate, State or potentate hath, or ought to have, any jurisdiction, superiority, pre-eminence, authority, dispensing or other power, in any matter, civil, ecclesiastical or spiritual, within this Commonwealth . . ." [11] Forty-six years elapsed before Massachusetts abolished all religious tests for office.

But unable to divest themselves of partiality or bigotry, various other States explicitly specified the Protestant as the only religion to be countenanced and protected. Neither the Catholic nor the Jewish religions were definitely recognized as entitled to consideration. In prohibiting the State establishment of any religious sect, Article XIX of New Jersey's Constitution of 1776 then went on to reserve rights all-inclusively to Protestants. No Protestant, merely because of his religious principles, was to be excluded from any civil right; only those professing a belief in the faith of a Protestant sect could be elected to the Legislature or to any other office. They alone "shall fully and freely enjoy every privilege and immunity, enjoyed by others of their fellow subjects." [12]

William Livingston was Governor of New Jersey at this time and until 1790. A long article ascribed to him and supposedly written in 1778 violently attacked priesthood as having confederated with kings in the past to make "an iniquitous coalition of spiritual and temporal dominion" and crush liberty. Commenting upon this blast, which he later published, Matthew Carey, editor of the *American Museum or Universal Magazine*,[13] asked regarding the clause in New Jersey's Constitution: "Are Protestants, then, the only capable or upright men in the State? Is not the Roman Catholic hereby disqualified? Why so? Will not every argument in defence of his exclusion tend to justify the intolerance and persecutions in Europe?" However, the criticized provision

[11] Ibid., Vol. 3, p. 1908.
[12] Ibid., Vol. 5, pp. 2597-2598.
[13] This was an important magazine of national prestige. In a formal letter George Washington welcomed its entry as deserving of the public encouragement. Virtually all of the founders of the Republic and many other public men were patrons.

in New Jersey's Constitution remained intact until a new Constitution adopted sixty-eight years later—in 1844—omitted all matter as to Protestants having exceptional rights.[14]

Under Article XXXII of North Carolina's Constitution of 1776 no person denying God or the truth of the Protestant religion or the divine authority of either the Old or the New Testaments was capable of holding any office or place in the State's government. This interdiction was not amended until 1835 when, by special act, it was changed to read "or the truth of the Christian religion."[15] South Carolina's Constitution declared the Christian Protestant religion to be the State's established religion. In Maryland, by Article XXXIII of the Constitution of 1776, only persons professing the Christian religion were "equally entitled to protection in their religious liberty."[16] This restriction led to considerable subsequent agitation; in January, 1823, the Maryland House of Delegates passed a bill approving the relief of Jews from the wholly pro-Christian discrimination; but it was not until Maryland's Constitution of 1851 was adopted that remedy to Jews was afforded. Article 33 of this Constitution omitted all reference to exclusive protection for those of the Christian religion. No other test or qualification was now required than belief in God and a declaration of faith in the Christian religion; and special provision was made for Jews by the insert "and if the party shall profess to be a Jew, the declaration shall be of his belief in a future state of rewards and punishments."[17] By Vermont's Constitution only Protestants could hold office. Of all of the States restricting office-holding rights to Protestants, New Hampshire had the most sweeping stipulations and clung to them the longest. No man could be elected a member of the lower legislative house, Senate or as Governor unless he were a Protestant, and respectively owned freehold estates ranging from £100 to £500.[18] This exclusion of Catholics and Jews remained until 1876, when the New Hampshire Constitutional Convention abolished all religious disqualifications with one exception. This was a clause em-

---

[14] Federal and State Constitutions, Vol. 5, p. 2599.
[15] Ibid., Vol. 5, pp. 2793 and 2799.
[16] Ibid., Vol. 3, p. 1689.
[17] Ibid., p. 1715.
[18] Constitution and Laws of the State of New Hampshire, etc. (edit. of 1805), pp. 8-10.

powering towns to tax all citizens, whatever their religion, for the support of Protestant teachers of religion which exclusively was construed as morality.

We have thought it advisable to overlap mere chronological arrangement to show by the foregoing sequels how long the bigotry there exemplified remained anchored in organic law. But did Protestant majorities actually think themselves bigoted? The expressed sentiment among them seems to have been one of self-accredited breadth of view because Protestant sects now could exist side by side without open warfare. Thus a Boston publication, in 1785, elatedly informed its readers that the greatest number of churches in that city were the Congregationalist, besides which there were three Episcopalian, two Anabaptist, one Presbyterian and a Quaker. There was no mention of Catholic church or any synagogue. The article rapturously concluded: "Each of these persuasions live together in the greatest harmony. A striking proof of the candor and liberality of the present age!" [19] At nearly the same time when Jews in Philadelphia sought to build a synagogue they not only had to ask for permission but also for protection in undertaking the venture; the Supreme Executive Council of Pennsylvania ordered their petition filed.[20]

A sensationally violent eruption of bigotry in Britain at this time had its repercussions in America. For politically independent as was the United States, it was and long remained, as has been said, a cultural dependency of England, the literature of which was dominant.

Led by liberal members, Parliament, in 1778, had under consideration a bill to relieve Catholics from a few of the many severe laws in the statutes. One of these was a law (hitherto here described) which punished the saying of mass with perpetual imprisonment. Ever since the passage of that law and supplemental law, priests had to conceal themselves in garrets or other sequestered places, or to get protection had to act as servants to ambassadors from foreign countries. Two organizations, both named the Committee for the Protestant Interest, had been formed, one in Edinburgh, the other in London. Publications issued by these Committees or by their partisans now resorted to every means to inflame

[19] The Boston Magazine, August, 1785, pp. 21-22.
[20] The Colonial Records of Pennsylvania, Vol. 13, p. 367.

the worst passions against Catholics. One of these screeds advised Protestants to have no dealings or other intercourse with Catholics. All opponents of repeal were urged to prepare a list of "papists" within their districts and make it public, and even to include as "papists" those who favored the repealing act. However the use of the characterization "papist" goaded the narrow and backward population, it was now disclaimed and deplored by leading English statesmen and clerics. "Papist," said Charles James Fox in Parliament, "is an invidious name, and by no means applicable in its strict sense to the English Roman Catholics." In the House of Lords, Bishop Horsley scored the term "papist" as opprobrious." [21]

Unawed by stentorian protests, Parliament in 1778 repealed some of the old anti-Catholic laws. Although many more and severer laws were left in the statutes, Protestant bigots would not stomach even this partial recision. Early in the following year there was distributed in Edinburgh a circular urging Protestants to pull down a recently built "Pillar of Popery." This was a house built in Leith Wynd occupied by a Catholic bishop and in which one room was set aside as a chapel for his small congregation, consisting partly of four Catholic families living under the same roof. A crowd, composed at first chiefly of boys, collected around the house. At this point the mob could have been dispersed, "but," the account related, "the town council had all along openly leagued themselves with the Protestant Committee in whose name and at whose incitement the work of destruction was now about to be commenced." The bishop's house was set on fire, and soldiers summoned to the scene merely stood by.

Subsequently, the mob started to attack an old house which was a Catholic place of worship in Blackfriars Wynd but a party of magistrates, backed by troops, prevailed upon the mob to retire. Then it proceeded to the poorer districts in other parts of Edinburgh to assault Catholics. Houses and shops occupied by these were plundered and then set afire. "At first," said the account from which we quote, "the sole passion seemed to be a hatred of popery. In truth, thieves had been among them [the rioters] from the first." Setting up the cry "No Popery" the ringleaders now led their followers to

[21] *The Parliamentary History of England,* Vol. 19, pp. 1373-1376.

the houses of some conspicuous Protestants known or believed to favor the removal of disabilities upon Catholics. But anticipating such an attack, these Protestants had surrounded themselves with armed friends, and the mob was foiled. The next morning, however, the chapel in Blackfriars Wynd was fired and destroyed and shops in various parts of the town were sacked; soldiers, no doubt in full sympathy with the mob, stood looking on, even allowing the mob to pelt them with stones.[22]

Hailing events in Scotland as a triumph for the Committee for the Protestant Interest there, the organization of the same name in London set out to emulate exploits in Edinburgh. Lord George Gordon was in his twenty-ninth year and an erratic personage, but because of his vehement, in fact blatant, zeal for Protestantism as well as the prestige of his rank, he was asked to become President of the London Committee. He at once accepted.[23] Gordon proposed that every true Protestant follower should wear a blue cockade in his hat, and all should march in protest. At a meeting at St. George's Fields, on June 2, 1780, the multitude was reckoned at 40,000 or 50,000 carrying banners with the inscriptions "Protestant Association," "No Popery."

So far, the crowd was decorous enough. But later, marching in four divisions to Parliament to demand a repeal of the repeal act, it turned into a wild mob in which ruffians, blackguards and thieves briskly injected themselves. The Houses of Parliament were invaded and members insulted, maltreated and forced to don the blue cockade. On the appearance of the Foot Guards, the mob slunk away. But on the following days, spurred by leaders circulating inflammatory handbills, it looted chapels and other places, made bonfires of insignia, pulpits and benches, smashed altars and set the building on fire. As no magistrate would take upon himself the responsibility of ordering them to fire, soldiers brought to the scene stood passively by. When, however, on a subsequent day, the mob twice assaulted the Bank of England, a strong military force fired into it, killing and wounding many. But, at some places, with shouts of "No Popery" the mob, armed with iron bars,

[22] Citing *The Annual Register* for 1780, this account was set forth in the volume *Sketches of Popular Tumults Illustrative of the Evils of Social Ignorance*, pp. 33-40.

[23] Testimony of Rev. E. Middleton, Howell's *State Trials*, Vol. 21, p. 563.

oaken sticks, wheel spokes or cutlasses, tried to fight the soldiers. These are only some of the continuing outrages, the full
story of which would be a long one. The extent of havoc
wrought may be gleaned from a current account of merely the
result of the first day's outbreak. ". . . After the close of the
riots the metropolis presented in many places the image of a
city recently stormed and sacked, all business at an end, houses
and shops shut up and the Royal Exchange, public buildings
and streets possessed and occupied by troops—smoking and
burning ruins—with a dreadful void and silence—in scenes of
the greatest hurry, noise and business." [24]

Finally, after days of this devastation, the soldiery at all
points in London were sternly commanded to subdue the rioters, which was done and wholesale arrests were made. Fifty-
nine ringleaders were hanged, and others imprisoned at hard
labor or transported. Sent to the Tower of London, Gordon
was tried on a charge of high treason, but as the jury could not
be convinced of any intention on his part of waging war
against the State, he was acquitted. He was, however, later convicted of grossly libeling the French Ambassador, and sentenced to a long term in prison. Cherishing a deep grievance
against Protestantism for not shielding him from his plight,
and loathing Catholicism, and further to exhibit himself in a
new and startling role, what did Gordon now do? While imprisoned in Newgate he announced his conversion to Judaism,
and the English world had curious occasion to learn of his
scrupulously practicing all of the observances of the Jewish
religion. So he kept himself before the public until his death
in prison in 1793. To the end he was gratified by the talk and
notice evoked, for the last report issuing from his cell was that,
when death was almost imminent, his uppermost troubled
thought was his fear of not being buried in a Jewish cemetery.

Departing from America as this digression seems, the effects
of these riots which, of course, received wide publicity, were
diverse in the United States. The unyielding bigoted elements
read or heard with satisfaction of the forcible action taken by
their Protestant brethren in Scotland and England, and con-
doned the excesses on the ground that any measures to keep

[24] *The Annual Register for 1780,* cited in *Sketches of Popular Tumults,* etc.,
p. 85. Also citing *A Plain and Succinct Narrative of the Late Riots,* etc. by
William Vincent which account was really written by Thomas Holcroft, a
noted contemporary English dramatist and miscellaneous writer.

Catholicism down were legitimate and justifiable. On the other hand, deeply perturbed by the occurrences, the liberal groups evinced all the greater determination to remove in America the cancerous conditions of religious hate which could produce such enormities.   *

CHAPTER VI

LIBERALISM MAKES PROGRESS

WHEN, in 1787, Congress adopted its ordinance for the formation of the Northwest Territory, consisting of the present States of Ohio, Indiana, Illinois, Michigan, Wisconsin and Minnesota east of the Mississippi River, the principle of full religious freedom was incorporated. "No person, demeaning himself in a peaceful and orderly manner shall be molested on account of his mode of worship, or religious sentiments in the said Territory." In the Federal Constitutional Convention in the same year Charles Pinckney moved the adoption of a clause that "no religious test shall ever be required as a qualification to any office or public trust under the authority of the United States." This clause, Roger Sherman said, he thought unnecessary because of what he viewed as "the prevailing liberality being a sufficient security against such tests." [1] But the convention did adopt Pinckney's clause, and wisely.

As has been here shown, such liberality as existed was partial, not general. Moreover, the embodying of the full religious rights in such Constitutional or other instruments as did give them was a guarantee against law's reprisals but not a guarantee against the retention of individual or collective bigotry. This, as events sadly proved, remained in many sections of the country. The generation of this time was one which had imbibed the narrow, intolerant ideas hitherto fixed in law as well as in belief and custom. If broadminded and flexible men and women now took a different attitude, there were considerable numbers of people who adhered to the old traditions and prejudices and sought to perpetuate them. Migrating from the East to the Middle West, settlers could change their locale, but this by no means implied rid-

[1] Elliot's *Debates*, Vol. 5, p. 498.

ding their minds of inculcated religious bias. This, too often, was carried along and nurtured.

When consideration of the Federal Constitution was deliberated in the various State Legislatures, the clause against the test oath was differently viewed. In some of these the opinion was expressed that the clause did not go far enough in the direction of assuring complete religious equality. In certain other Legislatures, notably that of Massachusetts, fear of such liberty being granted to Catholics was portentously declared. "I shudder at the idea that Roman Catholics might be introduced into office," Major Lusk, a member of the Massachusetts Legislature, said with great emotion.[2]

In only three States—Pennsylvania, Delaware and Maryland—did Catholics have the right to vote. In its Constitution of 1790 South Carolina gave Catholics the right of suffrage, and Georgia followed in 1798. New York repealed its law of 1700 proscribing Jesuits, yet in 1801 enacted a test oath obnoxiously unacceptable to Catholics; five years later, however, this law was repealed. The fact that Catholics now had a widening right to vote did not at all signify their full equality of rights with Protestants. While laws extended parity of rights to them, political parties or organizations, as a rule, in various places refused to nominate a Catholic for office. In exceptional circumstances a solitary Catholic might be chosen, but purveying to the numerically much stronger Protestant or "nativist" forces, nominating committees selected known Protestants.

This was typically shown by the consistent action of Tammany Hall, which has been erroneously represented in uninformed books as having always welcomed and enlarged the sphere of the immigrant. As a matter of fact, during its first decades, the Tammany Society, or Hall, was strictly a "nativist" organization. Intent upon getting votes, it humored the Catholic but would not risk Protestant antagonism by putting him in elective office. This aroused the enmity of naturalized American citizens, two hundred of whom finally lost patience and on the night of April 24, 1817, when Tammany Hall's general committee was in session, marched in a

---

[2] The U. S. Government publication *Documents Illustrative of the Formation of the Union of American States* gives a good recital of the proceedings attending the ratification of the Federal Constitution.

body to Tammany headquarters in New York City. The intention of the Irish leaders was to impress upon the committee the expedient justice of nominating for Congress Thomas Addis Emmett, an Irish lawyer and orator who, after suffering imprisonment in Ireland for political offences, had emigrated to New York in 1804. Also the leaders planned to urge the committee to nominate other Irish Catholics in the future. But infuriated at the course of Tammany Hall, which they regarded as a stronghold of bigotry, the bulk of the Irish allowed the leaders no time for words. A fight was at once started; in the scrimmage Irish assailants tore down the fixtures and broke the furniture, using the pieces as weapons or missiles which were hurled about, hitting heads as well as smashing windows. Nearly all present were bruised or battered. Strong reinforcements arriving at Tammany's behest drove out the intruders.[3]

This by way of exemplifying the difference between rights granted by law and the withholding of them in practice. The total yearly immigration then and in previous years was small and the number of Irish Catholics entering the United States was slight. It was to encourage immigration to forward the settling of vast undeveloped areas that, from its founding, the Federal Government announced as one of its prime inducements the religious freedom to be had in the United States. In the section dealing with means of promoting emigration from foreign countries, Alexander Hamilton, in his notable report on Manufactures, in 1792, had made this a predominant point. Not only, he wrote, would immigrants get relief from the taxes, burdens and restraints heaped upon them in the Old World, and greater personal independence and consequence in the New. "What is far more precious than religious toleration, a perfect equality of religious privileges would probably [cause them] to flock from Europe to the United States to pursue their own trades and professions, if they were once made sensible of the advantages they would enjoy . . ."

Along the same lines but in much more explanatory detail Tench Coxe, a political economist who became Assistant Sec-

---

[3] In recounting the circumstances of this affray *The National Advocate,* a New York City newspaper, averred on May 10, 1817, that the Irish entered Tammany Hall in bellicose temper shouting "Down with the Natives!" but this assertion was positively denied by Irish leaders.

retary of the Treasury under Hamilton, had written his *Thoughts on the Present Situation in the United States*. Referring to vain attempts of rivals or enemies of the United States to mislead or deceive their peoples, Coxe emphasized the religious more than the material benefits available in America. "A short residence gives the emigrant from any country, of every language, and every religion, the rights and privileges of a citizen. Whatever may be his faith or mode of worship, the laws place him beyond the reach of all interference . . ." And later in his *Notes* for the "Information of Immigrants," [4] he wrote: "The situation of religious rights in the American States, although well known, is too important, too precious a circumstance, to be omitted. Almost every sect and form of Christianity is known here—as also the Hebrew Church. None are tolerated. All are admitted . . ." Then, as if relating a condition startling and refreshing to Europeans irked by religious compulsions of their own countries, Coxe spread into particulars. "In this land of promise for the good men of all denominations are actually to be found the independent or Congregational Church from England, the Protestant Episcopal Church (separated by our Revolution from the Church of England) the Quaker Church, the English, Scotch, Irish and Dutch Presbyterian or Calvinist Churches, the Roman Catholic Church, the German Lutheran church, the Baptist and Anabaptist Churches, the Huguenot or French Protestant Church, the seceders from the Scotch Church, the Menomist Church, with other Christian sects, and the Hebrew Church. Mere toleration is a doctrine exploded by our general Constitution . . ."

Thus, at the origin of the Federal Government, the invitation to European peoples to come to America was to a large extent grounded upon the assurance of their finding complete religious liberty. But this, as we have seen, existed to a partial degree only in State Constitutions, and unfortunately, as evidenced by repeated sequels, immigrants of certain faiths, while protected by the aegis of law, were not sheltered

---

[4] *The American Museum or Universal Magazine* in 1788-1792 was conducting a campaign to encourage immigration, and largely emphasized the religious latitude newcomers would have in the United States in contrast with repressions in Europe. This magazine published Hamilton's report in full, and as to Coxe's articles it "ascribed" the second to him but this was a form then often used to indicate but not disclose the writer. Issues of *The American Museum or Universal Magazine*, November and July, 1790.

against incursions of bigotry deep-rooted in thought. Coxe's enumeration of churches was imposing and true in the sense of their coexistence. Yet underneath superficials, many of those different churches were themselves constant sources of prejudice or propagators of bigotry toward one another. This was demonstrated in attitude, openly or insidiously in sermons, and still more often in sectarian tracts which bristled with animadversions. Underneath the formal profession of religion, various of the sects kept acrimony alive, and the effect of the whole was to continue and renew a strong undercurrent of bigotry which needed only an opportune occasion to burst into action.

Novel as the doctrine then was, some advanced spirits attempted to impress upon all concerned a new definition of property rights applied to religious beliefs. And as religious rights were at that time as largely a topic of discussion as are economic rights in our own time, the stand of one writer may be illuminating. Religious opinion, he contended, was as much a personal property right as the ownership of real estate, merchandise or any other kind of property. He went on to propound this definition of property: "In its larger and juster meaning, it embraces everything to which a man may attach a value, and have a right, and which leaves everyone else the like advantage . . . He has a property of peculiar value in his religious opinions, and in the profession and practice dictated by them . . . As a man is said to have a right to his property, he may be equally said to have a property in his rights . . ." [5] Such a pronouncement, however, was scouted as untenable if not anarchic by clerical bodies maintaining that they alone, in synods and otherwise, had the sacrosanct right to determine what their associates and followers should think. One of a number of conspicuous evidences was the action of the Baptist Church in throwing out of its fold members who held the doctrine of the final restoration of all things. [6]

Although theocratic assumption was still strong, yet its

[5] Ibid., June, 1792. Whether this was an article or an editorial cannot be judged. It was unsigned.
[6] Elhanan Winchester, in University Hall, Philadelphia, preached a sermon, published as a booklet of twenty-four pages, in 1793, on this purgation. The sermon, addressed to rejected brethren, began, "The outcasts comforted," and proceeded to give consolation.

power of proscription over social institutions was waning, and correspondingly there came into triumphant action an opposing liberal element. Two signal defeats indicated this change. True, it concerned matters of amusement and entertainment and not essentials of religion, but in the ministerial view these were closely bound, as was clearly set forth in protests when the contest over the Pennsylvania law prohibiting theaters came to a climax in 1789. Signed by 1,900 citizens a petition requested the Legislature to repeal the law. Alarmed ministers of all Protestant sects busied themselves in churches and sent emissaries to collect signatures to a counter petition; 3,310 names were obtained.

The virulent feeling of religiosity against theaters was shown by, for instance, the declamatory language of the Quaker petition. Toward plays the public was represented as having "shown such an abhorrence of those ensnaring diversions that the stage actors did not find it to their interest to prosecute their corrupt employment." Denouncing theaters, the petition apprehensively declared: "Vice is gaining ground, and religion is in danger of being openly the subject of ridicule . . . by the introduction of those seminaries of lewdness and irreligion." And more of the same tenor. The counter petition contested the claim that the theater was a promoter of wickedness; it urged the vital and important need of relaxation from life's cares, to serve which means of recreation the drama was a rational amusement. "The Dramatic Association," now formed to push in increased agitation for the law's repeal, secured a majority of signatures; the final count of forces showed the proportion roughly of 6,000 for repeal, and 4,000 against.

The report of the Legislative Committee dismissed the claim that the stage was a corrupter of public morals; "the better opinion seems to be that dramatic pieces, in common with other works of taste and sentiment, tend to the general refinement of manners and the polish of society, than which nothing can be more favorable to the growth of the virtues.' Taking these as its main grounds, the Pennsylvania Legislature, on March 2, 1789, repealed the act of 1786, so far as it applied to Philadelphia and one circumjacent mile. In thus acting adversely to ecclesiastical pressure, the Legislature, in the act, further justified its course by this promulgation: "It is contrary to the principles of a free government to deprive any of its citizens of a rational and innocent entertainment, which at the same time affords a necessary relaxation from the fatigues of business [and] is calculated to inform the mind and improve the heart." Then to meet fearsome plaints of opponents that, if legalized, the stage would degenerate into giving indecent and immoral performances, to the scandal of religion and virtue, corruption of morals, and destruction of social good order and decency, the act of repeal went on to tender a mollification. This provided for a board of censors without whose license no play could be exhibited, and, if it were, the offender was liable to £200 fine and imprisonment.[7]

The opening of the South Street Theater in Philadelphia was a gala event. Among a notable audience the most eminent was George Washington. Actor Wignell dressed in black, his hair elegantly powdered and carrying two silver candlesticks bearing wax candles, ceremoniously escorted Washington to his box which was adorned with the United States coat of arms.[8]

The experience in Boston somewhat resembled that in Philadelphia. Ministerial cohorts had succeeded, in 1784, in having re-enacted the earlier Massachusetts law prohibiting theaters. Much agitation ensued in Boston and came to a definite head in the autumn of 1791. At a regular town meeting called to consider this prohibitory law, the citizens voted in favor of the law's repeal, and gave instructions to their representatives in the General Court to act accordingly. When the question came before the appointed Legislative committee, John Gardiner thus stigmatized the law: "The illiberal, unmanly and despotic act which prohibits theatrical exhibitions appears to me to be the brutal, monstrous spawn of a sour, envious, morose, malignant and truly benighted superstition which, with her inpenetrable fogs, hath too long begloomed and disgraced this rising country . . ." After an acid debate, the committee voted against repeal of the law. Whereupon there was great rejoicing among the aggregated pastors.

But although defeated, the promoters of the stage were not

---

[7] *The Statutes at Large of Pennsylvania*, Vol. 13, pp. 184-186.
[8] A graphic description of this occasion is contained in Charles Durang's *History of the Philadelphia Stage*.

disconcerted. Evasion of the law's specifications was their next move. Styling it a "New Exhibition Room," a place of entertainment was opened in August, 1792, and under the guise of "moral lectures and dialogues," a medley of song, ballet, acrobatics and rope dancing was performed. Manager Joseph Harper later distributed handbills announcing that he as leading actor, and five other males and three females, would deliver at the Exhibition Room "a moral lecture in five parts, wherein the pernicious tendency of libertinism will be exemplified in the tragical history of George Barnwell or the London Merchant." This ruse aroused the suspicions of the watchful opponents; waiting until they found their fears confirmed by the playing of the first act, they hastily called in a sheriff armed with a warrant, and had Harper arrested. He was allowed to explain the circumstances to a greatly excited audience which he asked to withdraw. Popular sentiment made itself powerfully felt; when after being freed on bail, he was haled to court, Harper was discharged on a technicality. The law became innocuous, and when the Federal Theater, at the corner of Federal and Franklin Streets, was opened in 1794, it was hailed by exultant pro-stage Bostonians "as an era, a revolution" effected by defiant public opinion.[9]

[9] Sydney Willard, *Memoirs of Youth and Manhood* (Cambridge, 1885) Vol. 1, p. 321.

CHAPTER VII

COLLIDING FORCES

IN the treaty for the acquisition of Louisiana, in 1803, and in the subsequent one for the cession of Florida, the Federal Government embodied provisions for assuring the principle of religious equality. And successive Presidents of the United States were vigilantly on guard against any Congressional legislation infringing upon the clause in the Federal Constitution that "Congress shall make no laws respecting a religious establishment." Two such bills were actually passed by Congress and both were vetoed, in 1811, by President Madison. One bill incorporated the Protestant Episcopal Church in Alexandria, Va.; the other made a grant of land for the Baptist Church at Salem Meeting House. The first bill, President Madison declared, was an open violation of the Constitution; in appropriating funds, or the equivalent in lands, the second comprised a principle and precedent equally contrary to the Constitution.[1]

Two years afterward there came in New York City a noteworthy case evincing the cleavage in the public attitude toward full religious freedom. Massed on one side were the noisy, importunate bigots, and on the other a group of liberals resolved to surmount their own religious predilections. Transcending merely local interest, it was a case attracting wide attention. Daniel Phillips and his wife had received goods stolen from James Cating to whom, a police investigation disclosed, the property was returned by the intercession of his pastor, Rev. Anthony Kohlmann, Rector of St. Peter's, a Catholic Church. Summoned to court, Father Kohlmann was questioned touching the identity of the persons from whom he had received restitution of goods. Upon the ground

---

[1] *Documents Nos. 294 and 295,* 11th Congress, 3rd Session, *American State Papers, Miscellaneous,* Vol. 21, pp. 152-154.

that the secrets of the confessional were inviolate, he excused himself. Likewise, in respectful terms, he declined telling the Grand Jury. He was indicted.

At the utmost the matter of the theft was trivial, and the whole proceeding could have been easily dispensed with, since upon information otherwise obtained, two men responsible for the theft were arrested and indicted. But the shrieking opponents of Catholicism saw an opportunity to vent their animus and make capital. Here, they clamored, was the pernicious confessional in stark operation as a shield of thieves, and they summoned up all of the old stock charges against it even as a conferrer of outright absolution for murder and assassination. From such sources came the insistent demand for Father Kohlmann's indictment. This, to his assailants, seemed rather a foregone conclusion from the composition of the Court of General Sessions. The judges were Mayor DeWitt Clinton, Recorder Josiah Ogden Hoffman, Richard Cunningham and Isaac S. Douglass, all Protestants. But the Board of Trustees of St. Peter's Church were fully as anxious as the opposition to have a speedy determination. In a formal communication to the District Attorney this Board requested a trial as soon as possible so as to secure a judicial finding which should secure to all Catholics as well as to all others "the free exercise of their religious profession and worship." When the case came to trial on June 7, 1813, those who had been hopeful or sanguine of Father Kohlmann's conviction were bewildered to see two noted Protestant lawyers volunteer to defend him. One was Richard Riker, the other William Sampson.

Sworn on the stand, Father Kohlmann asked leave to state his reasons for refusing to answer. If, he said, he were a purely private individual, he would have unhesitatingly complied. But as a minister of the sacrament, a perpetual and inviolable secrecy was enjoined upon him.

> . . . It would be my duty to prefer instantaneous death or any temporal misfortune, rather than disclose the name of the penitent in question. For, were I to act otherwise, I should become a traitor to my church, to my sacred ministry and to my God. In fine, I should render myself guilty of eternal damnation. . . . If I should ever so far forget

my sacred ministry and become so abandoned as to reveal, directly or indirectly, what has been entrusted to me in the sacred tribunal of penance, I should forever degrade myself in the eye of the Catholic Church, and I hesitate not to say, in the eye of every man of sound principle; the world would justly esteem me as a base and unworthy wretch, guilty of the most heinous prevarication a priest can possibly perpetrate, in breaking through the most sacred laws of his God, of nature and of his Church.

According to the canons of the Catholic Church, I should be divested of my sacerdotal character, replaced in the character of a layman, and forever disabled from exercising any of the ecclesiastical functions. Conformably to these same canons I should deserve to be lodged in close confinement, shut up between four walls to do penance during the remainder of my life. Agreeably to the dictates of my conscience, I should render myself guilty, by such a disclosure, of everlasting punishment in the life to come.

In opening for the defence, Richard Riker spoke of the novelty and magnitude of the cause. New York's Constitution, he contended, protected Father Kohlmann in the exemption claimed by guaranteeing the free exercise and enjoyment of religion. The Catholic religion had existed for eighteen centuries; the Constitutional Convention knew that auricular confession was a part of the Catholic faith. "If they had intended any exception, would they not have made it? If they had intended that the Catholics should freely enjoy their religion, excepting always auricular confession, would they not have said so? By every fair rule of construction we are bound to conclude that they would have said so. And as the Convention did not make the exception, neither ought we to make it.

"Again there is no doubt that the Convention intended to secure the liberty of conscience. Now, where is the liberty of conscience to the Catholic, if the priest and the penitent be thus exposed? Has the priest the liberty of conscience if he be thus coerced? Has the penitent the liberty of conscience if he is to be dragged into a court of justice to answer for what has passed in confession? If this be religious liberty—which the Constitution intended to secure—it is as perplexing as the liberty which, in former times, a man had of being tried by the water ordeal, where, if he floated he was guilty, if he sank he was innocent."

There was nothing to show, Riker went on, that auricular confession excused acts of licentiousness. "Catholics do not hold that the confessor can unconditionally forgive every or any sin which might be committed. If that were so, a sinner might repeat his sins at pleasure. But the Catholic creed (Council of Trent) held that priests could absolve no one but 'the truly penitent sinner,' making a sincere and humble confession of his sins, with a true repentance and the hearty resolution of turning from his evil ways. According to our [Protestant] faith give me leave to ask whether a sinner, under such convictions and resolutions, looking to and confiding implicitly in the Savior of the world, would not, through the merits of that Savior, be absolved from his sins? I answer he would. It is the faith of all Protestants."

Citing Sir William Blackstone to the effect that if Catholics could be brought to renounce the supremacy of the Pope, they might quietly enjoy their religion, confession included, Riker continued:

"With regard to the supremacy of the Pope, we know that to be merely spiritual. They consider him the head of the Church; but politically, or as connected with government, or civil society, they acknowledged no supremacy whatever in the Pope. History shows us that Catholic princes have oftentimes gone to war against the Pope in his character of a temporal prince.

"The great body of the American people are Protestants. Yet our Catholic brethren have never hesitated to take up the sword with us, and stand by us in our hour of danger." Then Riker told how, in answer to the congratulatory Address sent to him by Catholics, in 1789, George Washington, "did not hesitate in the face of the nation to do justice to their revolutionary services—to their good conduct as citizens—and to the aid which they rendered us in the establishment of our free government."

Summing up, Riker declared: "I consider this a contest between toleration and persecution . . . To compel the Reverend Pastor to answer, or to be imprisoned, must either force his conscience or lead to persecution. I can conceive of nothing more barbarous, more cruel, or more unjust than such an alternative. To compel him to answer, against his religious faith, or to confine his person, would be the highest violation of right that I have ever witnessed. It would cast a shadow upon the jurisprudence of our country. The virtuous and the wise of all nations would grieve that America should have so far forgotten herself as to add to the examples of religious despotism."

William Sampson's argument was much along the same lines. The judges of the Court of General Sessions unanimously decided in favor of Father Kohlmann. The decision concluded: "Although we differ from the witness and his brethren in our religious creed, yet we have no reason to question the purity of their motives, or to impeach their good conduct as citizens. They are protected by the laws and Constitution of this country, in the full and free exercise of their religion, and this court can never countenance or authorize the application of insult to their faith or of torture to their consciences." [2]

Heartening as was this culmination to the broadminded forces, and establishing as it did, a precedent of immense importance, it was counteracted by the stream of publications whetting and intensifying the prejudices of all who wanted to stay in that condition. Biased historians of the partisan although not professedly sectarian type wrote distortions enough. But they were exceeded by the ministerial self-styled historians loosening their prejudices to indulge in orgies of exaggeration and defamation. One such book, written by David Benedict, A.M., pastor of the Baptist Church of Pawtucket, R.I., was published in Boston in 1813. This book is not to be slighted as an ephemeral production; it was preserved in many Baptist homes and in private and public libraries; and a century later the evidences of its living influence were to be found in the fanatical agitation of a vehement bigot who, in his magazine in America, followed the lines charted by this book, making the same charges but amplified and vulgarized.

[2] In response to a considerable demand, William Sampson embodied the whole proceedings in a book published in New York City, in 1813, entitled *The Catholic Question in America—Whether a Roman Catholic Clergyman Be in Any Case Compelled to Disclose the Secrets of Auricular Confession.* It is from this book of more than 114 pages that the above material is cited. *The Portfolio* (Magazine) in December, 1813, also published the proceedings.

Purporting to be a historical survey of the Baptist sect, the book opened with a bitter assault upon the Catholic Church. The attacks were only a revamp of the outpourings of seventeenth-century English writers when the prevailing fashion was to decry and besmirch everything connected with the Catholic Church. That there was ground for criticism was self-evident, but the writers in question missed the actualities and descended into crass abuse. One leader of such vituperative writers, referring to England's past, described the Catholic clergy as "lazy dignitaries and rich prebends," and convent inmates as "glouting nuns," and both were "lusty, lazy and lustful." On this writer went: "He is a great stranger to history and our English records that cannot tell us with what arts, tricks, cheats and pious frauds the priests of old did use to gull the silly laity out of their lands, manors, money and revenues, beggaring their heirs to make the priests rich and proud, lazy and insolent; in hopes, their prayers and masses to climb to heaven"—and more in the same vein.[3]

But English records gave a very different account. The king and nobles and their ancestors, a Parliamentary act began, had given away a large portion of their lands to monasteries, priories and other religious houses. These gifts, it was stated, were made with the intent that sick and feeble men might be maintained, hospitality, almsgiving and other charitable deeds might be done, and prayers said for the souls of the founders and their heirs. "But that," the preamble continued, "certain aliens, the Superiors of these Orders—such as the Abbots and Priors of the Order of St. Agustine, St. Benedict and others—have at their own pleasure laid various unwonted, heavy and importable tillages, payments and impositions in subjection to them in England, Ireland, Scotland and Wales without the consent of the king and his nobility and contrary to the laws and customs of the realm." These levies, the preamble further complained, had miserably diminished the resources of the monasteries and their capacity to give aid, and the original purpose was thereby "now converted to an evil end." It was therefore enacted that no abbot, prior or other should directly or indirectly, secretly or openly,

---

[3] Hickering's *Essays Concerning Excommunication in Times of Popery*, pp. 34-35. In his *Constitutional History of England*, Henry Hallam at a later time similarly wrote of "the enormous, and in a great measure, ill-gotten opulence of the regular clergy [of England]," Vol. 1, p. 93.

or by any device of merchants send such rent, tillage or other imposition to Superiors beyond the sea. All alien abbots and priors were prohibited from imposing or assessing tillages, payments, charges or other burdens. This law was further confirmed by Parliamentary acts in 1331 and 1332.[4]

That corruption in monasteries and other such institutions did exist was an established fact attested by other laws, but this could not be twisted into a sweeping arraignment, nor into an ignoring of humanitarian and other activities carried on. Considering monks as a whole, they assiduously studied and improved methods of agriculture and were often leaders in the development of products. Manual toilers then worked from sunrise to sunset; and comparing the life of monks with that of brawny drudges, the duties of charitable care, pastoral work, devotion to literature and art and other such occupations did not, in the sight of these disparaging writers, rank as work at all. When the time came, after the dissolution of the monasteries, the resentment of the illiterate mass against literary and artistic labor had occasion to display itself. Valuable manuscripts were seized and used for paltry and utilitarian purposes. This was a notorious condition.

Making no qualifications or allowances, a herd of anti-Catholic campaigners had, in slavish similarity, all contributed their indictments which amounted to sheer perversions. These came down unalloyed by reasonable inquiry, were accepted by Catholicism's bigoted opponents as indubitable truth, and, reinforced by current writings on the same plane, were grounded in the belief of a large number of people in America. When Benedict's book railed at the Catholic Church as "this idolatrous and corrupt communion," and particularly when he declared that "the religious orders of priests, monks, friars and so on form an innumerable company of lazy, ambitious and unprofitable beings," no reviewer evidently had the erudition to point out his rank imitation of bygone jaundiced writers. Without reservation of any kind he indiscriminately condemned clerical celibacy "as the means of a torrent of lasciviousness, debaucheries and crimes." Citing as his authority Robinson's *Ecclesiastic Researches,* which declared that not a single Pope possessed "any godliness," and "many wonder that any Christian can remain

[4] *The Statutes at Large, Great Britain's Parliament,* Vol. 1, pp. 160-162.

in a church so superstitious and vile," Benedict proceeded to build an almost entire structure of vilification on the career of a single Pope. Audacity and usurpation could justly be laid to Pope Gregory VII, whose grand object was to establish complete papal supremacy. But to adduce the example of one or even more in a long line of Popes was a method as far-fetched as it was culpable.[5]

Inasmuch as these and like representations instilled into much of the public mind had their subsequent evil results in America, we cannot leave this book without a glance at more of its contents. Of cruelties and killings the Catholic Church unquestionably had been guilty, but from what source did Benedict get his statement that "three millions of lives have been sacrificed to the persecuting rage of the papal power"? Included in his total figure covering different periods were the executions which he ascribed to Jesuits. "The single order of the Jesuits alone are [sic] computed, in the space of thirty or forty years to have put to death 900,000 Christians who deserted from popery." He then dealt with the Inquisition "the bloody instrument of papal vengeance which, in the space of about thirty years destroyed by various torture 150,000." [6]

These egregious exaggerations went undisputed and were believed by many to be authentic, since they came from a rather prominent minister. To explain the excessive preponderance of such books published in America at this time and until the third decade of the nineteenth century, it is necessary to point out that they were written by Protestant theologians, nearly all saturated with bigotry. "Most of the books written in America during the past century have been upon theological subjects; and books of this character have

---

[5] Benedict's *A General History of the Baptist Denomination in America and Other Parts of the World*, Vol. 1. pp. 21, 22 and 31. Here, perhaps, is an appropriate place to insert a view of the successor of the Catholic Church in England a few years after Benedict's book was published. *The Edinburgh Review*, September, 1826, (pp. 592-593) stated: "The Church of England is unpopular. It is connected with the Crown and the Aristocracy, but it is not regarded with affection by the mass of the people. . . . The system of church patronage, while it makes many of the clergy dependent upon the rich and the great, makes all of them independent of popular favor; and their course of life keeps them somewhat remote from the contact of public opinion . . . Birth, habit and education have identified them with the higher orders;—they share their feelings and enjoy their pleasures. . . . Their style and manner of preaching are unpopular."

[6] Benedict, Vol. 1, pp. 29-31, 134-135.

ever continued to form a great part of the production of the American press." So commented a current periodical in itemizing a "List of American Authors," comprising 496 names.[7]

In addition to books, many sermons were published as pamphlets or booklets. Some pastors did not stop at attacking the Catholic Church but would combine in their so-called sermons denunciation of all liberals. A typical such output was that of the Rev. William Cogswell, pastor of the South Church in Dedham, Massachusetts. First caustically condemning the "Church of Rome and its popery," he proceeded to impeach "those enemies of the church arrogating to themselves the style of Liberal." Every man who had positive religious convictions, he complained, was called by Liberals a fanatic, a bigot and an exclusionist. "For a person to believe that the whole Bible is given by the inspiration of God, they consider the grossest superstition . . . In their pretended zeal for religious liberty they would deprive all others of such freedom." [8]

But in various States, thanks to the unremitting efforts of these same ministers, Liberals, so-named, had slim freedom, should the severe laws be enforced. Vermont, New Hampshire, Massachusetts, Connecticut and a number of other States had all re-enacted old laws penalizing unbelievers who expressed their views by heavy fines or by imprisonment or both. Most of these laws long continued in force, some until late in the nineteenth century. One feature, embracing old as well as newer States, was that in Delaware and Arkansas unbelievers were held not competent to testify in any court, while in Maryland, North Carolina and Mississippi denial of the existence of God entailed disqualification from office. Yet this denial might not be one of a supreme Deity but only a refusal to accept the God as conventionally preached and the Bible as literally of divine inspiration.

Furthermore, all who favored the moderation, or opposed the strict enforcement of old constricting Lord's Day laws,

[7] *The American Quarterly Register*, August, 1833. And this item may be interestingly added. "There is, in this country, no class of men that can be styled authors by profession. They are engaged in other professions and employment."

[8] *Religious Liberty, A Sermon Preached on the Day of the Annual Fast in Massachusetts*, by Rev. William Cogswell, A.M., Pamphlet published by request, Boston, 1828.

were branded by the ministerial forces as Liberals bent on undermining religion. Only when their joint interest was involved did ministers of the different sects agree to act in concert. One of such occasions was in July, 1821, when to devise ways of ensuring better attendance at the churches by rigorously enforcing Sunday laws, the clergy of all denominations in New York City proposed to call a meeting in City Hall Park. Immediately there came a large anti-clergy counter meeting at which "huge outcries" were raised against the tyranny of the clergy who were denounced as "Puritan, persecuting, hypocritical and intolerant." The clerical movement was nullified.[9]

Aside from such a special cause for joint action, the unvarying attitude of many of the sects was one of distrust toward one another. In 1825 six denominations managed to get together in organizing the American Tract Society. At a later time a New York City magazine, running a series of eulogistic articles entitled "Pulpit Portraits, or Sketches of Eminent Living Divines," could not refrain from noting the course of the sects in the American Tract Society. Each of these had a veto power upon all tracts issued, and each member of the Examining Committee vigilantly studied every line written to see that the dogmas of his particular church were not impaired. And all—so the review of the American Tract Society ran—kept the most jealous eye upon one another to exclude any possibility of what each considered its own inhibited heresy getting into the publications.[10]

In a population in the United States of 9,638,453 in 1820 there was only a scattering of perhaps 10,000 or 15,000 Jews, 6,000 of whom, it was estimated in 1824, lived in New York City. A negligible factor in point of numbers, they were not the object of any confederated denunciations and any vestige of even a tentative movement against them was absent. In the larger contests going on they were subordinated to an obscure position except in one respect which seemed to furnish a sufficient outlet for lurking bigotry. If a Congregationalist, Baptist, Methodist, Episcopalian, Catholic or other Christian embezzled, or otherwise committed felony, no men-

[9] *Thoughts on the Anglican and American-Anglo Churches,* by John Bristed, Counsellor at Law, New York, 1823, pp. 149-150.
[10] *Holden's Dollar Magazine,* December, 1848, p. 751.

tion was made in the published reports of his religious faith or connections. But let a Jew slip even into a misdemeanor, the fact that he was a Jew was prominently heralded. From this habitual and prejudicial course one variation is to be noted. It announced: "A Jew! A Presbyterian Church was lately sold off by auction, at New Orleans, to pay off the debts of the trustees, and purchased by Mr. Judah Touro, a native of New England and a Jew, that it might not be converted to any other use than that for which it was intended; and the society still worships in it." [11]

[11] *Niles' Register*, December 7, 1823.

CHAPTER VIII

UPHEAVAL AGAINST MASONS

A TORRENT of bigotry now burst forth in a new direction. The Masonic Order or the Order of Free and Accepted Masons were the victims. The sudden loosening of an intense campaign of vituperation and odium against this body was certainly a bizarre development. It was a body that in America as well as in parent countries had long enjoyed high prestige. It had seemed remote from any possibility of attack, at least in a democratic country. Its membership had included or now included many eminent Americans—George Washington, Benjamin Franklin, John Marshall and others in the illustrious list.

The onslaught was marked by paradoxes. As nearly as can be judged from the currents of the times, the preliminary feeling against Masons began with the filtering in of propaganda from France particularly. At the resumption of Bourbon rule after the Napoleonic regime, a systematic effort was made to represent the Masons as having been the conspiratory power promoting the French Revolution. Masons were depicted as an arch-plotting organization in the arcana of which the darkest deeds were planned under an iron-clad oath of secrecy, the violation of which meant death. The linking of Masons with the impetus to the French Revolution was fabricated. In reality, before 1789 the membership of the French lodges was composed largely of beneficiaries of the old order—nobles, officials, rich men and not infrequently priests. That many of them became emigrés during the French Revolution proved on which side lay their adherences. Reactionary forces in Europe after 1815, however, were not concerned with admitting but with suppressing facts. The aim was to divert attention from the actual causes of the French Revolution. And since Masons were under the ban of the Catholic Church in some countries, it was an easy channel to pick upon them as a disapproved if not a discredited institution.

No doubt such reiterated charges, well embroidered, had weight in supplying some groundwork for the ensuing outbreak of prejudice. But why, among a people committed to republican institutions, could any kind of hearing be given to charges with such an origin? The same question could have been asked as to a population predominantly Protestant. This incongruity seems to present itself as an enigma. But the explanation was simple. Whatever preparatory molding was done by propaganda from Europe, its absorption was not related by anti-Masons to the superinducing local causes.

Foremost among these was the deep chagrin of a host of ministers and their devotees at the passing or extinction of their political power and the decline of the church's hold. With resentment they beheld many of the most important offices in New York State and elsewhere filled by members of the Masonic fraternity. Superior to creed and extraneous to all churches, here was an organization with simple fundamental principles. One was belief in God. Acceptance of the Book of the Law was another. Among Masonic Christians the entire Bible denoted the Book of the Law, and the Old Testament to Jewish members. Immortality of the soul and resurrection were accompanying Masonic principles represented by impressive symbols. As fuel for clerical restiveness there was a large part of the population with latent receptivity to sensational appeal to emotions or fears. Finally, there were the calculating men—mostly starting out on their careers— seeking notoriety or personal political advancement. Seeing the prospects offered by a spectacular movement assuming the proportions of a whirlwind, they ranged themselves as its leaders.

Convinced that the time was ripe for such a venture, William Morgan, a tailor of Batavia, New York, had, in 1826, set out to give lectures and to write a book upon Masonry, disclosing what he alleged were its usages, oaths and obligations. He was arrested at Batavia upon a criminal charge, on September 11th of that year, by a posse from Canandaigua who took him back to that place for examination. He was acquitted, but immediately re-arrested upon a civil process for a trifling debt. Judgment was obtained and he was imprisoned. On the next night those who had brought the action caused him to be discharged. When he left prison he was seized, gagged, thrust into a carriage, and conveyed by relays to the magazine of Fort Niagara. From that point on his fate remained a permanent mystery.

The general agitated speculation over Morgan's disappearance was such that *Niles' Weekly Register,* on March 24, 1827, was moved to comment: "It is no uncommon thing, so great is the excitement, to find from five to six columns in one New York newspaper about it. For example, the *Albany Observer,* of March 16th, has seven and a half of its capacious columns filled with it . . ." Himself a Mason of high degree, Governor DeWitt Clinton offered $1,000 reward for the discovery of Morgan alive, and, if murdered, $2,000 for the discovery of the perpetrators, and a free pardon to any accomplice who made a full exposure.

In various New York towns committees to investigate the crime were appointed. According to a political historian of the time, Masons took too high-handed or aloof attitudes in refusing to assist and in contenting themselves with ridiculing charges that they could lend themselves to so base a crime. In consequence, the impression that the Masonic institution itself was responsible took a strong hold upon popular judgment. "Heated by the novelty of the crime, the mystery in which it was shrouded, the thousand wild and exaggerated rumors which such novelty and mystery were well calculated to set afloat and keep alive, there were not wanting those who denounced the institution in the severest terms as blasphemers and murderers, and every member as a traitor and a murderer, and this language was not only used in public meetings and through the columns of newspapers, but in oral discussions and social intercourse and boldly avowed face to face." Further, the same historian related, "mutual crimination stimulated excitement to the highest pitch of violence ever witnessed in America, entering into all the religious, political and social relations of society." [1]

Morgan's abductors were detected and arrested. Under

---

[1] Hammond's *History of Political Parties in the State of New York,* Vol. 2, pp. 374-375.

New York law up to 1827 abduction was accounted a misdemeanor only. Three of the convicted men were sentenced
to short terms in jail. At the trial, one of these men, a former
sheriff of Niagara County, testified that the object was to get
Morgan on a farm in Canada; he did not know what happened to Morgan after being placed in Fort Niagara. Public
excitement was acute, and to support the theory of murder a
much decomposed body later found on the shore of Lake
Niagara was identified from the teeth by Morgan's wife and
others as that of Morgan. The Coroner's jury so found.[2] But
the jury, it was soon established, had been mistaken in its
verdict or deceived by witnesses; a second examination, after
the body was disinterred, showed that the teeth were unlike
those ascribed to Morgan; the body was three and a half
inches taller than Morgan's; and the clothing was different
from that worn by Morgan. That the body was that of Timothy Monro was positively testified to by his wife and son.[3]

At first the movement against Masonry was more ecclesiastical and moral than political. Although the Masonic order
contained a sprinkling of minister members, the campaign
against it was pushed by the numerous non-attached ministers
backed by their church organizations. The methods smacked
of the whoop of revivalist meetings and the fervor of temperance exhortations.[4] A troublesome member, a Presbyterian
pastor, Lebbeus Armstrong, was expelled by the Royal Arch
Chapter at Saratoga. He affected that he had renounced
Masonry, and two days later he delivered his invective in a
long sermon at the Baptist Meeting House at Edinburgh,
Saratoga County. Characteristic of many other sermons, some
extracts may be reproduced with edification, especially as it
was published as a booklet and considerably circulated. "I
am convinced," he said, "that the whole system of Masonry
belongs to the power of darkness . . . of iniquity, com-
pounded of Judaism, Heathenism, Infidelity and (of late)
professed Christianity . . . and that its tendency is to subvert the moral government of God . . . the Scriptures are
now fulfilling before our eyes in the present indications of
the final overthrow of that long celebrated Institution . . .

[2] *Niles' Weekly Register,* November 8, 1827, p. 147.
[3] Ibid., November 28, p. 162.
[4] Alexander's *Political History of the State of New York,* Vol. 1, p. 371.

Freemasonry, unmasked and exposed to the glare of the world, is incontestably proved to be the Man of Sin." [5]

The developing political movement against Masonry began with the effort of voters in many towns in Western New York to keep known Masons out of office. The New York Senate appointed a select committee to investigate the abduction of Morgan. One of the members was Thurlow Weed, an ambitious young editor-politician. As Hammond related the circumstances, certain politicians on the committee used the anti-Masonic excitement for their own purposes. A reputed union was under way between DeWitt Clinton and Martin Van Buren to secure New York State's vote for Andrew Jackson. In the effort to squelch this, the committee opponents of Jackson emphasized the fact that both Clinton and Jackson were high in the Masonic order, and represented the projected union as another proof of the covert and perilous workings of Masonic influence. [6]

The committee's report, on February 14, 1829, was drawn in such a way as greatly to intensify feeling against the Masonic Order. Invidiously utilizing a deep-set popular notion as to Jesuit artifice and device, the report coupled Masons with Jesuits as intrinsically the same. "The Jesuits," the report elaborated, "secured unity of design and secrecy of action which used the most solemn sanctions of the most high God to subserve purposes the most selfish and profane. The Jesuits presented to the sixteenth century a moral power greater than the world has ever known. It penetrated with the silence and certainty of fate the secrets of every court in Europe, and subjugated, without force of arms, one-half of the continent of America as the dominion of the Pope. This order has been crushed, but within the last 120 years another has arisen—the Society of Free and Accepted Masons. This institution . . . adopting sanctions similar to the order of the Jesuits and commanding a secrecy still more profound, have recently made demonstrations of a power,

[5] Booklet published at Waterford, *Armstrong's Sermon on the Revelation and Destruction of the Man of Sin . . . Or, the Total Overthrow of the Institution of Freemasonry, Predicted by St. Paul.* Under the title was a woodcut with the caption, "The Hydra-headed Monster, with his tail coiled round the Tree of Liberty, is designed to represent the Institution of Masonry, which for ages past has been concealed under a mask of disguise, except the human head representing its professed virtues and union with Christianity."
[6] Hammond, Vol. 2, p. 380.

astonishing in its effects, upon the social and political compact of a character such as the friends of free institutions cannot fail to deplore. Formerly, one-half to two-thirds of the justices belonged to the fraternity of Masons—now not one in twenty are of the initiated; and this change has been chiefly produced by the entire [public] conviction that Masonry pervades and influences the courts of justice." [7]

In the wake of the publication of Morgan's book came a deluge of other melodramatic books all purporting to expose Masonry's innermost and most startling secrets. Of the list of these books, the Anti-Masonic General Central Committee of New York State went to the length of formally urging the public to read *Free Masonry, by a Master Mason,* a volume of 400 pages. No intelligent person, was the committee's assurance, could read it "without being convinced that the Institution is a rank imposture and a dangerous cheat." Not the least consideration whatever was given to the actual fraternal principles or moral precepts of the Masonic order. As the rage progressed, it swept into a new field. Suspecting the Odd Fellows to be Masonry under another name, the Anti-Masonic Convention at Albany in March, 1829, condemned that Order, and also in general terms other societies having secret oaths.[8] Unable to withstand the cyclone of denunciation and reprobation, a number of Western New York influential Masons whose business, professions or standing were jeoparded, issued an address recommending the abandonment of their chapters and lodges.[9]

The defection of such men was due to pressure and intimidation. All that they sought was relief from these. But there was another type of quitter who, succumbing to the pervasive mania, turned against the Masonic organization and vilified it to the extreme. They made their renunciation an ostentatious affair, and instead of seeing in these renegers pliant opportunists, anti-Masonic sentiment hailed them as valiant spirits whose testimony could not be refuted.

One of these characters was Henry Dana Ward who vauntingly signed some of his editorials "A Renouncing Ma-

[7] *Report of the New York Senate Select Committee,* pp. 5-8.
[8] *Niles' Weekly Register,* March 14, 1829.
[9] Ibid., March 21, 1829.

son." Launching an anti-Masonic magazine in New York City, he announced in the intial issue: "The American people are awakening to the development which Free Masonry has made of its licentious tendency; and also to the investigation of the principles of this prodigious society." Anti-Masonry, this magazine pledged, "will seek Free Masonry wherever the creature will lurk, in the hall of legislation, on the bench of justice, or in the chair of the Executive; wherever Free Masonry with its iniquitous oaths may hide." Further came the boastful claim: "The people are jealous of this institution. More than fifty newspapers have opened their columns to portray its character; they will give it no rest in any public place. . . . Free Masonry . . . must be sought out and destroyed . . ."[10] The next month's number declared that the magazine would "fully unfold the lawless, immoral and irreligious tendency of this secret society; it will dissipate its mystery and bring its glorious pretensions to the bar of public judgment and its boasted light to the test of truth. . . . It will show the institution to be shamefully false, and as false it will treat it, paying respect only to the respectable men who belong to the society and none to the falsehood itself."[11] But the revelations thus promised never eventuated; nothing more than high-pitched abusive generalities could be offered.

A little later came a public letter which the anti-Masonic forces triumphantly exploited. It was from Cadwallader D. Colden, several times in the past Mayor of New York City. Not by popular vote but by choice of the Council of Appointment—a State body then having the power—had he been selected for that office. Now a derelict politician, he fell in with what he viewed as the winning side. Yes, he wrote, he had been a Freemason when twenty-one years old, but "after the buoyancy of youth had passed," he began to see "the vanity and folly and the evil tendency of Masonry." This he condemned as "arrogant and impious in its pretensions, and its peculiar science and morals are alike worthless." A long rambling letter, it further charged that Masonry's "titles and

[10] The Anti-Masonic Review and Monthly Magazine, February, 1829, pp. 10, 71, 75-76.
[11] Ibid., March, 1829, p. 131.

trappings are vain, foolish and inconsistent with republican institutions." [12]

In Western New York the chief anti-Masonic publication was the *Anti-Masonic Inquirer,* of Rochester, founded and edited by Thurlow Weed. For his own reasons or purposes he had early sped to the conclusion that Morgan had been murdered by Masons. Constitutionally obstinate in his opinions, Weed retained or professed to retain this belief throughout his life.[13] His vitriolic attacks upon Masons and Masonry were relished by large numbers of people who found in them a valve for the release of their propensity to be against something or other. If principle was involved it was artificially nursed, and if a craving for sensation it was a natural outlet. The circulation of Weed's paper reached proportions esteemed huge in those times. It spread rapidly into the other Western and Northern counties of New York, penetrated widely into Ohio and Pennsylvania, and had its eager following of subscribers even in distant Vermont. Influenced by Weed's success, Ward decided to publish a weekly New York newspaper, *The Anti-Masonic Beacon.* Supplementary to regular newspapers in New England, Pennsylvania and other States battering at Masonry, a miscellany of anti-Masonic periodicals had come into mushroom existence.

Proclaiming a relentless warfare for "the overthrow and extinction of the government and laws of Free Masonry," the anti-Masons of New York, Pennsylvania, Massachusetts and Connecticut now invited delegates from other States to assemble in a congress in September, 1830, at Philadelphia. "The organization and principles of the society of Free Masons," the resolution declared, "are inconsistent with the genius of our republican institutions," and the outgrowing evils should be abated.[14] Similar action had already been taken by several State conventions. Evidently harkening to the criticism that the Masons were not the only secret society, the National Anti-Masonic Convention, at Baltimore, in September, 1831, broadened its resolutions to include all "secret and affiliated societies" as hostile to liberty and free

[12] This letter received widespread publicity. It filled nearly five pages in Ibid., May, 1829 (pp. 175-179).

[13] See pp. 313-318 of his *Autobiography,* published in 1884, two years after his death.

[14] *Pennsylvania House Reports, 1833-1834, Doc. No. 198,* p. 867.

discussion. Then the resolutions proceeded to specify the Masonic institution as "dangerous to the liberties and subversive of the laws of the country." [15]

That the underlying grievance was as much if not more church-bred than political was evident from this editorial comment on a preliminary anti-Masonic meeting in Baltimore: "When upon earth before has a body of men been assembled, from many hundreds of miles around, smarting under insult and oppression, their *sole object* to prostrate a tyrannical power, and to annihilate a social and political evil of the greatest magnitude . . . The ministry is corrupted, the church is defiled, Christianity is supplanted in the affections and confidence of this generation, by the arts of Free Masonry." [16]

The extent to which public feeling was wrought into a febrile state was shown by the near-victory of the anti-Masonic forces in the New York State election of 1831. Granger, Anti-Masonic candidate for Governor, received 120,361 votes to 128,842 cast for his opponent. In the next year the Anti-Masonic Party nominated William Wirt, an old Virginia lawyer, for President, but his only electoral vote was that of the State of Vermont. Early in 1834, a bill was introduced in the Pennsylvania Legislature to debar Masons from the right to vote, to act as jurors or witnesses or to hold office. Disclaiming that any of its members were Masons, the majority of the Pennsylvania House of Representatives committee reported adversely. "Anti-Masonry," it declared, "comes from the land of notions. It envies the possessors of office. It is ignorant. It absurdly denounces as a mysterious institution full of guilt and blood a society of which your committee suppose ten or fifteen thousand of our most useful, intelligent and eminent citizens of all parties are members. . . . No facts have come to our knowledge which imputes [to] or establishes guilt on any Mason in Pennsylvania. Certain books, romances, pamphlets and almanacs have been sold with regard to Masonic crimes in New York, where society has been in a measure disorganized." The minority report, that of a lone member, was a wild production. Its essence was

[15] Ibid., p. 867.
[16] *The Anti-Masonic Review and Monthly Magazine*, October, 1830, pp. 315-318.

that Freemasonry had its own secret code of criminal laws and its secret tribunals "in whose hands are placed the character and life of its members." [17]

Overawed by the agitation against them, Masonic lodges in sundry States surrendered their charters. The Grand Lodge and many subordinate lodges of Rhode Island did so.[18] A mass meeting of Worcester, Massachusetts, Masons resolved that although in practical operation the Order had done nothing conflicting with its moral, social and civic duty, yet it was no longer considered expedient to sustain that Order "at the expense of the peace and harmony of society." Therefore, in view of this and the spirit of recent legislative enactments, the institution should be voluntarily dissolved by its members.[19]

What was the definite effect of the anti-Masonic movement upon the enrolled membership of the Order? Some particulars as to the result in New York State are available. At the time of the "Morgan affair" a New York newspaper was quoted as saying, "There were 600 regular Masonic lodges in New York State; in 1834 only fifty were in operation." But Masons brave enough to face hostility were not wanting. For to show further the diminution of members the account read on: "And at a late grand procession in the city [of New York] in honor to the memory of Lafayette, only about 100 Masons marched in it." [20]

After all the years of uproar, what now happened? The politicians dominating the Anti-Masonic Party in New York State delivered it bodily to the National Republican, or Whig Party, as it was now called, and in it those same politicians, in due time, became bosses or attained high political office. In relating the fusion of Anti-Masons with the Whigs in 1834, Hammond trenchantly related the nature of the somersault by which the Anti-Masons instantly disbanded. "They seemed, as if by magic, in one moment annihilated. That party . . . comprising many thousands of electors . . . who had repeatedly, most solemnly declared that they would never

[17] *Report upon the Subject of Anti-Masonry*, April 1, 1834, *Journal of the 44th House of Representatives of the Commonwealth of Pennsylvania, 1833-1834*, Vol. 2, Doc. No. 196, pp. 856-862, *et seq*.
[18] *Niles' Weekly Register*, March 17 and May 7, 1834.
[19] Ibid., August 30, 1834.
[20] Ibid., July 19, 1834.

vote for an adhering Mason for any office whatever, in one day ceased to utter a word against Masonry, assuming the name and title of Whigs, and, as it were, in an instant amalgamated with National Republicans composed of Masons as of other citizens." [21] After some political successes in other States, Anti-Masons there mostly followed the same course, and in a few. years after 1835 the Anti-Masonic Party became entirely defunct. An American Party, organized in 1875, tried to resuscitate the agitations against Masons but the effort was futile.

If contemplation of a past folly's failure can afford satisfaction, the Masons now can serenely indulge in that feeling. The Masonic membership in the United States in 1939 (the latest figures obtainable) embraced 15,518 Lodges and a total membership of 2,484,062.[22]

---

[21] *History of Political Parties in the State of New York*, Vol. 2, p. 439.

[22] Benito Mussolini, dictator of Italy, from 1922 had proscribed Masonic organizations. With his advent to dictatorship in Germany in 1933, Adolf Hitler did likewise. The time-worn charge that Masons were a secret body of plotters was revived, and all of the old canards were equally and systematically disseminated in Germany and the countries which it later overran. To this propaganda there was no cessation. Hitler had not then made his pact with Communist dictator Joseph Stalin of Russia. To make Masons seem accomplices of Communism, the newspaper *Angriff* of Berlin, on September 15, 1937, published a dispatch, represented as emanating from New York. American Masonic lodges, this dispatch averred, were continuing to give supplies of war equipment to the Loyalist (Revolutionary) Government in Spain in return for assurances of a grant of complete freedom to the Masonic movement in Spain. The dispatch itself disclosed its invented substance in its further preposterous assertion that European Masonic orders were collecting "gigantic sums for the purchase of influential American newspapers."

Chapter IX

CONVENT BURNED

AGITATION against Masonry had not yet subsided before it was obscured, then superseded, by outbreaks of an enduring and more formidable type of bigotry. Fierce as had been the movement against Masons, it was, after all, but a fleeting phenomenon. Against Catholicism, however, animus was abiding. Back of it was the whole force of inherited prejudices and ceaseless diffusion of antagonisms. Smoldering, this animus needed but a breath of an excuse to burst forth.

One such occasion was now found at Charlestown, Massachusetts. There had been a modest Catholic school in Boston, but in 1820, with funds supplied by a Boston supporter, the Ursuline Convent had been founded. Its buildings at Charlestown were opened to pupils in 1827, and later enlarged. Four Ursuline nuns had been brought from Europe. In 1834 the Community consisted of ten members and three domestics, all women, and fifty-four pupils, girls whose ages ranged from six to eighteen years. Daughters of residents of Massachusetts and adjacent States, their parents were of all shades of religious belief; not one-eighth of the pupils came from Catholic homes. By their religious obligations, the nun instructors were bound to devote themselves to the education of young girls. The vows taken did not especially impose the same strict seclusion from the world as did those of other Catholic orders.

To put the consecutive details in sequence, we have to consult the several official and legislative committee reports irrespective of their chronological appearance. One report, prepared long after the event in question, was a more complete summary and gave details lacking in the hastily submitted earlier reports and was more impartial. On a July day in 1834, a quarrel between convent laborers and neighbor-

ing brickyard workmen arose and ended in a riot. Then came
rumors "industriously spread by the workers" reflecting upon
"the moral purity of the convent's inmates." [1] Dovetailing
with ideas sowed from the time of Henry VIII that all convents abounded with vice, these rumors were believed with
alacrity. The narrow-minded foes of Catholicism had for
some years been chafing because of the presence of a convent
which to them traditionally signified a noxiously alien institution.[2] Only the semblance of a provocation or, rather, pretext was needed to cause agitation, and this was now supplied.

Scandalous gossip went the rounds that Elizabeth Harrison, a convent teacher, had strangely disappeared. All Boston
and environs buzzed with talk. Bishop Fenwick, of Boston, in
a letter on July 31, 1834, notified Miss Harrison's father in
New York City of the circumstances. In a fit of hysteria she
had left the convent and gone to a neighbor's house, then was
conveyed to the residence of the parents of one of her pupils.
On a later day the Bishop and her brother had taken her back
to the convent. "I saw her yesterday after her physician had
left her," the letter stated, "and found her again rational and
considerably better in health. She appears quite amazed at
the step she had taken, and does not know how to account for
it . . ."

Although there was not a shred of truth in the rumor, two
Boston newspapers, treating it as a fact, published in duplicate a false and inflammatory article. This began: "Mysterious! We understand that a great excitement at present exists
in Charlestown, in consequence of the mysterious disappearance of a young lady at the nunnery at that place. . . . After
some time spent in the nunnery she became dissatisfied, and
made her escape from the institution, but was afterwards persuaded to return, being told that if she would but continue
three weeks longer she would be dismissed with honor. At
the end of that time, a few days since, her friends called for
her but she was not to be found, and much alarm is excited
in consequence." [3]

---

[1] *Massachusetts House Document, No. 75,* 1853, p. 2. Benjamin F. Butler
was chairman of the legislative committee reporting. The reason why this
report was made nineteen years later appears further on in this chapter.
[2] *The Boston Atlas,* August 13, 1834, told how "the convent was by its nature unpopular and a strong feeling existed against it."
[3] This article appeared in *The Boston Mercantile Journal,* on August 9,
1834, and was copied by another Boston newspaper the next day.

A public declaration by Bishop Fenwick that the story was unfounded produced no effect. On the contrary a new and more alarming version was set afloat. Elizabeth Harrison, rumor No. 2 charged, was held in durance in one of the secret cells which, it was awesomely asserted, were in the convent's basement. "These accusations, exaggerated as they flew from mouth to mouth, engendered a highly inflamed state of feeling against the Community. To silence this, the town authorities of Charlestown visited the institution [on August 10th] and made the most inquisitive search for every secret place, therein accompanied in their labors, however, by the same Miss Harrison, *whose hard lot as a prisoner in one of its dungeons, the citizens of the neighborhood were then lamenting and for whose imaginary wrongs they were preparing the signal and unjustifiable vengeance which followed.*"[4]

The five selectmen who had made the investigation published a jointly signed statement in Boston newspapers, on the morning of August 11th. Upon examination, this set forth, nothing in the least objectionable had been found, "and they have the satisfaction to assure the public that there exists no cause of complaint on the part of the said female, as she expresses herself to be entirely satisfied with the present situation, it being that of her own choice, and that she has no desire to alter it." Ignoring or not choosing to believe this finding, a crowd, estimated at from forty to sixty persons in ugly mood converged, at 9 o'clock on the night of August 11, 1834, upon the convent. Coming from different sections of Charlestown, they arrived on foot or in wagons, and stationed themselves in front of the convent, shouting abusively and threateningly. Some newspaper accounts asserted that all had painted their faces in Indian fashion or otherwise disguised their identity,[5] but if this was so no verification is to be found in the official reports. Facing the crowd, the convent's Superior asked what were its wishes. Angry voices informed her: the purpose was to enter the place and rescue the secreted young lady. Selectmen, she told them, had already inspected the convent and their report should be convincing.

While this parley was going on another and larger crowd

<hr/>

[4] *Massachusetts House Document No. 75*, pp. 2 and 3. Italics in the original.
[5] *The Boston Daily Advertiser*, August 13, 1834, was one of the newspapers so stating.

arrived, mounting soon to between one and two thousand, some joining the attacking mob, others as spectators. As the ringleaders were about to break into the convent, Thomas Hooper, a selectman, arrived at the scene. "I told them," he later testified, "the story about the lady was all false, that the selectmen had examined the building and found everything to their satisfaction; told them that there were fifty children and a sick lady, besides other nuns in the building. One replied that no female should be injured but that the cross must come down (meaning the cross on the building). They were at this time breaking up the furniture, and several voices called out, 'Now for the torches.' The idea of setting fire to a building with fifty children in it sensibly shocked me, and to induce them to desist, I told them that if they contented themselves with what they had done, they might possibly escape, but if they brought torches they would certainly be detected." Hooper's assurances of the utter untruth of the circulated story and his warnings only brought forth, as an investigating committee later reported, derisive expressions of distrust and shouted insults. Strong in its preconceptions, the assailants had been schooled in the idea that vile misdeeds must necessarily be a regular performance in convents. And no plea could have any dissuasive force. At the convent gate before 9 o'clock, John Runey, another selectman, spent ineffectual time in trying to impress upon the mob the story's falsity as established by the selectmen's inquiry.[6]

For perhaps two hours the mob churned in tumult. Several nuns fainted but recovered in time to join with associates in speeding the children out of the building to near-by friendly families giving them refuge. Late at night the mob kindled a bonfire of fences. This, both newspaper reports and official investigations declared, was most probably a prearranged signal to summon all concerned in the plot. Torches were brought. Rushing with a roar into the convent the mob rifled every drawer, desk and trunk and wrecked furniture. Then heaping these together with books and religious objects in the center of several of the rooms, the building was set on fire. "Finding it impossible to save the building, now completely on fire," Hooper further testified, "I returned home."

[6] This and other testimony taken at the time was embodied in *Document No. 75.*

Another selectman, Abijah Monroe, testified: "I was in the road on the night of the fire from 12 to 3 o'clock. I did not do anything to stop the riot." While the convent was blazing, the mob fired the bishop's adjoining library or lodge, and a farmhouse and barn. The burning "was in the presence of a vast concourse of spectators, and of the civil authorities." [7] No attempt was made to restrain the mob.[8] Ten or eleven fire engines from Boston, five from Charlestown, and some from Cambridge arrived, but as they could not act without orders from a Charlestown magistrate, the firemen had to stand by idly.[9] No Charlestown police were present, and no militia.

On the day after the fire, a mass meeting of Protestants, under the leadership of Mayor Theodore Lyman, Jr., of Boston, was hurriedly held in Faneuil Hall. Unanimous resolutions were passed denouncing the attack upon the convent as a "base and cowardly act." All citizens were called upon to express their abhorrence of the act. "That we, the Protestant citizens of Boston," the resolutions read, "do pledge ourselves individually and collectively to unite with our Catholic brethren in protecting their persons, their property and their civil and religious rights." A Committee of Twenty-eight was appointed to investigate the riot proceedings, use every suitable means to bring those responsible to justice, and to consider providing funds to reimburse the Ursuline Community for the damage done. A reward was offered for the conviction of the culprits. Charlestown and Cambridge passed resolutions similar to those adopted in Faneuil Hall and offered a reward, and Governor John Davis of Massachusetts likewise posted the offer of a reward for the conviction of the perpetrators.

But such was mob confidence in impunity even from arrest that on the day after the Faneuil Hall meeting, a mob of men and boys, partly armed with pistols and knives, paraded Boston streets at night and menaced the Catholic Church in Franklin Street. Finding it defended, the mobsters slunk away, then marched to the convent's ruins where they further

---

[7] Statement in *Report No. 22, Massachusetts Legislative Documents*, Feb. 4, 1841.
[8] *The Boston Gazette*, August 13, 1834.
[9] Testimony of Warren Draper, reporter for *The Boston Mercantile Journal*, and also testimony of volunteer fireman.

destroyed whatever they could find in the grounds.[10] Upon learning of the convent's destruction, squads of infuriated Irish laborers employed on construction work in Worcester, Lowell and Providence railroads were, it was reported, hurrying to Boston on a mission of revenge. Learning of this, Bishop Fenwick sent priests in different directions to intercept the laborers and instruct them "not to raise a finger." As for Boston Catholics "so great was the excitement" that, on the afternoon of August 12th, Bishop Fenwick called upon them to assemble in the Franklin Street church. There, while denouncing the incendiaries he judiciously urged his hearers to observe the utmost self-restraint.[11]

His address called forth this comment from *The Boston Gazette:* "The destruction of the convent was an act of the most degraded of the human species but he impressed the fact that it was not their [Catholics'] duty to seek revenge for this vile act, and said that the man was an enemy to the religion he professed, and would put the Catholic religion in jeopardy, who would raise a finger against their opponents at this time. We hope the bishop will furnish us with a copy of his address for publication. It would be read with a high degree of satisfaction by his Protestant fellow citizens."

With Mayor Lyman as chairman the Committee of Twenty-eight examined 140 persons and submitted a report narrating the circumstances of the assaulting, plundering and burning of the convent. It is partly from this report that some of the foregoing facts have been derived. In reporting results the committee took pains to give assurance that it had no "disposition to aid in the dissemination of the Catholic faith, being *unanimously* opposed to its characteristic tenets." Nevertheless, "whatever might have been the convent's characteristics, that did not sanction high-handed violation of the law." The whole number of arrests and commitments made, the committee stated, was thirteen, of which eight were for arson, a crime punishable by death. Concluding its report, the committee deplored the cowardly outrage "perpetrated in the presence of multitudes of our fellow citizens and in the presence of magistrates." The committee recommended enactment of a law penalizing magistrates thereafter for not using their power to suppress riots.[12] Such a law was passed in 1835.

Reprobation of the riot and its consequences by public meetings and newspapers reflected nothing more than the views of a mere minority which, in turn, was indisposed to take measures counter to strongly dominant anti-Catholic sentiment. At trials at Concord four of the rioters were acquitted, and a boy found guilty was pardoned by the acting governor and council of Massachusetts. Yet at about the same time two men, convicted of arson in Boston, in no wise associated with the convent's burning, were hanged in the prison yard there.

Only one Protestant pastor in Boston, as far as can be learned, remonstrated forcibly against the apathy of the authorities, and he took care in his published sermon to keep himself anonymous. Speaking in the Brattle Square Church, on June 17, 1838, he denounced the "gross, brutal and unprovoked outrage" committed against a "devoted body of Christians." In nearly four years, he complained, "nothing had been done about the matter; the Legislature had afforded no relief and had given no assurance that Catholics would be better protected in the future. Some few of the citizens meet together and express their indignation, and here and there a clergyman notices the event in his sermon; the law officers of the State, after weeks of persevering and unremitting labor, succeed in getting one boy condemned, who is shortly after pardoned. But nothing is done to redress the injured individuals, nothing is done to reinstate them in their religious rights, and to vindicate the cause of outraged civil and religious liberty. The community, the State, as a whole, was shamelessly supine and indifferent, and to the encouragement given to the lawless and violent by that supineness and indifference may be traced the growing prevalence of riots and disorder from that hour to this." [13]

Tardily the Massachusetts Legislature did get to the point, in 1839, of remedying defects in existing legislation by the

[12] *Documents Relating to the Ursuline Convent in Charlestown, Comprising the Report of the Committee Appointed by the Mayor in Response to the Resolutions of the Faneuil Hall Meeting, August 12, 1834.* Published as a pamphlet by Samuel N. Dickinson, Boston, 1842, pp. 8-15.
[13] Sermon on *The Nature and Extent of Religious Liberty.* Pamphlet published by request by I. R. Butts, Boston, 1838, pp. 16-17. No hint of the preacher's denomination is given in the pamphlet.

passage of an Act Concerning Riots. This allowed indemnification for destruction of property. A petition in 1841, signed by John G. Whittier, the poet, and others, urged the reimbursement of the Ursuline Convent Community. The minority of the House Committee to which the petition was referred agreed that if the Community should seek indemnity, it should be the State's duty to provide it.[14] But, as a body, neither this committee nor other House committees three and nine years later[15] were willing to approve recoupment.

Finally, in 1854, the question came before another House Committee of which, as we have noted, Benjamin F. Butler was chairman. He had already shown the independent, fearless liberal qualities later distinguishing him as a General in the Civil War, and still later as Governor of Massachusetts and a third-party candidate for President of the United States. Public belief in the charges of immorality against the convent's inmates had been so strong, this committee declared, that not for twenty years did any legislative committee venture to favor indemnification. "Although catering to the popular curiosity, a Miss Reed published her *Six Months' Residence in the Convent* [not the correct title as published] in it was no charge against her associates. And during the time that has elapsed, no person has come forward before any of the numerous committees who have had the subject in charge to indicate the evidence of such crimes. From these considerations and a calm review of all the circumstances, your committee are led to the most settled conviction that no suspicion, even of impurity of life, attaches to the members of the Ursuline Convent of Charlestown. Justice requires that the Ursulines be paid for their loss." [16]

But, despite the committee's urgent recommendation, pressure in and out of the Legislature by inexorable anti-Catholic forces caused the defeat of the move to grant an indemnity.

[14] *Massachusetts House Report, No. 22*, 1841, p. 6.
[15] Ibid., *Document No. 32*, 1844, and *Document No. 210*, 1852.
[16] Ibid., *Document No. 160*, 1854. (This is textually the same as *Document No. 75*, heretofore cited.)

CHAPTER X

CRAZE FOR "DISCLOSURES"

THE casual reference in the committee's report in the previous chapter to the book *Six Months in a Convent* gives no adequate idea either of that production or of the succession of other books, all professing to expose convent life. Although these screeds were designed to pander to a furore of the particular time, their malignant influence far outlived that era. After a quarter of a century and again sixty and more than eighty years later, some were cited in anti-Catholic movements as accredited and standing authorities. That the vitality of these books was anything but transient was shown by the issuance of editions long after the original publication.

To discern the impetus to such writings we have to transfer attention to England. The republication or rather pirating of English books in America was carried to such an extent that an American magazine was prompted to deplore "the mania for reprinting works of every kind from our trans-Atlantic brethren . . . taking for granted that all that comes from that nation of bookmakers [England] will not only be acceptable, but find ready sale here." [1] Long agitation to remove some remaining disabilities in Britain upon Catholics had aroused the bitterest antagonism, and the passage of the emancipation bill, as it was called, by the House of Commons, in 1829, only the more accentuated the fears of those irreclaimable opponents who visioned Catholicism wedging itself into power. The daughter of a minister and in her bloom a Sunday-school teacher, Mrs. Martha Butt Sherwood joined a disposition to be of practical help to the needy with the deepest bigotry against Catholics. Her first book, to "inculcate religious principles in the poor," printed in 1802 was followed by many other books in the ensuing decades. She

[1] *The American Monthly Magazine*, April, 1833.

became one of the most prolific of English writers, and her popularity was also widely established in America.

One of her books was *The Nun,* of which multiple editions had already been published in America by 1835. Purporting to be a personal history, it was, however, put in the form of a romance, narrated in the first person. The heroine presented herself as having been a Turin heiress, brought up "according to the strict principles of the Roman Catholic faith." Left an orphan, she had been induced by the loss of a sister to enter a convent. At the time she was "a devoted Papist." This assurance prepared the way for reaping public belief in the chapter of horrors provided. In gruesome detail the book told of trapdoors leading to dungeons in which inmates were chained to stone pillars and in other cruel ways compelled to do penance. We are tempted to reproduce *in extenso* the absurdly sentimental strain of Chapter VII entitled "Deliverance," but must refrain from giving more than a fragment. Seeking to escape, the heroine had taken refuge in a "charnel house filled with moldering bones" and was about to yield, in utter despair, to her doom when she heard a dulcet voice: "The lady of the knotted veil has no reason to fear the person who now addresses her." Managing—because she was so slight—to get her over the walls, he turned out to be the brother of a nun who had died in a dungeon. Then overcoming all manner of further obstacles, they got to safety, were married, and in due time had a blissful household of two sons and three daughters.

"Thus," the book flourishingly concluded, "I terminate my history, trusting that those things respecting the Roman Catholic Church which I have faithfully recorded may tend to fill the inhabitants of this Protestant land with a sense of that gratitude to God who has liberated this country from the slavery of the great apostasy whose name is Mystery." [2]

To return now to *Six Months in a Convent.* The full name of the author, as inscribed, was Rebecca Theresa Reed. Brought out in Boston, in 1835, the book was also contemporaneously published in London, England. Its main object, set forth in the preface, was "to counteract the prevailing

---

[2] To exemplify the continuing popularity and sales in America of Mrs. Sherwood's books, all, after each had long had independent sales, were brought out in a collected edition of sixteen volumes by a New York publisher in 1855.

passion among Protestants in favor of a convent education for their daughters, which, among other things, appeared to be giving an impulse to the advances of Popery in that quarter of the world." [Boston] The book dealt with what Miss Reed portrayed as the characteristics of the Ursuline Convent. It dwelt upon the disciplinary harshness of the rules; the Superior's severity in exacting cruel, heartless penances. Pupils, she represented, were sometimes punished for refusing to say prayers to the saints which, they said, their parents disapproved. Further, they at times were punished for refusing to read Catholic history. In the transparent aim to incite indignation, she recounted many more alleged incidents. A pupil who said she would be glad to leave the convent was compelled to kneel and perform an act of contrition by kissing the floor, apologizing to her teachers and begging forgiveness. However, to quote precisely some of what Miss Reed wrote will furnish a better idea of the kind of charges which haters of convents were greedily eager to accept as veracious:

I was particularly hurt in witnessing the austerities put on a religieuse, named sister Mary Magdalene, who came from Ireland. Once, while reciting the office, she, by accident or losing breath, spoke in a lower key than she should. At a signal from the Superior she fell prostrate before her desk, and remained so for an hour, until the office was finished and she had permission to rise.

She [the Superior] seemed determined to know my thoughts, and put many questions to me that were hard to answer. I complained of my strength's failing and of my diet, and she immediately imposed the following penances: to make the sign of the cross on the floor with my tongue, and to eat a crust of bread in the morning for my portion.

On one of the Holy Days the Bishop came in, and after playing on his flute, addressed the Superior, styling her Mademoiselle, and wished to know if Mary Magdalene wanted to go to her long home. The sister beckoned to her to come to them and she approached on her knees. The Bishop asked her if she felt prepared to die. She requested that she be anointed before death. The Bishop said: "Before I grant your request, I have one to make; that is, that you will implore the Almighty to send down a bushel of gold for the purpose of establishing a college for young men on Bunker Hill. . . ." After she had given her pledge she kissed his feet.[3]

At the close of her book Miss Reed declared: "If in consequence of my having for a time strayed from the *true religion*, I am enabled to become an humble instrument in the hands of God in warning others of the errors of Romanism, and preventing even *one* from falling into its *snares*, and from being *shrouded* in its delusions, I shall feel richly rewarded." [4]

A signed notice published by Mother Mary Edward St. George of the Ursuline Community in nearly all of the Boston newspapers, on March 20, 1835, stigmatized Miss Reed as an impostor, declared her stories false and the title of the book a falsehood. Miss Reed, this notice further stated, had first come into the convent as a domestic, and had not been there more than four months and one week. Mother Mary announced that she would answer the book. In reply came this statement published the next day: "The Committee of Publication declare that the title was affixed by the committee and not by Miss Reed."

Just who composed this committee was not made clear. Denouncing Miss Reed's book as "an impotent and impudent falsehood." *The Boston Literary and Catholic Sentinel,* established by Bishop Fenwick, depicted Miss Reed as "having become the tool and dupe of an ignorant fanatic person of the name of Croswell who rants and roars every Sunday in a Methodistical psalm-house in Charlestown, and at his instigation obtruded on the public attention an infamous and libellous book . . . for that despicable fanatic is the real author of the vile work. . . ." *The Boston Traveler* "thereupon called attention to the fact that Croswell was not a Methodist preacher but rector of the Episcopal Christ Church in the north section of Boston. Croswell's greatest offence, this newspaper said it suspected, was in giving a public certificate of character to Miss Reed who had been a communicant of his church for two years. Admitting its having "imbibed the false impression from mere hearsay stories," *The Boston Literary and Catholic Sentinel* retracted its charge against Croswell.

[3] *Six Months in a Convent,* pp. 29, 48-50.
[4] Ibid., p. 86.

Ruminating over these bitter exchanges in Boston, a national periodical disclaimed taking any part in the quarrel but felt obliged to moralize on "the love that these people owe one another." [5]

In her extended reply to *Six Months in a Convent* Mother Mary stated in her "Preliminary Remarks": "It is an old adage that a lie will travel many leagues while truth is putting on her boots. No doubt such will be the case with the stories of Rebecca T. Reed, aided as they are by men who have enlisted in the crusade against Catholics and Catholic institutions. It is believed no book professing to state facts ever issued from the press containing so little truth in proportion to the whole." Taking up the main question whether Miss Reed's stories were true, the Lady Superior first established Miss Reed's identity. The daughter of a poor farmer, she had been baptized first in the Episcopal, then in the Catholic Church. She had been fed, clothed and instructed by the Ursuline Sisters whose only motive was charitable. She had not been noted for her obedience. As to the alleged brutal treatment of Mary Magdalene when dying, the Lady Superior pronounced this incredible for a community of well-educated and well-mannered women, all under the influence of religious duty. "Does," she asked, "the religion of the cross so brutify the gentle nature of women?" Moreover, two of Mary Magdalene's own blood sisters were novices in the convent at the same time. "Would they have continued there and taken the black veil afterwards, if there had been a particle of truth in that portion of the 'narrative'? Add to all this the testimony of Miss Alden and Dr. Thompson and the solemn declaration of these own sisters of Mary Magdalene made in writing and exhibited to contradict the lying report." Point by point the Lady Superior went on to deny in detail other of Miss Reed's assertions.[6]

By way of answer came an anonymous pamphlet. Much of the first part of this was quibbling, and concerned with minor and irrelevant points. Would Miss Reed have left had she not reason? Her motives could not be justly impugned, and

[5] *Niles' Weekly Register*, April 4, 1835.
[6] "An Answer to *Six Months in a Convent* Exposing Its Falsehoods and Manifold Absurdities," by the Lady Superior, pamphlet published by James Monroe & Co., Boston, 1835, p. xxxvi.

the truth of her story about Mary Magdalene was reiterated. From this point on the bulk of the pamphlet was an attack upon the Catholic Church. The grounds given are well worth some extended reproduction as they show the nature of a widespread inculcated sentiment. If American liberty was to be preserved, the pamphlet maintained, the Catholic religion could not be suffered to prevail to any considerable extent in the United States. "For what is the support of the Catholic religion? It is ignorance; it is hostility to all mental improvement; it is superstition, and how can liberty and these qualities breathe the same air. . . . The character of the monasteries and nunneries in Europe is well known. They are described as being the abodes of indolent and licentious people—the nurseries of vice. We do not say that this description can be proved to apply to the religious establishments of Catholics in this country. The Papists here, being in a minority and opposed by public opinion are obliged to proceed with secrecy and caution. But we do earnestly ask Protestant parents whether they are justifiable [sic] in patronizing convent schools and thereby lending their aid and countenance to a religion incompatible with our institutions, and to the foundation of establishments that may become the haunts of iniquity." If due care were not taken, the pamphlet concluded, Americans would see Catholic establishments scattered in every direction throughout the country, and then the American "may feel the chill of rayless winter under the icy grasp of Catholic oppression." [7]

Persistently trying to allay the suspicions expressed by fair-minded Protestants that her charges were a string of the merest fabrications, Miss Reed or her mentors now felt impelled to produce a new book entitled *Supplement to Six Months in a Convent.* A strained attempt to justify her accusations, it was replete with prejudice, malice and colossal exaggerations. In, for instance, the aim to show how the Pope's "faithful subjects" from Ireland were swamping America, the Appendix represented Irish immigrants as "coming to us at the rate of 200,000 per annum. In the last thirty years 600,000 have found their way into the United

---

[7] "A Review of the Lady Superior's Reply to *Six Months in a Convent,* Being a Vindication of Miss Reed." Unsigned pamphlet of 51 pages, Boston, 1835.

States." As a matter of fact, official figures of immigration into the United States from all countries showed 58,640 in 1833, 65,365 in 1834, and 45,374 in 1835. From 1820 to 1830 the total number of immigrants from all countries was 151,824, and from 1831 to 1840 the figure was 599,125. Equally wild was the assertion that within two years, six hundred Roman Catholic priests, chiefly from the abolished monasteries of Portugal and other countries, had come to the United States "and dispersed themselves over the valley of the West."

However, the number of individuals or groups making diagnosis of *Six Months in a Convent* and its sequences was relatively small, and the discredit expressed did not affect the general public. In other cities as well as Boston the demand for copies of *Six Months in a Convent* was importunately large. Partiality for such disclosures joined with curiosity and a lively taste for scandal, and all of these enhanced by the ardent controversy, induced a rush to get such a much-discussed book. Inability to procure copies caused impatient complaints in New York, reported *The Journal of Commerce* of that city. "We learn by gentlemen from Boston," it said in explaining reasons for this scarcity, "that forty men are employed day and night in working off and binding this work without being able to supply the demand in the city of Boston alone. We booksellers in many instances have bought up second-hand copies and sold them to new readers, being unable to obtain a full supply from the publishers. Between 7,000 and 8,000 copies, we understand, have already been published and the work has been stereotyped. About half a dozen copies have reached this city (one of which we have) and more are promised. They will be gone in a trice. A thousand copies is the least that ought to be sent here to begin with . . ."

Edition after edition run off the press gradually satisfied the ubiquitous demand. Nor did this grow stale with the passing years, as instanced by the publication of an edition at Halifax, Nova Scotia, in 1865, and further revival by another edition in Boston, in 1893.

The prevalent craze for "convent disclosures" brought forth another book: *Awful Disclosures of Maria Monk, As Exhibited in a Narrative of Her Sufferings, During a Residence of Five Years as a Novice, and During Two Years as a*

Black Nun, in the Hotel Dieu Nunnery at Montreal. A volume of nearly 250 compact pages, some of the salient points only can be noted here.

First of all, a few words as to Maria Monk. A Canadian of Scotch ancestry, she was about twenty-one or twenty-two years old when the book ascribed to her was published in 1836. Found in a pregnant condition in what were then the outskirts of New York City, she had been taken to Bellevue Hospital. There, representing herself as a nun who had escaped from the convent in Montreal, she claimed that a priest was the father of her child. Clearly she was not qualified to write a book; diction, style and arrangement throughout were unmistakably those of a practiced, if not of a professional, writer.

Opening sentences of the Preface alone were calculated to have aroused misgivings of a deliberate effort to avert suspicions. "It is hoped that the reader of the ensuing narrative will not suppose that it is a fiction or that the scenes and persons that I have delineated had not a real existence. It is also desired that the author of the volume may be regarded as a voluntary participator in the very guilty transactions which are described; but receive sympathy for the trials which she has endured. . . ." A further suspicious feature of the Preface was a warning to readers that, following her disclosures, structural alterations to conceal interior parts of the convent as described by her might be made. This notification, as events tended to prove, was shrewdly made to forestall the results of any investigation dissecting her story.

Maria Monk's book did much more than make the now somewhat perfunctory allegations of subterranean passageways, cells, and brutal penances exacted. She accused visiting priests and the nuns of licentious practices, and, going still further, definitely made charges of infanticide. According to the narrative to which her name was signed, she, while in the convent, came upon a book which she examined. It "was a record of the entrance of nuns and novices into the convent, and of the births that had taken place in the convent. . . . The period the book embraced was about two years . . . but I can form only a rough conjecture of the number of infants born, and murdered of course, records of which it contained. I suppose the book contained at least one hundred pages, and one-fourth was written upon, and that each page contained fifteen distinct records. On this supposition there must have been a large number, which I can easily believe to have been born there in the course of two years." Elsewhere she asserted: "At least eighteen or twenty infants were smothered and secretly buried in the cellar while I was a nun." How did she know this? She had "learnt it through nuns," and, moreover, she professed to have seen herself several cases of infanticide. Enlarging upon the theme, she told of observing a place in the cellar covered with lime; this, it occurred to her, "must be the place where the infants were buried, after being murdered, as the Superior had informed me." Much lurid space was devoted to the alleged mysterious disappearance of a number of veiled nuns.[8]

William L. Stone was editor and part owner of the New York newspaper, *The Commercial Advertiser,* and an author of various books. His intense skepticism was aroused, as he wrote in the preface of an account of his investigation, by two circumstances. "I was most unexpectedly thrown into the company of a second impostor of kindred character, who has either come to this city to try her hand in the same business, on speculation, or who has been brought hither by the associates of Miss Monk, to sustain her wretched inventions. I allude to Miss Frances Partridge, or St. Patrick, as she says she was called in a convent, in which, although an inmate for twenty years and upward, she was yet ignorant of the location." The second circumstance propelling Stone to action was his unwillingness to believe that nuns could become "willing instruments of lust and murder."

"But," his account went on, "my prejudice against the Catholic faith was strong. Its monstrous corruptions in the Old World were notorious. The work of Maria Monk I knew to have been written by one of our most estimable citizens— a gentleman of character and approved Christian piety—who had taken every pains, as he supposed, to record the exact truth. I knew from his own lips that he was a religious believer of all he had written. I knew that other intelligent and

---

[8] Inasmuch as this book ran through many editions, numerous of them with paper covers of different paging, it is advisable here to refer solely to the headings of the chapters in which these allegations were mainly made. They were Chap. XVI, "Treatment of Infants," Chapter XVII, "Disappearance of Nuns," and Chapter XIX, "Imprisoned Nuns."

pious gentlemen had, by repeated examinations, endeavored to detect the girl's imposture, if impostor she was, without success. I knew that these men and multitudes of others, were firm believers in the truth of her revelations. . . ."

Stone determined to make a personal investigation in Montreal. Associated with him were John Frothingham, president of the City Bank of Montreal, and Duncan Fisher. At the Hotel Dieu convent, Miss Beckwith, an English-speaking nun who had been in the convent ten years, informed them that Maria Monk had never been there as a nun, although it was possible she had been in the hospital; no inquiry was made into the names of patients there. As to the assertion of nuns becoming mothers and infants murdered, Stone and his fellow investigators found that of the thirty-six nuns, more than half were past the child-bearing age. "Certainly not more than fifteen of them could 'in the natural course of human events' become mothers. Taking Maria's statements therefore as correct data, and each of these fifteen nuns—striking the average—must give birth to two and a half children every year! A most prolific race, truly! What nonsense, and how great the popular credulity to swallow it!!"

By the bishop's permission, Stone and his party painstakingly scrutinized every wall, the mortar and other factors in the cellars and vaults, and minutely inspected every door and passage. There were no such trapdoors and secret passageways as described in the Maria Monk book. And regarding the statement in it that Maria formerly helped whitewash the walls: "All that she has said is false. Not a single cell or vault of the convent has *ever* been whitewashed. The walls are as dark and bare of lime as when they were first built, a century ago."

After this inspection, came an interview with Maria Monk and Frances Partridge. At the hearing were three ministers and three laymen "of whom," Stone wrote, "one was the writer of Maria Monk's *Awful Disclosures*." Asked how she was able to escape over a massive outer wall some twenty feet high, she said she went through the gates. When it was pointed out to her that there were no gates, she replied: "It was so then; I don't know what alterations have been made since." Turning to the assembled company, Stone said: "Gentlemen, this is utterly untrue. There is no passage in that direction. There are no gates. The wall is as solid as built a century ago."

Stone's report of the entire investigation concluded: "I will therefore now close this protracted narrative by expressing my candid opinion, founded not only upon my own careful examination, but upon the firmest convictions of nearly the entire population of Montreal[9] embracing the great body of the most intelligent evangelical Christians, THAT MARIA MONK IS AN OUT AND OUT IMPOSTOR, AND HER BOOK IN ALL ITS ESSENTIAL FEATURES A TISSUE OF CALUMNIES. However guilty the Catholics may be in other respects, or in other countries, as a man of honor and professor of the Protestant faith, I MOST SOLEMNLY BELIEVE THAT THE PRIESTS AND NUNS ARE INNOCENT IN THIS MATTER."[10]

The American Protestant Vindicator now issued a challenge to Catholic prelates of Montreal and elsewhere to appoint an "impartial" committee to investigate charges in the Maria Monk book. Not waiting for the outcome of this proposal, a number of predeterminate Protestants held a meeting at Broadway Hall, New York City, on January 16, 1837, and promptly passed resolutions. These asseverated: "The more profoundly the testimony of Maria Monk respecting the Canadian priests and nuns is searched, the more lucid and irrefragable it appears." The resolutions further requested *The American Protestant Vindicator* and the editors of all other religious periodicals in the United States to publish the proceedings of this meeting. To the end "that those of our Reformed Brethren who are yet 'incredulous' concerning the true attributes of Popery and the doings of the Jesuits may be enlightened and convinced; and those who are doubtful may be decided and confirmed."[11]

---

[9] In Toronto an edition of *Awful Disclosures* was published at a later time "for the trade." The date was not given.

[10] First published in *The New York Commercial Advertiser,* the whole account of the investigation and of the examination of Maria Monk and Frances Partridge was later issued as a book entitled *Maria Monk and the Nunnery of the Hotel Dieu. Being an Account of a Visit to the Convents of Montreal, and Refutations of the "Awful Disclosures,"* by William L. Stone, New York, Howe & Bates, 1836. See particularly pages iv, 9, 15, 32-34, 38-39, 42-45. Words in capital letters as above were as originally published.

[11] These proceedings were published in a pamphlet, *Evidence Demonstrating the Falsehoods of William L. Stone Concerning the Hotel Dieu Nun-*

A new and sensational turn soon developed in the Maria Monk episode. With every possible embellishment, the story was given out and widely published that on the night of August 15, 1837, six priests abducted Maria from New York City and conveyed her to the Catholic Asylum in Philadelphia. One of these priests, it was alleged was the Rev. Mr. Phelan, the father of her child. The ascribed purpose was to get her out of the way and put her under Catholic duress.

"A sterling Protestant conscientiously opposed to the views of the Catholic Church," as he wrote of himself, Dr. W. W. Sleigh, a leading Philadelphia physician, was beset with doubts regarding the published story. Up to this time, as he further wrote, he "had been a firm believer in the truth of the substantial facts recorded in Maria Monk's works." He decided to make a thorough investigation. The result of this was embodied in a pamphlet which moreover was also signed by two Protestant ministers and several lay Protestants. He proved that she had left New York City alone, and her entire story otherwise, he declared, was utterly false. In view of these findings "now he entertains no other opinion of the said Maria Monk's works but that they are, in every important statement, a mass of falsehoods." At the end of his pamphlet he thus pictured Maria: "This creature has been so dragged about by various parties and her mind kept in such a perpetual state of excitement for several years, that she could have been made to say or consent to anything." Dr. Sleigh did not know "who induced her to fabricate her fables," but he did declare his conviction that "she is at present incapable of taking care of herself." [12]

nery of Montreal. The "evidence" incorporated was nothing more than a lot of hearsay matter or testimonials "on belief" of various persons that they thought Maria Monk was telling the truth. The whole would have been inadmissible in any court of law.

[12] Pamphlet _An Exposure of Maria Monk's Pretended Abduction and Conveyance to the Catholic Asylum, Philadelphia, by Six Priests, on the Night of August 15, 1837,_ by W. W. Sleigh, Philadelphia, pp. 34-36.

CHAPTER XI

SAMUEL F. B. MORSE'S BOOK

MEANWHILE, the career of an influential and formidable movement, aimed primarily at Jesuits but practically at Catholicism as a whole, had been started. The individual who came forward to vocalize pervasive fear and enmity was none other than Samuel F. B. Morse. As a portrait painter he had been for many years the first President of the Academy of Design in New York City, and he already had conceived the idea of the electric telegraph which before long he made a practical invention.

As casting light upon his formative period and heritage of bias, his parentage and environment are weighty factors. Born at Charlestown, Massachusetts, in 1791, his father Jedidiah Morse, was a militant Congregational minister, and the household temper was one of the deepest animosity against other faiths, particularly Catholicism. Permeating the whole community, this attitude, with all of its prepossessions, left its indelible impress upon Morse's mind. This in maturity, was a strange mixture of pliancy to new ideas in the realm of invention and imperviousness to any fresh ideas in the religious or social field. Just as he believed in the divine ordination of his invention and of God directly planning his trials and successes, so, too, he persisted in holding slavery as ordained from the world's creation by God for wise, benevolent and disciplinary purposes.[1]

At Yale College the lectures on electricity especially interested him, but choosing to slight this innate appeal, he cherished an ambition to become one of the world's greatest painters. In England where he later began to study painting, he, on May 13, 1815, wrote in grandiose fashion to his parents:

[1] See *Samuel Finley Breese Morse, His Letters and Journals*, Edited and Supplemented by his son, Edward Lind Morse, Vol. 2, pp. 19, 46-48 and 331.

". . . My ambition is to be among those who shall revive the splendor of the fifteenth century; to rival the genius of a Raphael, a Michael Angelo, or a Titian . . ."[2] He had a great love for his native country but it was not disassociated from an enormous egotism. Pertaining to America he wrote from London to his home folk: ". . . How shall I raise her name, how can I be of service in refuting the calumny, so industriously spread against her, that she has produced no men of genius?"[3]

Returning to America, he had indifferent success with his painting, which he now alternated with pursuing studies in electricity. Going to Europe in 1829, he traveled in many countries there. His experiences in Rome brought all of his underlying prejudices to a climax of anger. Of artistic decoration he, of course, had an appreciation, but he lacked even a glimmering of the inner meaning and symbolic significance of Catholic ceremonies. Looking with hostile eye at the presentation of Cardinals' hats at the Vatican Consistory, he was repelled by what he ignorantly supposed was the barbaric splendor of the attire of Pope Pius VIII and that of his retinue. He did not see the Pope as the spiritual head of a great church but as a very decrepit and tottering being. Beholding the Cardinals in rotation kiss the Pope's hand and the new Cardinals approach his toe, Morse's "countenance had an expression of pain."[4] On other days he made a point of stationing himself where he could see more ceremonies and pageants but with no other motive than to find ground for strictures. A procession of brown-robed and head-shaved Franciscan and Capuchin monks chanting their liturgy thus impressed him: "They seemed, many of them, like disinterred corpses, for the moment reanimated to go through this ceremony and then to sink back again into their profound sleep."[5]

On the same day while watching a sacred ceremony on the Corso, Morse laid himself open to an experience the utilization of which later had a telling, in fact, a prodigious effect in heightening anti-Catholic feeling in America. He made him-

[2] Ibid., Vol. 1, p. 177.
[3] Ibid., Vol. 1, p. 133.
[4] Ibid., Vol. 1, pp. 339-340.
[5] Ibid., pp. 352-353.

self conspicuous by keeping his hat on. As Morse related the incident, his hat was abruptly struck off "by a poltroon in a soldier's costume, with a gun, accompanied with curses and taunts and the expression of a demon . . ."[6] Morse, as his letters told, was further disgusted by the shameless begging by great numbers of monks and priests in Rome. All of which threw him into a highly combative mood. Meeting Earl Spencer's son, who had been converted to the Catholic faith, Morse engaged in a three hours' argument with him "concerning the idolatry of the Virgin Mary and the results of the Catholic religion in other countries."[7]

Morse arrived in New York late in 1832 and there buried himself with further experiments on the electric telegraph. But this sole preoccupation did not last long. A little later he was writing his book *Foreign Conspiracy Against the Liberties of the United States*. Originally, this was published, under the name of Brutus, in *The New York Observer*, in 1834, and brought out as a book, under Morse's name, in 1835. As his main premise, Morse used a fear besetting Americans at an earlier time, not much earlier, it is true, but still one which in the intervening time had shrunk almost to the proportions of a relic. This was the Holy Alliance formed after Napoleon's downfall by a confederacy of European sovereigns. At that time American newspapers had denounced it as a deadly conspiracy against mankind's liberties, especially those of America. But the Revolution of 1830 in France expelling the Bourbon dynasty had torn away one of the Holy Alliance's essential props, and it no longer functioned.

Assuming, however, that its machinery was still intact, Morse pictured the Holy Alliance bent upon the destruction of liberty in America and the substitution of a priest-ridden, tax-burdened condition of despotism. He represented Austria as leading in the plot or "grand scheme," as he termed it. "She has her Jesuit missionaries traveling through the land; she has supplied them with money, and has furnished a fountain for a regular supply." The Pope, Morse went on, would require all whom he appointed to support the agents that Austria was sending to the United States to accomplish her own purposes. "And who are these agents?" Mostly the Jesuits, he

[6] Ibid., p. 353.
[7] Ibid., p. 377.

repeated, and then proceeded to reassert the hackneyed characterizations. "They are an ecclesiastical order, proverbial through the world for cunning, duplicity, and total want of moral principle; an order so skilled in all the arts of deception that even in Catholic countries . . . it became intolerable, and the people required its suppression." [8] In point of fact, so far as Austria was specifically concerned, it was the insistence of other religious orders, jealous of Jesuit services to science and education, as these were understood at the time, that had induced the Empress Maria Theresa to suppress the Jesuit order.[9] Backed by Austria's machinations and funds, Morse continued, a constantly increasing host of Jesuits was invading America; they were forwarding the organization of "popery," and were a danger to free institutions.

In all of these assertions, Morse drew heavily upon conjecture or imagination; for one thing, in the entire United States including, of course, the French and Spanish cessions, a Catholic census could show no more than 382 churches, 342 priests, twenty colleges and seminaries for men, sixty seminaries for women, and seventeen convents.[10] But just how were Jesuits to get control of America? Morse had this figured out to his own satisfaction. Their plan, as he proclaimed it, was to marshal the influx of Catholic immigrants and secure control of the Government through the ballot box.[11] Morse singled out the Irish Catholics in America as the element which could be thus used with facility. They "in an especial manner clanned together, and kept alive their foreign feelings, associations, habits and manners." [12]

These are only a few typical extracts from this book which had all the effects of an incendiary torch. After putting forth every possible representation that could make Protestants shake with alarm, he proceeded to offer a practical suggestion for united action. Disregarding the plain lessons of history in his own country, not to mention some other countries, he

---

[8] *Foreign Conspiracy Against the Liberties of the United States*, 1835 edit., pp. 21-22.
[9] Frederick von Schlegel, who made a thorough study of such affairs, in his *Lectures on the Philosophy of History*, 1810; edit. of 1849, p. 305. The son of a Lutheran minister, Schlegel was received into the Catholic church in 1808.
[10] *Niles' Weekly Register*, March 28, 1835.
[11] *Foreign Conspiracy Against the Liberties of the United States*, 1835 edit., p. 47.
[12] Ibid., p. 24.

dogmatically declared: "Our religion, the Protestant religion, and Liberty are identical, and liberty keeps no terms with despotism." To buttress this postulate with what he considered would be the final authority of a great scholar, he professed, in a later edition, to quote Schlegel, whom he had met in Europe. Schlegel, Morse wrote, viewed monarchy and "popery" as sustaining each other in their contest against the hated Republicanism the great nursery of which was in the United States. This alleged citation was spurious, as anyone consulting Schlegel's work could easily have ascertained. As a historian Schlegel could not have presumed to represent Protestantism as an ally of Republicanism, seeing that England, Prussia, Sweden, Denmark and some other countries all were both Protestant and monarchical. This was only one of the fictions set afloat by Morse; no one then made any critical analysis; and years later an anti-Catholic member of Congress gravely used the Schlegel story as if it were an established fact.

Since, Morse contended, "popery" neither acknowledged the right of the people to govern themselves, nor "tolerated liberty of the press or of conscience or of opinion," why, he asked, should not Protestants form an Anti-Popery Union? He did not favor its entering the storm of politics; it should, he advocated, align itself as a Christian Party; and its weapons should be the Bible, Sunday school, common school, college and university.[13] These were to be made the propaganda agencies to offset intrusions of "popery." Qualified as was this proposal, it nevertheless made its deep and ultimate impression. Subsequently it took concrete shape in the formation of a powerful organization which, although at first modeled on lines of secret operation, yet branched out to wield a direct and potent sway over politics.

The influence of Morse's book was indubitably great; nor was it confined to its particular era. Successive editions were issued; it was also published by the American and Foreign Christian Union in 1841; more regular editions followed in the next decade and afterward. As in the case of the books on convents, Morse's book was copiously to be found in Sunday-school, public and school libraries; such productions riveted in the minds of many of the youthful readers distinct preju-

[13] Ibid., pp. 119-122.

dicial ideas which remained to animate them as adults, and which in turn were often transmitted to their children. Without venturing to question any of Morse's premises or seeking to tally fact with assertion, many an editor shaped his comments in accordance, and many a preacher found in Morse's book matter for thunderous sermons. And especially after Morse proved the correctness of his electric-telegraph theory, it was more strenuously assumed that he, now risen to a superlatively distinguished position, must have been equally right in the things maintained in his book.

Dealing pre-eminently with this, as we here do, we should not be misled into overlooking the output of other books, all contributing in one way or another toward aggravation of prejudice. One of these productions, appearing in the very year in which the Inquisition was abolished in Spain, was entitled *The Holy Inquisition*. Inclusive of a multitude of victims burnt alive or otherwise punished, it placed the total number of sufferers directly or indirectly involved at the impossibly precise figure of 3,410,215. In reproducing such assertions, numerous American periodicals accepted them at their face value, and they became fixed in expanded popular credence already disposed to believe the worst.[14]

[14] For example, see *Niles' Weekly Register*, May 25, 1835.

CHAPTER XII

NATIVISM

IN SOME of the larger cities a political party calling itself the Native Americans had come into aggressive action. The principles of this party were at first confined to two demands. One was the exclusion of all foreigners from office, the other a change in the naturalization law. After the French Revolution the Federalists under President John Adams passed an act requiring fourteen years residence in the United States before naturalization papers were granted. With the election of Thomas Jefferson as President a law was enacted reducing the term to five years. The Native American Party called for a twenty-one-year residence as an indispensable requisite for citizenship.

At its inception and for some years afterward this party did not take the anti-Irish, anti-Catholic stand which later signaled its course. The bulk of immigrants was from England; there was only a small infiltration from Ireland, Germany, France and some other countries. These English immigrants were mostly weavers, spinners, cabinet makers, watch makers and other kinds of artisans, and some farmers and laborers.[1] Accustomed as these were to lower wages and poorer living conditions than the American worker, their competition caused much dissatisfaction.

But although the economic pinch was severely felt the formal objections were not, at this stage, put upon that ground. The arguments now advanced against the foreigner may be gleaned from a memorial, signed by 900 members of the Native American Association, to the House of Representatives at Washington. The foreigner, the memorial urged, was inured to monarchical governments. Worn by oppressions

---

[1] Report of U. S. Secretary of State Edward Livingston, February 21, 1833, *Document No. 119*, House of Representatives, 22nd Congress, 2nd Session.

and toils, he sought a new home in America. He brought along "all his foreign habits, prejudices and predilections 'lumbring' at his back." This being so, "can it be believed that he can disburden himself so completely of these, and have so learned to fulfil the duties of a citizen of the United States, in the very short term of five years as to be qualified to exercise all the political privileges of one?" The memorialists expressed their fears over "the rapid and extraordinary increase of the foreign population." It would, they prognosticated, "ere long expose the institutions of the country to serious danger." How? Led by artful demagogues, foreigners might eventually be used "as the instruments of the overthrow of this now happy and envied republic." Then to meet expected criticism, the memorialists noted that they "were not to be reminded that all—without exception—of the native citizens of the United States are themselves descended, mediately or immediately from a foreign stock." But—and an emphasized *but* it was—Native Americans would welcome foreigners as friends and companions, yet the relation should end there. Foreigners should "mingle not in our political affairs; [they should] be content to be governed and seek not to govern" those who entertained and afforded them shelter and protection.[2]

To these arguments was added another plea mainly from New England. A report of a committee of the Massachusetts House of Representatives, sent as a memorial to Congress, complained of the "host of foreign paupers with which we are already infested" coming into the United States via Canada. Yet this "host," according to the figures given in this memorial, comprised fifty actually entering into the United States of a total of 320 who had landed in Canada.[3]

The Native Americans made headway variously in a number of cities. In New York, for instance, in the election of 1835, they polled some 9,000 votes in a total of 23,000. By 1841 the movement had become avowedly anti-Catholic, and by 1843 definitely anti-Irish.

The first of these results was quickened by the far more than local perturbation caused by a Catholic petition pre-

---

[2] *Document No. 98*, January 1, 1838, House of Representatives, 25th Congress, 2nd Session.
[3] *Document No. 219*, House of Representatives, 24th Congress, 1st Session.

sented by Archbishop Hughes, of New York City, to the
Board of Aldermen, on September 21, 1840, for the appropriation of public funds for Catholic schools. Public schools, the
petition complained, were uniformly opened with the reading of Protestant selections from the Scriptures to which
Catholics objected. Also that many of the elementary reading
lessons contained matter prejudicial to the Catholic name
and character; the term "popery" was repeatedly found in
them. "This term," the petition went on, "is known and
employed as one of insult and contempt toward the Catholic
religion, and it passes into the minds of children with the
feeling of which it is the outward expression." Furthermore,
stated the petition, both the historical and religious portions
of the reading lessons were chosen from Protestant writers
"whose prejudices against the Catholic religion rendered
them unworthy of confidence in the minds of your petition-
ers." The petition specified a number of examples of such
offensive books, one describing the "deceitful" Catholics as
having burned John Huss, and others ridiculing "popery." [4]

Immediately there came a protest by a committee of pastors
of the Methodist Episcopal Church against any sectarian division of the school fund. The Roman Catholic Church, this
memorial charged, aimed to use public funds to teach their
dogmas not only to their own children, but also to Protestant
children. "Such a grant of public funds would be utterly
destructive of the whole scheme of public instruction. If Roman Catholic claims are admitted, all the other Christian
denominations will urge similar claims." [5]

Addressing the New York Board of Aldermen, on October 29 and 30, 1840, Archbishop Hughes said that he took no
stand whereby he could lay himself open to the Protestant
charge of "enmity to the word of God" by excluding the
Protestant Bible. "I would leave the Protestant Bible to those
who reverence it; but for myself it has not my confidence." He
disclaimed all intention "to bring anything from Rome, except to those who believe in its spiritual authority." As vigorously he also denied the charge of his planning to preach the
Catholic religion in the public schools. Catholics, he said, ob-

[4] *Document No. 40*, Documents of the [New York] Board of Aldermen,
1840-1841, Vol. 7, pp. 569-576.
[5] Ibid., pp. 580-585.

jected to the use of books in which they were branded as "papists." A book in which this was done might not be a textbook but it was in the school library supported at public expense to which Catholics had to contribute. One book so used was *The Irish Heart* which, describing an Irish Catholic, made fun of the Catholic doctrine of substantiation. "Now suppose," Archbishop Hughes commented, "Catholic children hear this in the company of their Protestant associates! They will be subject to the ridicule of their companions . . . and they will become ashamed of their religion." Notwithstanding all that Father Matthew (an Irish priest who then long carried on a crusade for temperance) had done, the same book, the Archbishop said, thus pictured intemperance: "It is more probably a part of the papal system." The Archbishop could have cogently pointed out that in the years following 1838 when Father Matthew began his temperance work in Ireland, large numbers of Catholics there had joined his movement, and the consumption of liquor as shown by excise statistics had greatly dropped.

Reluctant as we are to enlarge too much upon a phase or subject, yet if the matter at hand sheds needful illumination upon the spirit, foibles or peculiarities of a period, the advantages of dwelling upon it are manifest. To go on, then, we follow Archbishop Hughes' reading from the same book:

> For when drunkenness shall have been done away, and with it, that just relative proportion of all indolence, ignorance, crime and misery and superstition of which it is the putative parent: then truly a smaller portion of mankind may be expected to follow the dark lantern of the Romish religion. That religion is most likely to find professors among the frivolous and wicked which, by a species of ecclesiastical legerdemain, can persuade the sinner that he is going to heaven, when he is going directly to hell. By a refined and complicated system of Jesuitry and prelatical juggling, the papal see has obtained its present extensive influence throughout the world.

After reading these extracts, the Archbishop caustically remarked: "And, unless we send our children to imbibe these lessons, we are going to overturn the system!"

Much more had Archbishop Hughes to say, but we shall confine ourselves to one more of his points, saying:

Suppose the Presbyterians were in the minority, and Catholics were numerically what Protestants are now, and therefore able to decide what lessons these children should read in the schools, I ask if the gentlemen [opponents] would not conceive they had reasonable objections if they [the Catholics] forced upon them a system of education which taught that their denomination, past, present and to come, was deceitful. Now take up these books which teach that all is infamous in our [Catholic] history . . . If such a practice were reversed what would they [Protestants] do? Would not Presbyterians have a right to complain . . . if we spread before *their* children lessons on the burning of Cervetus by Calvin, and on the hanging of members of the Society of Friends by those who held Calvinistic doctrines? . . . How was it that after the Protestant Bible, "without note or comment" came into use, every denomination of Protestants in *the whole world* that had the misfortune to be yoked to civil power, wielded the sword of persecution, and derived their authority for so doing from the *naked text* [of their special Bible] . . .[6]

As a basis of compromise, a committee on behalf of the New York Public School Society offered to remove from school textbooks all contents offensive to Catholics. Furthermore, to exclude from all school libraries every work the aim or tendency of which was to create prejudice against Catholic tenets or practice. Finally, that all books would be carefully examined to see if they did contain offensive matter.[7] With this decision before it, the Special Committee of the Board of Aldermen submitted its report on January 11, 1841. Conceding the Catholic complaint "to be not wholly unfounded," it pointed to the resolution of the School Society to expunge all prejudicial passages as one sufficient reason why no ordinance was necessary. Another reason given was the rule of American government not to recognize sectarian difference. "When it begins to legislate with reference to any particular denomination of Christians in any manner which establishes their religious peculiarities, it oversteps a boundary which

[6] The whole of Archbishop Hughes' speech with other addresses was published in 1864 by the American News Company as a book, *Lectures of Archbishop Hughes, Etc., Containing His Speech on the School Question.* The above citations are from pp. 56-57, 68 and 71.

[7] *Document No. 40*, Documents of the [New York] Board of Aldermen, 1840-1841, Vol. 7, pp. 565-566.

public opinion has established. . . ." That Catholics largely withheld sending their children to the public schools was a charge in the report thus stated: "It is a melancholy fact that in neighborhoods where Catholic children are numerous, the public schools number but few children whose parents profess the Catholic faith. . . ." [8]

What neither this committee nor any other body saw fit to comment upon was the pregnant fact that in a country professing to protect all religions, only one religion was at this juncture recognized as the well-established religion of the communities. All of the States had advanced to the point of leaving maintenance of church, religious institutions and ministers entirely to voluntary support. But at least twenty-four State Constitutions specifically recognized Christianity as the exclusive religion.

Whatever was the degree of effectiveness in barring the offensive books from school classrooms and school libraries in New York City they still remained in Sunday-school and other libraries there, and they were similarly in circulation throughout the United States. Indeed the demand for those books became stronger with the widespread dissemination of an alarming report erected on nothing more than the petition of Archbishop Hughes. Catholics were represented as plotting to undermine the public-school system, or such as it then was in embryo, with the ultimate aim of securing control. Passions were aroused to venomous bitterness. Presently, too, there came into vigorous action ministerial associations called Lord's Day Associations. The avowed object of these was to keep strict Sunday laws on the statute books and see to their enforcement. But these groups also proved themselves centers to focalize anti-Catholic sentiment.

The antagonistic course toward Irish immigrants which Morse charted in his book now began to take general effect. Many of that nationality who had come to America lived in the most squalid manner—"shanty Irish" they were dubbed —but their supreme objective was to save all that they could from their slight earnings to send remittances to relatives in Ireland to pay for passage to America. And as fast as more of the Irish came, the process cumulatively increased. Both economic and religious conditions in Ireland had long been des-

[8] Ibid., pp. 558-563.

perate. Testifying before a Select Committee of the House of Lords appointed in 1825 to investigate the state of affairs in Ireland, Daniel O'Connell, noted Irish leader and orator, made these statements: Taxation was terrific; the peasantry suffered great distress from the tithe on potatoes; it was very rare to find an Irish peasant having any money; not one in twenty of the peasantry could find constant employment; there were three times as many people in Ireland as were necessary for the purpose of cultivating the land; Ireland was infested by traveling beggars; one million out of seven millions of Irish existed entirely by charity and plunder. Religious oppression, O'Connell further testified, was ruthless. Catholics were excluded by British law from every possible opening or office; could not qualify at elections; were not eligible to become guardians to their own children without taking certain oaths repugnant to their conscience. To get employment, O'Connell stated, some Irish Catholics conformed to Protestantism but when taken seriously ill sent for the priest and died in the Catholic faith. And O'Connell mentioned another and most distressing fact: Weighted by drastic laws of every kind, it was, he said, a "common practice for the peasantry to make presents, and females, their chastity, to magistrates, to influence decisions." [9]

Foes of Irish immigrants in America did not give the slightest thought to the aspirations of these seekers of religious liberty. Neither was any understanding evinced of the results of centuries of persecution in making Irish Catholics all the more determined to cling to their faith. That they were and staunchly remained Catholics was held a prime reason for condemning them as menaces. To this was added the fear of many American workers that with the influx of Irish immigrants now beginning in force, native workingmen would soon have to descend to a wage of a shilling or twenty cents a day instead of the $1.50 they were daily receiving.

The sweep of the Native American forces was rapid. One of their leading orators in the New York City mayoralty campaign of 1843 gave assurance in a speech that "the American Republicans will not be found with Roman Catholics in the same ranks." [10] At the same time, by promising much-needed municipal reforms, the Native American Party gained the support of numbers of voters not intensely swayed by bigotry. Native Americans elected James Harper mayor, and for many years afterward were a strong, although not victorious, party in New York City. In Boston and elsewhere throughout parts of the country they made initial or sizable showings, and some constituencies began sending Native American members to seats in Congress. The Native American Party's hold was chiefly in cities and manufacturing centers; unsettled regions in some sections of New York and especially in the middle and farther West favored immigration to develop lands and increase population. Opposing any impediment tending to discourage immigration, those sections were averse to the Native American demand for a long probation as preliminary to naturalization.

Yet in some of those Western areas the already resident settlers manifested strenuous objection to one kind of immigration which touched upon their own sort of bigotry. Born of the preaching of Joseph Smith, Jr., in 1831, Mormonism held itself to be a Christian religion but with its own revelations. These, was the claim, were based upon writings on long-hidden golden plates the location and purport of which were revealed to Smith by a prophet Mormon. He, it was asserted, had lived in America some time after Christ, and in some mysterious way had preached Christianity. Frequent doubts cast upon this story had no effect in retarding the growth of Mormonism. This had its own distinct theology of a highly esoteric nature.

In the earlier stages, the feeling against Mormons was not dominantly because of polygamy. Although this was somewhat in practice, it was not openly proclaimed until 1852 as an ordained institution. Animus was directed at Mormons partly because their ideas and ways differed so greatly from the customary, and in part because of their phenomenally industrious co-operative system which, while essentially individualistic, was planned harmoniously for the common benefit. At the time this was viewed by outsiders as communism. As the Brook Farm experiment in Massachusetts had aroused the intense envy and resentment of farmers there, with evil

[10] See *The History of Tammany Hall*, 1917 edit., p. 135.

consequences to the Brook Farm equipment, so was the experience inflicted upon Mormons.

Driven by persecution from their prosperous settlement at Kirkland, Ohio, where they had built a temple, the Mormons, led by Smith, migrated to Missouri, then Far West. Forced by outrages to leave that place, they went to Nauvoo, Illinois. Numbering now nearly 20,000, they created an extraordinarily efficient community. Brigham Young, who combined the fervor and power of a missionary with great proficiency as an organizer, went to England, in 1840, to make converts. Within a year he had baptized between 7,000 and 8,000 persons into the Mormon Church, and of these more than 1,000, mostly women, were assisted in emigrating to the Mormon settlement. It was this species of immigration that aroused the virulent opposition of settlers of contiguous sections, connecting it, as they did, with the speedy growth of Mormonism which they reviled as a cult battening on immorality.

Dissensions stirred by a disgruntled Mormon induced an appeal by the community in 1844 to the civil authorities to enforce order. This opening gave a mob of outlying settlers the opportunity for which it had been eagerly waiting. It stormed the Mormon settlement and shot Smith. With him no more, the expectation was that the Mormons would be leaderless and disrupted. But Brigham Young stepped forward as leader. In 1845 he led the community to Council Bluffs, thence in 1847 on the memorable and stupendous march across the prairies and over the mountains to a refuge in the wastes then far beyond the limits of the United States. There the Mormons founded what became Salt Lake City, Utah, and, safe from assault, were securely able to devote their collective enterprise to creating a notable, flourishing, enduring community.

This, but the barest summary, although a departure from the main narrative, needs reference here as a timely interpolation of a contemporaneous and different kind of bigotry. To treat of later developments as to agitation against the Mormon doctrine of polygamy and the results would, at this point, be premature.

CHAPTER XIII

THE FRUITS OF NATIVISM

RETURNING to the career of the Native Americans: An era of turbulence disgraced by a succession of murderous riots now attended their operations. These scenes began in Philadelphia, on May 3, 1844, when the Native Americans, as if inviting trouble, sought to hold a street meeting in the Kensington district, in a neighborhood largely populated by the Irish. The mere presence of the Natives acted as an instant provocation; enraged opponents broke up the meeting. Dogged in purpose, the Natives, three days later, held a meeting in the same place. A shower forced them to adjourn to Washington Market. As Representative L. C. Levin was about to make a speech, an Irish Protestant and an Irish Catholic engaged in a heated argument in which other men quickly participated. Resenting an effort to pull him away, one of the young men so engrossed became wildly excited, and drawing two pistols threatened to shoot anyone molesting him. Dared to fire, he did so, wounding the face of a volunteer fireman from a near-by hose house.

A furious mêlée now took place. Hearing continuous pistol firing, Irish men, women and lads rushed out of their abodes carrying firearms or clubs and bludgeons. Irish women fought by the sides of their husbands, directing them where to fire or whom to strike, and even the small Irish boys took a conspicuous hand in the affray. There was at least one death and, it was believed, more than fifty wounded.

The report of this affair rapidly spreading, a mob gathered, and late at night on the same day attempted to fire the fence in front of a Catholic schoolhouse. Forewarned, the Catholics had on hand armed defenders who fired a volley, killing two persons and wounding several others, some of whom were bystanders. A brigade of volunteers was now ordered out by the authorities and violence seemed quieted. But on the next day it was resumed. Meanwhile, Cardinal Francis Patrick, of Philadelphia, had issued an exhortation for the observance of peace and earnestly urging Catholics to avoid places of excitement. And to make a show of force, Brigadier-General Cadwallader had his brigade parade in the afternoon.

Despite which, a Native American procession paraded the streets. It carried an American flag and a placard bearing the inscription in large letters: "This is the flag that was trampled by the Irish papists." Previously a call for a Native American meeting in the State House yard at 3 P.M. on May 7th, had been made, and all adherents were formally notified to be "prepared for defence." Accordingly some came with concealed pistols and knives, others with visible muskets. Circulating among the crowd, Mayor Scott ordered the arrest of such as could be detected carrying arms.

The mass meeting was one of large numbers. The Rev. Mr. Perry offered resolutions denouncing the "gross and atrocious outrage" of the previous day at Kensington, and "considering the Bible in the public schools as necessary to a faithful course of instruction therein." These resolutions were adopted by acclamation; a collection was taken up for widows, mothers and children of Native Americans described as murdered, and a reward of $1,000 offered for the arrest and conviction of the guilty.

What the gathering then actually did was to resolve itself into a mob. Most of the audience went in a body to Kensington, and, at the corner of Second and Master Streets, defiantly proceeded to organize a meeting. From houses and roofs in the vicinity a number of shots were fired. Frantic for revenge, many Native Americans rushed about, a frame dwelling was set afire, and the flames spread until twenty-nine houses were consumed. Taking fire, the market house was totally burnt. Early in the evening militia under command of General Cadwallader arrived and deployed in the neighborhood, and stationed cannon to range the streets. Making a brief address, General Cadwallader urged compliance with the law and gave notification that he was determined to enforce it at all costs. During the day's riot eight men were killed, and the wounded were fourteen men and two boys. Of the slain nearly all were artisans. A great amount of property had been destroyed since it was not until late at night that fire companies with apparatus belatedly appeared, and the work of staying the flames took several hours more.

During the night large numbers of people remained on the site, but, as by daylight the violence seemed to be quelled, the troops, excepting two dozen men, were gradually withdrawn. However, at 2 o'clock on the afternoon of this day—May 8th— a mob fired a row of houses, in which Irish families had taken refuge, at Ninth and Poplar Streets. While this was going on, another mob burned St. Michael's church to the ground, and likewise the pastor's adjoining dwelling. The fire spread, destroying ten frame houses. Late in the afternoon a dense, clamorous crowd threatened the church of St. Augustine, on Fourth Street, between Rose and Vine Streets. Mayor Scott had taken what he supposed were adequate police measures to protect the church. The mob drove away the police by a shower of bricks, stones and other missiles, broke down the iron gates, and some of the mob rushed into the church which they had already set on fire by the time the First City Troop galloped to the scene. When the fire enveloped the base of the cupola "the sight was hailed by a loud cheer," and when the cross fell into the street, another cheer resounded.[1] Many of the adjacent houses took fire but the firemen's efforts saved them from serious damage. In the case of burning houses, one a priest's residence, the other the church's seminary and library, north of the church, "none of the engines threw water upon them because they were the property of the church." [2]

The mob then went to the corner of Second and Phoenix Streets where stood a finely designed Catholic schoolhouse which was set on fire. "This beautiful building was also consumed without any effort being made to save it—the firemen throwing water upon the adjoining buildings, to guard them from the flames. At 6 o'clock the bare, blackened and tottering walls alone remained." [3] However, the fire spread in another direction, and, before being brought under control,

[1] So reported *The United States Gazette*, a Philadelphia newspaper, which gave the most detailed accounts, on May 7, 8 and 9, 1844, of the successive riots. It is from this newspaper that the foregoing and other facts here related are taken.

[2] Ibid., May 9, 1844.

[3] Ibid.

destroyed fifteen frame houses. Attacks were also made upon stores kept by Irishmen, and their goods thrown into the streets.

Cavalry now appeared, and by night were patroling the city. During the night two Catholic churches were threatened by mob demonstrations. At the Cathedral of St. John, on Thirteenth Street, General Cadwallader, at the head of his troops, announced martial law, and gave the mob five minutes to leave the place. It left. At St. Mary's Church, on South Fourth Street, the commander of U. S. Marines which guarded the streets ordered a charge which dispersed the mob.

The accounts in the Philadelphia newspapers were copied fully in newspapers throughout the country, and caused the greatest excitement. But even more of this was in the offing. Elated and heady over what they considered their great successes, Native Americans were in no mood to cease attacks, and only needed a ground or a pretext to resume. This was found on July 5, 1844, in a rumor that, by order of General Porter, muskets obtained from the State arsenal had been stacked in the Catholic Church of St. Philip de Neri, in Queen Street, Philadelphia. A shouting crowd in the Southwark section immediately beseiged the church, a delegation ransacked it, and did, or professed it did, find muskets. The turmoil continued through the next two days.

For the sequel we now turn to Major-General Robert Patterson's report to Governor Porter. Unable to make any impression upon the howling mob, now equipped with muskets and with three cannon, two masked, one concealed in a dray[4] —the sheriff, on the evening of May 7th, called upon General Patterson for troops. He ordered General Cadwallader to march with his brigade to the church, take possession of it, defend it at all hazards, and, if necessary, fire upon assailants. Colonel Pleasanton, of the first regiment of artillery, received instructions that, if as reported, the insurgents had cannon to be used against the troops, to open fire upon them without parley.

"General Cadwallader," General Patterson's report went

[4] But, according to *The United States Gazette* the armed mob of 3,000 "had beyond doubt at least six cannon." One of these was taken from the brig *Venus*.

on, "had scarcely taken possession of the church when his troops were attacked by showers of missiles from a savage and infuriated mob. Self-preservation, if nothing else, rendered necessary that the soldiers should fire. The first fire caused the insurgents to recoil; but they soon rallied and opened a scattering fire from small arms and field pieces." This combat continued for several hours. The troops "firmly performed their duty under a galling fire, poured upon them from various directions in the darkness of the night." At the same time the cavalry made a highly effective charge. At 10 o'clock that night Brigadier-General Poumfort arrived with the remainder of his brigade and fresh supplies of ammunition. By the afternoon of July 8th, the troops had mastered the situation, and, upon the sheriff's request, were withdrawn by General Patterson.

On the two days of fighting two soldiers had been killed and twenty-six wounded.[5] "Of the number of the killed and wounded of the rioters," General Patterson reported, "I, of necessity, can have no official information, but I believe it to be far greater in amount than that of the soldiers on duty. Concealment on this subject has been the policy of the survivors of the insurgents in order to avoid legal punishment." [6]

The reverberations of these riots sounded throughout the country, yet Native Americans, ignoring the provocations they themselves had furnished, persisted in putting the entire blame upon the Irish. Thus, the Native American Convention held at Harrisburg, Pennsylvania, on February 22, 1845, declared that in Kensington, which it described as the "Irish Quarter," Native American meetings "were met by foreign aggression . . . broke [sic] up by the physical force of foreigners." Constituting themselves the sole defenders of the American flag, the Convention members in formal resolution further represented the flag as having been defaced by Irish Catholics who had murdered martyrs to American freedom —"slain by the rifles of foreign mercenaries." At Southwark also, it was held, Native Americans had been unlawfully attacked. The address of the Convention to the citizens of Penn-

[5] This small number of casualties was accounted for by the fact that the mob overshot its cannon.
[6] "Report of Major-General Robert Patterson in relation to the Philadelphia Riots, Document No. 2, Journal of the 55th House of Representatives of the Commonwealth of Pennsylvania, 1845," Vol. 2, pp. 13-15.

sylvania demanded twenty-one years' residence "as a necessary defence against the swarm of aliens, who, like a deluge, annually poured moral and political corruption upon us from the tainted shores of monarchy-ridden Europe." [7]

At that juncture there were few Native American members of Congress. When, on December 18, 1845, a move was made for an act to extend the naturalization period to twenty-one years scathing remarks were made about the Native American Party. Much choler was roused by the opening speech of Representative Levin, of Philadelphia, who eulogized his party, the Native American, as "embodying all that was pure in patriotism, all that was lovely in virtue." And it was these high-minded men whose aim it was to protect American institutions from foreign influence, that had been attacked by "drilled bands of armed foreigners." Then came this deep-throated warning: "Unless some remedy be applied to this great and growing evil, the day is not far distant when the American-born voter will find himself in a minority in his own land." [8] Scornfully, Representative Chipman, of Michigan, asked: "Who are Native Americans . . . but those who derived their very existence from foreigners?" Representative Gordon of New York ridiculed Levin's panegyric; Native Americans were a "busy, talking, agitating, fanatical, proscribing" party, and he pointedly inquired: "Was it not they who were setting man against man, all over the land, and trying to excite our native-born citizens against their naturalized brethren?" Representative Grover, of New York, succinctly characterized the spirit of Native Americanism "as made up of religious bigotry and political intolerance." [9] More denunciations were forthcoming in the debate of December 30, 1845. One of these was the speech of Representative Dixon, of Connecticut who thus placed responsibility: "These Native American meetings were the cause of that excitement which ended in the riots, the murders, the burning of churches, with which we are too familiar." [10] The argument of Representative Campbell, of New York, on April 8, 1846, favoring

[7] Pamphlet, "Proceedings of the Native American Convention Held at Harrisburg, February 22, 1845, Printed by Order of the Convention," pp. 11, 12 and 24.

[8] *Congressional Globe*, 1st Session, 29th Congress, Vol. 15, pp. 46-50 and 63. Also Appendix.

[9] Ibid., pp. 79, 80 and 82.

[10] Ibid., pp. 68-69. Also Appendix.

Native American demands hinged partly on his assertion that Thomas Jefferson had been "a most zealous Native American," but more so on his strong opposition to Tammany Hall which he said—and not without good reason—was now making a brisk, systematic business of naturalizing thousands of foreigners, a number sufficient to swing an election.[11]

Unlike the Ursuline Community's experience, the Catholics of Philadelphia did receive indemnity for destroyed property. Native American enmity could not vitiate the provisions of an already-existent Pennsylvania law requiring each county to pay for mob damages. Claims for the destruction of two Catholic churches, two Catholic schoolhouses, and a large number of dwellings, all owned or occupied by Catholics, were allowed to the amount of $245,750. Independently of large expense incurred by the city and county of Philadelphia in dealing with the riots, the State of Pennsylvania's bill for troops engaged in suppressing the riots was $53,333.

Unable to impress an adverse, even contemptuous Congress, the Native American Party nevertheless succeeded in its campaign of inciting many communities. While aimed at Irish Catholics, this was not without its affrightment to German Catholics. Yielding to the hurricane of bitterness aroused, a group of these assembled in the Broadway Tabernacle, New York City, and formally announced their "secession" from Rome.[12]

Famine, added to oppression in Europe, conspired to augment greatly the hordes of immigrants, largely Irish. In the three years 1847-1849 inclusive, 758,519 immigrants came, and many more in following years. The bulk of these aliens landed at the port of New York. That many of them had no capacity to compete with American skilled workers and that there was little ground now for economic fear in such a respect was indicated by a report on their qualifications. "Great numbers of those who come here from abroad," it stated, "are entirely ignorant of the first elements of common school education, cannot even read and write, and are by their ignorance compelled to resort to inferior employments . . ." It was this exigency, the report noted, which, in 1848, induced the New York Legislature to authorize the Board of Education to or-

[11] Ibid., 1846, Appendix, pp. 619-620.
[12] Niles' Weekly Register, October 13, 1846.

ganize evening schools "open to all and the right of all without any distinction of race or religion or national character." [13] And, indeed, while Native Americans were furiously preaching enmity against Irish Catholic immigrants, these, as well as others, were the unsophisticated victims of "runners and keepers of lodging houses who practiced abuses and frauds" upon them. So reported a committee of the New York Board of Aldermen in response to complaints made by the Irish immigrant societies.[14]

That, irrespective of immigrant attachment to Catholicism, there was a considerable amount of apprehension over the enormous inpouring of immigration was evidenced by the editorial scares expressed by a New Orleans magazine—a city in which Catholicism had an old solid grasp. Pointing to the "daily increasing tide of foreigners," this magazine went on to declare: "It is for republican institutions we fear most." [15] But Native American declaimers had now reached the point where they no longer deemed it necessary to becloud their real object. This was not the foreigner, but the Catholic foreigner.

A proposition before Congress to establish an American Embassy to Rome, then a Papal State, gave Representative Levin, who seems to have been a national Nativist mouthpiece, a long-awaited and much coveted opportunity to vent himself openly. He began his speech on March 2, 1848, in the pathetic pose of having been a frequent victim of misrepresentation "by the paid agents of Jesuits who hang around this Hall and who swarm over this land." This was news to Congressmen; they were familiar enough with lobbies of manufacturers, railroad promoters and land-grant seekers, but they had never seen a Jesuit lobby. Levin forthwith plunged into vilification of the character and motives of "priest-politician" Pope Pius IX who, he said, "was not bound to keep faith with heretics." Then Levin harped upon "the flood of immigra-

---

[13] *Annual Report, New York Board of Education, 1854*, p. 8.
[14] *Documents of the* [New York] *Board of Aldermen, 1844-1845*, Vol. 2, pp. 837-840. After describing how these immigrants were thus further reduced to utter impecuniousness, the report, assuming that they could pluck the necessary means out of the air, "directed" them "to seek a home on the cheap and productive lands at the West where every immigrant, with moderate industry, can speedily become a landowner, and an independent farmer."
[15] *De Bow's Magazine*, February, 1848.

tion sweeping its millions of foreign Roman Catholics over the land . . . this country seems destined to be the grand theater of Roman Catholic power." Back to the Jesuits Levin now went. They, he asserted, maintained an oath that Protestant governments were illegal without the sacred confirmation of the Pope. In like recklessness, Levin fantastically declared: "Every shipload of immigrants was and would further be accompanied by the necessary numbers of Jesuit priests who are to locate them judiciously, with a view to the political control of certain States, or the organization of new ones in the West." Taking this as a certainty, Levin somberly exclaimed: "How many Jesuit Senators shall we have in the course of the next twenty years!" Professing to quote from Schlegel's eighteenth lecture, Levin read a passage the alleged import of which was: Jesuits, acting for Catholicism, were scheming to attain their ultimate end of extinguishing republicanism in America.[16]

Other members of the House of Representatives were impatient enough at Levin's attacks and disposed to waive them aside as the spawn of limitless bigotry, but this specific charge excited the skeptical curiosity of Representative Maclay of New York. For some days he preoccupied himself with a minute search of Schlegel's writings. Prepared by March 8, 1848, Maclay, on that day asked Levin if his remark about Schlegel was correctly reported in the *Congressional Globe*. Reading the extract, Levin said it was. "I assert," Maclay challenged, "that there is no such passage in Schlegel's eighteenth lecture nor in any other. I have the eighteenth and other lectures in my hand, and I defy the gentleman to verify the quotation." Levin admitted that he might be mistaken as to the name of the author, but he would produce the work from which the quotation was drawn.[17] That would have been simple. Morse's book would have supplied the explanation not only as to the origin of this item, but in fact the basis of all the rest of Levin's extravagances.

The next move was characteristically in keeping with the deception. Levin's speech was published in pro-Nativist periodicals, and widely distributed as a pamphlet, with the *Con-*

[16] *Congressional Globe*, 30th Congress, 1st Session, pp. 418-421, and Appendix, pp. 437-442.
[17] Ibid., p. 442.

gressional Globe cited as the source. But all mention of the passage in that record of Levin's admitting error when confronted by the proofs was entirely suppressed.

What, may here be the query, was the strength of the various denominations and religions in the United States? The census of 1850 showed a total of 36,011 churches. Of this number Catholics had 1,112 churches and Jews thirty-one synagogues. Methodist churches—12,467—were the most numerous; Baptist—8,791—came next, and below them the 4,584 Presbyterian churches. There were 1,674 Congregational, and 1,422 Episcopal, and 1,203 Lutheran churches. The remainder of the sects, each with a varying few hundred churches were Christian, Dutch Reformed, Quaker, Unitarian, Universalist and others. The total value of all church property in the United States was $86,416,639. Of this, the value of Catholic churches was $8,973,838 and that of synagogues $371,600.

Chapter XIV

KNOW-NOTHINGS

AFTER the election of Franklin Pierce as President of the United States, in 1852, a secret organization, naming itself the Grand Council of the United States of North America, was formed. Because of its members consistently refusing to divulge information concerning it, always replying that they knew nothing, they were popularly styled Know-Nothings. As we have seen, Morse in his book had proposed an Anti-Popery Union; the Know-Nothings followed his council in arraying the power of a concealed society against Catholics. In fact, Morse gave the Know-Nothings his endorsement. In a letter in 1854, he wrote that as far as the Know-Nothings were "resisting aggression of foreign influence and its dangerous assaults upon all that Americans hold dear, politically and religiously, the Know-Nothing Society has my hearty concurrence." [1]

The very nature of such a body, with leaders and members taking every precaution to hide their identities, precludes any correct ascertainment as to what man or set of men were the actual founders. We need not, therefore, be impressed by the legend created in biographical notices in later years that one Edward C. Z. Judson was the originator. Throughout his life he was a confirmed sensationalist. When in the Navy he had been a hotspur, fighting duels with other sailors for the merest fancied slight. As an outcome of the riots at Astor Place, New York City, in May, 1849, Judson was arrested for having, in a paper published by him, incited the outbreak, and was sentenced to a year's imprisonment and a fine of $250. After his release he converted himself into a manufactory of thrilling stories for weekly periodicals; under the pen-name of

---

[1] *Samuel Finley Breese Morse, His Letters and Journals,* Edited by his son, Edward Lind Morse, Vol. 2, p. 332.

"Ned Buntline" he produced more than four hundred of these slap-dash serials. These references to his career may tend to dispel the large claims made for his ingenuity and craft in creating such an organization which obviously was the product of other kinds of mentality finding satisfaction in self-effacement.[2]

The precursor of the Know-Nothings seems to have been the Order of United Americans founded at the residence of R. C. Root in New York City, in December, 1844, by Root, James Harper, C. A. Whitney, Daniel Talmadge and others.[3] Evidently this order existed side by side with the Know-Nothings and was not secret since the list of officers was published as a matter of public information. According to *The Know-Nothing Almanac or True Americans' Manual* for 1856, each State had its separate organization, and the leading officers were entitled Grand Sachem, Grand First Chief and Grand Second Chief.

In here giving the contents of the Know-Nothing constitution and rituals, elucidation as to how these became public in 1855 is necessary. They first were handed over to Governor Saybrook, of Illinois, who exposed them in that State. A copy was then sent to Henry A. Wise, long a Democratic member of Congress from Virginia and now a candidate for Governor on an anti-Know-Nothing platform in that state. The constitution and rituals were published in *The Richmond Enquirer* and *The Richmond Examiner* and in other Virginia newspapers. This might suggest the use of the documents as campaign material. But after the campaign and the election of Wise, they were published next year in a book in which this explanation was made regarding why and how the innermost Know-Nothing secrets had been revealed. ". . . There were many true patriots that were deluded into the organization, some of whom had and many of whom had not the courage to withdraw. . . . Many who went through these cere-

---

[2] Judson gloried in showmanship. During the Civil War, he, with the rank of Colonel, was a chief of scouts among the Indians. He was the first biographer of William F. Cody, the Buffalo Bill of Wild West Show fame. In full cowboy regalia, he and Cody, in the 1890's used to dash on horseback through New York streets. Ostensibly, their purpose was that of speeding to the offices of the publishers of their stories to transact business of the greatest importance. Actually, the performance was one for spectacular publicity.

[3] Such was the origin stated in a book published in New York, in 1856—*The Great American Battle or the Contest Between Christianity and Political Romanism*, by Anna Ella Carroll of Maryland, pp. 252-253.

monies were offended with their puerility, and it is not surprising that some few, shocked at the incendiarism thus inculcated should, from a patriotic conviction of duty, have resolved to lay them before their countrymen. We here introduce the ritual in full as published in various Democratic papers in the State; the authenticity of which was repeatedly acknowledged by members of the Order . . ." [4]

Among the other qualifications required by Article II of the Know-Nothing constitution, every member had to be a native-born citizen, a Protestant, born of Protestant parents, reared under Protestant influence, and not married to a Catholic. Section I of Article III declared: "The object of this organization shall be to resist the insidious policy of the Church of Rome, and other foreign influence against the institutions of our country by placing in all offices in the gift of the people, or by appointment, none but native-born Protestant citizens." Other sections of this article empowered the Grand Council to establish signs, grips and passwords, and to prescribe the mode of punishment to be inflicted upon members or officers for any dereliction of duty. Article VII directed the Grand Council to levy a tax upon State, Territorial or district organizations.

Under General Rules and Regulations came the requirements for outside and inside rituals. Candidates for membership were asked by the Marshal to take a solemn oath of obligation. This pledged them never to divulge the organization's secrets, and never mention the name or names of any person they saw present, or even to admit elsewhere the existence of such an organization. Candidates had to vouch for themselves as stalwart Protestants, and swear that they would use their influence to exclude from office Roman Catholics in particular without regard to party preferences. Having thus complied, the applicants were conducted to the inside ritual. Here, before the president, they had to take an oath that they would not reveal any of the organization signs, secrets, mysteries or objects, nor would they support any Catholic or non-native-born person for office, nor ever acknowledge to any outsider the organization's existence. The president then gave

[4] *A Biographical Sketch of Henry A. Wise, with a History of the Political Campaign in Virginia, in 1855,* by James P. Hambleton, M.D. Published by James Pinckney Randolph, Richmond, Va., 1856, pp. 46-47. The entire Know-Nothing constitution and ritual were incorporated in this volume.

this notification: "To all the foregoing you bind yourselves, under the no less penalty than that of being expelled from this order and of having your name posted and circulated throughout all the different councils of the United States as a perjurer and as a traitor to God and your country, as a being unfit to be employed and trusted, countenanced or supported in any business transaction, as a person unworthy the confidence of all good men, and as one to whom the finger of scorn should ever be pointed. So help you God!"

Having signed the constitution, candidates were delivered to the Instructor. He informed them of the passwords, and how to tell from certain cryptic signs posted around that a meeting was to be held. To know where, the inquirer was told to ask of "an undoubted brother only," "Have you seen Sam today?" The reply would be, "Go to — at — o'clock." A piece of red paper, displayed around would signify suspected danger, while if the paper had an equilateral triangle cut out, it would denote actual trouble, requiring all members to come prepared to meet it.

As further set forth in the published exposures the Instructor would proceed:

It has no doubt been long apparent to you, brothers, that foreign influence and Roman Catholicism have been making steady and alarming progress in our country. You cannot have failed to observe the significant transition of the foreign-born and Romanist from a character quiet, retiring or even abject, to one bold, threatening, turbulent and even despotic at its appearance and assumptions. You must have become alarmed at the systematic and rapidly augmenting power of these dangerous and unnatural elements of our national condition. So it is, brothers, with others besides yourselves, in every State of the Union. A sense of danger has struck the great heart of the Nation. In every city, town and hamlet the danger has been seen and the alarm sounded. And hence true men have devised this Order as a means of disseminating patriotic principles, of keeping alive the fire of national virtue, of fostering the national intelligence, and of advancing America and the American interest, on the one side, and on the other of checking the stride of the foreign or alien, of thwarting the machinations and subverting the deadly plans of the Jesuit and Papist.

Over the platform of the president's dais in each council room an American flag was festooned. Upon taking the second degree, all members had to take an oath that they would support members of that degree for all political offices, and that all such elected to any office would—if it could legally be done—remove all foreigners, aliens or Catholics.

Soon come a development in public life which made Know-Nothings frantic with rage and otherwise opened the floodgates of the wildest bigotry. This was the appointment by President Pierce of Attorney-General James Campbell of Pennsylvania, a Catholic, to be U. S. Postmaster-General. While through a multitude of underhand machinations the Know-Nothings were inciting popular passion and influencing the press, they were openly abetted by Alessandro Gavazzi —Father Gavazzi, as he was still called—an apostate priest. Vehement anti-Catholics assailed Campbell's appointment as one which would surely place at the disposal of the Pope all of the secrets of American diplomacy; while taking somewhat of a parallel line, Gavazzi urged the American people to keep Catholics out of the Post Office and, above all, not to allow them to hold positions of trust there, for whenever the Jesuits found a "Romanist" there they used him to obtain information.[5] Indeed, the rumor was assiduously spread that President Pierce intended to become a "Romanist." To all attacks either upon Campbell or himself, Pierce remained undaunted; as one who had tried hard but unsuccessfully to have ratified a new constitution freed of religious tests, for his native State—New Hampshire[6]—Pierce was not the man to be swayed by the din aroused. That the Pope was burned in effigy at various places was a fact.

Preaching against what he termed "the errors of Popery" Gavazzi began his operations in England. Queen Victoria had issued her proclamation against Roman Catholic ecclesiastics wearing the habits of their order and exercising the rites and

---

[5] See *Biographical Sketch of Hon. James Campbell, Postmaster-General of the United States, 1853-1857*, by his son, John M. Campbell, 1894. It was during Campbell's administration that stamped envelopes were introduced. Previously postage stamps were in large solid sheets the separation of which required a knife or scissors.

[6] In the New Hampshire Constitutional Convention of 1850 he had denounced the religious test clause as undeniably "a stigma upon the State at home and abroad." The convention did draft a Constitution abolishing religious and property tests, but it was defeated by popular vote.

ceremonies of the Catholic church in highways and places of public resort.[7] Nevertheless the tide had been running in favor of some considerable share of civil rights for Catholics, although granting of these to Jews was still obstinately opposed. More than twenty years before this time the precedent of a Catholic becoming a member of the House of Lords had been established when the Earl of Surrey took his seat. A note to the *Debates* recorded: "The circumstances occasioned some sensation, and the noble earl was warmly greeted by his many friends."[8] Jews were still exiled from Parliament, the House of Lords, in 1851, refusing to pass an empowering bill, and Alderman Solomons, Jewish member elected for Greenwich, was not permitted to take his place in the House of Commons. Finally, deciding to wait no longer, voters of London's financial quarter requested Baron Rothschild, whom they had elected, to present himself in the House of Commons to take his seat. He did so and was not disturbed.

There was not lacking a strong current of envenomed opposition in England to Catholics, and every move, then and long afterward, to extend their rights was painfully viewed by adversaries as a "Vatican or Anglo-Catholic plot." Nevertheless Gavazzi did not get an encouraging reception. The fury of his outbursts made an adverse impression upon audiences accustomed to restraint of expression. Although discreetly tempering his remarks in Ireland to suit conditions there, they met with cold disdain from Catholic inhabitants whom he expected to incite. Seeing in notoriously inflamed conditions in America a more propitious field for his agitation, he went thither, signalizing his entry, in May, 1853, by the delivery of nine lectures. As such they were advertised, but actually they evidenced themselves as nothing more than tirades.

Gavazzi charged that the Bible used by Catholics was corrupted; that the papacy was usurped and enthroned tyranny; that monks and nuns were not only useless but dangerous, and, in particular, nuns were "miserable slaves"; that the "Satanical Jesuits" were the synonym of oppression and

---

[7] This action was taken under a sixteenth-century law prohibiting priests being seen in their robes outside the churches or officiating in a building having a steeple or bell. This law remained in the statutes until the second quarter of the twentieth century.

[8] *Parliamentary Debates*, 1829, N. S. No. 21, p. 1106.

death, and as they had ruined other countries, "would ruin
America if allowed to go on." He stigmatized Cardinals as
modern types of ancient Roman pagan Senators; a Cardinal
"was really a spy and inquisitor for the Pope" and came to
America "for the sole purpose of opposing, persecuting and
fighting against the Protestant portion of the community."
Lecture VII dealt with what he described as the Inquisition
building on the left of the Vatican "with its fine and rich
apartments for the inquisitors, and its cells, prisons, racks,
ovens, pitfalls, living tombs for the destruction of the people.
Here men were tortured, scourged, chained, burned, murdered to the greater glory of God by order of the Pope."
Gavazzi charged Rome "with striving against all schools not
controlled by her, especially the American schools; Jesuits
throng to America to support and glorify the Popish system. . . ." In the next lecture Gavazzi denounced the auricular confession as immoral; "in astute hands, especially Jesuit,
it has become a political instrument, making the priest master
of the secrets, the conscience, the soul of his penitent." In Lecture IX Gavazzi returned to the Inquisition. "Generally, the
Romish clergy are cruel by second nature and system. A
clergy, bachelor by system, must necessarily be cruel." Gavazzi enumerated and described fourteen kinds of alleged
torture by masked Dominican friars; one of the worst of these
tortures, he said, was not allowing sleep for fourteen, twenty
or thirty days and nights continuously. "If," he lugubriously
warned, "the Inquisition be near being introduced in England, beware for your America."

This is but an outline of the substance of Gavazzi's so-called
lectures. His audiences seem to have been altogether receptive, according to a report of one of his lectures published by
The New York Daily Tribune, on May 9, 1853.

But Gavazzi's experience in at least two Canadian cities was
disconcertingly different. Twice speaking from a pulpit in
the city of Quebec, he was on the second occasion attacked by
a crowd of Catholics and roughly handled. The loud applause
his two lectures in Protestant Toronto evoked reassured him,
and he sanguinely went to Montreal. There, on June 9, 1853,
he began his lectures at Zion's Church. The hostile crowd
which gathered outside the church was of such numbers that
the police were overpowered after shots had been fired from

both sides. Troops ordered out by the Mayor suppressed the riot by firing several volleys.[10] The casualties seem to have been seven killed, including some substantial city residents, six mortally wounded, and ten injured.

Gavazzi now returned to New York City where, at Metropolitan Hall, on June 22, 1853, with a cordon of police surrounding the place, he lectured on "Freedom of Speech." His harangue was published in full in *The New York Daily Tribune* the following day. "While in America," the account of his comments read, "I will enjoy the freedom of America." [A whirlwind of applause, with the waving of hands, hats, handkerchiefs etc.] When the whirlwind had subsided, Father Gavazzi remarked—"This is better than the stones of Quebec!" [Renewed applause.] In this so-called lecture Gavazzi represented that the riot in Montreal was not against him individually but against freedom of speech. In the Introduction to his book later, however, he declared: "The Romish priests in both Quebec and Montreal connived at, and even instigated, the riots which occurred in both cities." [11]

Editorializing on these riots *The New York Daily Tribune*, on June 11, 1853, had said that its readers were well aware that it had not approved the system adopted by Gavazzi in his lectures. "This system is one of reckless denunciation and appeals to passion. Accordingly, we doubt whether he has much strengthened the Protestant, or weakened the Catholic, side by his declamations, while certainly he has not gained for himself a very high place in public esteem. In the United States Signor Gavazzi pursued his course not without remonstrance on the part of the press, but without riots . . ."

Evidently realizing the force of such criticisms, Gavazzi now endeavored to put himself forward in a character that might enlist the sympathy or admiration of the American people at large. After the revolution of 1848 in various European countries, many participants in the unsuccessful revolution had fled to America, and here these refugees enjoyed high prestige in public regard. In a preface to Gavazzi's book, G. B. Nicolini described Gavazzi as having long been a revolutionist in Italy where he had attacked "the corruption and

[10] *The Montreal Herald,* June 10, 1853.
[11] *Authorized Edition of the Lectures Complete of Father Gavazzi,* etc., 1854, p. v.

tyranny of the Court of Rome" and had been repeatedly imprisoned. He had also, it was represented, preached in the
middle of the Coliseum against the Austrian oppressors, and
when the Austrian army had put down the movement for independence, he had been immured in the inquisitorial dungeons of Corneto from which he was released when Rome
was taken by the French.[12]

We need not enter into the question of the truth of this
virtual self-certification, nor indeed linger upon Gavazzi's
further career, for he soon vanished from public appearance.
But his volume of lectures did not. It was pushed by the
Know-Nothings, and in advertisements by the publishers,
DeWitt & Davenport, headed the list as among the "very popular anti-Catholic works." [13] Catering to other readers who
liked to have their bigotry administered to in the form of
entertainment, the same firm brought out a number of novels. The sale of 40,000 copies was announced of Miss Sinclair's
Beatrice, or the Unknown Relatives, the "object of which was
to expose deceptive arts of Popery and the Jesuits." Another
book advertised as highly popular was *Helen Mulgrave, or
Jesuit Executorship, an Autobiography of a Young Lady; a
Seceder from Romanism.* This "showed the intrigue and ras-
cality of Jesuit priests in the case of wills and getting estates.
It is a tale to harrow up every generous and honorable
feeling." [14]

Equally effective in deepening bigotry but among supposedly more cultured groups was, for instance, a book by the
Rev. John Dowling, a minister acclaimed as an unimpeach-
able scholar. Reviewing this volume, published in New York
City, a magazine began by this exaltation: "The reputation
of Dr. Dowling's great work on the Papacy would ensure him
the attention of readers . . ." [15] In this particular book—
The Life and Reign of Pope Pius the Ninth, etc.—Dowling,
referring to the prayer for the Pope ordered by Archbishop
Hughes, of New York City, wrote: "In spite of these hypocritical prayers of the cringing slaves of papal despotism, however, the days of the apostate church of Rome are numbered;
and soon shall the prediction of her fall in the eighteenth

[12] Ibid., p. xxiv.
[13] *The Know-Nothing Almanac or True Americans' Manual* for 1856.
[14] Ibid.
[15] *Holden's Dollar Magazine,* March, 1849.

chapter of Revelation be accomplished"—and a torrent of abuse followed. Taking their cue from such allegedly reputable writings, pastors and street preachers went to greater excesses, using all of the power of emotional appeal to excite the listening audiences or mobs.

A typical specimen of anti-Catholic sermons was that of the Rev. B. C. Cutler, D.D., Rector of St. Ann's Church, Brooklyn, on June 13, 1853. The subject was "The Duty of the Protestant Church." "History," he said, "will mark the middle of the nineteenth century as the period of the commencement, God grant the period of the conclusion of the modern conflict with Anti-Christ. Hundreds of our laymen and hundreds of our clergymen have, after aping Popery for a time, gone over to it. . . . Behold the Papists themselves! They have come to this Protestant country, and without the shadow of a doubt to convert us to the Catholic faith . . . and alas! my brethren, what is to be the end of all this? Strife, strife, strife!" [16]

Accelerating this spirit of strife were the periodicals and often newspapers disseminating Know-Nothing aims and passions, but posing as independent publications. Published at Washington, D. C., *The American Organ* was practically the central mouthpiece of the Know-Nothings and had a national circulation. *The American Crusader* served Know-Nothing purposes in Boston and vicinity. In New York *The Herald* came to be regarded as the most powerful and influential of newspapers devoted to Know-Nothingism.

No matter how obscure anyone who took on the calling of a street preacher might be, however irresponsible or shady his career, he at once was accorded conspicuous notoriety in these publications if he attacked Catholicism, and should he do so in an Irish neighborhood he was extolled as a person of God-given intrepidity.

One of these street preachers was J. S. Orr whose mental equipment can be judged from the fact that he styled himself "The Angel Gabriel, or the Trumpeter for the King that is to come." At noon on May 7, 1854, he harangued for an hour and a half in Winnissimet Square, East Chelsea,

---

[16] It was the custom of metropolitan newspapers at this time to print in full the sermons of prominent ministers. Cutler's complete sermon was published in *The New York Daily Tribune,* June 14, 1853.

near Boston. Then, in a carriage drawn by six horses, he and his associates pompously went to East Boston, where, on the same afternoon, he delivered his usual thunders against the Pope and priestly rule. At this date Boston contained perhaps 32,000 Catholics. As Orr proceeded, there were signs of disturbance, at which the police dispersed the crowd. On their way back to East Chelsea, Orr and his party were subjected to a shower of stones and brickbats. Upon reaching Mt. Bellingham, Orr again spoke, denouncing in the most violent terms all foreigners, especially the Irish, numbers of whom, as he well knew, worked in the neighboring rolling mills and lived near by. Sallying forth, the Irish hurled all available kinds of missiles at him. A crowd of Nativists or Know-Nothings drove the Irish away, smashed the windows of Irish-populated houses, and then hastening to the Catholic church, demolished its windows. Shinning up the church's rain-gutter, a lad wrenched the cross from the gable, and swinging it two or three times over his head, threw it to the ground, where the crowd seized it and shivered it to pieces. Seven of the ringleaders were arrested but Orr was not molested.[17]

[17] *The Boston Journal*, May 8, 1854.

CHAPTER XV

PREJUDICE ADVANCES

RIOTING spread in many cities. On Sunday afternoon, May 28, 1854, a street preacher, one West, declaimed against Catholics at the junction of Grand Street and East Broadway, New York City, opposite the Mayor's residence. A mob collected, marched to the City Hall and there assaulted men who looked like Irishmen. Dispersing the mob, police arrested two assailants, both carpenters.[1] A week later there was a severe riot in Brooklyn when a New York preacher, flanked by a bodyguard, went on June 4th to an Irish neighborhood in Brooklyn, and there harangued against what he termed the errors and vices of "Romanism." A crowd of 1,000 or more, including a procession of 200 Know-Nothings who had marched thither, loudly applauded him. Meanwhile the crowd was continually increasing until it reached an estimated 20,000. Edging their way forward as best they could the Irish began to object. As soon as he saw blows exchanged and bricks flying, the preacher slipped away from the scene. Presently came pistol shots. The disorder was so general and violent that the police could not cope with it. National guardsmen did not arrive until the mob had exhausted itself with fighting. Many persons were injured and sixty rioters arrested but the disposition of their cases was not reported.[2]

Again in Brooklyn on June 11, 1854, J. S. Orr, self-styled "Angel Gabriel," mounted a stand on a vacant lot at Atlantic Avenue near Hoyt Street, blew his trumpet and commenced to inveigh against "Romanists." After he left, the crowd, estimated at 10,000, was addressed by the Rev. John Booth of the Primitive Methodist Church. Among his auditors were Catholics who restrained themselves; on the previous day

[1] *The New York Herald,* May 29, 1854.
[2] Ibid., June 5, 1854.

Bishop Loughlin had visited all of the Catholic congregations, warning them against any demonstrations. But as Orr started to go over the ferry to New York, two fiery Irishmen were discovered by his supporters waiting to heave paving stones at him. When the police arrested them, other Irishmen formed a rescuing party; there was a pitched fight, and many were wounded, including police, Irishmen and Know-Nothings. The Fourteenth Regiment was hurriedly sent for, and twenty-three arrests made.[3]

Near the steps of the Sagadohec House, Bath, Maine, a street preacher, on successive days, kept inflaming crowds by denunciations of Catholics, the Jesuits and foreigners. By 7 o'clock on the evening of July 6, 1854, he had worked a crowd of 1,500 persons to such a ferment that it made a rush for the Old South Church, a large old frame building now under lease to a Catholic congregation. Using heavy timbers as battering rams, the mob demolished pews and everything else it could, and then burned the church. "Engines," the newspaper report read, "made only feeble attempts to put out the fire." [4] Another street preacher caused trouble when, opposite the American Hotel, in Buffalo, on July 13, 1854, he caustically attacked "Romanism," priestcraft and papacy. Upon a number of angry Irishmen seeking to interrupt, a fight ensued in which much mauling was done by fists, brickbats and clubs.[5]

But whether or not inflamed by street preachers, Know-Nothings found some pretext for rioting. Usually the blame was cast upon the Irish. Such an outbreak occurred in Lawrence, Massachusetts, on July 11, 1854. A rumor was spread that an Irishman had turned an American flag upside down and so hoisting it threatened to murder anyone taking it down. Such was the account in the pro-Know-Nothing Boston newspaper *Bee*. Later, however, Thomas D'Arcy McGee, of New York City, received a letter from a correspondent in Lawrence, giving the other side and what he vouched for as the facts. Afraid to give his full name, this correspondent

[3] *The New York Daily Tribune,* June 12, 1854.
[4] *The Boston Mail,* July 9, 1854.
[5] *The Buffalo Commercial Advertiser,* July 14, 1854. Although, it was said, the Irish had a right to attend such meetings, this newspaper urged them to keep away as they only became excited. Nowhere, in any city, was action taken against the street preachers as disturbers of the peace and inciters of riot; they were treated by the authorities as privileged and sacred characters.

signed his initials only. According to him the Know-Nothings had tried every means to raise a fight with the Irish, but Father O'Donnell had held these in check. It was, he went on, a Know-Nothing named Goodrich who had reversed the flag. Finding that they could not fasten the incident upon the Irish, the Know-Nothings formed a procession, headed by a brass band, and marched through the streets firing pistols and shouting abuse at the Irish. Accosting the mob, the Mayor read the riot act but that was no deterrent. Claiming that it was being assaulted by the Irish from alleyways, the mob attacked twenty houses occupied by Irish and considerably wrecked them.[6]

The worst of all the riots began on election day, August 7, 1854, at St. Louis, Missouri. The immediate cause seemed to have been a rumor which was only a survival or recrudescence of the canards of former centuries which depicted all Catholic churches as arsenals and resulted, as we have seen, in laws for the disarming of "papists." Out this old notion now burst again.

Throughout St. Louis had flown the report that arms and ammunition were concealed in the Catholic College and in St. Patrick's church. Mayor John How appointed a committee to investigate the premises. Archbishop Peter Richard of St. Louis put every facility at its disposal and called upon Catholics to avoid as much as possible assembling on the streets. There was no foundation, the committee reported, for the absurd rumors. But many men chose to believe otherwise and came armed to the polls. The instigation of what followed was imputed to an Irishman stabbing an American in the back. This was but a stale repetition of charges elsewhere that the Irish began the quarrels. However, it suited the purpose. A mob, in which were many youths, ransacked steamboats at the wharf, supplied itself with axes and other implements, and looted and hacked whole rows of houses—fifty to sixty—in which the Irish lived. Naturally the Irish fought back.

"For forty-eight hours," a St. Louis newspaper reported, "the city has been the scene of one of the most appalling riots that has ever taken place in the country. Men have been

[6] *The Boston Bee,* July 12, 1854. Also *The New York Herald,* July 14, 1854, in which issue McGee's letter was published.

butchered like cattle, property destroyed and anarchy reigns supreme. . . . The military and police have, thus far, been unable to check the onward march of lawlessness and crime. The scenes of last night were terrible, never, we hope to be enacted again." [7] Estimates of casualties were eight or ten persons killed, thirty seriously wounded, and a large number injured. There were many arrests for disturbing the peace and for riot and murder, but available records of the disposition of these cases is lacking.

Almost a year later, on election day, August 6, 1855, in Louisville, Kentucky, where a Know-Nothing administration was in power, came another formidable but lesser two days' riot of Know-Nothings against foreigners. This riot had been organized in advance; a mob brandishing bowie knives and muskets and pulling a brass cannon sought to ravage a Catholic church, but was dissuaded by the Mayor; it did, however, attack the Irish quarter, burning down houses. In the fierce outgrowing fight fully twenty persons comprising both sides were killed and many more injured.[8] During this period, a Catholic Church in Sydney, Shelby County, Ohio, was blown up with gunpowder, and at Ellsworth, Maine, the Rev. John Bapst, a priest of Bangor, Maine, was tarred and feathered, and ridden out of town on a rail.[9]

When, on October 3, 1854, a Know-Nothing Convention of Pennsylvania lodges was held at Philadelphia, a newspaperman of that city,[10] supplied from some inside source with the information, exposed the passwords, signs and grips. Also the fact that a Professor Tiffany of Carlisle College was the convention's president, whereat he was highly wrathful, saying serious harm would come to him at college now his position as head of a secret society was revealed. The formal name now used by the body directing the Know-Nothings was Grand Council of the Supreme Star Spangled Banner. In Pennsylvania alone it claimed 635 lodges with 110,000 members, 80,000 in good standing. Upon its secret rituals being made public, the convention adopted a denunciatory resolution: "The aroused malice of the sleepless dis-

---

[7] *The St. Louis Evening News,* August 9, 1854. Also accounts in *The St. Louis Intelligencer,* August 8 and 9, 1854.
[8] *The Louisville Courier,* August 7 and 8, 1855.
[9] *Niles' Weekly Register,* for 1856, p. 367.
[10] *The Pennsylvanian,* October 6, 1854.

ciples of Loyola, the foes of God, of man and of liberty, has been directed against us. Every means, however atrocious, will be adopted, and the spirit which has enchained the world and washed its fetters in gore, will be on the alert to discover your secrets, to thwart your action, and to destroy your fortune, your reputation (and, it may be done in cowardly security), your life. . . ." A solemn warning was issued that dire retribution would be inflicted upon any traitor-informer. The convention adopted new passwords, signs and grips; these were promptly revealed to the same newspaper which exposed them.

The strength of the Know-Nothings was shown in the elections of 1854. Operating furtively through the American Party, organized in that year, they elected Governors in nine States, and filled Legislatures and Congress with Know-Nothing adherents. A clear majority of 33,000 was reaped in Massachusetts. In Congress eight of the sixty-two members of the Senate were avowed members of this party, and 104 of the 234 members of the House of Representatives.[11] Many other Congressmen were too timid to oppose Know-Nothingism.

In the House, Representative William H. Witte, of Pennsylvania, on February 5, 1855, introduced a motion calling for the House disapproval of the Know-Nothings. It declared "the existence of secret oath-bound political associations . . . inconsistent with, and dangerous to the institutions of republicanism and directly hostile to the genius of this Government." Further, "That every attempt to proscribe any class of citizens on account of their religious opinions or to favor or injure any religious denomination by national legislation is in direct violation of the Constitution of the United States." Still further, "That every interference with the guaranteed rights of naturalized citizens is inconsistent with the plighted faith of the nation. . . ." Immediate objections were made to the motion, consideration of which was defeated by a vote of 103 to 78.[12]

Later in the same year Representative Howell Cobb of Georgia made his protest. He told how in that State and elsewhere a secret political organization had sprung up "and

[11] *The Know-Nothing Almanac or True Americans' Manual* for 1856, pp. 62-63.

[12] *Congressional Globe*, 1855, pp. 571-572.

before we were aware of it, a large part of our people were bound by solemn oaths and obligations to subject their fellow citizens to a new test unknown in the political history of the country." Cobb read to the House two of the oaths administered by the Know-Nothing Party of Georgia. One ran: "That you will not vote nor give your influence to any man for any office in the gift of the people unless he be an American-born citizen, in favor of Americans ruling America, nor if he be a Roman Catholic." The other oath required: "You will, when elected or appointed to an official station, conferring on you the power to do so, remove all foreigners, aliens or Roman Catholics from office or place in your gift." An attempt to apply these oaths to himself and his friends, Cobb stated, was rejected, and the Democratic Party in Georgia triumphed. None of the many Know-Nothing members of the House disputed the fact of these oaths.[13]

In Virginia, Henry A. Wise, Episcopalian and Mason, pointedly asked in a public letter why there was such persecution of a mere minority. The number of natives to persons of foreign birth then in the United States, he wrote, was as eight to one, and most of these immigrants were naturalized. In Virginia the proportion of natives to that of residents born in foreign countries was nearly thirty-eight to one. Taking the full number in the United States, there were 17,737,578 native-born whites, and 2,210,839 foreign-born persons. Of 14,234,825 church members in the whole country, or persons for whom church accommodations were provided, the Roman Catholics could claim only 667,823. The ratio of Protestants to Catholics was twenty-one to one. "Now," Wise went on, "what has such a *majority* of numbers . . . to fear from such *minorities* of Catholics and naturalized citizens? What is the necessity for this master majority to resort to a *secret organization* against such a majority? I put it fairly: Would they organize at all against the Catholics and naturalized citizens if the Catholics and naturalized citizens were in the like majority in numbers and of wealth, or if the majorities and minorities were reversed? . . ."[14]

[13] Ibid., p. 66.
[14] *A Biographical Sketch of Henry A. Wise, With a History of the Political Campaign in Virginia, in 1855,* by James P. Hambleton, M.D., Richmond, 1856, pp. 9-10.

Saying that it was essentially a survival of theocracy, Wise denounced the Know-Nothing organization as wholly anti-American. An erudite but unsigned letter published in *The Richmond Enquirer*, on March 19, 1855, explained why it was so. The writer reviewed at length the long course of anti-Catholic legislation in England, and traced the transplanting of this with all of the accompanying proscriptions to America. Even the exclusion of all foreigners and Catholics from office was, he demonstrated, not an American but essentially a British idea. "All of its [the Know-Nothing] principles were borrowed from Britain. There is not an original plank of native growth in the whole platform."

Yet underlying much Southern opposition to Know-Nothings was a belief or apprehension that they were connected with the Abolitionist movement against Negro slavery. In one of his speeches Wise directly made this charge which, however, was only partly true. The Know-Nothings soon began to slough their secret trappings and come more into the open as a well-disciplined force merged into the American Party. Holding its convention at Philadelphia, in June, 1855, this party, among other articles adopted, demanded "resistance to the aggressive policy and corrupting tendencies of the Roman Catholic church in our country," the exclusion from all offices of persons of non-American birth and education, and also of those who held allegiance to any foreign power, civil or ecclesiastical. A twenty-one-years' residence was demanded for naturalization. But the Know-Nothings were already split, as was evidenced by the holding, a few days later, of a convention of the anti-slavery branch of the American Party at Cincinnati. This branch, as distinguished from the parent Know-Nothings, was in the North greeted by the laudatory name of Know-Somethings.

From Springfield, Illinois, Abraham Lincoln on August 24, 1855, had written a letter denouncing Know-Nothingism: ". . . How can anyone who abhors the oppression of Negroes be in favor of degrading classes of white people. . . . As a nation we began by declaring that 'all men are created equal'. We now practically read it, 'all men are created equal except Negroes.' When the Know-Nothings obtain control, it will read: 'All men are created equal except Negroes, foreigners and Catholics . . .'"

But such an utterance was lost on great numbers of voters swayed by the prejudicial books and other matter which they had absorbed or were newly so doing. Notwithstanding the fact that Maria Monk's *Awful Disclosures* and other such books had been effectively exposed at the time of their publication, these "revelations"—as they were blatantly advertised —were widely used as campaign material. *Awful Disclosures* was distributed or sold with the announcement that this was the bomb "which threw the greatest consternation into the ranks of the papal priesthood." The assurance went on: "Nor is the evidence given by Miss Harrison, Miss Monk and other escaped nuns the only testimony we have which goes to show how extremely immoral are the practices of the conductors of convents." Only recently new screeds had supplemented the collection. One—"a book that the Jesuits cannot suppress"— was *The Escaped Nun, or Disclosures of Convent Life.* According to the advertisement, this gave "a more minute description and a bolder revelation of the mysteries and secrets of nunneries that has ever before been submitted to the American public." By 1856—so the publishers, DeWitt & Davenport avouched—20,000 copies had been sold. This book was a refurbishing of all of the tattered banalities: Girls were inveigled into convents which were prisons; nuns were held in cruel bondage; lecherous priests infested nunneries; immorality was rife in those places; and more of the salacious like, all "designed to create a profound sensation."

To impress the eye as well as warp the mind, woodcut prints were extensively displayed. One was that of "Sick Lady Confessing to a Priest." It carried a long admonition, part of which was: "Roman Catholic servants employed by careless Protestants are constant spies and informers—telling their priests in the confessional all the secrets of the family circle." Woodcut prints of the Inquisition horribly torturing its victims were common. The inscription to one of these woodcuts contained this unfounded assertion: "One of the Romish Editors in the United States has recommended the Inquisition as a valuable auxiliary to the Papal system." To another such woodcut print this was part of the appended account: "The priestly professors of this papal system are the loudest in their whining and hypocritical cries of persecution in the United States, when American Protestants, in self-defense, oppose the encroachments of Papacy, and seek to save their country from its pollution."

If any such whimperings had been done, we, as a matter of strict historical fidelity, should record it, but a thorough search has revealed no evidences; in the face of majority malignity, Catholic leaders everywhere were counseling forbearance. Also, on the other hand, if any body of ministers had formally opposed or denounced this unmeasured sweep of bigotry, we should be eager to record that manifestation; some individual pastors no doubt there were who deplored the excesses, but no group or other collective action was discernible.

To get back to the profuse use of woodcut illustrations: One of the most efficacious in making popular anger boil was a picture bearing the inscription: "Procession of the Wafer Idol—Professor Morse Outraged." Here a man considered one of America's foremost personages was portrayed in the scene which we have earlier noted when his hat was knocked off by a gun in the hands of a soldier in Rome; in the print Morse was shown as meek and stunned, and the soldier as a ruffianly brute.[15]

During the height of the Know-Nothing agitation, in 1855, the Legislatures of New York, Massachusetts, Connecticut and Ohio enacted in common a stringent law aimed at the property interests of Catholic churches. That title to Catholic church grounds was only nominally vested in the bishops who never received a dollar from the ownership was a thoroughly well-known fact. But the acknowledged object of these laws was to preclude any further acquisition of property for the support of the Catholic church. Catholics were prohibited from devising, conveying, donating or transferring any property to their bishop or clergy.

[15] Without looking further, the curious may find the foregoing advertisements and descriptions of anti-convent and other such books and reproductions of woodcuts with inscriptions, in the current *Know-Nothing Almanac or True Americans' Manual,* all prominently featured.

CHAPTER XVI

THE TWILIGHT OF KNOW-NOTHINGISM

OF PRO and anti Know-Nothing feeling there had been bitter demonstrations all along in Congress, but none so stormy as those which continued for three days, beginning January 7, 1856, arising from the contest over the choice of Speaker of the House. A Presidential election was to be held this year, and the American Party was straining itself to gain every point of vantage, seeking in this case "to organize the House on American principles."

Deriding this design, Alexander H. Stephens, of Georgia, pronounced these so-called principles in direct opposition to the Constitution. "It is the political character of the Papacy," interjected Representative Whitney of New York, "which affords the sole basis of my opposition to its encroachments in this country." Stephens replied to some extent; the gist was: "Thousands of Catholics are as true patriots as ever breathed American air." Eulogizing the American Party, Representative Brown of Philadelphia, fervently exalted it as "sentinels between the priesthood and the civil institutions founded by our fathers." This irritated Representative Cadwallader who, also a Philadelphian, had never recovered from his indignation over the riots in that city, in 1844. Native American "outlaws," said he, had caused them by unprovoked insults which goaded Irish Catholics into fury. Representative Florence of Pennsylvania scoffed at the American Party's pretensions; invoking the spirit of Americanism, he said, was only a mask for its ulterior Abolitionist purposes.

Each member grew more restive as the debate went on. In particular, Representative Eustis, of Louisiana was exasperated by the accusation that right in the House itself papal power was intrenched. Yes, he broke forth, he favored the established order of complete separation of church and State.

149

"But, sir, that very same reason which makes me a deadly enemy of Catholic interference with our institutions makes me blush for my countrymen when I see the Protestant church soiling its robes by dragging them into the mire of politics. [Cries of 'Hear, hear' and 'Good'.] Your legislatures are filled with gentlemen who wear white cravats and black coats. ['Hear, hear' and laughter.] Your Congress has a large proportion of these clerical gentlemen. And I ask you with all due respect and all due courtesy to gentlemen of the cloth to show me a Catholic priest or an accredited agent of the Church of Rome in this Hall." This challenge, the notation in the *Congressional Globe* reads, drew laughter and cries of "Hear, Hear."

In sheer fanaticism all of the Know-Nothing speakers were surpassed by Representative William R. Smith of Alabama. The only rejoinder that he could make to Eustis was that priests had sat in the legislatures of other lands. A favorite with Know-Nothing auditors in the galleries, Smith had hardly spoken before applause began. From his reservoir of enmity to Catholicism, Smith poured forth invective. "I hope that," he shouted, "should this Republic stand a thousand years, a Roman Catholic priest will never be a member of Congress . . . I ask any member of this House . . . if they can point me to an instance when the Roman Catholic clergy, in any convention or any assembly in the world, ever arrayed themselves on the side of liberty? [Renewed applause in the galleries.] When, in any country, in the history of legislation of the world, were the Roman Catholic clergy arrayed on the side of the people on the great questions of civil and religious liberty?"

Representative Davidson reminded him of Magna Charta. Totally ignorant of the enforcement of Magna Charta by a wholly Catholic Parliament in the face of the Pope's attempt at negation, Smith contented himself with triumphantly pointing to the papal interdiction as final proof of Catholic opposition to liberty. Depending upon conventional, partisan or partial historians, not one of Smith's oppugners could make refutation by citing the actual circumstances.[1]

[1] These debates are spread over pp. 152-167, *Congressional Globe*, January 5, 7 and 9, 1856.

In the midst of this national explosion of bigotry came a supplication petition from Jewish citizens of Washington, D. C. It requested the passage of an act enabling them to build a synagogue in that city. "I understand," explained Senator Lewis Cass, of Michigan, in presenting the petition to the U. S. Senate, on February 5, 1856, "that the existing law in this district makes provision . . . only in relation to Christian denominations. Such a distinction is an act of gross injustice, and if continued after our attention is directed to it, would be a disgrace to our jurisprudence." Senators listened in silent embarrassment, and agreed to refer the petition to the Committee on the District of Columbia.[2]

Baltimore soon became the scene of rioting. A Know-Nothing mayor of that city had been elected in 1854, and in the State election of 1855 the American Party had been victorious. Governor Lignon, however, had his own independent views, and in a message to the House of Delegates pressingly urged the investigation of secret societies. These, he declared, "have already been productive of more baneful consequences than anything which has occurred since the organization of our Government." The House of Delegates appointed a Committee on Secret Societies which, on March 3, 1856, handed in a report, or rather a semi-report. For, it turned out, the committee's majority refused to make any investigation. Vaunting themselves as adherents of the American Party, the majority's members asserted that this alone was enough of an authoritative denial of the Governor's charges. The American Party's policy of "resistance to the aggressive policy and corrupting tendencies of the Roman Catholic Church," the majority gave notification, met with its enthusiastic approval. Lastly, the majority considered the Governor's message "an assault upon a large number of people of Maryland . . . and an insult to their intelligence." In detail, the minority report described the organization and sinister machinations of the Know-Nothings who, it said, presumed to call themselves the American Party, and it denounced the system of proscribing Catholics. As one of the means to accomplish its ends, the minority further stated, organized clubs were banded to disfranchise the naturalized

[2] Ibid., February 5, 1856, pp. 357-358.

voters, and city police were affiliated members of these terroristic bodies.[3]

On election day in Baltimore, on October 8, 1856, a premeditated and concerted move to prevent naturalized citizens from voting resulted in hours of desperate fighting. City authorities made no effort at suppression. Pummeling with fists, clubs and blackjacks was interspersed with pistols and muskets fired by snipers from behind trees and skulking at corners. The fiercest encounters were hard by Lexington market, in the public squares surrounding Washington Market and in two wards elsewhere. "Each party," reported a local newspaper, "struggled to make their way to the polls, but the Americans, being in superior strength, generally prevailed." Of a total vote of 24,938, the American Party's candidate received a majority of 2,846 over his Democratic opponent. A Maryland historian represented that the bloodshed was unprecedentedly great [4] but this was much stretching the facts. Casualties listed by Baltimore's leading newspaper were four men killed and twenty wounded;[5] and undoubtedly many not too seriously injured went to their homes and were not reported.

The American Party's national convention nominated President Millard Fillmore as its candidate for the Presidency. Its campaign was one of unmitigated appeal to bigotry, slander, hatred and fear. But it was not alone in this course. In the aim to discredit John C. Fremont, the Republican candidate, a Philadelphia German-language organ of the Democratic Party, the candidate of which was James Buchanan, spread the report that Fremont was a Jew and had been educated in the Mosaic faith. From other Democratic organs came the more weighty charge of Fremont's being a Jesuit. Much was the discussion generally in newspapers teeming with editorials and correspondence on the subject.[6] From ministers came formal statements denying Fremont was a Catholic; he himself denied that such was the case; in fact the simplest inquiry could have ascertained his Episcopalian affiliations in youth, and his total lack of church connections

[3] *Maryland House Documents*, 1856, pp. 10, 14, 17, 24, *et seq.*
[4] Scharf's *History of Maryland*, (1879) p. 250.
[5] *The Baltimore American*, October 9, 1856.
[6] For instance, *The New York Times*, October 9, 10 and 14, and *The Philadelphia Times*, October 9, 1856.

in maturity, although he had his children baptized in the Episcopalian church.[7]

Accusing the Democratic Party of cultivating the favor of naturalized citizens to the injury of American workmen, the American Party made an impassioned appeal "To the American Mechanics." These were urged to unite against ruinous foreign labor, and not to be driven from their employments "by cheap-working foreigners." [8] Simultaneously, greater exertions were made through more books and pamphlets, which were quoted by Know-Nothing speakers, to frighten people into belief that their national security was being subtly undermined. In the main, the book, *The Great American Battle or the Contest Between Christianity and Political Romanism*, published this year, was a trite paraphrase of much of Morse's book, but written in popular, tawdry style. The subject of Chapter XIX, however, was new. It purported to expose a Jesuitical attempt to destroy the American navy,[9] and it was upon this alleged plot that many a Know-Nothing declaimer expended his vehemence. Nor, it may be added by the way, did the fabrication die with this campaign; in one phase or another it pursued its tortuous underground way to spring into life decades later.

At the election the American Party succeeded in polling 874,534 popular, but only eight electoral votes. A minority, it was, as signs clearly indicated, on the wane especially as the far more pressing issue of slavery was irresistibly pushing it into the background. Yet, unaware that its force had reached the crest, ministerial associations still kept on the same line of bigoted outcries. The annual published proceedings of the

[7] Misstatements concerning Fremont's religion long survived this campaign. On October 13, 1928, his granddaughter, Juliet Fremont Hull, found it necessary to write a public letter—which was published in the *New York World* October 16, 1928—correcting some erroneous assertions.

[8] *The Know-Nothing Almanac or True Americans' Manual*, for 1856, pp. 19-20.

[9] Trivial as it may seem, the whole foundation upon which this charge was built was: A bill creating a Navy Board had been introduced by a Catholic, Senator Mallory of Florida; two members of this "scarlet board" were Catholics, and the head of it was so connected by marriage. With nothing more than these facts to draw upon, the chapter went on: "Why were Romanists thus anxious to subjugate the American navy? . . . It was to sap the foundations of our democratic liberty and our glorious Constitution of Government, which is hateful to European State-Absolutism, and the cunning disciples of Jesuitism who run wild with delight in crippling the only arm of the national defence. . . ." (pp. 277-278.)

American Foreign and Christian Union, for 1857, 1858, 1859 and subsequent years, were prolific with expressions of alarm at the increasing number of Catholics, their growing material strength and their public exhibitions. Not giving the least consideration to the fact that Catholics had the fullest right to demonstrate their religion as they saw fit, one of these reports ominously itemized "the multiplication of Roman Catholic public processions, pompous displays at church dedications, consecrations of burial grounds, laying of cornerstones of churches, celebrating festivals, importing relics . . ." In another report came the equally querulous deprecation: ". . . Rome, too, has pursued here a different policy. She has arrayed herself in shining garments and gorgeous trappings. She strives to make her religion fashionable. She builds her stately cathedrals . . . and adorns them with jewel and tinsel, and hires the most expensive and superb music . . ."

Some New York publishers, also, failed to see the engulfing of this bigotry by a vital and genuine issue. Forth, in 1859, came an anonymous volume with the raw and challenging title, *Pope or President? An Appeal to the People of the United States.* The preface began: "The extreme incredulity of the American people to believe that their civil and religious liberty is eminently perilled by the Roman Hierarchy has induced the publication of this volume. . . . The Papal Church has become a destined and formidable power in this republic. It therefore becomes vitally important that someone should dare assume the responsibility of revealing the astounding mysteries of the Vatican." But the expected effect of this appeal, backed by a conglomeration of contents in the text, did not materialize. Making no nominations in 1860, the American Party, now considerably shorn, fused with the Constitutional Union Party, which received 590,631 popular and thirty-nine electoral votes. In the next year, headed by Morse—the same Samuel F. B. Morse—as president, came the organization of the American Society for Promoting National Unity. Its announced aim was to restore and preserve unity by converting all who opposed Negro slavery to the conviction that this institution was ordained by God for the improvement and blessing of both races.[10]

The Civil War, or War Between the States, as the South

---

[10] Horace Greeley's *The American Conflict,* Vol. 1, pp. 438-439.

preferred to call it, caused a suspension of anti-Catholic bigotry and the repeal of the laws (heretofore described) directed at acquisition of property by the Catholic Church. The condition impelling this and some other changes in the law in the North was that Catholics were fighting side by side with men of other faiths for the preservation of the Union. This was the argument successfully made on March 14, 1862, by State Senator Richard B. Connolly in urging the New York Legislature to repeal the Church Property Bill of 1855. In New York, he said, whole regiments were composed entirely of Irish-American citizens, and in his district there was hardly a Catholic family a member of which was not in the Union Army.[11] On the like grounds Governor Andrew of Massachusetts, in a message to the Legislature in 1862, recommended effacement of such a discriminatory law in that State. In the same year the Massachusetts Legislature passed an act removing two other long-enduring discriminations. The school committee was enjoined from requiring any scholar to read any particular version of the Bible of which his parent or guardian disapproved. And no school books calculated to favor the tenets of any special sect of Christians were to be purchased or used in any of the public schools.[12]

The Civil War was barely ended when voices were raised for resumption of the campaign against what they condemned as "Romanism." One of these agitators was the Rev. Henry M. Scudder who, at the annual meeting of the American and Foreign Christian Union, at New York City, on May 9, 1865, recited how Negro slavery had been killed; God had a great work ahead for the American nation in propagating republican principles throughout the world; and papacy was now the great enemy of liberty.[13] But the country at large was too preoccupied at this stage with great problems ensuing from the war to give heed to such incitations. In many sections anti-Catholic bigotry was by no means absent, but it was virtually in a dormant state, subordinated by the critical and immediate problems of reconstruction after the havoc of a long war. Prostrated and destitute, the South especially had to occupy its attention with adjustment to a totally new social system

[11] Pamphlet, *Speech of Senator Richard B. Connolly in Favor of the Repeal of the Church Property Bill of 1855, State of New York, in Senate.*
[12] *Laws and Resolves of Massachusetts,* 1862, pp. 41-42.
[13] *The Christian World,* June, 1865, p. 163.

compelled by the abolition of slavery. The American Party entirely disappeared, and an attempt, by unseasonable revival in 1880, made it worse than a fiasco by its polling the infinitesimal and ludicrous vote of 707 in the entire country.

The one notable and tragic demonstration of bigotry in the long period following was more the outcome of a transplanted feud than anything else. Because of their support of William III of England, Prince of Orange, Catholics, at the end of the seventeenth century gave the name Orangemen to Irish Protestants. In 1795 these instituted in Ireland the Society of Orangemen, a secret politico-religious society, for the purpose of upholding the Protestant religion, of striving for its ascendency, and of opposing the Catholic influence in the government of Ireland. Originating in Ulster there, this Society, as emigration proceeded, spread itself in other countries, with local branches called lodges throughout the British Empire and in many parts of the United States. An important change in the character of law as affecting religion had been made in Ireland in 1869. No longer did Catholics there have to pay tithes for the support of an established Anglican church which they never attended. The act of 1869 put the maintenance of all religions in Ireland on a voluntary basis. But neither the passage of time nor the influences of the institutions of other countries in which they resided tended to diminish the hostility of the two Irish factions, one living in tradition, the other in memory of long oppression.

At an annual celebration of the Battle of the Boyne (in which, in 1690, the army of William III defeated that of James II) a party of Orangemen, on July 12, 1870, wended their festive way to hold a picnic in a park on Eighth Avenue near 92nd Street, New York City. As they marched up the avenue their band kept playing airs intensely obnoxious to Irish Catholics. When a gang of these working on the nearby boulevard heard these provocations, their anger flared. Hurling stones and then brandishing shovels and crowbars, the, made for the Orangemen, who resisted. The few police escorts were powerless. Some of both sides carried pistols which were now used. Three persons were at once killed, and of the array of wounded some afterward died. The Orangemen had to retreat, but this attack made them all the more determined to parade on the next July 12th.

Mayor A. Oakey Hall, however, committed himself to the other side by marching at the head of the St. Patrick's Day procession, and doubtless with his consent, tacit or other, the police commissioner issued an order forbidding the Orangemen's parade. A mass meeting at the Produce Exchange denounced this action, and there were further expressions of public indignation. This was the period of the Tweed regime's great thefts of public funds. Already confronted by a public movement dangerously inquisitive regarding the city's huge debt and outlays, the political machine feared antagonizing public opinion further. A policy of conciliation presented itself as the wiser course. Responding to an urgent request, Governor Hoffman came to the city, and a consultation with city officials resulted in the revocation of the prohibitory order. A proclamation was issued notifying all citizens to keep the peace, and conveying a warning that the paraders would be protected in their rights by the State's full civil and military powers.

Flanked by five National Guard regiments, the Orangemen, in full regalia, paraded up Eighth Avenue which was lined with spectators. From a tenement house between 24th and 25th Streets a shot was fired. This provoked an instantaneous assault, first by missiles of various kinds thrown from abutting buildings, and then scatterings of shots from the greatly excited crowd. Two of the regiments poured volleys which had deadly effect. Including three members of the Ninth Regiment, fifty-four persons were killed and mortally wounded, and many soldiers injured.[14] Although done without express authority, firing by the regiments was justified by dominant public sentiment as imperative in preventing a much worse riot. Escorted to the Seventh Regiment armory over Tompkins Market, the soldiers cleared the streets, allowing the Orangemen to strip themselves of their insignia and singly betake themselves to their homes.

In refreshing contrast to the bigotry erstwhile displayed in Congress was the action of that body in protesting against the

[14] Wilson's *Memorial History of the City of New York,* Vol. 3, p. 534. This account needs a slight amplification. Two policemen were among the fifty-four killed, and the injured numbered sixty-seven persons, including women and children. Catholic Irish sympathizers made the funerals on the following Sunday of those killed by the militia an occasion for vigorous denunciation of the Orangemen, militia and police, while obsequies for the soldiers and policemen slain were eulogistic of their heroic devotion to duty.

robbery, brutal treatment and massacres of Jews, accompanied by destruction of their homes in various towns in Bessarabia, Rumania. Responding to a U. S. Senate resolution of March 28, 1872, President Grant transmitted the report of the U. S. Consul at Bucharest. This report stated that the outrages originated in a rumor of the theft of 100 ducats by a Jew and profanation committed by an alleged Jew in the cathedral at Imail. Pointing to the immunity enjoyed by the perpetrators of the violence, the note of the U. S. and other national consuls to the Rumanian Government declared it unworthy of a civilized country. On May 20, 1872, the House of Representatives passed a resolution requesting the President to join with the Italian Government in protesting against "the intolerant and cruel treatment of the Jews of Rumania." President Grant replied that the Italian consul had, on April 18, 1872, acted with the consuls of the United States, Great Britain, France, Austria, Germany, Greece and Hungary in making a joint protest.[15]

But the main reason for the subsidence of organized bigotry not only during the Civil War but for nearly three decades later was that numerous religious and other movements were actively engrossed with the aim to extirpate the Mormon practice of polygamy. This, taking its rank as a preeminently moral crusade and having no tincture of religious contest, enlisted the combined efforts of associations and bodies of otherwise diverse interests.

The proportions of the agitation induced Congress, in 1862, to enact a prohibitive law. This penalized polygamy and, declaring theocratic institutions inconsistent with American principles, annulled the Utah Act of 1851 and other acts incorporating and empowering the Church of Jesus Christ of Latter Day Saints. Further, the act forbade any ecclesiastical corporation in a Territory from holding more than $50,000 of real estate.[16]

The scope of this act was inherently defective. For while penalizing actual polygamous marriages, it did not make

---

[15] U. S. Senate *Document No. 75*, 42d Congress, 2d Session. *House Executive Document No. 318*, Vol. 15, 42d Congress, 2d Session.

[16] The object of this provision, Senator Bayard explained, was to prevent the wealth of the community from accumulating in the hands of a theocratic body; were this action not taken the Mormon Church would ultimately become owners of all the valuable land in Utah. *Congressional Globe*, 37th Congress, 2d Session, Part 2, p. 2506.

polygamous cohabitation unlawful. At the same time, the Government had no adequate or expedient means of enforcing the law; there was no railroad to Utah until 1869; and all power of every kind was concentrated in the Mormon priesthood which could effectively withstand inroads upon its institutions. Favorable to them as were these circumstances and deficient as was the law, both polygamous and non-polygamist Mormons were angered by the obloquy thus put upon their faith, and both sincerely believed such a law a gross infraction of their constitutional rights. The validity of the act was hotly contested, but the Supreme Court of the United States, in 1878, upheld the act's constitutionality.[17]

Nevertheless, polygamous marriages not only continued, but, in 1880, John Taylor, leader of the faction sustaining polygamy, became president of the Mormon Church.[18] Seeming a deliberate defiance, this choice enraged a co-ordination of anti-polygamy forces which now multiplied efforts to get Congress to pass a new and more drastic act. Meetings denunciatory of polygamy were then and thereafter held in many places; members of Congress were deluged with letters; and religious and other bodies passed resolutions and sent memorials to Congress. A memorial of Methodist Episcopal Church ministers condemned polygamy as "a high crime against society and in antagonism to Christian civilization." [19] Claiming to represent 1,000,000 persons, the American Baptist Home Mission Society memorialized Congress to take sufficient measures to suppress the "pestilent system" of polygamy and its "attendant monstrosities." [20] Similar memorials flowed from the General Assembly of the Presbyterian Church, the Conference of the Church of Christ, the Reformed Episcopal Church, and other such bodies, and dozens of petitions from committees of farmers and other citizens.[21]

Senator Edmunds introduced the bill called by his name. In the debate Senator John Sherman suggested that the extent of polygamy was much overrated; according to Utah sta-

---

[17] Reynolds v. The United States, 98 *United States Reports*, p. 145.
[18] Taylor's pamphlet, published by the Deseret News Company, Salt Lake City, indirectly affirmed the legitimacy of polygamy or "celestial" marriages, or at least did not repudiate them.
[19] *Congressional Record*, February 18, 1882, p. 1258.
[20] Ibid., p. 1259.
[21] U. S. Senate *Miscellaneous Document No. 30*, 47th Congress, 1st Session, 1882, p. 343, *et seq.*

tistics, he said, there were in all about 2,500 polygamists against ten times as many Mormons who had but one wife or were wifeless.[22] (A later Government investigation substantially confirmed this statement.) The Government of Utah, Senator Edmunds replied, had been for a long time a theocracy in the hands of polygamists who monopolized all places of power and influence.[23]

Passed by Congress, in 1882, the Edmunds Act, applying to all Territories, penalized bigamy, polygamy, cohabitation with more than one woman, disfranchised polygamists, deprived them of the right to hold office, and contained other sweeping provisions.[24]

Finally, it created a Utah Commission to supervise elections and report on conditions in Utah.

The report of this body to the Secretary of the Interior, on April 29, 1884, noted progressive improvement. Older and leading Mormons, the report said, still agitated for polygamy, but nevertheless the effects of the stigma placed upon plural marriages by the Edmunds Act had been "a heavy blow against their dominating influence." Evidences tending to show the efforts of these elders to retain their prestige were stated by the commission which pointed out: "Among others, their newspaper diatribes and pulpit harangues against the [Edmunds] law, and their exhortations to the (non-polygamist) Mormons to stand by their (polygamous) leaders and elders." Evidently, the commission commented, the meetings in which these discourses were delivered were concerted by the leaders because of their alarm at the effects of the law upon the mass of Mormons, only a small part of the adults among whom had entered into polygamy. No longer, also, did polygamous Mormons hold nearly all principal political offices; since the commission had begun its work there had been elected in Utah 1,351 officials, not one a polygamist. On the other hand, 12,000 polygamists, including women voters, had been disfranchised. In the more rural and remote districts, chiefly in Southern Utah, there had not been much decrease

[22] *Congressional Record*, February 16, 1882, pp. 1211-1212.
[23] Ibid., p. 1213.
[24] For instance: All jurymen believing in polygamy could be challenged; special oaths were required from voters that they were not polygamists; adultery and fornication were made criminal offences; children born before January 1, 1883, were legitimatized, but those born thereafter were not allowed the right of inheritance.

in polygamy, but elsewhere the "old theological tyranny was no longer nearly so powerful." Many Christian denominations had established colleges, schools and churches in Salt Lake City and in various other places. This influx, together with the operation of the law, the development of mines and the establishment of banking and mercantile interests, were gradually giving Utah a character very different from that in its original years when, to a great extent, it was isolated from the rest of the world and under the imperious leadership of a fanatical leader.[25]

In 1886 Congress received petitions asking for further legislation against the Mormon Church, chiefly to deprive it of the economic support it had in its campaign of proselytism. Senator Edmunds introduced a bill, one clause of which dissolved the Perpetual Emigrating Fund Company. Two reports were submitted by the House Committee on Judiciary. The majority report made the mistake of attacking the Mormon religion as such and of bringing in matter extraneous to the point at issue. Equally condemning polygamy, the minority report declared the existing law sufficient for all purposes; the Salt Lake City penitentiary was overcrowded with inmates convicted for violating that law; the U. S. Government had no interest in Mormon property and there was no reason why oppressive proceedings should be begun. "It is positively childish," the minority report went on, "to insist that there is now or ever can be any danger to our civilization or our institutions from the exertions of the Mormon people . . . who number less than 250,000 souls." [26]

However, insistent public demand prevailed; the Edmunds-Tucker Act, as it was called, became law on March 3, 1887. It annulled Utah Territory laws creating the Perpetual Emigrating Fund Company, and prohibited Utah from passing any laws promoting immigration into its borders. It struck again at foundation powers of the Mormon Church, and effaced Utah laws creating a Mormon militia. Rules of evidence were changed so as to make less difficult the securing of evidence in cases of polygamy and cohabitation. Adultery

[25] *Document No. 153*, 48th Congress, 1st Session, pp. 1-5. Christian small businessmen complained, however, of the clannishness of Mormons in trading with one another rather than do business with gentiles, p. 4.
[26] *House of Representatives Report No. 2735*, 49th Congress, 1st Session, Vol. 9, Part 2.

was made liable to a term of not more than three years in prison. Every marriage had to be fully certified; violation entailed $1,000 fine or not more than two years in prison or both. Female voting was prohibited. The delicate question of the status of children was met by a provision legitimatizing all those issue of plural marriages born twelve months after the act's passage.[27]

Although not completely eradicated, polygamy was effectively broken by the year 1890. An estimated 1,100 persons had been convicted under Federal laws; much Mormon church property confiscated; and for the first time gentiles in that year obtained control of Salt Lake City's municipal government. The Supreme Court of the United States having declared the Edmunds Act constitutional,[28] Wilfred Woodruff, President of the Mormon Church, issued, on September 26th of the same year, a manifesto advising Mormons to refrain from contracting any marriage forbidden by the laws of the land. This proclamation, he later testified, he expected to be obediently observed.[29] At a great conference of many thousands of Mormon church members, a motion that Woodruff's declaration be regarded as authoritative and binding was unanimously adopted.[30] The enabling act of July 6, 1894, authorizing the people of Utah to adopt a Constitution and form a State government, secured perfect religious freedom but prohibited polygamous marriages.

From time to time later came rumblings here and there against Mormons, but they were merely diminishing remnants of a once mighty agitation that, by the early 1890's, had attained its object and spent its force. The way was now conveniently open for the pushing of an organized and definite bigoted movement which, in the meantime, had been busily preparing itself for action on a national scale.

[27] United States Statutes at Large, Vol. 24, pp. 635-641.
[28] Murphy v. Ramsey, 114 United States Reports, p. 45.
[29] House Report No. 85, Part 1, June 20, 1900, p. 41.
[30] Statement of Delegate Joseph L. Rawlins of Utah in the House of Representatives, December 12, 1893. Congressional Record of that date.

CHAPTER XVII

THE A. P. A.

IN the prosaic town of Clinton, Iowa, on the night of March 13, 1887, seven men headed by Henry F. Bowers founded the first national council of an organization which, despite its insignificant beginnings, was loftily termed the American Protective Association. This name was ere long abbreviated by the organization itself to the initials A. P. A., and thus it became known in popular usage. A Marylander by birth, and a lawyer at Clinton, Bowers was now about sixty years old. In writing nine years later of the formation of the A. P. A., Bowers related that of the seven initiators one was a Methodist, one a Baptist, one a Presbyterian, one a Congregationalist, one a Lutheran, and two of no professed sect. Two were Republicans, two Democrats, one a Populist, and one a Prohibitionist.[1] The central idea cohering them was opposition to Catholicism, and the definite aims were the curbing of its numbers by a more rigid restriction of immigration, and the preservation of the public schools from what was viewed as the Catholic purpose to subvert them.

Doubtless the founders of the A. P. A. had no expectation that a movement so obscurely launched as a secret order would reach the redoubtable proportions that it did. Yet they were not unaware of anterior movements which, from a meager start, had in due course spread powerfully. More than one of the seven had been contemporaries of the Know-Nothing outburst and the American Party's campaigns, and doubtless had absorbed their ideas and spirit, and at least a portion of the "literature" then put forth.

But Bowers and his colleagues did not have to depend upon the still extant writings of an earlier period for the source of their impressions or convictions. Since that era there had

---

[1] *The California Standard,* one of the organs of the A. P. A., June 6, 1896.

been a lessening of the quantity of new anti-Catholic productions. Yet swamped as it was by agitation against polygamy, anti-Catholic enmity was able to obtrude itself at times in rancorous utterances and irrepressible action in politics and industry.

One of a number of current diatribes was a voluminous pamphlet published in Milwaukee, in 1883. The work of George P. Gifford, a lawyer, it was alarmingly entitled, *Our Republic in Danger—A Clarion Charge to the Rescue*. The prefatory note explained that the contents originally had been delivered as an address to "an Association of Patriots," but that in response to an "urgent demand for its publication and circulation," it had been brought out as a pamphlet. The Introduction emphasized the "superabundant evidences of the wicked designs of the Roman hierarchy encouraged by every European monarchy against our Republic, with palpable proofs of the destructive workings of Jesuitical emissaries in nearly all of the ramifications of our liberal and exposed institutions." The main points of the text were: There was a "Romanist" movement "directly intended for the overthrow of the common schools of America, conceded to be and consecrated as the main pillar of our Republican edifice." The Roman Catholic hierarchy was "a separate political government, despotic, tyrannic, absolute and anti-republican." In method it was "aggressive, undermining, arrogating, and always seeking international conquests." Against this peril, the pamphlet exhorted, "the votaries of liberty should rise up." [2]

Looming as the prospective Republican candidate for President, James G. Blaine was attacked in an Appendix to this pamphlet. Although, it declared, Blaine himself was a Protestant, his mother was a Catholic; he had sent one of his daughters to Paris to be educated in a "Romish" convent, and recently another daughter had been married in his Washington mansion by a "Romish" priest to an ex-officer of the Papal Guard.[3] Becoming alarmed for his political future, some of Blaine's personal friends, on April 5, 1883, made public a letter he had written, on March 10, 1876, to Professor James King, of Pittsburgh. The charge of Catholicism, Blaine wrote,

[2] *Our Republic in Danger*, etc., pp. 5 and 11.
[3] Ibid., p. 17.

was a plot of his enemies; his ancestors on his father's side were Presbyterians; he abhorred religious tests in a republic where perfect freedom of conscience was the birthright of every citizen; he would not speak disrespectfully of his mother's faith; and no pressure would draw him into any avowal of hostility or unfriendliness to Catholics, though he had never received, nor did he expect, any political support from them.

This was really the preliminary to an episode in next year's campaign when Blaine was the Republican nominee. Nobody then or since has seemed to understand why the Rev. Samuel D. Burchard, a Presbyterian clergyman in New York City, should have made his "famous bull" in a speech, on October 29, 1884, when, in company with other ministers, he called to see candidate Blaine at the Fifth Avenue Hotel. "We are Republicans," said Burchard, "and don't propose to leave our party and identify ourselves with the party whose antecedents have been *rum, Romanism and rebellion*." Seeing the enormous probable effect of such an expression upon Catholic voters, William C. Whitney, campaign manager for Grover Cleveland, the Democratic candidate, gave the damning alliteration the utmost publicity throughout the country. Many Democrats who expected to vote for Blaine became angry, but the political effect, in measurably helping to elect Cleveland, was perhaps exceeded by the religious and social effect in giving a new and national impetus to the rekindling of organized bigotry.

A glimpse of one of the existent and underlying results of anti-Catholic prejudice in industry was given by the testimony, before a U. S. Senate committee on October 15, 1883, by Father William McDonald who had served as a priest for thirty-two years at Manchester, New Hampshire. Although, he said, there were many skilled Catholics in the factories there, yet he never knew a Catholic to be appointed foreman.[4] Senator Henry W. Blair, of New Hampshire, chairman of the committee, interposed these remarks which throw a valuable light upon an attitude: "I have taken some pains during this investigation to become acquainted with Catholic priests— something that I had not done before—and I think that priests are not, many of them, inclined to assert the political

[4] *Report on Relations Between Capital and Labor,* U. S. Senate Committee on Education, Vol. 3, p. 215.

influence they once did. . . . I should be glad to see the time when Catholics will be considered in the same light as the rest of the population. I think the more people mingle together, the more they will think alike. I do not belong to any church or denomination, although my early affiliations were Congregational, and I attend the Methodist church now. My affiliations are principally Protestant, but it is not a bad thing to associate a little with people of all opinions . . ." [5]

Seeing that such were the views of one of America's leading public men, the prevalence of a considerable body of people enclosed in prejudicial insularity was not surprising. It was these that the A. P. A. set about gathering to its fold. Transmitted religious hostility was reinforced by another set of factors. Humphrey J. Desmond, who made a study of the A. P. A., noted a compound of envy of the growing social, professional and financial prestige of American Catholics and, at the same time, resentment at the spoliation of cities by political bosses and their machines composed of men of immediate Irish descent and supported largely by an Irish-American vote.[6] The arising scandals were given the fullest publicity everywhere in the country, but to accuse such politicians of having originated corruption was altogether untrue; They were merely the successors of American and non-Catholic bosses who, in previous eras, had used their political machines to loot municipalities.[7] This plain fact, however, was forgotten or ignored, and onus placed upon them as Catholics.

Trenching upon the interests of many non-Catholics in a personal way throughout the Western States was the entry of Catholics as lawyers, doctors, editors, merchants and in other lines. These, the second generation removed from the impecunious immigrant, had fully availed themselves of opportunities afforded in America, but far from being given credit for their self-advancement, they were looked at askance by Protestant competitors who could not extricate themselves from their fixed idea that America was rightfully a Protestant land and Catholics were intruders. This rankling feeling was deftly accentuated by the A. P. A. organizers and lecturers,

[5] Ibid., p. 668.
[6] The A. P. A. Movement, 1912, pp. 9-10.
[7] See, for example, the facts narrated in my History of Tammany Hall, particularly as regards Fernando Wood and William M. Tweed.

more by invidious comment than by outright presentation.
As membership dues, first coming in slowly, kept expanding
the A. P. A., leaders took on a paid staff, the mission of which
was to stir up communities, establish branches in various
States and expedite membership. This was not difficult among
that part of the population whose plastic mentality in youth
had been fundamentally molded by the antecedent line of
preachments, books, pamphlets, legends and traditions. As
adults these people were ready to accept any representation
or misrepresentation in accordance with their preconceptions.

Every passing and relevant event was seized upon by the
A. P. A. which, making it appear of the most portentous
character, used it for a double purpose. On the one hand, it
was made the ground for a fresh attack upon Catholics, while,
on the other, it was held aloft as full justification furnished
of the urgent need for such an organization as the A. P. A.
To attribute sincerity to leaders of that body is to disregard
the shifts and devices deliberately employed. Archbishop Ireland made an address before the National Educational Association assembled at St. Paul. Actually he praised America's
public school system. The exception taken by him was that
of deploring lack of provision for religious instruction which,
in his view, sustained his making a plea for Catholic schools
to exist side by side with public schools. Over this proposal
there could be differences of opinion in respect to public policy, but no disputing the right of any religious or non-
religious body to conduct its own educational institutions.
Archbishop Ireland's expression was completely distorted by
A. P. A. lecturers and publications and affrightingly presented as a living proof of the Catholic Church's fixed aim to
destroy the public-school system. And, as we shall see, this
charge was supplemented by the widespread distribution of
what were exposed as forged documents.

The coming of Archbishop Satolli to America, in November, 1892, as papal ablegate, was likewise depicted as an enormous peril to America. Satolli's mission was to use his authority to settle certain problems within the Church. He, in the
next year, was made apostolic delegate. In a letter to him, on
May 30, 1894, Bishop A. Cleveland Coxe, of the Protestant
Episcopal Diocese of Western New York, took the position
that Satolli was a Vice-Pope. (Other like-minded writers were

terming him a Sub-Pope.) "But," Coxe wrote, "we cannot allow two governments of the American people. The inevitable consequences—'the irrepressible conflict'—must come." Then—and this is surely worth adverting to as showing one of the avowed instances of such early effects—Bishop Coxe, in the same letter, told of the influence which Professor Samuel F. B. Morse had upon him when he (Coxe) was an undergraduate in New York City. Morse "had recently published, as a result of his long residence in Europe his *Proofs of a Foreign Conspiracy* and other works on the same subject, and from time to time he tried to enlist my interest in his views, forewarning me that if I lived long enough they would turn up in forms not wholly theoretical. . . ." [8]

As will be later noted, aspersions upon Satolli's visit increased in virulence. For the nonce, it will be elucidative to turn to one of the many anti-Catholic addresses to note the simultaneous efforts toward creating fear of imminent Catholic control of the United States. This particular address—it was glorified as such by its author, the Rev. A. W. Drury—was delivered before the Seminary Conference of the Union Biblical Seminary at Xenia, Ohio, on November 3, 1893. It was entitled "Romanism in the United States and the Proper Attitude Toward It." So valued was the screed by the anti-Catholic forces that it was soon rushed into pamphlet form, widely quoted as finality coming from a renowned minister, and even more widely circulated.

Drury imputed to Archbishop Ireland the declaration that "it is the purpose of the Romanists to make America Catholic." Another alleged announcement ascribed to "a leading Romanist," one Dr. Brownson, was: "Undoubtedly it is the intention of the Pope to possess this country. In this intention he is aided by the Jesuits and all the Catholic prelates and priests." From where Drury obtained these ideas he did not explain, nor did his hearers or readers ever ask such a pointed question; they were only too inclined to believe. But we should be guilty of an inexcusable omission did we not quote these further extracts, important in showing the utterly heedless assertions used in rousing racial hatred as well as religious bigotry:

[8] Coxe's letter in full was printed in *The A. P. A. Magazine*, September, 1896. This periodical was published in San Francisco.

. . . The Irish world constitutes a very large part of the papal army in the United States . . . The political dangers of Romanism are greatly increased by the concentration of Romanists in the large cities and in particular parts of the United States. Roman Catholic saloon keepers determine largely the nominations and elections in our cities. The Romish population furnish the kind of material with which the ward politician delights to reckon. The Old World has unloaded upon us its paupers, criminals, illiteracy and Romanism, including its Jesuits and multitudinous orders. Washington, the capital of the nation, is a Rome-dominated city. The departments swarm with Romanists. Protestants and Romanist alike are in the most oppressive ways bled for the support of Romanist institutions.

And now came a variation of the old charge of Jesuits seeking to dominate the American navy:

It is said that priests see to it that Romanist applicants are supplied with examinations lists in advance; that the Romanist heads of departments, in advance of reports to their superiors of vacancies to occur, give information to the Romanist bureau; that the visits of Cardinal Gibbons to the White House are followed by the speedy appointments of Romanists as heads of departments. . . . The Roman Catholic Church is the enemy of our public-school system. . . . The nine per cent of illiterates in the United States are very largely Roman Catholics.

The oracular Rev. Mr. Drury seemed to have been totally unaware of the fact known to all familiar with the situation that illiteracy was and continued to be strikingly abundant in the Southern States, preponderantly and intensely Protestant. He went on with this dictum: "Where ignorance and Romanism prevail, crime multiplies." [9] The most casual consultation of the U. S. census returns for 1890 would have informed him that the percentage of criminals was highest in the South Atlantic States, and almost wholly native-born.

Drury was by no means the only minister to declaim along these irresponsible and venomous lines. Of the number a particularly conspicuous example was the Rev. Madison C.

* *Romanism in the United States*, etc., pp. 11, 12, 16, 17, 18 and 27.

Peters whose utterances received prodigal newspaper publicity. From his pulpit in the Bloomingdale Reformed Church, New York City, on April 23, 1894, Peters declared ". . . Silently and patiently the Jesuits have massed the Irish Catholics in the great cities of the United States, and from the grog shops and damp ditches, the Irish have come to rule our cities in all their departments from Mayor to school teacher." Evidently unaware that of all cities Philadelphia was pillaged by the most corruptly intrenched political machine, Peters certified Philadelphia as "the only city in America that is distinctly American." Peters' sermon-pronouncements, like those of other ministers talking in similar vein, were republished in full in the leading A. P. A. organ, *The American Patriot*,[10] reaching a wide receptive constituency over the country.

Enough, however, of ministerial rant which nonetheless had its authoritative and cumulative effect in firing the worst passions of bigotry. A condition of which the A. P. A. editors, lecturers and emissaries made great capital was the rapid spread of the Knights of Columbus, a fraternal and benevolent society of Catholic men. From an original membership of eleven, when it was founded in New Haven, in 1882, it had expanded from city to city and from State to State. Its four degrees of ceremonial were the teaching of charity, unity, fraternity and patriotism. Saloon keepers were not eligible for membership, and the order's rule forbade its activity in politics. And in organizing a Commission on Religious Prejudice to combat, through platform and publications, the spirit of bigotry and thereby setting forth the Catholic position, the order was only acting in legitimate and necessary self-defense. A. P. A. periodicals and speakers, however, affected to detect in the Knights of Columbus a huge ramification, the object of which was to install papal control of America. Unlike anti-Catholic organizations, before this time and afterward, the Knights of Columbus required secrecy but no oath whatever from members.

According to W. J. H. Traynor who, from his post as editor of *The American Patriot*, was, in 1894, elected the A. P. A.'s supreme president, the A. P. A.'s membership dur-

[10] Issue of September 12, 1894, copying from *The New York Tribune*, April 24, 1894.

ing its nascent years was 70,000, mainly in the North Missis-sippi Valley and reaching eastward and westward. In Boston, Massachusetts, however, a Committee of One Hundred, of which the Rev. James B. Dunn was Secretary, had been formed, and it published tracts, which it sent throughout the country, urging the need of such an organization as the A. P. A. Giving quotations from Catholic sources upholding the claim of papal infallibility, Dr. Dunn stated:

> In view of such declarations and teachings, we ask, Can a good Romanist be at the same time a loyal American citizen? . . . The Vatican claims absolute and supreme authority in all things, civil as well as spiritual, and every member of that Church is bound to render to the Pontiff absolute and unquestioning obedience. This being true, is it not quite certain that whatever his personal opinions and feelings may be as an American citizen, he must support the Church against the State? . . . Can any person who is loyal to Romanism be true to Republicanism? Can a Romanist be a good citizen of America? The United States Supreme Court has decided that the law . . . dis-franchising Mormons is constitutional, on the theory that the men who take the oath the Mormons are required to take cannot be good citizens. Why should not this principle be applied to those who confess allegiance to this Papal hierarchy? How much longer will this flagrant violation of citizenship be permitted in America? . . . Romanism is a political system . . . as a political power it must be met . . . *No ballot for the man who takes his politics from the Vatican.*

This assumed the existence of a Catholic political party in the United States. Of course, there was no such entity. Like Protestants, Catholics voted for one or the other of both parties or for another when there was a third party. But repre-sentations like the above were taken literally by swarms of amenable people who, at the same time, were bombarded by the A. P. A.'s official "Declaration of Principles" and the ex-hortations of its speakers. That "Declaration" did not come into the open by specifying Catholics. "The support of any ecclesiastical power of non-American character," it held, "which claimed higher sovereignty than that of the United States, is irreconcilable with American citizenship. Therefore, the A. P. A. is opposed to trusting any official position or functions to such subjects or supporters." Non-sectarian schools were upheld by the "Declaration" as the bulwark of American institutions, and opposition expressed against "the employment of the subjects of any ecclesiastical power as officers or teachers of our public schools." By indirection, the "Declaration" protested the enlistment of Catholics in the U. S. Army or Navy. More directly a demand was made for the prohibition of the importation of pauper labor; restriction of immigration to those proving their qualification to citizenship; and for a change in the laws so that no aliens would be naturalized or allowed to vote unless they spoke the English language and had lived seven continuous years in the country.

These were but some of the A. P. A.'s formal "Declaration of Principles" but its editors and speakers used more forthright phraseology. They harped upon what they affirmed was the Roman Catholic attack on the public-school system, and the attempted foreignizing, by force, of whole communities, in language and religion, by "Romish" priests. They inveighed against what they declared was the complete control of American great cities by Romanism; Jesuit control of the heads of the Government at Washington; the almost complete success in "Romanizing" the U. S. Army and Navy; and other assumed conditions all luridly described with frenzied positiveness.

Adherents flocked to the A. P. A. which, by 1893-1894, had implanted its organization in perhaps two dozen States and was even edging its way into Canada. Fully seventy weekly publications were diffusing its propaganda. Separately, the circulation of most of these was not large, but often they were passed from hand to hand, and in the aggregate the number of readers was very considerable. Aside from news items chosen or doctored to suit the purpose, the main contents were columns of "plate" matter defaming the Catholic church and its prelates and scurrility concerning priests, convents, the confessional box and other such choice subjects.

Elaborating its activities and to impress people all the more with testimony from persons who could be exploited as sophisticates from the ranks of the "enemy" itself, the A. P. A. employed several ex-priests and some putative ex-nuns on its lecturing staff. Of the whilom priests, two had been definitely ousted from the Catholic church for serious misconduct, and to prove their total detachment both had wives who abetted their apostate attacks. Another ex-priest, Chiniquy, of French-Canadian origin, had, it was openly charged, been suspended from his functions; he himself took refuge in the claim that, after coming to the United States, he had voluntarily quit the priesthood, in 1858, and had joined the Presbyterian Church. In 1890 he was past his eighty-first year. A fourth ex-priest pluming himself as "Bishop" McNamara, had of his own accord left the Catholic Church, in 1875, to found an independent "Catholic Church," in New York City, and he had later gravitated into the Baptist Church. At least four men exhibited as "ex-priests" had never been ordained but had merely dipped into studies at Catholic institutions.

Chiniquy's specialty was a two-fold performance. Portraying himself as one whom Abraham Lincoln had befriended when he, Chiniquy, had been persecuted by the Catholic Church, he sought to propagate the idea that Lincoln's assassination was a Catholic plot. The set of circumstances he wove to support this canard ran to this effect: A Canadian Jesuit priest, converted by his teachings, had told him, in 1862, that he (the Jesuit priest) had been informed of the plot by Samuel F. B. Morse who—so the assertion went—had heard it by chance in Rome. Just when Morse was supposed to have heard it was not stated. Yet on this fragile and no doubt mythical basis, Chiniquy represented himself as having sped to Washington to warn President Lincoln. Afterward, Chiniquy proceeded, he heard the same information from two more Jesuit priests, and he again went to Washington to repeat the warning. To climax his story Chiniquy offered this addendum: After the assassination of Lincoln he met the Rev. F. A. Conwell, of Chicago, who, he said, assured him that priests at St. Joseph, Missouri, had reported the event two hours before it happened! [11]

Through the columns of *The American Patriot* and like publications the A. P. A. used this string of assertions as grim fact. Also directed to the same end was a book by two military officers on Lincoln's assassination. Profusely advertised

[11] See particularly Chiniquy's statements soberly set forth in *The Baltimore Morning Herald*, January 24, 1890, in which city he was then lecturing.

in *The A. P. A. Magazine,* which made a business of selling the volume, this book was heralded: "No unbiased man, after reading this vivid yet truthful account of the Great Conspiracy, will for a moment doubt the connection of the Jesuits with this hellish plot of assassination of America's greatest and most beloved President." [12]

Simultaneously with the story of the Lincoln plot, Chiniquy produced a series of other plots. One of these was a decision of a secret conclave of Catholic prelates, at Buffalo, New York, in 1851, to concentrate Catholic immigration from Europe in large American cities and by its vote to seize them for the Catholic Church. This alleged project was, as we need hardly note, merely a stale repetition of fears expressed in Morse's book, and of foolish charges which, years previously, had been made by Know-Nothings in Congress. To recount other of such so-called plots spun by Chiniquy would, indeed, be superfluous. But flimsy, or even ridiculous, as they now expose themselves, they had weight at the time with numbers avid to believe.

The tirade of two other ex-priests were of such a violent nature as to provoke riots. One of these was occasioned by Joseph Slattery, at Keokuk, Iowa, in 1893, followed by a similar disturbance at Kansas City, when "Bishop" McNamara was sentenced to a year's imprisonment. Thereafter Slattery went to great lengths to laud McNamara as a martyr in the cause. Thus: ". . . He was imprisoned by a Romish crowd of officials; his wife could only see him once a day for a short space of time, but every ruffian could come to the door of his cage and spit tobacco juice at him. . . . He had been shot at on the streets of New York, his head had been broken with a glass bottle on the streets of Hartford, Connecticut; he had escaped almost miraculously of being thrown by Romanists under a passing train in Newark, New Jersey . . ." [13] Altogether, a wondrous record.

[12] This book, issued subsequent to Chiniquy's lectures was utilized by the A. P. A. as substantiating his charges. The advertisement in *The A. P. A. Magazine,* April, 1896, for instance, associated the contents with Chiniquy's accusations.
[13] Slattery's letter published in *The A. P. A. Magazine,* November 15, 1895.

CHAPTER XVIII

THE A. P. A. AT ITS CREST

DECIDING that circumstances urgently called for an inquiry into the methods of the A. P. A., the Rev. Washington Gladden, a Congregational minister and a voluminous writer of books and articles, applied himself to the task. Reflecting progressive although not radical Christian thought, Gladden was shocked by the sweep of bigotry. The result of his investigation was embodied in a comprehensive article.

For any such rampant bigotry, he commented at the outset of this, the time seemed strangely inopportune, seeing that the Pope Leo XIII was perhaps "the most enlightened and most progressive pontiff who ever occupied the throne." That Pope, Gladden wrote, was abreast of modern civilization. He had affirmed the right of people to govern themselves under republican institutions. He had shown an intelligent understanding of the great social questions of the time and had manifested a warm human sympathy with them. In this course the Pope, it was authentically reported, had the hearty support of the whole Curia, or papal court. "This," Gladden noted, "is the administration which the anti-Catholic zealots have chosen to attack." [1]

Gladden detailed how the A. P. A. already controlled municipal elections in various Middle Western and Western States, and he described its initial electioneering methods. Leaflets containing copies of what were audaciously represented as "documents" issued by Catholic authorities and secretly obtained by A. P. A. stalwarts were circulated. In one of these inventions Cardinal Gibbons, Archbishop Ireland and other Catholic prelates were quoted as advising American Catholics of their alarm at "the rapid spread of educated in-

[1] "The Anti-Catholic Crusade," article in *The Century Magazine*, March, 1894, p. 790.

telligence, knowing that wherever the people are intelligent, the priest and the prince cannot hope to live on the labor of the masses . . ." Further, "the people must not think; that is a privilege that belongs only to the Pope, who, by divine right is the only person appointed by God to do the political and religious thinking of this world."

Then the same "document" condemned any school system teaching the youth anything other than the Roman Catholic catechism, or accustoming the youth to think. "This is unnecessary and a waste of time and money, when the holy father has been appointed by God, especially at the Vatican council, in 1870, to do the thinking of this world." The action to be taken was thus incorporated as an explicit order: "Therefore, we call upon our subjects to do all they can to break down and destroy the free schools of this Protestant nation, which has compelled us to set up and maintain at great expense parochial schools to defend our faith, thus lessening the income of the clergy." Having gone so far, the fabricator or fabricators of this "document" now threw in a passage craftily designed to perturb the non-Catholic elements among the multitude of unemployed. Even in normal times lack of employment was always considerable, but during and after the great industrial panic of 1893 it swelled to abnormal and even affrighting dimensions. Jobless Protestants now read in the "document" the command that employment must be found for the mounting ranks of faithful Catholics, who, in due time, would possess the land. How was this employment to be assured? The means by which they were to attain the grandiose object was not explained, but this bald course was prescribed: "Catholics must secure control of all the cities, railways, manufactories, mines, steam and sailing vessels— above all, the press. . . . This will render it unnecessary to remove or crowd out the American heretics who are now employed. You need not hesitate; it is your duty to do so . . . but be careful to do nothing that will create scandal."

Had Gladden been somewhat better acquainted with the tissues of more or less equally spurious matter put forth in the past, he might not have been so astonished at this recrudescence. And, in fact, a point escaping him was that some of those old false tractarian publications were even now revived for current use. However, he did not fail to note the fatuity with which such a "document" was widely accepted as bona fide. He sorrowfully commented:

American Protestants, the graduates of our public schools, are expected to believe that Roman Catholic prelates are in the habit of talking in this way to the people of their charge. The men who forged this precious manifesto . . . seem to have had no misgiving that those to whom it was shown would laugh in their faces. And the melancholy fact is that they were justified in their confidence. The forgery has been taken seriously by tens of thousands of American voters. No man can intimate a doubt of its genuineness without being denounced as a Jesuit or an ally of the Pope. It is published week after week in scores of journals with large circulation. There are great masses of people to whom it does not seem improbable that the Roman Catholic archbishops would publish such a document as this. . . . Who could have imagined that credence would be given to a document which represents them as preposterous fools?

An even more insensate forgery was an "encyclical" alleged to have been issued by Pope Leo XIII. This, of all occasions, was represented as being promulgated on Christmas, 1891. A clumsily worded contrivance, its import was to instruct all American Catholics that on or about the feast of Ignatius Loyola, in July, 1893, *"it will be the duty of the faithful to exterminate all heretics found within the jurisdiction of the United States."* [2] (Italics were employed in A. P. A. publications.) After quoting the entire substance, Gladden stated: "This document has been published in many of the anti-Catholic newspapers; [doubtless meaning A. P. A. periodicals]; in some of them it has been standing week by week for months at a time; in leaflets and handbills of every form it has been distributed throughout the whole country." [3] To say

---

[2] Ibid., 790-791.
[3] Ibid., p. 791. Other forthcoming forgeries were alleged oaths taken by Catholic prelates and priests, by Jesuits and Fenians binding them variously to persecute all heretics and destroy all governments not having the sacred confirmation of the Pope. The Fenians' oath allegedly began: "I will fight till I die, wading in the red gore of Sassenach (Protestants) . . . and of . . . Orangemen and heretics who do not join us and become ourselves . . ." These elaborate fabrications, represented as Catholic canon law, were published as standing matter in *The American Patriot*, November 8, 1894, and in later issues, as also in other A. P. A. publications.

that it has spread terror in some communities is no over-statement; in small towns not reached by counteracting influences this was a proved condition. People in those places never saw the editorial comments of outside journals of their own denominations. For instance, *The Christian Advocate,* which was very far from approving anything connected with Catholicism, said, scoffing at the alleged "encyclical": "We do not know of a more transparent fraud. It is the work of some-one whose mendacity has intoxicated his own mind to such a degree that, although he obviously wanted to lie, he could not do it shrewdly."

Visiting a friend in Illinois, early in 1893, Elbert H. Hubbard asked him whether he was going to see the Chicago Fair. "Not he—he dared not leave his home a single day; did I not know that the Catholics had been ordered by the Pope to burn the barns and houses of all heretics? It sounded like a joke, but I saw the gray eyes of this old man flash and I knew he was terribly in earnest. With trembling hands he showed me the Pope's encyclical printed in a newspaper. . . . I was taken to the two clergymen in the village, a Presbyterian and a Methodist; both were full of fear and hate toward Catholics, with a little left over for each other. They were sure that the order to kill and burn had gone forth." Hubbard went on to relate how he found this quaking fear in many towns and villages. Men there were arming themselves with Winchesters, and "many preachers never spoke in public without fanning the flames." Meanwhile, A. P. A. lodges were initiating new members, and "lurid literature which was being vomited forth from presses in Louisville, Chicago, Omaha, and Kansas City was being sent forth." [4]

Having pursued its serpentine way through the ages, there came into new life the hoary charge of Catholic churches converted into arsenals. "Disarming-the-Papists" legislation and Catholic "plots" had left their deep undercurrents in persistent tradition, and out they now burst from their cerements. In many a community wild-eyed alarmists broached

[4] Although Hubbard was somewhat of a literary poseur, we may accept this account as within the truth, confirmed as it was by much evidence from other sources. Hubbard's ignorance of precedent conditions was shown by his entitling his article "A New Disease," published in *The Arena* (Magazine), June, 1894. See p. 79. Gladden's article cited a letter from a small-town Ohio physician who wrote that some people there were "almost prostrated with fear."

tales of a consignment of arms to the local Catholic church and of nightly drillings in its basement as preparation for war. Searching of churches by invitation of priests revealed no shred of evidence; nevertheless the circulation of such stories was pushed as a steadfast policy.[5] Hubbard wrote that he had repeatedly sought proof of charges boldly made by the A. P. A. leaders of arms and drilling in Catholic churches; given permission to inspect these and monasteries and convents, his search had been in vain.[6] Susceptible to stories going the rounds, Deputy-Sheriff Stanberry, of Lucas County, and Rev. W. S. Brackney, a West Toledo, Ohio, minister, felt certain that a search of St. Heding's Polish Catholic Church would disclose arms and ammunition stored there. Much discomfited after their inspection, they admitted having been deceived.[7]

As the year 1893 came and went without the least sign of the supposedly appointed massacre, the absence of this was coolly explained by A. P. A. speakers. It was only deferred, they said, because of fear of the A. P. A.'s vigilance and strength; should these decay, and no other obstacle intervene, slaughter would surely come. Now it happened that, in his article, Gladden, himself hailing from Columbus, Ohio, had included the statement of a Protestant minister in that city in an ecclesiastical assembly that he had bought a Winchester rifle to defend himself against the "Romanists." In many instances, Gladden charged, the Protestant pulpit was silent regarding the forged "documents" because members of the church were enrolled in the A. P. A., and the pastor did not care to alienate his supporters. "For the honor of Protestantism," asked Gladden, "is it not high time to separate ourselves from this class of 'patriots'? In any large town, if the leading Protestant clergymen will speak out clearly, the plague will be stayed or abated." [8] Galled by such criticism, the Protestant ministers of Columbus, Ohio issued a public statement. Recounting how the "encyclical" had been kept standing in many newspapers and scattered broadcast by means of leaflets and handbills, the statement pronounced it a stupid forgery. Likewise the "document" of the Archbish-

[5] Gladden, *The Century Magazine*, March 1894, p. 791.
[6] *The Arena* (Magazine) June, 1894, p. 79.
[7] Desmond, *The A. P. A. Movement*, p. 57.
[8] *The Century Magazine*, March, 1894, p. 795.

ops. Faced with this effective exposure, a characteristic way of escape was charted by one of the leading A. P. A. weeklies, *The American Citizen* of Boston. All along, it now solemnly declared, it had known that the "encyclical" was fraudulent. Who concocted it? None other, averred that periodical, than the Jesuits "to bring discredit on the A. P. A. movement." [9]

President Traynor of the A. P. A. now came forward to avail himself of national publicity in defence of that organization. The May, 1894, issue of *The North American Review,* had published an article on "Hostility to Roman Catholics." It had asked: "Why should not Catholics enjoy equal freedom, as citizens, to hold opinions on morals or education, to engage in politics or government to advance them?" Traynor's article, in reply, was published in the same magazine two months later. The Papal hierarchy, he contended, asserted its complete sovereignty over the State, disregarded the Constitution and laws, and a papal fiat was superior to the people's voice. He denied any A. P. A. commercial proscription of "papists," maintained that the A. P. A.'s secrecy was due to precaution against boycotting, and he also denied the purchase of arms by the A. P. A. In a later article in the same magazine, Traynor accused Catholics of carrying on "a policy of positive antagonism to the American public-school system," and charged that priests were "interfering in American politics." To what end? "The Papacy seeks to renew in the New World the power of which she has been denuded in the old." It was to prevent this, he explained, that the A. P. A. was organized.[10]

This endeavor at self-vindication was designed as much for general public consumption as to screen its full purposes. To perceive the A. P. A.'s character as it now stood and its intrinsic objects, it is only necessary to turn to Traynor's manifesto—or "official letter" as it was euphemistically styled—to the A. P. A. membership. Sent from Detroit, Michigan, on August 1, 1894, this long-drawn letter began with a disclosure. Traynor was much disturbed at a class of self-seeking adventurers, "hungry for office and the franchises of the Association," clamoring to use the A. P. A. for their purposes. As a matter of fact, these men had already slid into an organiza-

[9] Desmond, *The A. P. A. Movement,* pp. 24-25.
[10] *The North American Review,* July, 1894, pp. 69-74 and August, 1895, pp. 132-140.

tion which could be made to yield them profit in several ways as well as notoriety. The same rapacious inrush had signalized previous movements of the kind, but this was the first time the head of any of them was either candid or unwitting enough to make the damaging admission.

The prime duty of the next Congress, Traynor urged, should be to close America's portals against Europe's pauper and ignorant immigrants, but how, by the exclusion of such penniless "refuse" the papacy would be robbed "of a rich source of revenue," he did not clarify. Next he dealt with Satolli. Here we may inject the fact that, according to the written statement of Henry A. Bowers, the coming of Satolli "very materially" augmented the growth of the A. P. A. "We looked upon Satolli," Bowers wrote on March 1, 1899, in reply to a questionnaire which Humphrey J. Desmond had sent, "as a representative of the Propaganda at Rome to direct and influence legislation in this country, more especially his settling down in the City of Washington and several moves which he made. . . ." [11] Inasmuch as fear of Satolli's mission was thus conceded to be so fruitful a factor in advancing the A. P. A.'s growth, Traynor's emphasis upon his presence was part of the continued plan to keep the subject red-hot. ". . . The papacy," he warned members, "is a cat upon the watch, which never tires or relaxes its vigilance. If Satolli is silent at present . . . he is merely observing a masterly inactivity . . . In other words, he patiently awaits the dissolution of the A. P. A., and the subsidence of awakened public opinion." Following Satolli's elevation, in 1895, to be a Cardinal, that step was viewed by A. P. A. publications as furnishing more proof of its deep suspicions, and attacks grew apace.[12]

Next, in his official letter, Traynor emitted this grievous complaint: "The mighty and subtle Jesuit is stealing into our

[11] The A. P. A. Movement, p. 15.
[12] A leading A. P. A. official in the State of Washington and a member of its Legislature agitated, in 1895, the passing of a resolution requesting Congress to order, on the ground of his being "a menace to our free institutions," the removal of Satolli from the United States. "Satolli came to these shores because it was desired that one man should have control of all the Catholic people," stated an Address "The Political Situation and Duty of Patriotic Americans," published in The A. P. A. Magazine, January, 1896. "The Pope sent Satolli over to destroy our public schools. Let Americans retaliate by overthrowing his nunneries" counseled another writer in Ibid., March, 1896. Etc., etc.

labor unions, into our churches—aye, even into our very councils [of the A. P. A.] that they may divert the tide of opinion which they are powerless to stem. Knowing the utter futility of nominating for office papists of acknowledged affiliations with the papal church, they substitute those, who, while being nominally Protestant, are as much the creatures of the papacy as the papacy itself." Tacked on to this generality was the even more gratuitous charge that, to divert the public mind from its present channel, the papacy would welcome civil war as a boon and a blessing.

Assailing parochial schools, Traynor, in the same breath bewailed the degeneracy of the public schools in which, said he, history falsified by "papists" was being taught. No "papists" he demanded, should be allowed on any board of education. Turning his attention to the confessional box, he described it as "that relic of the inquisition where treason is hatched . . . where the secrets of commerce and the delicate purity of the connubial relation are betrayed to the unsexed delegates of a foreign power . . ." Then, as if having the mandatory power of command, he declared: "The confessional box must go!" And summoning other imaginary reasons he pronounced it "a public nuisance and a debaucher of purity by its teachings alone—what its practical results are, the daily press, replete with priestly scandals, in which female penitents figure prominently, is unanswerable authority." This, of course, was sheer falsehood, as scrutiny of the press attested; one could pore over files of newspapers without finding a single case of the kind. Some instances of priests succumbing to human weaknesses did occur, but they were solitarily exceptional and the rare records in the press made no mention of the confession box as instrumental.

Tedious as it may seem to enlarge upon Traynor's letter, yet it is important as showing the particular ideas possessing the head of a then powerful organization, and in showing, too, how from era to era outworn charges were revitalized to do new service. Traynor traduced convents and monasteries as "these parasites of paganism" where tender women and girls were "immured in a living tomb . . . with celibate priests as their sole companions." The laws permitting this "are monstrous, unnatural, cruel and un-American," and "each candidate for the State Legislature should be pledged to their end." Traynor represented that, by "playing upon the super-stitions of dying penitents, priests secure magnificent for-tunes." (We, who have made a lifelong study of great Amer-ican fortunes, never discovered any such fortune thus ac-quired.) But after treating this absurdity as truth, Traynor called for a law in every State rendering invalid any bequest made by a dying testator—now he suddenly ceased involving the priest personally—to any ecclesiastical institution.[13]

Concomitantly, during these years, the A. P. A. publica-tions were busily pursuing a two-fold course in what they called exposure of convent conditions. One line of action was their own editorials. A sample of these will show their un-speakably vicious nature. "Rome's seraglios," was the head-ing of this particular abomination. "In America today we have ten thousand American women shut up in convents and nunneries of the Roman Catholic church. They are white female slaves in this land of freedom. . . . They are victims of a lecherous priesthood, a carnal class of so-called celibates who retreat under the garb of sanctity to conceal their de-basing work . . . How long will the six or seven thousand stall-fed priests of Rome in this country be allowed to travel up and down the United States of America, recruiting Amer-ican daughters for these retreats of priestly lust and religious mockery? Shall the great mother of harlots multiply her harlotry?" [14]

The accompanying line of action was in A. P. A. periodi-cals pressingly recommending the purchase of books, old and new, purporting to turn the searchlight upon convent life. One of these books was our old acquaintance, Maria Monk's *Awful Disclosures*. In either utter ignorance or wilful per-version of the fact that it had been thoroughly disproved, *The A. P. A. Magazine* eulogized it as: "The most famous of the Escaped Nun Books. Not a line of its three hundred pages has ever been disproved. The only full unexpurgated

---

[13] In its entirety, Traynor's official letter was published in *The American Patriot*, September 6, 1894, pp. 6-8. Another favorite charge usually leveled at persecuted minorities was contained in an editorial, December 28, 1895: ". . . Popery is essentially a filthy religion, both morally and physically. The cabins of the Irish papists are embowered in dirt. . . . This is not true of Ireland alone but of all other popish lands. . . . The popish quarters of all our large cities are abodes of filth. They reek with physical and moral pollu-tion. . . ."

[14] *The American Patriot*, October 19, 1895, which republished it from *The Independent Loyal American*.

edition." Among the list of other such outflow was *Confessions of a Nun,* by one Sister Agatha, and a pamphlet *Convent Horrors,* by W. J. Phillips, editor of *The Protestant American.* Taking advantage of a created legend, Phillips, giving the fullest rein to his verbose defamation, broke out: "Similar scenes to those described by Maria Monk are today being enacted behind the prison walls which screen cloistered communities in this country from the indignant eye of public decency. We openly charge that the cloistered nunneries are maintained for the purpose of entrapping confiding females in order that they may serve to gratify the carnal propensities of a self-indulgent celibate priesthood." And much more of the same wallowing. He "dared the Roman priesthood to disprove the charge." Had he given specific cases tending to show a chronic condition, his effusion might have had value despite its extravagant invective. But he could adduce nothing more than a few suppositious cases in Poland, and in Rome and other parts of Italy, and a single definite American case, that of Edith O'Gorman. She, we may add, exploited what she presented as her experiences in a New Jersey convent and her "escape" therefrom in her book *Convent Life Exposed* now boomed by A. P. A. publications. Basing his entire attack upon a series of assumptions and a clutter of gossip jaded by long use, Phillips, to give them an evidential air, demanded a Federal investigation of convents.[15]

Seldom deigning to give the volume of attacks any notice which might be construed as imparting substance to them, the Catholic clergy preserved a scornful silence. And, it must be acknowledged, the Catholic laity contained itself in the face of a campaign of abuse and falsehood which might well have caused forceful retaliation.

A truculent exponent of A. P. A. conception, the Rev. Q. A. Henry, toured much of the United States. The very titles

[15] The contents of this pamphlet were reprinted in *The A. P. A. Magazine,* March, 1896. Since, as time recedes, posterity is disposed to wonder what kind of incitements underlay great outbreaks of bigotry, constant elucidation is a much-needed part of this history. Phillips' particular audience was as starkly ignorant of the actualities of convent life as he so exhibited himself. He could, therefore, indulge in the irrationality of representing, as a regular practice, women having been kidnapped and lugged into convents, and of nuns who had escaped being dragged back screaming. He could audaciously claim that "women are tortured and murdered in these institutions and no coroner's jury ever views the remains."

of his lectures were provokingly offensive to Catholics: "The Crimes of the Confessional," "Rome and Rum, the Twin Devils in the Republic," "The Jugglery of Jesuitism," and sundry others in the same vein. These abounded with the rashest assertions. For "his infamous and nefarious purposes" the priest used the confessional which was "a school of vice"; "most liquor dealers were Roman Catholics"; and the Irish were "corruptionists." Treating the Rev. Mr. Henry as a noble evangelist, *The American Patriot* published his lectures in full. While thus evincing his own brand of tolerance, Henry berated the Catholic Church in America as having "grown increasingly intolerant and insolent" and as having "passed the limits of conscientious forbearance." [16] He sought mightily to betake to himself the character of a man exposed to violent threats by the "Pope's vassals." [17] As a matter of fact, only one effort was made to break up his meetings.

Similarly a lecturer who passed herself as an ex-nun had complete immunity in city after city where she spoke, and it was not until she reached Geneseo, New York, in December, 1894, that she had her experience of being pelted with rotten eggs. Whereat, the A. P. A. press howled at this mistreatment and infringement of free speech. Real trouble did ensue when on February 26th next year, ex-priest Slattery, accompanied by his wife, started to make his usual rancorous lecture in Masonic Temple, Savannah, Georgia. Shouting "Down with Slattery," "Death to the renegade," a crowd hurled bricks and cobblestones at the windows. Bustling into the hall, police silenced Slattery. But the crowd was in vengeful temper, and Vicar-General Cafferty was hurriedly sent for to exert his influence. In the uproar only some could hear his admonition. "This man Slattery," he said, "can do your church no harm. You are bringing disgrace upon your religion by your conduct here tonight. It can meet with nothing but condemnation. I plead with you to disperse and go home. . . ." Nevertheless, the potent aid of the militia, advancing with fixed bayonets, was required to get the Slatterys and their audience out of the place and escort them to safety

[16] *The American Patriot*, October 11, 1894, "The Impending Conflict Between Americanism and Foreignism."
[17] Henry's signed statement in Ibid., October 18, 1894.

Reprinting details of the occurrence from daily newspaper accounts, *The American Patriot* and other A. P. A. organs raged at this demonstration of mob unreason.[18]

But the palmy years of ex-priests and ex-nuns were closing. Becoming disillusioned as to their value and methods, some State branches of the A. P. A. demanded cessation of their services. The head of the Iowa branch openly stigmatized the average ex-priest as a leech intent upon his own enrichment. The supreme convention of the A. P. A. followed with this resolution: "That whenever an ex-priest or ex-nun is lecturing, or claims to be lecturing under the auspices of the A. P. A. that we denounce and show him up." Appertaining thereto, Slattery on November 15, 1895, wrote a long letter for publication. Daring the A. P. A. to show up the ex-priests, he accused a "certain clique" as having been responsible for the resolution. And now came a droll development. To discredit that alleged clique, Slattery reprobated it for putting forth, through *The American Patriot* "a bogus encyclical letter," and for "never saying a word about showing up the forger or denouncing the paper." Slattery himself had said no word until now. He accused the A. P. A. officials of misappropriating the order's funds, and asked: "Were the men who in many places ran away with the money of the order ex-priests? Were the forgers, compilers and publishers of the bogus encyclical letter of the Pope an ex-priest?"[19] In another letter dated February 20, 1896, Slattery took exception to statements by Traynor who had characterized several A. P. A. lecturers (without mentioning names) as unscrupulous, mercenary, of immoral character, and traitors to the A. P. A. "Clap-trap denunciations" Slattery retorted.[20]

Flushed with confidence, A. P. A. leaders were in boastful mettle. This prediction was made on December 29, 1895, by the Rev. Ray Palmer, in a church at San Francisco: ". . . The day is soon coming when this country is to be ours. In a very short time we will number in this country six million of members. It is no secret, my friends, that during the last year we have grown a thousand a month in the State

[18] Ibid., March 9, 1895.
[19] Slattery's letter was prominently featured as an article "Ex-Priests and the A. P. A.," in *The A. P. A. Magazine*, January, 1896.
[20] Ibid., April, 1896.

of California. I will tell you the time is coming when the Jesuit will be in mourning." [21]

In a magazine article six months later, Traynor exulted over the great growth of the A. P. A. in the years 1894 and 1895. The organization, he boasted, had solidly planted itself in every State and Territory. It had been instrumental, he claimed, in overturning political regimes in New York, Massachusetts, Michigan, Tennessee, Kentucky, Ohio, Minnesota, Pennsylvania, Wisconsin, and partially in California and Oregon. Nearly 100 members of the lower branch and several Senate members, he stated, had been elected on a pledge to support the A. P. A.'s platform, either in whole or in part. Then in the tone of a disabused leader, he found himself obliged to acknowledge that the great majority of these Congressmen could not be regarded as "honestly the friends of the A. P. A. or imbued with its principles." Many, he ruefully admitted, had "accepted A. P. A. principles as a means to the end of obtaining A. P. A. votes, and lost no time in repudiating the principles when their political interests suggested the repudiation." [22] In concrete fact, only about twenty actual and dependable members of the A. P. A., although elected on regular party tickets, sat in Congress. Obviously, this was far below the record achieved by the prior American Party. And unlike the Congress of Know-Nothing times, the Congress in session was unruffled by discussions of issues dear to the A. P. A.

In a self-laudatory strain, little removed from braggadocio, Traynor soared to the superlative in extolling the A. P. A. as "the strongest and purest political force the world ever knew." [23] Parenthetically, however, his panegyric was indeed modest compared to the glittering testimonial going the rounds of the A. P. A. publications. We must restrain ourselves from giving the whole of this composition; but this

[21] Ibid., February, 1896. Address, "The Clarion Call of the Country." It was on this occasion that the Rev. Mr. Palmer gravely declared: "Not for thirty years had there been a Congressman who has not been under the thumbscrew of the Jesuits." This was followed by the inspirational assurance: "God has raised up the A. P. A., and around this great order is being crystallized the highest thought of this civilized nation."

[22] The North American Review, June, 1896. Traynor's article, "Policy and Power of the A. P. A." pp. 663-664.

[23] Ibid., p. 666.

rhetorical flourish should be sufficient: "The American Protective Association is chiefly composed of the most public-spirited, broad-minded, loyal-hearted patriotic men of the Nation; God's noblemen, who are devoting their energies and abilities to the welfare of the whole people. It is beyond all precedent the largest living body of men on earth, united by the nobler virtues, demanding for mankind Mutual Freedom, and according equal rights and protection to every inhabitant of the land, unforfeited by treason or crime." [24]

Perhaps it was because of such charges as Slattery's that A. P. A. spokesmen felt impelled to trumpet the surpassing virtues of their organization. Be that as it may, Traynor added to the intended effect by picturing prominent members of the A. P. A. in a pathetic light. Nearly every one, he wrote, had been boycotted, personally, politically, socially and in business, by "Irish Papists" especially, and had been forced to retire "absolutely ruined." [25] But in the very act of claiming inroads by boycotting, Traynor crowed over the A. P. A.'s huge strength.[26] "It holds the balance of power in the United States, with its membership of nearly 2,500,000 persons, who influence at least 4,000,000 voters." [27] Indubitably the A. P. A. had a large following, but the validity of these expansive figures was open to serious questioning. In keeping with the tactics of leaders of various organizations at all times, the roster of reputed membership was fabulously swelled. In all likelihood a million or so actual members was nearer the authentic mark.

At this identical time, however, the A. P. A. was beginning to disintegrate. At a meeting of its Supreme Council in Washington, D. C., on May 12-18, 1896, Traynor, in his address announced: "A well-meaning and by no means unimportant section of the Order has arisen which advocates peace with the priest and his subjects and members of the Order. Some would even go so far as to negotiate with them politically, than which nothing could be more dangerous to the perpetuity of the organization. . . . The keystone of the A.

---

[24] This piece of rapture seems to have been originally printed in the periodical *Freedom's Banner*, from which it was copied and featured by *The A. P. A. Magazine*, September, 1896.

[25] *The North American Review*, June, 1896, p. 661.

[26] *The A. P. A. Movement*, pp. 66-67.

[27] *The North American Review*, June, 1896, p. 666.

P. A., in fact, is that a papist, no matter how liberal nominally, is not a consistent citizen of the United States. Entire renunciation of the papacy must precede his acceptance as a candidate worthy of its suffrage." [28]

Because some of William McKinley's intimate friends and backers were Catholics, the Supreme Council of the A. P. A., scoring him as a tool of the Catholic hierarchy, refused to support his nomination for the Presidency. This led to a split in the A. P. A. organization, in which partisan feelings now considerably supplanted religious animus. One faction of the A. P. A. endorsed McKinley's nomination, while another faction formally condemned that action as based upon disreputable methods. In the fiercely fought campaign of 1896 with William J. Bryan as the Democratic candidate, the funds of massed capital supported McKinley, and the passionate issues drove great numbers of A. P. A. members to aligning themselves with one side or another. Still functioning as a body, A. P. A. leaders, after McKinley's election, severely denounced him for his appointment of several Catholics to important offices. The recall of Cardinal Satolli to Rome, in 1896, dissipated one of the main justifications utilized by the A. P. A. for its existence, and proved to many the hollowness of the fears expressed as to his presence in the United States. Two years later came the Spanish-American war. The excitement and the problems of this, crowding out other agitations, became the preponderant theme of public attention and political grouping.

The disruption of the A. P. A. proceeded at a gradual although a telling enough pace. Recalled in 1898, to be again its president, Henry F. Bowers managed to maintain the organization as a national body, but much debilitated by the falling away of State branches and active councils.

Now that the heat of attacks was fast sinking and he could, with quiet dignity, present the Catholic stand, unaffected by a controversial spirit, Cardinal Gibbons of Baltimore, contributed an article "The Church and the Republic" to *The North American Review*. Published in March, 1909, it was later issued as a pamphlet by the International Catholic

---

[28] *The California Standard*, May 30, 1896. This periodical was the successor, in the previous month, to *The American Patriot* and *The San Francisco American*.

Truth Society. The fifteen million Catholics in America, he wrote, had all the greater appreciation of the liberty they and their Church enjoyed in America because their fathers had known persecution in the British Isles, in Germany, in Poland and elsewhere. Usually, he went on, Catholics ignored the occasional insults directed at them by that part of the community "not yet emancipated from ancestral misconception and prejudices, and still wedded to the conviction that the Gospel is to be propagated by slander and the fomentation of religious strife." Such outbreaks, he said, Catholics knew to be abhorrent to the spirit of every true American. They relied upon that spirit "to nullify the spasmodic efforts of bigotry; for though a large proportion of Christians do not sympathize with Catholic doctrines, this dissent is not carried over into political or social life." American Catholics naturally resented charges against them, but they believed pronouncements of antagonistic ministers did not represent the general American attitude which was one of religious liberty and equality before the law. A proposal solemnly made by Lutheran and Baptist synods to exclude Catholics from office was, of course, incompatible with American ideas of religious freedom. That Americans at large did not believe in these synodical principles was shown at every election, when, as President Theodore Roosevelt pointed out, districts predominantly Catholic had repeatedly elected Protestants to office, and *vice versa*. Several strongly Protestant States had elected Catholics as Governors and U. S. Senators. Two Chief Justices of the Supreme Court of the United States were Catholics—Taney and White. The Catholic doctrine held, Cardinal Gibbons continued, that the Church could not intermeddle in affairs purely civil nor the State in affairs purely ecclesiastical; Church members were bound to obey the State in all things not contravening the moral law.

Dealing with the Catholic Church's past Cardinal Gibbons commented: "Popes are human, and it is plain from history that some of them did not always act moderately, wisely . . . But they had to do with a crude, brutal power which would have enslaved religion; and in a fierce struggle for the life of the Church such mistakes, humanly speaking, were inevitable." Just so; but it might have been better had Cardinal Gibbons touched upon the great persecutions of helpless peoples by the Church merely and wholly because of their different religion. These are only some vital extracts from the Cardinal's long article which ended by thanking God that Catholics lived in America, "this happy country of ours." [29]

After 1900 the A. P. A. dwindled by quick stages into a mere vestigial remnant over which Bowers, loath to detach himself from a thing he helped to create, presided until his death eleven years later. But as we shall instantly see, the agglomeration of prejudices, misrepresentations and hatreds on which the A. P. A. had thrived were far from moribund. Already a new super-agitator and a new movement had made their advent.

[29] In pamphlet form this article covered eighteen compact pages. Necessarily, the whole would have to be read to get the full scope of Cardinal Gibbons' thesis.

Chapter XIX

WATSON'S DUAL CAMPAIGNS

THE personage who now vehemently revivified and widened the campaign of bigotry was Thomas E. Watson. Not abating in the least degree attacks upon Catholics, he expanded the scope to include Jews.

His was not the case of a nonentity. Before flaming into action as an arch propagator of a double bigotry, he had climbed into the wide prominence afforded by an outstanding public career. His birth, in 1856, was in a log hut near the small town of Thomson, Georgia. His ancestors were Quakers; he himself grew up a Baptist. He managed during two of his adolescent years to take a course in an out-of-the-way Georgia educational institution of Baptist foundation which long since had been glowingly termed by its originator a university. Whatever the other effects were upon Watson's mentality, his studies there all the more sharpened religious antagonisms already inhering. Sectarian books absorbed by him were exactly the kind to fasten and deepen animus, and, as the sequel disclosed, he never outgrew their sway. In notable particular, one of these abiding influences was the book of that early Baptist minister, David Benedict, the acidulous contents of whose production we had occasion to examine in a prior chapter. Watson became a school teacher in his native locale, then equipped himself for the law business, and budded as a backwoods attorney in Thomson. Highly emotional, he adapted this quality to his profession. As his clientage later grew he specialized in trial cases, and his success in manipulating the sentiments, partialities and aversions of jurors gave him the rank of a wily pleader, and in time his services yielded large fees.

In the South, especially, the ambitious young lawyer, as a rule, looked forward to the éclat of a political career as the proper adjunct of his vocation. Watson joined law with politics. Elected, in 1882, to the Georgia Legislature, he served a term. After a lapse of eight years he became a member of Congress during the session of 1891-1893. Closed as his mind was in the religious or racial field, it was open to new ideas in the political. In conformity with reforms advocated by Populists, with whom he ranged himself, he espoused its platform. At a time when the U. S. Senate was considerably an oligarchy of millionaires, often corruptly elected by Legislatures, he supported the proposal for the popular election of Senators. To satisfy the agrarian vote he pressed in Congress the passage of an act making the first appropriation of funds for rural mail delivery. In 1897 he bought an Atlanta newspaper which he now named *The People's Party Paper*, and when, in the presidential election that year, the People's or Populist Party polled a vote of more than 1,000,000, he stood out as a political luminary. That Party chose him as its candidate for Vice-President, in 1896, and eight years later as its candidate for President.

Whether it was his conceit or his aim to avail himself of new sources of revenue that led him into pretentious authorship is not clear. Perhaps a combination of both. At intervals he wrote various historical and biographical books much boosted at the time, but the hackneyed nature of the subjects and their declamatory and partisan treatment did not commend his works to the judicious. His paramount interest, however, was in periodical journalism. In conjunction with an associate, Major Charles E. McGregor, who had newspaper experience and made the arrangements, Watson, in October, 1906, started a weekly, *The Jeffersonian*. By December of that year, according to McGregor's enthusiastic account, this periodical "permeated nearly every State in the Union," and it was decided to launch a monthly, also at first called *The Jeffersonian*, and later named *Watson's Magazine*. Both of these periodicals were now published in Atlanta. It was not until much subsequently that their place of publication was transferred to Thomson. Speedily, McGregor related—doubtless overdrawing the facts—"the Watson publications enjoyed a national circulation, reaching every community in America." [1]

---

[1] Contained in McGregor's posthumous account of Watson's career, and inserted in the *Congressional Record*, January 21, 1923, pp. 2119, *et seq*.

By 1908 Watson was credited with having amassed more than $250,000, much of which was invested in plantations operated by tenants. He insatiably craved more riches. How was he to get them? He had seen newspapers, magazines and book publishers reaping fortunes from sensationalism. Exposures of corporate and political abuses and corruption had, however, much passed their zenith. Now labeled "muckraking," their very excess and fury cloyed the popular mind. The Populist Party, too, had sunk low to a meager 117,000 votes nationally in 1904, and in 1908 was fading away entirely. The sensationalism of bigotry appealed to Watson as a fertile means. One of his biographers seemed to think that Watson was animated by sheer calculation in proceeding to exploit the bigotry of a half-illiterate Southern rustic population. But this assumption was a mistake. Watson was merely and finally reverting to his youthful and fixed prejudices and giving them expression. As another of his biographers rightly wrote: "The positing of the Watson mind in enmity to the Romish church had been accomplished long before. In his researches, in his mental ruminations, the die had been cast and irretrievably so." [2] And, moreover, as to the charge of his deliberately setting out to make his appeal to the rural "red necks" as the one backward constituency upon which he could depend, that was disproved by a pregnant fact. For it was in Atlanta itself that his magazine had its largest local circulation. To use a colloquialism, it was a "best seller" there.

While, in one place, admitting the petrification of Watson's mind in the respect mentioned, one of the authors cited above sought to endue Watson with impartiality by saying that he attacked Protestants before he did Catholics. The so-called attack upon Protestants was nothing but a left-handed part of his campaign against Catholics. It dealt with Protestant foreign missions, warned Protestants that they were "walking right into the trap" and declared: "The Roman Catholics are encouraging Protestants to concentrate their attention on foreign countries while the Romanists are concentrating on the United States." Under the misleading title of *Foreign Missions Exposed*, this "study" was later published

[2] William J. Brewton, *Life of Thomas E. Watson*, p. 326. This book was published in Atlanta, by the author.

in a book of 158 pages, the advertisement of which said: "Mr. Watson is appealing to Protestant churches to save America from the wolves of Rome." [3]

The literary attitude of the aforesaid biographer toward Watson may be judged by his laudations. Watson was "richly gifted in intellect"; he had "the most positive, absolute and daring *courage* known to his generation." The attribute of "genius" was even suggested.[4] But we may judge these high-sounding tributes to have been as much designed to invest the subject personality with superior importance as to evidence a mark of the writer's friendship with Watson. Obviously, Watson was but one of a succession of vociferous bigots. He fell into an established groove, substantially repeating what had often been said previously. Most trite was a leading editorial headed: "The Roman Catholic Hierarchy; The Deadliest Menace to Our Liberties and Our Civilization." With politic consideration, he disclaimed any ill-feeling toward the individual Catholic, but he pronounced the Catholic organization "the object of my profoundest detestation." [5] Never did the thought enter his mind that such a feeling might well be reciprocated.

For years, from 1910 onward, he plowed the old, worn furrows, turning up in the process a mass of matter which could not possibly be designated by any other word than filth. Indeed it is no improper diagnosis to say that in his attacks both upon the confessional and convents and later upon Jews he evinced or seemed perilously to betray the deep workings of a sex complex. That he manifested these in his imputations regarding the confessional would not be conclusive proof, since the same had repeatedly been said before. To this extent it was a traditional course. But the application, in different circumstances, to adherents of another religion, gives weight to the suspicion of a prurient mentality. The license he allowed himself in his pornographic accusations showed, at any rate, the quality of his thought. To him the confessional presented itself as a place "in which a lewd priest sows the minds of girls and married women with lascivious suggestions." It was "an open way to

[3] Advertisement in *Watson's Magazine*, April, 1912.
[4] Brewton, *Life of Thomas E. Watson*, pp. 3-6.
[5] Watson's *Jeffersonian* (Magazine), August, 1910.

damnation along which untold thousands of our sisters have traveled to hell." It was a snare where were made "secret confessions to unmarried Lotharios, parading as priests and enjoying themselves carnally with the choicest women of the earth." In unconscious self-revelation he went on with this assertion which significantly imaged his particular standards: "At the confessional, the priest finds out what girls and married women he can seduce. Having discovered the trail, he wouldn't be human, if he did not take advantage of the opportunity." [6]

In another issue, Watson sneeringly asked whether superstition had not precluded scholarship among priests, but he could not hold to this line before sliding into his favorite topic. "Is there none among them," he queried concerning priests, "to point out the absurdity and ludicrousness of their wearing a garment emblematic of sexual intercourse? . . ." [7] And in the studied aim to roil the susceptibilities of Southern whites viewing miscegenation with horror, Watson artfully broke forth: "Not always will we tolerate the *kidnaping of our children* by these *Romanist* priests. Not always will we submit to their polluting the flower of our womanhood. . . . *Heavens above! Think of a negro priest taking the vow of chastity and then being turned loose among women who have been taught that a priest cannot sin. It is a thing to make one shudder.*" [8]

Presuming upon his standing and popularity, Watson continued his foul attacks upon priests and Catholic women. But his popularity was not quite what it had been. Many a balanced Populist, disgusted at his ravings, quit adherence. But as fast as one of these fell away, his place was taken by a number of raw bigots reveling in Watson's ultra-sensationalism. Watson's hold in the South was no security against forces in the North. One of these was Anthony Comstock, Secretary of the Committee for the Prevention of Vice, which had been founded in the early 1870's. He hated Catholicism, but he detested obscenity far more. To root out obscenity was the

[6] Ibid., March, 1911.
[7] Ibid., July, 1911.
[8] *Watson's Magazine,* April, 1912. Italics in original. The fatal consequences which such incitations were likely to have in intensification of race enmity may be indicated by the prevalence of lynching in the South. The greatest number of lynchings was in Georgia.

great, unflagging passion of his life, and in his auxiliary capacity as a post-office inspector he had Federal power to take
action. That Comstock sometimes overdid his appointed task
was a patent fact; so bent was he in warring against his re-
pugnance that he occasionally could not discriminate between sheer pictorial obscenity and decent nudity in true
works of art. But, on the whole, his vigilance did much in
keeping down commercialized obscenity. He caused Watson's indictment for sending obscene "literature" through
the mails. Previously, the National Federation of Catholic
Societies had called the attention of advertisers in Watson's
magazine to his "vile output." At the consequent diminution
of advertising, Watson grew exceedingly wrathful. He denounced the Catholic priesthood as never tolerating "any
criticism of their pagan creed or their heathenish ceremonials." With fine self-righteousness he declared: "It is Protestants who furnish the toleration; the Roman wolves never
furnishing any." [9]

The indictment against Watson, on his own motion, was
dismissed in November, 1913, on a technical ground.
Namely, that the entire article complained about was not
contained in the indictment. Meanwhile and later, Watson
was complaining mightily of being persecuted on the one
hand by Comstock, and, on the other, by "the Roman Catholic priests [who] were trying to ruin, disgrace and penalize
Watson for uncovering the prostitution of the confessional."
Crying that the liberty of the press was menaced, he put
forth this absurdity: "It is not by accident that the Pope is
demanding of Congress a law to close the mails to all such
Americans as Watson." [10] Assuredly, there was no such demand; the law barring obscene matter had long been in the
statutes.

A new and rectified bill of indictment against Watson was
drawn by the U. S. Attorney for the district. In a spirit of
defiant bravado, Watson not only refused to desist his smut
but made it even more obnoxious. Again the confessional as
a "sink of perdition," amplified by "No man can imagine a
woman who could maintain her self-respect, after being compelled to act as a sewer pipe for a bachelor priest's accumu-

[9] Ibid., August, 1911.
[10] Ibid., October, November and December, 1913, and January, 1914.

lated garbage." [11] The case against Watson before a jury resulted in a mistrial. Subsequently pressed, the case came to trial in November, 1916. Watson produced a train of witnesses to testify to his good character, and represented that he had merely quoted the language complained of from an old book copied and re-copied ad lib from an ancient tome. Upon Watson's acquittal, the U. S. Attorney declared that the Government could not bring Watson to justice in Georgia, and announced his intention of transferring the case elsewhere for fair trial. Through an intermediary Watson notified the U. S. Attorney-General of his determination to resist any attempt to take him out of Georgia for trial. The case was dropped.[12] However, Watson, as we shall duly note, encountered positive action from the Government on other grounds.

In the main, Watson's articles and books on cognate subjects followed the lead of Benedict's book. The Massacre of St. Bartholomew's Day and other subjects as therein dealt with formed the pattern of many of Watson's attacks. These were varied by frenzied comments on current events. Because the head and an employe of the nation's highest tribunal happened to be Catholics, therefore the Pope's "chief servant" was Chief Justice of the Supreme Court of the United States and its chief clerk was likewise so. Because Joseph Tumulty, Secretary to President Wilson, was a Catholic, accordingly the Pope had access to the Government's secrets. Along with such other rabidness Watson trotted out that threadbare fiction as to armed Catholics. *"The Pope's secretly organized traitors, the Knights of Columbus, are armed to the teeth with the best of modern rifles."* [13] But Watson's ever-recurring themes were indicated by titles such as: "What Goes On in the Nunneries," "The Roman Catholic Confessional, the Open Door to Perdition." [14]

Another reference to Maria Monk's *Awful Disclosures* may

[11] Ibid., December, 1913.
[12] Brewton's *Life of Thomas E. Watson*, pp. 335-337.
[13] *Watson's Magazine*, December, 1913. Italics in original. Viciously inscribed caricatures and photos were freely used. A caricature of Tumulty was captioned: "Is My Halo on Straight?" Under a photo of Cardinal O'Connell was an inscription beginning "A Papal Virgin." Affixed to a photo of the Pope was this ribaldry: "The Pope Has Photographs Taken, As He Makes God Out of a Pancake." Ibid., January, June and July, 1915.
[14] Ibid., June and July, 1915.

now seem in the nature of a bore, but it is unavoidable. And later, again, the mention of it will be indispensable. Linked with Watson's attacks upon the confessional, priesthood and convents was his unshakable reliance upon that book as infallible authority. Her assertions concerning infant murders in convents were, as we have related, proved to have been the ghoulish fancies of a sensation monger. To bolster belief in the truth of her book, Watson now had recourse to a clumsy maneuver. He published letters from two aged men avouching that fifty years past they had "heard" or "learned" reports of infantile remains discovered in the Hotel Dieu convent. And further to perpetuate the matter Watson wrote a book entitled *Maria Monk and Her Revelation of Convent Crimes*.[15]

Synchronously, beginning in 1913, Watson ferociously attacked Jews. Following the great persecution of Jews in Russia in the 1880's and 1890's there had been a mass immigration of Jews to America. Congressional committees did not remain indifferent. Resolutions reported by the House Committee on Foreign Affairs, in April, 1892, stated that the time had arrived when the United States Government was entitled to take an interest regarding continued persecution of Jews in Russia. This, the report went on, was a bounden duty inasmuch "as vast numbers of Jews driven from Russia are continually seeking refuge here." While, the report explained, the United States appreciated the fact that it had no right to interfere with a foreign Government's treatment of its own subjects, yet a cruel fact remained to temper this policy. Russia's laws were not directed against Russian citizens but specifically were enacted to bear upon the Jewish population. The committee favored requesting the American minister to St. Petersburg to find out from the Russian authorities whether there was any possibility of repealing the oppressive anti-Jew laws decreed in May, 1882.[16] For the

---

[15] For years later, this was one of "five exposing books," written by Watson, and advertised as "filled with dynamic revelations of the working intrigue of the Roman Catholic Church." Advertisement of *The Fellowship Forum*, Washington, D. C. (Book Department) 1928.

[16] *Report No. 1177*, 52nd Congress, 1st Session. The laws referred to established ghettos, and otherwise restricted places where Jews were allowed to live. They were held down to certain occupations, could visit certain cities only, and in other ways were subject to the most rigid regulations. Pogroms were frequent.

lack of a sufficient quota of members to vote, the report was not passed by the House.

"Russia's peculiar laws," said another report of the same committee, was causing great uneasiness among American Jews, especially those engaged in commerce. If Russia persisted in those laws, the Executive branch of the U. S. Government should make an authoritative inquiry as to the status of American citizens of Jewish faith in Russia. "Every citizen of the Republic is entitled at home and abroad to the exact treatment and protection which are the full right of citizenship under the Constitution and our treaties with foreign powers. Our Government can make no distinction based on creeds or birthplaces of its citizens, nor can it permit such distinction to be made by foreign powers. . . . This much is due to the commercial greatness, the usefulness and patriotism of American Jews." [17]

Yet while this important committee was thus acknowledging the valuable contribution to the country of Jewish industry, this very condition became a growing grievance on the part of numbers of the envious. By dint of privation, living in congested quarters, and hard work, many of the earlier Jewish immigrants or their sons had saved enough money to go into the manufacturing business, chiefly clothing, or into jobbing or retailing. Others of the progeny had studied for the professions or arts. The same course developed after the Jewish mass migration of the 1880's and 1890's, and further was in conspicuous evidence following another such migration in 1907 and thereafter. Yet the ratio of Jewish immigrants in the United States in 1908-1914 was not 10 per cent of America's entire immigration in that period. Jewish people in the United States numbered less than 4,000,000 in a total population of 91,972,266 (census of 1910). The newly arrived Jewish immigrant, straight from ghettos in Poland and elsewhere, too often retained outlandishness of appearance and customs. Yet with few exceptions, the Jew born in America took naturally to the deportment, ways and standards of his cherished country, priding himself, in fact, upon his Americanism.

But in certain essentials anti-Semitism repeated the tactics formerly used against Irish Catholic immigrants. Long before

[17] Ibid., *Report No. 1000.*

Watson's outbreak, occasional articles accused Jews of being physically filthy. The writers would visit the East Side of New York City, where in old, decayed tenements devoid of conveniences, immigrant Jews in their poverty had to herd. The wonder was that in such squalid habitations—slums judged by the most ordinary rules of decency—Jews or any other class of immigrants could maintain the degree of personal attention and cleanliness that they did. As, too, in the case of Irish immigrants, the speedy success of second-generation Jews in applying themselves to advancement in manifold channels of business and in the professions excited growing animosity among many already infected with the blindest bigotry.

The old legend of Jewish extortion and fraud, perpetuated by such a production as Shakespeare's *Merchant of Venice*, had been noised for generations among the prejudiced. By a strange perversion of facts, those practices were lumped together as distinctively, exclusively and inalienably a Jewish trait. Consultation of reports of U. S. District Court judges in the early decades of the nineteenth century on bankruptcy frauds would have shown prevalent conditions. Hardly a Jewish firm was concerned; Jews were rare in business. The pseudonymous Walter Barrett's work *Merchants of Old New York* gave a graphic picture of unscrupulous business men, not one of whom was Jewish. Of the many official reports bearing upon the subject, one only need be convincingly cited. At a time when all important business of every kind was in Christian ownership, fraudulent bankruptcy was a festival. Why? With such looseness was a bankruptcy act of Congress drawn in 1841 that it contained no penalizing for fraud on the part of banks, manufacturing or trading companies—in fact, it omitted corporations in general. Reports of the U. S. District Attorneys in various cities set forth the consequent unmitigated swindling of the public by a multitude of irresponsible concerns.[18]

With the widening entry of Jews into business in subsequent eras there did come frequent cases of Jewish fraudulent bankruptcy, but non-Jewish firms were involved as well, and the practice was, we need hardly repeat, a long-estab-

---

[18] Particulars were set forth in U. S. Senate *Document No. 19*, 27th Congress, 3rd Session, 1842.

lished condition prior to the Jewish immigration. In the industrial field, great railroad systems, dominated by non-Jews, often had been and were being plunged into bankruptcy, usually preceded by shameless stockjobbing, looting of shareholders and plundering of funds.[19] These were notorious scandals, yet despite these and many other proofs to the contrary, Jews were picked upon by the biased as the sole perpetrators of fraud, and the more their initiative and enterprise carried them to the front in various lines of industry, the more was the old, enduring charge given increased prominence. A standardized slander, those who wanted to accept it as a fact were easily able to do so because it was a thing that from early years they had repeatedly heard in current chatter.

For an organized movement against Jews the time was nearly, but not quite ripe, yet the volume of pre-existent and gathering prejudice was an invitation to a spokesman who presumably could command a sectional if not a national hearing. Watson filled the role, and a tragedy, in 1913, gave him his coveted opportunity.

Following his marriage, Leo Frank, a Jew, had moved to Atlanta. He became manager and part owner of a pencil factory at Marietta, Georgia. A graduate of Cornell University, he was not twenty-nine years old, and of an intellectually serious disposition. On April 27, 1913, the dead body of Mary Phagan, fourteen years old, was found in the pencil factory's cellar. She had been misused and strangled. Before dying she managed to scribble on a pad two notes, one of which charged an unnamed Negro with having assaulted her. Leo Frank and one Newt Lee were arrested, but Lee was released and the charge of murder was confined to Frank. Although it was rare in the South to accept a Negro's testimony against a white, Frank was speedily convicted on the bare word of Jim Conley who, equally with Frank, was in the factory at the time of Mary's death.

Analyzing the testimony, prominent lawyers throughout the country pointed out that it indicated Conley as the guilty

<hr />

[19] Edifying accounts, from the records, of these and many other kinds of fraud are contained in *History of the Great American Fortunes, History of the Supreme Court of the United States,* and *The Ending of Hereditary American Fortunes.*

man. "Hang the Jew, or we will hang you," was the purport of notifications to court officials, and these menaces were reinforced by threatening mobs choking the area around the courthouse and adjacent approaches. In the courtroom itself spectators were allowed to give free vent to their prejudicial demonstrations. An Atlanta newspaper reported mutterings of a riot should Frank be acquitted. When the jury's verdict of guilty was communicated to the huge mob of men and women in the streets, it, according to *The Atlanta Constitution*, whooped a terrific roar of approval and madly reveled in jubilant antics. Frank was sentenced to be hanged.[20] Conley was sentenced, as an accessory to murder, to a year in the chain gang; dismissing him from further consideration we need only and aptly point out that early in 1919 he was sentenced to twenty years in the State penitentiary for *attempted* burglary in an Atlanta drugstore.

Indignant leading editorials in newspapers throughout the country excoriated the persecution of Frank. That he was convicted in advance and the trial itself was a travesty was the point of many of these condemnations. Meanwhile, Frank's execution was delayed by an appeal to the Supreme Court of Georgia—a futile appeal. In the first stage of the Frank case, Watson had held aloof. But having seen the mob spirit in triumphant action, he forthwith catered to it by attacking not only Frank, but all Jews. "Leo Frank was a typical young Jewish man of business who lives for pleasure *and runs after Gentile girls*. Every student of sociology knows that the black man's lust after the white woman *is not much fiercer than the lust of the licentious Jew for the Gentile*." [21] Professing to quote from a book *The Old World and the New* by Edward A. Ross, Professor of Sociology in the University of Wisconsin, Watson further declaimed: "Here we have the typical young libertine Jew who is dreaded and detested by the city authorities of the North, for the very reason that Jews of this type have an utter contempt for law and a ravenous appetite for the forbidden fruit—a lustful eagerness

---

[20] The above is merely a condensation of the Leo Frank trial. The full circumstances may be found carefully related in such works as *The Truth about the Frank Case*, by C. P. Connolly, originally published by *Collier's Weekly*, 1915; and in the noteworthy book, *Trial by Prejudice*, by Arthur Garfield Hays, a leading New York lawyer, pp. 302-321.

[21] *Watson's Magazine*, January, 1915. Italics in the original.

enhanced by the racial novelty of the girls of the uncircumcised. . . ." [22]

This was the crassest garbling of what Professor Ross actually wrote. He was specifically referring to one group of East European Jews. It was the lower class of such immigrants "who reach here moral cripples, their souls warped and dwarfed by iron circumstances." These particular Jewish immigrants, Ross said, were the worst exploiters of their own race. Ross' observation on pleasure-loving Jewish business men was an isolated comment. His animadversions were not upon Jews in general but upon that unscrupulous type of Jews who went into fraudulent bankruptcy, fraudulently acquired insurance, made a traffic of white slavery and engaged in other criminal activities. [23] As, however, we have had occasion to note in a previous chapter, when Jews were involved, special and opprobrious attention was focused upon them as Jews, but in the case of non-Jews guilty of the like or other malefactions their religious-racial character was not thus singled out for especial remark. And it may be justly added, as a matter of contemporaneous observation, that the kind of Jew here referred to was supplanted later by much more dangerous gangster leaders of Italian extraction who pushed forward to systematic bootlegging of liquor, vice and other rackets, and in the process used the murderous methods of the Mafia in disposing of rival interlopers or informers.

That pre-arranged plans had been made to lynch Frank before the trial ended was no secret, and threats of this action persisted. It was to prevent such a probability that Governor John H. Slayton, of Georgia, with the object of getting Frank out of jail and into the supposedly safer confines of the State prison, issued a secret order commuting Frank's sentence to life imprisonment. For this he was denounced as "King of the Jews and Traitor." Even Brewton, so well disposed toward Watson, could not forbear deploring the venomous attacks as "unwarranted and most discreditable to Mr. Watson." [24] Week after week, Watson issued the most violent articles against Slayton, Frank and the Jews. On the one hand, representing rich Jews of other sections as interfering

[22] Ibid.
[23] See Professor Ross' book, pp. 149-154.
[24] Life of Thomas E. Watson, p. 342.

in Georgia's "sovereign" affairs, he pandered to the peculiar and provincial feelings against "outsiders" His course, on the other hand, was to work upon mushy sentimentalism, as, for instance: "Iron out the white dress, little girl. Iron it smooth, and see yourself wearing it in the Sunday school tomorrow. Spread it out on the bed and leave it there till you come home. Fate and the Jew have other plans for you, my child." In any rational community such devices would have caused revulsion. But—and a grim fact it was—Watson's following, already considerable in Georgia, now increased and he felt himself basking in greater popularity. Contrariwise, Slayton ere long had to suffer deprivation of office.

At this time the publication office of both Watson periodicals was at Thomson, Georgia, then having a population of 2,151 and a large cotton factory and cottonseed oil mill. The circulation of *The Jeffersonian* was rated at 40,000, and that of *Watson's Magazine* at 18,000.[25] But the influence of these organs was not to be reckoned wholly by sales. Often copies were passed from hand to hand, and even more the pith of his comments were matters of common talk and thus passing around became a general consensus.

In prison Frank was the object of steady assaults from both whites and Negroes. Considering that they had license in maltreating one who was not only a Jew but a Northerner, these base creatures mauled him with fists and subjected him to other harrowing experiences. Finally, after his throat had been slashed, he was transferred to the prison hospital. On August 16, 1915, an armed mob of twenty-five or thirty men, grandiosely styling themselves "a vigilance committee" arrived in a file of automobiles at the prison farm at Milledgeville. The warden and the superintendent were handcuffed and the guards overpowered—if, indeed, they needed overpowering. Taken 100 miles to the outskirts of Marietta, Frank was hanged. A Marietta jury later went through the formality of examining witnesses; then followed the customary verdict in such cases of no clue to the lynchers.

In post haste, the day after the lynching, Watson's weekly gloated: "A Vigilance Committee redeems Georgia and carries out the sentence of the law on the Jew who raped and murdered the little Gentile girl, Mary Phagan. . . . Let Jew libertines take notice. . . ." But from the nation at large came editorial expressions of horror. Denunciations in New York newspapers were equalled or surpassed by those in other cities. "The same bestial spirit that lashed and ravished the helpless slave," said *The Milwaukee Free Press*. *The Chicago Tribune:* "It [the South] is a region of illiteracy, blatant self-righteousness, cruelty and violence. . . ." *The Boston Traveler:* "In this crowning demonstration of her inherent savagery Georgia stands revealed before the world in her naked barbarian brutality. . . ." Many more were the editorials to the same scorching effect. One pointed out that the excuse of lynching as being the work of an ignorant mob could not be satisfactory; "ignorant mobs do not travel in automobiles."

Watson grew more defiant. Even after Frank's lynching he continued his attacks upon him, heading one of his articles "Leo Frank, A Jew Pervert." [26] But in general, Watson's course now was to use Frank's case as the pivot for indiscriminately reviling all Jews. He assiduously used every trick by which anti-Jewish prejudice could be kept boiling. He pushed to the fore and harped upon the old absurdity called ritual murder, and sought to fix it as a Jewish custom. This "scholar," as Brewton plumed Watson, did not know the elementary fact that the charge of ritual murder was often brought in Rome against the early Christians. Their assemblies were considered a dangerous conspiracy against the State, and they were accused of making bloody sacrifices and holding incestuous festivals at their religious gatherings, which necessarily had to be held in secret haunts. Spurious informers "pretended to confess or to relate the ceremonies of this abhorred society." [27] When Christianity became the all-powerful State religion, the charge was transposed to the Jews.

The latest of the long list through the ages of such charges was that against Mendel Beiliss, a case which made an international sensation in 1911. In a small cave outside of Kiev, Russia, the mutilated body of a boy was found. Rancor against Jews at once awoke the ever-lurking popular belief

[26] *Watson's Magazine*, September, 1915.
[27] Gibbon, *Decline and Fall of the Roman Empire*, Vol. 2, p. 170.

in ritual murder. Police investigation showed that the slain boy was tortured and murdered by a band of gangsters on suspicion that he tattled. But the Czaristic Government, engaged at that very time in fomenting massacres of Jews whom it doubly hated because of religion and fear of Jewish revolutionists, sought to fasten the crime upon a Jew.

Superintendent of a brickyard in Kiev and living near the boy's home, Beiliss was accused. Made public two years after his arrest, the indictment was a bizarre document. Largely it was a stock of assertions by Russian professors in Government service that ritual murder was a Jewish practice. When, in 1913, the case reached trial, all that the prosecution could do was to produce some old tomes containing vague and gossipy allusions to ritual murder by Jews. Such a boomerang did the so-called evidence of Government witnesses prove that nothing remained for the court but to acquit Beiliss.[28]

Notwithstanding the known fact that the whole power of the Czar's Government had tried to convict Beiliss, Watson persisted in assuming his guilt, and thus sought to explain the acquittal: "Apparently, the same mighty engine of agitation and suppression that had worked for Dreyfus was put in motion for Beiliss." [29] The reference here was to Jewish "pressure" upon Russia, as if Jews anywhere had influence with the Czaristic machine! Self-evidently the wave of astonishment and protest over the Beiliss persecution had been well-nigh world-wide, stirring the enlightened of all races and religions. Watson, however, proceeded to connect that alleged exclusive Jewish "pressure" with the "pressure" which he represented as having been brought to bear by rich American Jews to save Frank. He further ascribed to them a campaign to "indict a State and traduce the whole South."

This playing upon sectional pride and hypersensitiveness was only one of his methods to keep anti-Jewish mob spirit at white heat. He used all of the arts of the cheapest demagogery to intensify the class feeling of the abounding gudgeons. These by no means comprised only the cloddish "red necks," hard-driven tenant farmers, lowly factory and mill workers and slum dwellers both in cities and rural areas.

[28] Beiliss came to America early in 1921, lived in the Bronx, New York City, and supported himself chiefly as a life-insurance agent, and died in 1934.
[29] *Watson's Magazine*, November, 1915.

Surely and most obviously the great proportion of million-aire industrialists and bankers were not Jewish. Yet Watson indicted them sweepingly as such. Belying open records as to William R. Hearst's descent, Watson denounced the Hearst newspapers as "Jew owned" because Hearst had sent his lawyer, Clarence J. Shearn, to Atlanta, to review the Frank case. Watson vilified Shearn as "that miserable little Jew jackass." [30] The Frank case, wrote Watson, "has shown us how the capitalists of big money regard the poor man's daughter." Again: "Frank belonged to the Jewish aristocracy, and it was determined by the rich Jews that no aristocrat of their race should die for the death of a working-class Gentile —'nothing but a factory girl.' " [31] Furthermore, in Watson's wild-eyed vision, rich Jews were not acting alone. "There is no longer any doubt," he pronounced, "that the Roman priests and the opulent Jews are allies." The proof thereof? "These insolent Jews take it upon themselves to acknowledge the Pope as the true and only 'Head of the Church of Christ'." [32] Upon what was this wholesale conclusion based? Nothing more than a letter which *The Jewish Daily News* of Chicago had sent to the Pope requesting him to use his good offices in behalf of persecuted Jews.

Bellowing forth in other directions, Watson had caustically attacked Woodrow Wilson as a "smug Down-Easter" because in his history, Wilson, in Watson's insular opinion, had not been fair to the South. With the entry of the United States into the World War in 1917, Watson plunged into acrid criti-cism of Government war measures. He denounced President Wilson's requesting Congress to declare a state of war with Germany, and his expressed hostility to conscription was viewed as a step which might tend to encourage evasion of that requirement. As an urgent war necessity, Postmaster Burleson excluded his publications from the mails. This, as Major McGregor described it, was a "heart-crushing blow" to Watson. The withdrawing of advertising from his periodicals had already cost him heavily; to get funds to keep them going he had, from time to time, been forced to sell land holdings, so that his fortune was much depleted. But

[30] Ibid., September, 1915.
[31] Ibid., August, 1915.
[32] Ibid., October, 1915.

after the signing of the Armistice he still had enough to buy *The Columbia Sentinel* which he made the successor of his suppressed publications and transferred to his plant at Thomson. He now conducted a campaign against the League of Nations.

Years of instigating hatred did not evoke the least regret in Watson, but when a son and daughter died he actually made a parade of his "crushing sorrow." And no more telling commentary could be made upon the caliber of Georgia voters than to record the fact that when he ran for U. S. Senator, in 1920, he carried the primaries and was duly elected. This despite the opposition of all of Georgia's daily newspapers, except an Atlanta newspaper owned by the opportunistic William R. Hearst, who advocated Watson's election because of his opposition to the League of Nations. Watson died on September 26, 1922; an escort of fellow Senators and other Congressmen attended his funeral, and a throng variously estimated from 10,000 to 15,000 or 20,000 people crowded the town of Thomson where he was buried.

Memorial eulogies in both houses of Congress were conventionally lavish and nauseatingly fulsome. A few typical extracts will show this. Senator Harris, of Georgia, lauded him as "a leader in all things . . . in many ways the most remarkable man of my time in our State. He was always fighting for the masses of the people." Senator Trammel: "We have assembled today for the purpose of paying homage and loving tribute to a great and illustrious Georgian—a great American. . . . Even in my youth I delighted in reading *Watson's Magazine* and in reading his weekly paper because from those publications I gained inspiration." From Senator Heflin, of Alabama, who proved himself the rankest kind of bigot, came this token: "He was a wonderfully well-informed man . . . a great student and a great scholar." In the oratory of these and other Senators one gem was discernible. It came from Senator Willis who, aiming to show that Watson could fend for himself, declared, "he was a tremendous master of invective"—which was undeniable. And several of the Senators, surveying Watson's career with politician's eyes, told reverentially how he had wielded the power to make and unmake Governors, Senators, Representatives and other public officials—the great determiner in Georgia of political fortunes. In all of these panegyrics not a word was said of Watson's bigoted campaigns nor of the Frank case.[33] To cap the procedure the public funds were used not only to print these long effusions in the pages of the *Congressional Record,* but later to embody them in a special Government document of 294 pages.[34]

[33] *Congressional Record,* January 21, 1923, pp. 2120-2128, *et seq.*

[34] *Thomas E. Watson. Memorial Addresses Delivered in the Senate and House of Representatives in Memory of Thomas E. Watson, Late a Senator from Georgia.* Government Printing Office, 1924.

CHAPTER XX

FIRST AND SECOND KU KLUX KLAN

BEFORE the resuscitated Ku Klux Klan came into activity in 1915, other publications than Watson's had paved the agitative way. One of these was *The Menace*, established at Aurora, Missouri, in November, 1911. As the name implied, it saw overhanging America a peril which in its view was the might of the Catholic Church. Its own formulated reason was: "*The Menace* was launched in the belief that the Roman Catholic Political Machine, in its political intrigues and its interference with established American institutions, is the deadliest enemy to our civilization and liberties."

The first issue of this weekly opened with an entirely unfounded assertion. A Clerical Party, this maintained, was functioning in the United States. So far as the Catholic Church was concerned there was not the least evidence of any such organized body. Hedging in the next paragraph, *The Menace* interpreted the charge in this way: "The Roman Catholic hierarchy in America is the great combination of politicians in the United States." If that were so, then why, as was further charged, should it go to the trouble of resorting to the boycott "to compel subserviency on the part of politician and small business men"? The main purpose and means of this hierarchy, it was stated, was, by enrolling men in societies, to destroy the public schools and substitute Catholic schools.[1]

Consecutively, by the device of repetition, *The Menace* trumpeted its alarm at what it warned was Catholic control of politics and legislation. The gist of its series of highly colored articles was merely the dregs of prior campaigns. But its readers did not know this. The nature of such a publication was precisely adapted to low-grade intelligence, so cheap in

[1] *The Menace*, December 2, 1911.

appearance and of such shoddy contents it was. When *The Menace* raised it warwhoop against "Jesuit politics in Congress," its readers grasped at the belief that this invasion had finally been accomplished. Anyone bethinking himself of inquiring into the composition of Congress would have found but a proportionately slight number of Catholics. Forth, too, in *The Menace,* presented as a brand-new charge, came the well-worn accusation of Catholics controlling the American Navy. Repeated in issue after issue were spread in bold-faced type alleged malefic oaths taken by Jesuits, Catholic prelates, priests and laymen, the whole headed by the query "Are Men Who Take These Oaths Loyal Citizens?" [2]

Interspersed profusely with such material was the requisitioning of olden tales defaming convents. "Open Rome's Prison Houses in America; Let Light into the Dungeons," and "Open the Nunneries; Free the Slaves" were two of the melodramatic titles, with appended quotations from Maria Monk's *Awful Disclosures.*[3] Steadily, this advertisement pushing her book was run: "Five hundred thousand copies of this great book already sold in Europe and America. Thousands of helpless and defenceless American girls are deceived and decoyed into these priestly charnel houses every year. Price 50 cents." Endeavoring to make convent deeds most horrendous, one of *The Menace's* articles went to the length of attributing to "numerous witnesses" this condition: "That when nunneries were razed to make way for new buildings, in practically every instance the walls of the underground recesses were bespattered with the brains of children of recent birth, while in the muck and mire of water and quicklime the skeletons of those of varying ages are in many cases too numerous to count."

This passage in particular roused the ire of Rev. M. J. Foley, editor of *The Western Catholic* at Quincy, Illinois. Complaining to President Taft of such "diabolical libels," he declared the contamination of the mails by *The Menace* was "an awful disgrace to the present postal administration." The reply, sent by *The Menace,* on February 6, 1912, to President Taft was a long political argument almost entirely evading the point of the complaint. Dwelling upon the Cath-

[2] Ibid.
[3] Ibid., and February 3, 1912.

olic hierarchy, the reply asserted that it was in control of the press. (Watson, a little later, accused Jews of dominating influence over the press.) Rome's "subtle fingers" had, the defence went on, grasped many official places, and its avowed purpose to capture the political power of the Nation was obvious. There were, the reply continued, 17,000,000 Catholic communicants in the United States with an army of 3,000,000 voters who held the balance of power in any given election and could dictate who should be the officials of the Republic.

Anyone with a grain of sense knew, as we have said, that votes of citizens who were Catholics were distributed among all parties, and if Catholics held, as alleged, the balance of power, how did it happen that every President was non-Catholic and virtually every high official the same? From making these nonsensical accusations, *The Menace* made another charge equally untenable. "The Roman Catholic Church maintains in America the most gigantic graft extant." At first glance this would seem to signify political graft. But no, the reply precipitately took another turn. It fell back upon "cases of the sale of indulgences, masses, pews, holy bones, beads and other relics to a poor and benighted constituency of dupes." As to convent inmates, only two instances were, at the end of the reply, incidentally mentioned, and these were cases of runaways which *The Menace* had reported and construed in its columns. Now esteeming its reply incontestable, *The Menace* triumphantly published it in full.[4]

The Post Office Department took no action, and *The Menace* continued publication for thirteen years more. At this time—early in 1912—it claimed 250,000 circulation and more later. To recount its further career would be of no profit, inasmuch as the substance was all of a piece with that which has already been noted.

An organization calling itself "The Guardians of Liberty" had been formed with a set of propositions. One of these was to protect America and its free institutions from the efforts of any religious-political organization to manipulate or influence the country's political or social development. The confining of religious instruction of children as purely

[4] Ibid., February 12, 1912.

the duty of parents was another. A third was opposition to the appointment or election to office of any person who openly or secretly conceded superior authority to any foreign political or ecclesiastical power. Among the sponsors of this organization, it was said, was a cluster of prominent military and naval men but, savoring of an upper-class character, it was not of a kind to appeal to the elemental. Remaining embryonic, it was soon displaced by the belligerent and spectacular Ku Klux Klan.

The organization of this name was both a continuation and a revision in aims of the first Ku Klux Klan. This strange appellation was taken from the Greek word Kuklos, meaning a band or circle, but what erudite individual originally suggested it is not known. Formed in Tennessee, in 1866, by Confederates, the Ku Klux Klans, as they were then called, spread rapidly to other Southern States, and embraced a concatenation of local bodies each distinguished by a descriptive name. There were the "Pale Faces" in Tennessee; the "Knights of the White Camellia" in Louisiana; the "Invisible Empires" in North Carolina; the "Invisible Circle" in South Carolina; and other designations elsewhere.

As a secret organization, the Ku Klux Klan had its immediate predecessors before and during the Civil War. In the decades prior to that conflict many persons, mainly of Northern rearing and ideas, suspected of opposing slavery, were summarily lynched. Others caught distributing antislavery tracts met the same fate. Reported from time to time, these cases were undisputed matters of record. In the years leading up to the Civil War, there were a number of secret societies, the members of which were pledged to uphold "Southern Rights" and forward the design of secession. The most important of such societies was the "Knights of the Golden Circle" or "Knights of the Columbian Order." This, as well as kindred societies, like the "Minute Men" and "The Precipitation," had its network of lodges, passwords and more or less flamboyant ceremonials all converging upon one dire object. Anyone found criticizing or even questioning the wisdom of secession was forthwith doomed. In the States bordering upon the Gulf of Mexico many men, before 1861, were hanged by mobs for no other reason than their uttered attachment to the Union.

With the ending of the Civil War a mass of embittered Confederate soldiers sullenly returned home to find themselves confronted by a new and to them intolerable condition. The Negroes, upon whom they had been wont to look far down as servile beasts of burden, were now freed and, in Constitutional law, at least, were granted the equal right of voting. This abrupt transformation from slavery to suffrage was doubtless not the most sagacious course. The whites feared Negro domination, especially in States where they were a minority. To a large extent this problem was met later by local laws, the effect of which was to disfranchise many Negroes.

Meanwhile, however, the traditional weapon of violence assumed the upper hand, and reasons were conjured for its habitual use. In their ignorance, Negroes often did not know how to use freedom, and in the first taste took it as an opportunity to commit depredations or petty thefts. This situation could have been easily handled by arresting the offenders. But the Ku Klux Klan was not concerned with what seemed to it the slow tameness of lawful measures. Over and above all other fears much of the South was haunted by the perturbation of a possible Negro uprising. There was no ground for this fear except an inherited idea which had foisted itself upon the deep South from the time of the successful insurrection of Negroes in Haiti against the French, in 1803. The Ku Klux Klan's definite, relentless aim was to paralyze the Negro into abject submission by a process of terrorization, while at the same time to conserve Southern interests in the political field by wreaking vengeance upon incoming Northern office-seekers, called carpetbaggers because their scanty possessions could be packed into such a receptacle.

With a peculiar hankering after gaudy, pompous, fantastic titles, the Ku Klux Klan adopted a line of nomenclature meant to be awe-inspiring, but which to the observer was supremely ludicrous. The chief officer was a Grand Wizard of the Empire, surrounded by his ten Genii. Associated was a Grand Dragon of the Realm with his eight Hydras; a Grand Titan of the Dominions and his six Furies; and a Grand Giant of the Province with a suite of four Goblins. Further in this queer group was a Grand Cyclops of the Den,

watched over by two Night Hawks; a Grand Magi; a Grand
Exchequer: a Grand Turk; a Grand Scribe; a Grand Sentinel; and a Grand Ensign. But however much such comical
investitures were calculated to excite mirth in the outsider
perchance hearing of them, the operations of the Ku Klux
Klan were assuredly of no laughable order.

Testimony before a Congressional Committee which
brought to light the Klan's components revealed, at the same
time, its systematic barbarities. At night bands of Klansmen
would ride about bent upon their fell mission. Each member
was shrouded in a gown, his face was covered by a mask,
and even wearing a horn. He carried whip and pistol. Victims
were lashed and tortured; anyone interfering with Klan plans
was killed. Apart from the many murders by hanging or
otherwise, the Klan made a business of arson, firing any place
which it disapproved. Schoolhouses were destroyed and
teachers driven away in Mississippi. In Georgia, South
Carolina and other Southern States investigated, the majority of the committee noted, outrages, including murders,
were numerous and horrible. General Reynolds, commanding the Federal troops in Texas, reported: "Murders of
Negroes are so common as to render it impossible to keep
accurate accounts of them." In Louisiana alone, testimony
showed, fully 2,000 persons were killed, wounded and otherwise injured in a few weeks prior to the presidential election
of 1868. The Ku Klux Klan was branded as "a fearful conspiracy against society . . . it had demoralized society, and
held men silent by the terror of its acts and by its powers
for evil." [5] This Ku Klux Klan was finally disbanded by
Federal military forces, but its spirit and traditions remained
to serve as a model for the second Ku Klux Klan re-created
in 1915.

This organization came into activity with a four-fold
program of antagonism to Catholics, Jews, the foreign-born
and Negroes. A Congressional investigation brought out the
circumstances of its founding. The head and front was William Joseph Simmons of Atlanta, Georgia. "They call me
'Colonel,' largely out of respect," he testified. "Every lawyer

[5] *Report of the Joint Select Committee of the House of Representatives on
the Condition of Affairs in the Late Insurrectionary States*, February 19,
1872, 42nd Congress, 2nd Session, *Report No. 42*, and Testimony, pp. 21-22,
82-85, *et seq.*

in Georgia is called 'Colonel,' so they thought I was as good as a lawyer; so they called me that." However, to give some semblance to the title, he explained that he was a veteran of the Spanish-American War, and at one time held the rank of "Colonel" in the order of the "Woodmen of the World." Placing himself further, he went on: "I am a churchman and proud of it . . . I am a member of two churches—the Congregational Church, and a full-fledged associate member of the Missionary Baptist Church, given me as an honor." He was, he said, a member of various fraternal orders, the Masonic and the Knights Templar, and since youth had been a "fraternalist," believing in promulgating "the fraternity of nations, so that all people might know something of the great doctrine—the fatherhood of God and the brotherhood of man."[6]

These were the complacent, high-sounding professions of the man who, in October, 1915, launched the Ku Klux Klan, a movement signalizing its progress by campaigns of religious and racial hatred enforced by terrorism. A meeting called by Simmons to start the organization was attended, he stated, by thirty-four "splendid citizens of the State of Georgia" who signed an application for a charter which was granted by that State, on December 4, 1915, to the Knights of the Ku Klux Klan. Somewhat later in Simmons' testimony, it developed, one of these "splendid citizens" repeatedly came into that "Imperial Wizard's" office and "would tell me of the great money-making possibilities, provided certain plans that he had worked out should be authorized and enforced . . . finally stating that he could guarantee a cold $1,000,000 to myself and to himself if those plans were carried out." This man, older than himself, Simmons said, had been a successful organizer for fraternal orders. "Would you object to stating who the man was?" asked Representative Rodenberg. Simmons replied: "J. B. Frost, one of the men whose name appears here as one of the petitioners in this charter." Relating how he had expressed his great indignation to Frost, Simmons further testified: "Some time after that, sir, he stated to me that if I would appoint six men whom he should name as imperial officers,

⁶ "The Ku Klux Klan," Hearings Before the Committee on Rules, House of Representatives, 67th Congress, 1st Session, 1921, pp. 67-68.

he would see to it that $30,000 was put on a table in my room within twenty-four hours." No man, Simmons said he replied, could buy or use the organization for grafting purposes.[7] But, so Simmons' testimony ran on, money grabbing soon began. "For three years the work was a tremendous struggle, made more arduous by a traitor in the ranks who embezzled all of our accumulated funds in the summer of 1916 and went off and attempted to organize a counterfeit order. The treasonous [sic] conduct of the man left me penniless, with large accumulated debts against the order. . . . I was forced to mortgage my home to get money with which to carry on the fight against this traitor's counterfeit order and to assist in the work we had to do."[8]

A different version was testified to on October 11, 1921, by C. Anderson Wright, of New York City, who, prior to the investigation, had been King Kleagle of the New York Klan, and had been assigned to the imposing post of Chief of Staff of the Invisible Planet, Knights of the Air, a function which covered the United States. Together with Mrs. Elizabeth Tyler, as co-partner, Edward Young Clarke owned the Southern Publicity Association, headquarters in Atlanta. This pair had conducted successful World War drives in Georgia for the Salvation Army, the Y.M.C.A., the Red Cross and other organizations, and, now that the war was over, they "in Clarke's own words" to Wright "were looking around for something." They had joined the Klan which was in poor financial shape. "Colonel Simmons, while very sincere, had no money to go ahead with the work. Mr. Clarke told me he talked this over with Mrs. Tyler, and they saw the possibilities of a wonderful revival of this name—Ku Klux Klan—which would strike the public's fancy. So they went and made Col. Simmons a proposition to handle the business end. That was just a little over a year ago [in 1920]. At that time, as I am told by Mr. Edward Young Clarke, the Klan had about 1,000 to 2,000 members; today they boast of 700,000 members. . . . With the $10 initiation fee [called a donation fee] you can readily see how much money they have taken in. . . ."[9] This exclusive of the sales of robes

[7] Ibid., pp. 80-81.
[8] Ibid., p. 69.
[9] Ibid., pp. 16-17. The distribution was thus specified: Of the $10 fee, $4 went to the field man or Kleagle; $1 to the State man or King Kleagle; 50

(hooded gowns), the manufacture of which cost $1.25 and which Clarke compelled every Klansman to buy and pay $6.50 for; the price was $7.50 until lately." The price, Wright explained, depended upon the quality of the robes and the varying regalia required.[10]

But these figures were at variance with those secured by O. B. Williamson, a Post-Office Department inspector who made an investigation of the Ku Klux Klan. W. E. Floding, an Atlanta manufacturer of secret-order paraphernalia, had, Williamson testified, manufactured K.K.K. robes at a cost per robe, he thought, of $5 or $6; transferred to another Atlanta concern, the contract yielded to it $4 for robe and helmet, for which Klan members had to pay $6.50. A finan-cial statement secured by Williamson from Imperial Kleagle Clarke, and covering operations of the so-called "propagation [sic] department" from June 1, 1920, to September 24, 1921, showed receipts of $860,393.50. Of this sum more than $634,000 was paid in commissions to field agents and others; $103,000 for organization work; $49,875.46 for publicity; nearly $25,000 for executive and clerical salaries; the re-mainder for supplies, postage, rent, traveling and other expenses.[11]

What, inferentially, had been the total amount flowing thus far into Ku Klux coffers? A statement handed in to the Congressional investigating committee by Representa-tive James A. Gallivan, of Massachusetts, declared that un-contradicted testimony showed total collections of $8,000,-000.[12] But whether or not the amount reached such a figure, the clear fact remained that the Ku Klux Klan had large revenues and, without straining the point, could be classed, financially at least, as Big Business. Through Imperial Kleagle Clarke, Mrs. Tyler, according to Wright, "absolutely dominates and runs the Klan and everything is done by her direction."[13]

Sensitive to the charge which he cited that "the Klan

cents to the district Grand Goblin; the remaining $4.50 to the Imperial Palace, of which amount $3 went to Clarke (so he told Wright) to use in any way he saw fit for the Southern Publicity Association. The remaining $1.50 went into the main treasury and was subject to the check of the Im-perial Wizard.

[10] Ibid., pp. 17-18.
[11] Ibid., pp. 29-33.
[12] Ibid., pp. 30-31.
[13] Ibid., p. 16.

is a gigantic swindle, run solely to enrich a few of the inside ring," Simmons sought hard to dispel it. Testimony denoted Simmons as a mere figurehead, yet nominally he was the executive head of the Klan, and in that capacity, he said, his total salary for six years had been approximately $12,000, or an average of $2,000 a year. Which was probable enough, inasmuch as no witness accused him personally of seeking to enrich himself. Appertaining to the charge that Clarke and Mrs. Tyler had received many millions of dollars for their propagation [sic] work, Simmons entered into a lengthy rebuttal. The Klan contact, he said, was with Clarke; Mrs. Tyler was his first assistant and had no official connection with the Klan; she was "a splendid business woman." Since Mrs. Tyler had no official post in the Klan management, how then could she have placed her resignation, along with that of Clarke, in Simmons' hands, as he contended, when the charges were first made? And notwithstanding his claim of an investigation of the charges being under way by the Klan, Simmons waved them away as unproved, and took extra pains to praise Clarke and Mrs. Tyler. During his and the association of other Klan officials with them, "their conduct and character have been of the highest."[14]

Both at that hearing and subsequently Simmons indulged in denials which were fully refuted by the evidence. He disclaimed the charge of the Ku Klux Klan as organized to preach religious intolerance, and more especially as being anti-Catholic, anti-Jew and anti-Negro. Yet previously proof had been presented to the investigating committee of a pronouncement by him as Imperial Wizard—a pronouncement published throughout the country and never disowned. It read in part: "We exclude Jews because they do not believe in the Christian religion. We exclude Catholics because they owe allegiance to an institution that is foreign to the Government of the United States. To assure the supremacy of the white race we believe in the exclusion of the yellow race and in the disfranchisement of the Negro. By some scheme of Providence the Negro was created as a serf." And the pronouncement threatened "a great invisible and mysterious force" which could be used "to strike terror" when deemed necessary. Sixteen years later Simmons

[14] Ibid., p. 70.

ventured the public statement in his own defence that when
he started the Ku Klux Klan there was no thought on his part
of attacking Catholics or Jews. And "the Klan while I ran
it, was not a Negro whipping organization."[15] Simmons remained head until 1923. What were the actual conditions?

In Atlanta, a publication named *The Searchlight,* which,
however, the Ku Klux never admitted was their organ,
was carrying on a furious campaign of racial and religious
hatred. But in the North the public tactics were different.
In a series of articles, in January, 1921, *The Herald* of New
York City pictured the Ku Klux Klan as a patriotic organization, favoring the restriction of immigration and summary
action against Bolshevists, as Communists were then styled.
The K.K.K. was further represented as absolutely devoted
to the original principles and ideas of the founders of the
nation, and, as such, standing for white supremacy, and
against priest or preacher supremacy.

Whence emanated these flattering articles? Wright's testimony elucidated both this question and the results. Particu-
larizing *The Herald* as one of a number of newspapers pliant
to Mrs. Tyler's "cleverness," he told how it had sent a correspondent to Atlanta. "The publicity was shooting from
Mrs. Tyler with talk about this wonderful organization, and
this correspondent, of course, saw things from the outside,
and thought it a very good thing. . . . Of course thousands
of people read these articles, and I know from being in
Atlanta that membership from the East began to grow,
and request after request came in to know about it" [the
Ku Klux Klan].[16]

Previously, Wright had received certain instructions from
Klan headquarters to work up sentiment in New York
against Jews. He was directed to start in and give Jews "the
dickens." As preached in his presence and that of others, the
idea to be spread was the patronizing by Klansmen of real
100-per-cent Americans. The plan was to organize everybody,
either Klan members or persons sympathetically inclined, in
a movement which would "practice not only moral clannishness but also practical clannishness; in other words a Klansman would be compelled to buy from another Klansman,

[15] *The New York Times,* September 23, 1937.
[16] "Ku Klux Klan," Hearings, etc., p. 24.

if possible." In the course of these personal advisements, superiors in the Klan—so Wright testified—said to him: "In New York City we have all the Jews; they are controlling New York;[17] we will get under here and when we have 10,000 members here, if we do not want a certain man to do a certain thing, he is not very apt to do it." After quoting this, Wright elaborated his own interpretation. "In other words, if a member of the Klan should be brought to trial before a certain judge or jury, if that judge or jury received 10,000 requests from New York to do a certain thing, they would be pretty apt to do it. That was their idea of getting control of the courts."[18]

The pertinent query was put to Wright by Representative Snell: "What induced you to disclose the secrets of the Klan?" His answer was illuminative. Yes, he knew that the mass of Klansmen went into that order in ignorance; there were enough narrow-minded people glad enough to join a movement against Jews, Catholics, foreign-born and Negroes. In fact, the number of the narrow-minded was so great, said he, that the more the newspapers attacked the Klan as preaching racial hatred, the more would its membership grow. Implying that he has been influenced against the Klan by the consideration he now stated, Wright went on: "But when you can show them where their money goes and what a fool he is [they are] and the character of the people getting it, I think the Klansmen of the country will realize and wake up to what they have gone into."[19] At any rate the heads of the Klan were not apprehensive of such a revolt among the membership. At a recent big Klan gathering, one of its high officials publicly boasted of a forthcoming Klan control of Congress.[20] Representative Gallivan introduced a joint resolution in Congress to determine whether any members were Klansmen but it was not acted upon.

In his testimony Simmons had eulogized the Klan as com-

[17] The population of New York City at this time was slightly more than 6,000,000, of which an estimated 1,500,000 were Jews. In the above testimony we have definite evidence of Jew-baiting for self-seeking financial reasons. Had conditions in America made it possible, then or eventually, this baiting might have resulted in outcropping massacres. At that very time pogroms were in action in Poland and elsewhere. Everyone in America stirring prejudice against the Jew or anyone else was a potential mobster.
[18] "Ku Klux Klan" Hearings, etc., pp. 19-20.
[19] Ibid., p. 26.
[20] Ibid., p. 27.

posed of "as fine a body of representative citizens as there are in the United States." This, in the face of testimony of a number of witnesses exposing the Klan's performances. Rowland Thomas, one of the editorial staff of *The World*, of New York City, had been assigned to the duty of investigating the Ku Klux Klan. The undertaking occupied three months in Atlanta and elsewhere. He produced a list of sixty-seven outrages which had been committed at night by masked men. These were only the known cases. Rooted in hatred and prejudice, the Ku Klux Klan, he said, employed a variety of sinuous methods. To secure members, the Kleagles, or salesmen promoters, in New York City, used bitter attacks upon Catholics. Similar attacks were made upon Jewish citizens elsewhere, but, although persistent, such attacks were "not so open." At the same time the chronic effort was made "to play upon any prejudice which might exist upon foreign-born citizens." When, Thomas said, *The World* and other newspapers published exposés, Klan officials talked of bringing libel suits for an aggregate of $10,000,000, and engaged 200 prominent lawyers. "Apparently from the way the revenue was flowing, they could afford to talk in millions."[21]

In more vivid detail Representative Leonidas C. Dyer, of Missouri, gave a summary of the Klan's operations. "During the past year a constant succession of violent and criminal assaults on individuals, consisting of abductions, floggings, brandings, irreparable mutilations, application of tar and feathers to men and women, and, in several instances, murders, have been reported from various parts of the country. . . . Terrorization, active or passive, of the colored people in American communities, has been one of the Klan's principal objects. . . . The name Ku Klux alone is enough to thoroughly frighten the average ignorant Negro." Representative Dyer said he had received various letters from men in the South who had been ruined physically and whose homes had been broken up and businesses destroyed. They belonged to particular religious groups against which the Klan was conducting its violent propaganda. "Abundant evidence exists," Dyer went on, "that such propaganda, directed particularly against those American citizens who

[21] Ibid., p. 11.

happen to be Catholics or Jews, has been actively circulated by the professional solicitors who have been making a living getting members of the Klan on a commission basis. Corollary evidence that the Klan is systematically cultivating such militant bigotry is found in the contents of its semi-official publication, *The Searchlight* of Atlanta, the pages of which literally drip with venomous and frequently totally baseless attacks on the Catholics and Jews. . . ." [22]

Representative Peter F. Tague, of Massachusetts, testified that he had called the Department of Justice's attention to the "terrible things done to innocent people in the South by the Ku Klux Klan." Upon his expressing an intention of introducing a resolution in Congress for an investigation of the outrages, he had been asked to withhold it, as an investigation being made by the Department had not only shown the published reports true, but even an underestimate of the atrocities, including murders. But, Tague declared, in certain localities in the South, the courts were intimidated. Presumably by connivance, Klansmen went boldly in, took away and destroyed court records, and thus effectively shielded themselves. "They openly boast that not only members of Congress, but members of the judiciary, officers of the courts, and officers of the police departments in the towns in which they work are members of their organization. . . . Let the country know whether the laws of the country amount to anything or not . . . whether a black man can walk down the street without being molested or interfered with . . . whether a Jew can go through the street without being interfered with; let the country know that 30,000,000 Catholics in this country stand up and oppose their actions . . ." [23]

Barely two months elapsed after Simmons' effort to whitewash the Ku Klux Klan when, at the fourteenth annual conference of Governors, at White Sulphur Springs, West Virginia, the violence committed by the Ku Klux Klan was an uppermost subject of discussion. This came after Governor Allen, of Kansas, had made an address telling of the action taken by the Attorney-General of that State to oust the Klan on the ground of its operating without a charter. That organization, Governor Allen said, fought the Catholic

[22] Ibid., p. 7.
[23] Ibid., pp. 2-5.

Church and expressed its antipathy to the Jew and Negro "under the protection of a mask and through the process of terrorism and violence." When lawlessness developed, the Klan would disavow it, "and then give $50 to a loose-mouthed preacher who would thank God for the Klan."[24]

These were some of the emergent facts giving an insight—and it was necessarily only that—into the Ku Klux Klan's terroristic methods. But as events proved, this was only a beginning.

[24] *The New York Times,* December 17, 1922.

CHAPTER XXI

"INVISIBLE EMPIRE" NATION WIDE

FAR from hindering the Ku Klux Klan's growth, the revelations before the Congressional investigating committee and the exposés in some leading newspapers only hugely stimulated inflow of members. Droves throughout the country were stampeded into joining. In 1922 alone, according to figures subsequently made public by Simmons, the average increase in membership was 3,500 a day, the total new army of members during that year reaching 1,200,000. From membership dues and sale of paraphernalia the Klan's daily income swelled to $45,000.[1] At this time, as indited in the findings of Judge Slick, in the U. S. District Court at Indianapolis, four years later, the Klan was operating in forty-eight States, in Alaska and in the Panama Canal Zone. Judge Slick's decision credited the Klan with having enrolled approximately 5,000,000 members in the United States; in Indiana alone, it was juridically stated, it had a following of 200,000 men, of whom 50,000 were dues-paying members.[2] Likely enough the flood of money returns was a powerful inducement in causing a group of outsiders to attempt trenching upon so rich a field. Seeking to trade upon the name Klan, this group had organized, in Indiana, a similar body. By Judge Slick's decree the Klan with headquarters at Atlanta was entitled to exclusive use of the name Klan.

Dominating the politics of many States, the Klan increasingly drew into its fold receptively ambitious men who, in mental capacity, were much above the country and urban yokels. Perhaps prejudices early suckled gave the inclination, but aim for political advancement crystallized the de-

[1] *The New York Times*, September 23, 1937, reporting extended interview with Simmons.
[2] Knights of the Ku Klux Klan v. Independent Klan of America, 11F (2d) *Federal Reporter*, pp. 881-884.

sire to join so puissant an organization. Inasmuch as Klan members had to take an ironclad oath of secrecy, the identity of members was, in general, effectively concealed. But on one memorable occasion there did come a sensational leak. A public prosecutor in Birmingham, Alabama, Hugo L. Black was elected a U. S. Senator, and while in that body, was, in 1937, nominated an Associate Justice of the Supreme Court of the United States.

The disclosure was then made that he had been a Klan member; he himself admitted having joined about fifteen years since, which would denote his induction in 1922 or 1923. This information caused a nation-wide commotion. Evidently President Roosevelt had no prior knowledge whatever of Black's association with the Klan, and in the Senate Black had supported progressive "New Deal" measures. A published facsimile of minutes of a Klan meeting at Birmingham, on September 2, 1926, showed speeches made by Black and by Bibb Graves, later elected Governor of Alabama.

Replying to the added charge of his having been elected a life member of the Klan, Black proffered an explanation. He had, he said, resigned from that body "before becoming a Senator" and never attached importance to the card endowing him with life membership. A torrent of editorials in newspapers of all political parties and in periodicals in large sections of the country showed how profoundly public sentiment was stirred. Amazement was expressed that a man tainted with such an association of intolerance should be selected for so crucial a post, and biting criticism made of the failure to inquire into his antecedents before choosing him. On the part of some Senators comments were exceedingly bitter. Senator Copeland, of New York, for instance, on August 17, 1937, pointed to the Supreme Court of the United States as the high and final tribunal which had to be depended upon to safeguard the rights of Catholics, Protestants, Jews, Gentiles and Negroes. "Does the leopard change his spots?" he asked. "Will Mr. Justice Black be any different from Candidate Black who, according to the *Mobile Register,* of April 15, 1926, backed by the Klan, had a walkaway in the race for the Senatorial nomination?"[3] However,

---

[3] *Congressional Record,* 75th Congress, 1st Session, p. 9069.

the majority of Senators could not bring themselves to transgress the custom of favoring a fellow-Senator. At the time, too, the recomposition of the personnel of the Supreme Court of the United States was a predominant issue, and Black's alignment with new social and economic laws assured his vote on the Supreme Court upholding their validity or that of further like legislation. His nomination was confirmed by the Senate, on August 17, 1937, by a vote of 63 to 16.

Underlying the orgy of Ku Klux Klan terrorism arising from the year 1922 onward was a vast stratum of harnessed ignorance. From this arose the epidemic of intolerance which, sweeping over literate sections of the country as well as those in which illiteracy abounded, could not be laid to inability to read or write. Too often illiteracy was explained as the concrete cause, yet the fact was overlooked that large numbers of people who had received education were as susceptible to the impulse of bigotry as those who had never had schooling. The ability to read did not of itself give the quality of breadth of mind and of reason; on the contrary, in the case of those of bigoted predilections, the chosen reading was of a kind to furnish them with the supporting data and arguments fortifying bias already established. Although violence was by no means absent in stretches of the country from the East to the Pacific States, it was more marked as well as more conventional in the South, and it was there that the proportion of illiteracy among native-born whites ten years old or more was, as shown by the Census Bureau returns of 1920, much the greatest in ratio to population. The denominational composition of the South had its important bearing upon the dominion of bigotry. Perhaps 40 per cent of the South's entire church membership, either active or passive, was Baptist, with Methodists second in order.

Before epitomizing the Klan's record of violence during the decade of the 1920's it will be advisable at this point to deal with the exit of Simmons. In his subsequent "inside story" he told some details of the manner of his ousting. A contest, he said, had been in stiff progress for control of the Klan, and all but two of his fourteen "cabinet" associates had been ranged against him. "The men who ruthlessly took charge," he asseverated, "were moved by selfish aggrandizement, a desire for graft. They created a condition I could not endorse." Simmons branded these men as "traitors" seizing control in 1923. His successor as Imperial Wizard was Dr. Hiram Wesley Evans, a dentist of Dallas, Texas. Affidavits in a Federal Court alleged that Simmons was forced to sell his interest in the Klan for $146,000, but his own story gave a different figure. He had, he said, left the Klan under an agreement whereby he received $90,000, but he did not say who paid it to him.[4] He put, he asserted, the whole of this sum into creating an organization called "Knights of the Flaming Sword," which collapsed when, in 1925, an accident suffered by him compelled him to abandon his activities. Nevertheless, as the evidence shows, he was again engaged, in 1930, in his favorite occupation of forming organizations —the third attempted since his compulsory relinquishment of Klan leadership. The time it was the "White Band" to "preserve white supremacy in America."[5]

The Ku Klux Klan's power in overriding State authority in perpetration of violence was acutely brought to general notice by the supplication Governor Parker, of Louisiana, had to make, in 1922, to Federal officials at Washington. Admitting that his State could not cope with the Klan nor stop its widespread "horrifying crimes," he besought the aid of Federal action in the aim of ending both them and the Klan rule. In one parish alone in that State thirty-one bills of information charging crimes by masked bands had been filed, but no punitive steps against the Klan could be effected. Conditions in Louisiana were a duplicate of those in many Southern States.

But a new factor entered to influence public opinion as represented by some Governors there. The concern felt by these officials might have had a share of compunction yet the practical problem obtruding itself was the continued northward migration of Negroes, causing a growing scarcity of that class of labor. The consequences of the 135 cases of lynching in Georgia in two years were thus stated to a conference by Governor Dorsey of that State: "In some counties the Negro is being driven out as though he were a wild beast. In others he is being sold as a slave. In others no Negroes remain. In only two of the 135 cases cited is the 'usual crime'

[4] *The New York Times,* September 23, 1937.
[5] Details in *The World,* of New York, November 11, 1930.

[rape] involved." Whatever the nominal reasons or pretexts advanced to extenuate the estimated 4,000 lynchings in the South since the Civil War, one unvarying, impelling motive was largely that of seeking to palsy with terror an oppressed race striving to rise. At all times, any sign of this aspiration immediately aroused the fury of the shiftless and prejudice-poisoned whites, tacitly abetted by many of the so-called better class of their color. And as all of these elements were compacted into the Ku Klux Klan, hunting out of Negroes, made more efficacious by "exemplary" lynchings, continued as a fixed course. Against this some perceptive Southerners, alive to the results, protested in vain. A conscientious executive, Governor Dorsey had no easy time, in 1922, in causing the indictment of twenty-two mob participants, of whom four were sent to the penitentiary.

Such occasional punishments, there or elsewhere, did not deter the Ku Klux Klan from indomitably pursuing its campaign of brutality and intimidation. Lynching of Negroes was only one aspect. In many Southern States flogging of both white men and women as well as Negroes was a regular proceeding. Calloused in cruelty, Klan bands mercilessly lashed victims and then rode away satisfied, often leaving those lacerated alone, some to die of their injuries. Tarring and feathering was another Klan custom, likewise kidnapping as a prelude to murder. Maryland masked Klansmen, convicted of tarring and feathering and put in the penitentiary, were merely putting in force a general Klan practice and could condole with themselves as unlucky in having been brought to account while fellow Klansmen who did the same in other localities evaded arrest. The same observation applied to forty-three Klan members indicted in California on charges of kidnapping with intent to murder. While committing these atrocities, the Klan, then and later, would stage its processions by the display of a blazing cross as if that token were a complete warrant for its existence and its excesses.

The infamies above mentioned were only a fraction of the total. Not pausing to give superfluous space to the many such reported in the news, we pass on to revelations in a noteworthy action in the Federal District Court, in Pittsburgh, in 1928. For the cumulative evidence therein given was all sworn testimony, and had the convincing value of coming from Klansmen themselves. The facts thus coming to light related to the years 1922, 1923 and afterward.

A quarrel over revenues was the instigation. In 1927 the Ku Klux Klan brought suit against five ex-members, one a minister, formerly high factotums in the Pennsylvania Klan, to prevent them from using the name Klan. Further, the suit asked $100,000 damages from the quintette on the ground, that after their dismissal from that organization, they had collected that sum now claimed as having rightfully belonged to the Klan. Filing a counter suit, the five set out to expose Klan officials as financially irresponsible and the Klan as socially lawless. Misuse was charged of $15,000,000 alleged to have been collected in Pennsylvania by the Klan and for which no accounting was ever made. Part of that sum, it was set forth, was used in building a lavishly expensive palace in Atlanta for the Imperial Wizard, and a much lesser sum for the "purchasing of a diamond tiara, valued at $30,000 to $100,000, for the Imperial Commander, or chief officer of women, of the Klan." The five also charged the Klan with responsibility for riots, floggings, kidnappings and murders in Pennsylvania.

Witness after witness at the trial on April 9-12, 1928, gave the most damaging testimony, virtually all of which stood unshaken. Former Klan officials disclosed the circumstances of a riot at Carnegie, Pennsylvania, on August 25, 1923. This steel manufacturing place contained many Catholic families; the Klan had been warned by municipal officials not to provoke the townspeople by a parade. This was, in fact, formally prohibited. Nevertheless Klan massed forces did march into Carnegie. The march, it was testified, was ordered by Imperial Wizard Evans. Stationed near Carnegie, he was at first hesitant to give the order—doubtless because of the warning —but, it was testified, pressed by his importunate followers, he yielded.

Called as a witness, Evans admitted having had the power to stop the march. The resultant march caused at least one death, that of a Klansman, and injury to other participants. Evidently, according to the testimony of another witness, Evans was anything but averse to riots; he, this witness declared, had suggested to Grand Dragon Rich a repetition of the Carnegie riots as a means of increasing membership.

And, indeed, there did follow a succession of riots in various localities. Testimony implicating Evans as responsible described the burning at the stake in Texas of seven or eight men while hundreds of hooded Klansmen stood by oblivious to their dying agonies. Interviewed in Texas, Klan chiefs denied the occurrence, but their mere say-so had no weight against sworn testimony. Admitting membership in both the Klan and its roaming "Night Riders" executing decrees of vengeance, Captain J. R. Ramsey, of Dayton, Ohio, testified how these decrees were enforced against anyone considered detrimental to the Klan and "included burning barns, tar-and-feather parties and other ruthlessness." Accompanying testimony gave definite data on kidnappings and outrages upon Jews and others in various places.

Evans was produced as a witness by the Klan's chief counsel to refute the charges made. He denied having participated in any act of violence imputed to him, or having any knowledge of the atrocities described. He did admit being known as "emperor" of the Klan. Summing up for the defence, Attorney Van A. Barrickman denounced Evans as a monster under whose rule brutal and bestial acts had been committed by an organization which "is supreme in its rottenness." Evans, went on Barrickman, constituted the Klan; "he came from Dallas, Texas, a poor man who could not even pay his office rent. Now he wears sparkling diamonds, lives in splendor in the seat of the country's Government at Washington, and when seeking recreation whiles his time away aboard his palatial yacht which is always at his beck and call on the Potomac." The brief address of the Klan's chief counsel sought to establish the point that the charges made against that organization had not been sustained.

The decision handed down by the presiding judge, on April 13, 1928, W. H. S. Thomson, thoroughly disposed of this contention. Judge Thomson could not be accused, on religious grounds, of harboring any bias toward the Klan. He emphasized the fact that the testimony came from Klansmen themselves. First, Judge Thomson dismissed the cross-suit of the five expelled or "banished" (as the court record read) members. Their proper course, he notified, would be to seek redress in the State courts which alone had jurisdiction in revoking, for cause, the Ku Klux Klan's charter in Pennsylvania. Then passing upon the Klan's suit, Judge Thomson declared that by reason of its proved outlawry, such an organization had no standing in court.

The text of the decision, grounded upon the evidence, was a scathing arraignment of the Klan. Under, it said, the guise of being a charitable and patriotic corporation, the Ku Klux Klan had obtained a Pennsylvania charter protected by which it had acquired in that State a membership computed, at different times, of from 240,000 to 300,000. In violation of its charter and its own constitution it "had established and is maintaining a form of despotic rule, which is being operated in secret under the direct sanction and authority of the plaintiff's chief officers; that, in violation of the rights and liberties of the people, it has set up tribunals not known to the law, before which citizens of the Commonwealth, not members of the Klan are brought, subjected to some form of trial, and upon conviction, severe corporal punishments are imposed, painful, humiliating and often brutal in their character, and in some instances destructive of life itself."

Judge Thomson's decision proceeded: "That in the secret operations of the corporation's activities and in hostility to the civil authorities, military organizations are established and maintained, with arms, regalia and equipment, with officers of varying rank and military titles, these officers being bound to obey without question the commands of the superior officer in authority of the plaintiff corporation. In addition to this, bands known as 'Night Riders,' or the black-robed gang, armed, equipped and masked, are formed and operated here and there throughout the country, both organizations being used as instruments of terror, oppression and violence, and being thus a continued menace to the public peace and destructive of the public order."

Concerning Klan operations in the State of Pennsylvania, the evidence conclusively established, Judge Thomson went on, the atrocities committed upon a Negro near Beaver Falls, on July 6, 1923, and in the preceding month, the kidnapping, by order of Grand Dragon Rich of a Pittsburgh girl, three or four years old. Rich personally took an active part. The child was transported away, and her grandparents, from whom she was seized, had never been able to learn where she was, or whether she was alive or dead.

Judge Thomson continued:

I also find as a fact that Hiram Wesley Evans was present and spoke to the assembled multitude at Carnegie immediately before the riot.

That he and Rich were well aware that the civil authorities of Carnegie had forbidden the parade, and that in defiance of this position and in utter disregard of the consequences which might naturally follow he gave the order to march, which resulted in the serious riot in which men were beaten and severely injured. At least one other man was wounded by gunfire and another man was shot to death.

Under these circumstances, he was directly responsible for the riot and bloodshed which ensued.

The evidence also disclosed that in the State of Texas men were brought before the Klan, tried and convicted, And in some instances were subjected to brutal beatings and in others were condemned to death and burned at the stake.

In view of all the facts disclosed by the evidence, the plaintiff corporation, stigmatized as it is by its unlawful acts and conduct, could hardly hope for judicial assistance in a court of the United States which is highly commissioned to extend to all litigants before it, without distinction of race, creed, color or condition those high guarantees of liberty and equality vouchsafed by the Constitution of the United States . . .

This unlawful organization, so destructive of the rights and liberties of the people, has come in vain asking this court of equity for injunction or other relief. They come with filthy hands and can get no assistance here. . . .

Judge Thomson assessed the costs of the suit upon the Ku Klux Klan.[6]

From this denunciation we turn to a gathering of 75,000 Klansmen at Dallas, Texas, on October 24, 1923. In his speech Imperial Wizard Evans grouped Negroes, Catholics and Jews as undesirable elements "defying every fundamental requirement of assimilation." They could not "attain

[6] Knights of the Ku Klux Klan v. [Rev. John F.] Strayer et al. 26F (2d) *Federal Reporter*, pp. 727-729. This gives the decision solely. For the testimony and remarks of counsel dependence is placed upon the newspaper reports of the trial. All important American newspapers gave the fullest accounts. The meticulous inquirer may consult, in particular, *The New York Times* of April 14, 1928.

the Anglo-Saxon level." Inherent in the blood of the colored race in America was "the low mentality of savage ancestors." The Jews were another "absolutely unblendable element"; for them, according to Evans, "patriotism as the Anglo-Saxon feels it is impossible." As for the allegiance of Catholics, "the Presidency at Washington is subordinate to the priesthood at Rome." Following this enunciation of the Klan gospel of "100 per cent Americanism," and of other ceremonies, hosts of Klansmen, headed by bands, and burning red fire and singing "Onward Christian Soldiers" marched at night through the business district.

From the National Catholic Welfare Conference and the Executive Committee of Orthodox Rabbis of America came quick replies to Evans. In spite of evidence to the contrary, said Father Burke's statement, the Klan had denied persecution of anyone, but Evans' speech proved the Klan's intolerance for Negroes, Jews and Catholics. Challenging the Klan to a joint debate, Rabbi Simon Glazer of New York declared this the question at issue: Whether Jewish Americans were to be considered Americans, or whether, according to the Klan, they must first be converted as Americans. But there was a matter other than Klan fanfare and his uproarious reception at Dallas which made Evans "seem happy and contented." Interviewed at the gathering by a *New York World* reporter he declared that *The World's* exposé had earned for the order [Ku Klux Klan] $1,000,000, and had cost the publishers $5,000,000,"[7] but no explanation was offered supporting that attributed figure of cost or how the alleged cost had been incurred. That this whilom dentist stepping from the most indifferent circumstances could now blithely talk in terms of millions of dollars was a fertile source of editorial comment.

A few weeks after Evans' speech in Dallas there was formed in Washington, D. C., a National Vigilance Association to fight the Ku Klux Klan. Composed of many college presidents, business executives and political leaders in all sections of the country, it sought the co-operation of fraternal orders, civic, labor and other organizations in condemning the Klan and the expulsion of members who persisted in swearing allegiance to the "Invisible Empire." In fact, many of the

[7] *The World*, New York, October 25, 1923.

large fraternal orders had already formally condemned the Klan and other proofs of solid public opinion were forthcoming. Condemnatory resolutions were adopted by the National Executive Committee of the American Legion and by the American Federation of Labor. The President of the United States rebuked the Klan. But means far more effective than words were needed, and it was to bring about the passage of adequate laws that the National Vigilance Association applied itself. One demand was for a statute in every State making unlawful the wearing of masks or hoods upon highways. State laws compelling secret organizations like the Klan to make public their membership rosters was a second demand. A third was the enactment of a Federal law comprehensively drawn to cover mob violence anywhere within the nation and to empower Federal prosecution of offenders.

Already in this year—1923—the New York Legislature had struck at the Klan by enacting a law requiring all organizations except labor unions and benevolent orders to give publicity to their regulations, oaths and memberships. For any person knowingly to affiliate with an organization failing to comply was made a misdemeanor. Contending that this law discriminated against Klansmen, suit was brought in the name of an offender who had been arrested to have the law declared unconstitutional. New York courts upheld its validity, and the case, in 1928, finally reached the Supreme Court of the United States which did likewise. Unlike benevolent orders which, on the whole, had justified their existence, the decision of this final court held, the activities of the Ku Klux Klan were of a character to stimulate hurtful religious and race prejudices. Conducting a crusade against Catholics, Jews and Negroes, it also "was striving for political power and assuming a sort of guardianship over the administration of local, State and national affairs; and that at times it was taking into its own hands the punishment of what some of its members conceived to be crimes." Further, the Ku Klux Klan was of a classification which made the secrecy surrounding its purposes and membership a cloak for acts and conduct inimical to personal rights and welfare."[8]

Legislation outlawing masked organizations was adopted

[8] N. Y. ex. Rel. Bryant v. Zimmerman, 278 *United States Reports*, pp. 76-77.

in the early and mid 1920's by Iowa, Minnesota, Michigan and other States. Yet the political and social power of the Ku Klux Klan continued dominant in many other States. In Oregon, for instance, it was Klan control of the political machinery which effected the enactment of the School Law, aimed at parochial schools, but actually affecting all private schools. This law compelled all parents to send their children to public schools. Test cases brought in behalf of parochial and private schools resulted in the Federal court in Oregon pronouncing the law unconstitutional, and later, upon an appeal by the State of Oregon, the Supreme Court of the United States—on June 1, 1925—held the same. Parents and guardians, one point in the decision stated, had the right to direct the education of their children as they saw fit; the child was not merely the creature of the State. Also, the Oregon law would have destroyed the property of private school owners.[9]

Among the aims of the National Vigilance Association was that of using the arguments of reason against all movements and influences intent upon breeding class or religious discrimination. There came into existence private agencies which made a special endeavor to combat prejudice, at least against Catholic and Jew. One of these agencies was the Iconoclast Publishing Company which put forth a monthly magazine *Truth and Light,* of which C. A. Windle, a non-Catholic, was editor. "The Ku Klux Klan and its allies, through the press and from the lecture platform, have aroused a vast deal of hostility to Catholics and Jews by their well-organized campaign of propaganda. The spectacular nature of the Klux order, its secret and mysterious methods, insure a world of publicity. 'Knights of the Invisible Empire,' encouraged by ignorance, prejudice and inbred bigotry are conducting a nation-wide campaign to make the people think—in terms of hatred."[10] Excepting some priests, Windle complained, most Catholics as well as the average Jew did

[9] Pierce, Governor of Oregon v. Society of Sisters and v. Hill Military Academy, 268 *United States Reports,* pp. 534-535.
[10] Compared to the findings of another writer this attribution was mild. In his article "Ku Klux Klan Reign of Terror," published in *Current History* (Magazine) April, 1928, R. A. Patton, of the editorial staff of *The Chattanooga Times* more outspokenly or realistically gave Klan operations a distinctively commercial purpose. He described the Klan as having been engaged in "selling a triumvirate of hates" to the American people.

not seem concerned in countering the circulation of lies believed by millions of people "who, in the absence of contradiction, accept for truth any and every charge" made against Catholic and Jew. Aloofness on the part of these, Windle advised, was a mistake. "People persist in ignoring the fact that an uncontradicted lie has the same effect as truth." In issue after issue Windle dispassionately exposed the aggregation of slanders spread by Jew-baiters and anti-Catholic crusaders; he dissected Watson's writings; he chided the credulous with accepting on face value assertions in sheets such as *The Menace, The Searchlight* and the like "in which there is too much invention, fraud, exaggeration." For one thing, dealing with the charge of Catholic control of Congress he cited figures supplied by the Board of Methodists which showed in Congress 367 Protestants and twenty-four Catholics.[11] But reverting to Windle's urging Catholics and Jews to fight back hard, would such a course, in view of his own personal experience, have had much, if any, effect, in an era when bigotry, deaf to all else, was running amok? Harken to his lament: "Four years ago I was billed to deliver a speech at Portland, Oregon, on 'The Menace of Bigotry.' Less than fifty people were present."[12]

While combating some kinds of bigotry, Editor Wendle's own office was publishing a pamphlet advertised as "Fallacies of Christian Science . . . the truth about Eddyism." This was only one more in the long list of attacks which for many decades had been made against Christian Science. From the pulpit had come many a sermon, put forth promptly in published form, denouncing Christian Science, sometimes along with Theosophy and Spiritualism, as superstitions, sophistries and delusions, altogether contrary to the tenets of the Christian religion.[13] Such, in fact, was the enmity of some of these opponents that, to heap opprobrium upon Christian Science, they represented it as advocating and fostering a species of promiscuity called "free love."

[11] Pamphlet, *Straight Talk to Non-Catholics*, p. 10.
[12] *Truth and Light*, March, 1924.
[13] The outpour of anti-Christian Science "literature" by ministers, including bishops, was extensive. A few titles will suffice to signify the attitude: "Anti-Christian Cults"; "Delusions"; "Christian Science Not Scriptural"; "Christian Science Unmasked"; "Facts and Fallacies of Christian Science"; "Christian Science an Apostasy from Science and Christianity"; "Christian Science and Other Superstitions"; "The Religio-Medico Masquerade," etc.

When Christian Science made its advent and for years afterward, there were few psychologists and only scant practical recognition of the powerful influence, in many essentials, of mind over condition of body. In time the study of mind became as much a specialized course taken by some physicians as the study of body by others, and the superinducing causes of certain bodily disorders could be located by the psychiatrist in the individual operations of the mind.

In the bigotry against Christian Science one of the most persistent charges floated was that its devotees, if a child had a physical malady, refused to call in a physician to administer the requisite services, preferring to let the child die rather than admit the fell sway of matter. Repeated assurances from Christian Scientists of the utter groundlessness of this charge did not dispel it, so tenaciously does a slander, once set in vigorous motion, persist. In net terms, how did Christian Science fare against opposition? Progressively its adherents multiplied so that, at this writing, it has 2,181 churches in the United States, 682 in other countries.

With this discursive glance, fitting at this point, at a co-existent kind of bigotry, we shall route ourselves back to the further career of the Knights of the Ku Klux Klan.

Chapter XXII

THE DECLINE OF THE HOODED ORDER

Unsatisfied with the control of political machinery in many States, the Ku Klux Klan was intent upon dominating the National Democratic Convention in 1924. Klan forces aimed to prevent the apprehended nomination of a Catholic, Governor Alfred E. Smith of New York, for President, and preclude a possible adverse report of the Resolutions Committee on the Ku Klux Klan. For the matter of religious bigotry was now an outstanding national issue, and the Democratic Party was confronted with the need of declaring its attitude toward the Klan. How to word its stand perplexed the committee. But before this could report, it happened that a speech in open convention furiously denouncing the Klan had been made, and the conflicting demonstration evinced the strong counter currents. To mollify both, two-thirds of the committee voted for a non-committal resolution which, avoiding mention of any organization, condemned "any effort to arouse racial or religious dissensions." Led by W. R. Pattangall, of Maine, thirteen dissenting committee members moved the adoption of an explicit pledge in the platform "to oppose any effort on the part of the Ku Klux Klan or any organization to interfere with the religious liberty or political freedom . . ." A long and tense debate followed in the convention. The majority's report implicating the Ku Klux Klan by nothing more than indirection was approved by the narrowest margin; in the vote of 546.15 to 542.85 the Klan could not legitimately claim a victory. The Democratic National Convention of 1924 chose J. W. Davis as its candidate for President of the United States; at the election he was badly defeated.

However, the Ku Klux Klan was able to point, after elections, to its success in electing its candidates for Governor in

Indiana, Maine and Colorado, and to its power in causing in two other States the defeat of candidates it opposed. By 1925 the Klan attained its highest point. Figures later supplied by an "authoritative source" credited it with having 8,904,871 members, but whether it had this number at any one time, since membership was a shifting factor, was not explained. The same source estimated that between 1920 and 1925 inclusive, the Klan, from ordinary membership dues and additional fees of the Knights of the White Camellia and the Knights of the Great Forest, had taken in $90,000,000.[1] Be that as it may, the total unquestionably reached tens of millions of dollars. So much so that, according to the article cited, former Klan members were now not averse to giving detailed information exposing the organization as a huge money-making affair redounding to the benefit of a group of high leaders. But, as we shall see, exposés tending to de-note this had already been made in official investigations.

Now during this same time Hiram Wesley Evans was loftily representing the Ku Klux Klan as the quintessence of patriotic aims. Conducting an impartial discussion, the editor of *The Forum* sought some person combining courage with knowledge and restraint to analyze the Klan. "Few men in public life," significantly wrote the editor, "care openly to discuss the hooded order; fewer still have anything more valuable than vituperation to offer." The choice fell upon W. R. Pattangall, Protestant and Free Mason, who had shown his dauntlessness in the Democratic Convention and later in his campaign for the Governorship of Maine.

In an authorized interview with Stanley Frost, Pattangall set forth the facts published in an article "Is the Ku Klux Klan Un-American?" The Klan, he said, was more than an organization; it was a state of mind. Its propaganda had "caused a tremendous development of anti-Catholic, anti-Jewish, and anti-alien sentiment all over the country." Further it was "now the rallying point for all the religious and race prejudice in the country." But inasmuch, Pattangall stressed, as Americanism was faith in freedom, tolerance,

[1] *The Washington Post,* November 2, 1930, the article which gave specific figures of membership for each of the years for each State, as also the membership of the Knights of the White Camellia and the Knights of the Great Forest and the dues paid by them. The inflow of funds from these two orders to the Klan was placed at more than $10,000,000 annually.

humanity, it could not discriminate because of color, birth-place or creed. Yet the Klan avowedly did these things and exalted them as a virtue. Exploiting prejudice as a means to aggrandize itself in political power, it "seeks a secret hold on Legislatures, judges and other officials." Yet what, aside from a string of narrow laws the Klan had caused to be en-acted and the vast upsurge of bigotry, was the actual result? "The one thing the Klan has accomplished so far has been the enrichment, in money and power of certain persons who, before it was organized had neither." These were but a few of Pattangall's points in the indictment.[2]

The proper person to reply to this, the editor of *The Forum* announced, narrowed to Evans, "Emperor and Im-perial Wizard of the Klan." In an authorized interview with Frost, Evans gave a long disquisition. The same was pub-lished under the title "The Klan; Defender of Americanism."

Racial equality, Evans declared, was impracticable; white supremacy was essential; the pioneers who settled America bequeathed to their children a priority right which was bound up with the spirit of Protestantism. Apparently Evans did not know of Catholic pioneers, and did not bother to think, in putting forth his racial and priority dicta, of the antecedent and transcending rights of Indians. Evans went on to attack the Roman Catholic Church; ignorant of vera-cious history as he showed himself, that Church had, he said, always opposed the fundamental spirit of liberty for which America stood; disregarding the open fact that the Baptist and Methodist churches in the South were quasi-political machines, and effective ones, too, he picked upon the Catholic Church as "a church in politics; an organized, disciplined, powerful rival to every political government." That was the Klan's "real objection to Romanism." What, forsooth, of the Jew? Him "the Klan considers a far smaller problem . . . He is confined to a few cities, and is no prob-lem at all to most of the country. . . ." Above all, "if the Klan's efforts to save Americanism . . . is [sic] intolerance, we are proud of it."[3]

One of Pattangall's counts against the Klan was that its actual, underlying purpose was to crush the spirit of liberalism. This aim, Pattangall wrote, was exemplified by the school laws fathered by the Klan. The Tennessee Legislature had enacted a repressive law. In any educational institution, supported wholly or in part by public funds, it was made unlawful to teach any theory denying the Biblical story of man's creation or to teach the descent of man from a lower order of animals. Generally elsewhere in the country, little was known about the passage of such a law; interested organizations knew of it; but to the great public at large the first awakening came with the arrest and indictment of John T. Scopes, a young high-school teacher who, unable to take so irrational a law seriously, had suggested to his class the possibility of there being some basis to the theory of evolution.

Who was responsible for such legislation restricting freedom of education? One surmise chose William Jennings Bryan as the inspirer. A rigid believer in fundamentals as set forth in the Bible, Bryan was an inexorable opponent of evolutionary ideas. He was now a resident of Florida, the Legislature of which had previously adopted—in 1923— a resolution expressing its objections to the teaching as truths of "Darwinism, Atheism and Agnosticism" in the public schools or State institutions. Bryan's presence in Florida was, of course, no proof of his having any connection with that step. But his action, at the General Assembly of the Presbyterian Church, at Indianapolis, on May 22, 1923, did exhibit his passionate initiative in trying to suppress the heterodoxy taught in the name of science. He offered a resolution to bar from the use of school funds any school teaching the evolutionary hypothesis. Killing his proposal, the Assembly adopted a substitute. By this, it "withheld official approval" from any educational institution seeking to establish an evolutionary philosophy or attempting to discredit the Christian faith.

The passage of anti-evolution laws in various States could hardly be attributed to individual endeavor. It was more in the nature of an endemic movement in which Ku Klux Klan influences had no inconsiderable share. But intermixed was the potent force of the Baptist Church in the South and near South. This notably had long warred upon all agencies teaching even the slightest variation from its fixed doctrines, among which was the Biblical tale of creation. A searching criticism of this inveterate Baptist stand was written by one of their own sect who had carefully followed all of its developments. In an article, Rev. Joseph Martin Dawson, Pastor of the First Baptist Church, at Waco, Texas, set forth his indignation at the machinations of united groups of fellow Baptists. By name he specified four Baptist periodicals which, for years, had editorially condemned institutions of higher learning. "They have waged war upon damnable heresies which, according to these eminent savants, are being incubated in most of the colleges and universities in our land." They had favored schools "which are little jerkwater colleges with no academic rating." Dawson went on to relate how, because they had shown sparks of liberalism, certain professors had been "hounded out of Baptist colleges."[4] Yet such measures were ineffective, outside the special province of the Baptist Church, in preventing the teaching of evolution and other condemned ideas. Only proscriptive law could accomplish this comprehensive end, and by grace of the Ku Klux Klan's political power, a beginning was made in achieving this desideratum.

Constant a subject as it was for large newspaper notice, the Klan in this respect, suffered an eclipse during and for a while after Scopes' trial at Dayton. To the preliminaries and to the proceedings newspapers everywhere gave a vast amount of space topped by bold headlines. And not without good reason. Interest extended to many countries. In England, for instance, the Bishop of Birmingham, writing in *Nature,* was one of a number of churchmen condemning anti-evolution laws. They were, he declared, the product of "ignorant fanaticism." He went on: "The normal educated Christian regards the process of evolution as the machinery by which God created man. Every divine of any eminence among us accepts this point of view. . . ." The like was true of some American and other churchmen who had developed the same cosmic comprehension. But all, whether in or out of churches, who literally accepted every word of Genesis as final and immutable, and did not know or barely knew what evolution meant, looked upon that strange thing as the

[4] "Baptist Illiteracy in the South," *Plain Talk* (Magazine), October, 1928. Giving copious facts and figures, Pastor Dawson placed responsibility for illiteracy in the South upon the predominant Baptist Church.

great enemy of religion. On the other hand, scientists, educators, the mentally enlightened of every kind, were astonished and indignant. To them the action taken was a retrogression to the depths of medievalism, and the law itself the worst sort of anachronism. It was this joining of an issue which had the effect of making Scopes a minor figure in a collision of forces. Fundamentalism, as it was styled, was arrayed against Modernism, and Conservatism against Liberalism. The outcome was keenly awaited.

Upon learning of the Tennessee law, the American Civil Liberties Union, in New York, had declared its intention of backing any school teacher prosecuted for violation. Standing for freedom of thought and the right to express it, that body at once complied with a request from Scopes' local lawyer for additional counsel. At its behest the noted Clarence Darrow, of Chicago, hastened to Dayton, and from New York City, Dudley Field Malone and Arthur Garfield Hays, both able lawyers. Opposing them was William Jennings Bryan, confident that in his character of upholder of a holy cause he singly could defeat their combined efforts. As announced, these were: 1. To prove that Scopes was not guilty; 2. to admit his teaching of evolution but that the law was unconstitutional; 3. that, when the subject of evolution was properly presented and understood, there was nothing in it to undermine religious faith. The presiding judge, John T. Raulston, was a lay preacher in the Methodist Episcopal Church.

To unfold the circumstances of this extraordinary trial would compel a long account; adequate details may be found by the curious in two particular books.[5] Enough here to outline sketchily the main lines: Darrow's denunciation of the laws as a brazen attempt to destroy liberty and his scoring of ignorance and bigotry; Bryan's branding of Darrow as an atheist; Darrow's cross-examining of Bryan who asserted his literal belief in the Bible, including the story of Jonah, and doubted the existence of any civilization older than the flood; the explanation of evolution by a noted scientist— all of this and much more was crowded into the singular proceedings. Convicted, Scopes was fined $100 and costs,

[5] *Let Freedom Ring*, by Arthur Garfield Hays, and *Clarence Darrow* by Charles Yale Harrison. Consultation of newspapers of July 10-22, 1925, will give the amplest details of the case as reported from day to day.

whereupon he informed the judge that, adhering to the ideal of academic freedom, he would continue to oppose the anti-evolution law in every way possible. The case was carried on appeal to the Supreme Court of Tennessee. In a decision full of subtleties, this tribunal sustained the constitutionality of the anti-evolution law but reversed the conviction on the ground of its having been improperly imposed by the judge. At the same time, by thus acknowledging that the law was one which could not be enforced, the court directed the Attorney General to *nolle prosse* all proceedings.

Did the derision heaped upon the State of Tennessee discourage either anti-evolution sticklers there or tend to impede those in some other States? Not so. Within a few months after the Scopes trial, Judge Raulston, speaking in the much newspaper-noticed Calvary Baptist Church—Rev. John Roach Straton, pastor—New York City, disclosed his unchanged attitude. He urged New York State to prohibit the teaching of evolution in its schools as an all-important step to prevent corruption of society and the downfall of civilization. Defending his handling of the Scopes trial, he stridently denounced those who had characterized his fellow Tennesseeans as "yokels, hillsters, ignoramuses." With quavers of emotion he told of his mountain upbringing in which daily religious instruction was a regular part. "If," said he, "I listen to evolution and lose my faith in Genesis, I am afraid I will lose my faith in the rest of the Bible." These and other remarks in his discourse were frequently punctuated by soulful "Amens" from the audience, largely a Bible class conducted by Straton.[6] When, soon, Mississippi enacted a law prohibiting teaching of the theory of evolution in the schools, Straton hailed it as the harbinger of further State laws; the movement, he rejoiced, "is gathering strength in the South and West and eventually it will swing to the North."[7]

And now what do we observe? Forth comes Edward Young Clarke, whilom Acting Imperial Wizard of the Knights of the Ku Klux Klan. He, it was announced in a despatch from Atlanta, had organized an anti-evolution society called the Supreme Kingdom, and sought a fund of $5,000,000 "to

[6] *The New York Times*, November 9, 1925.
[7] Ibid., February 10, 1926.

awaken the South and the country from the lethargy into which they have fallen and issue a warning to the people against the dangers of evolution, atheism, modernism and communism."[8] The enterprising Clarke had hit upon an assortment of objects for a new "drive."

Certainly, Fundamentalists had been chagrined by the defeat of anti-evolution measures in the Legislatures of Georgia and North Carolina, and by a close vote in the Kentucky Legislature. Again plying the Kentucky lawmakers with appeals, the anti-evolutionists were rebuffed a second time, and also were obstructed in the Virginia and Louisiana Legislatures. But the Texas Textbook Commission was responsive; all references to evolution were ordered expunged from its books of instruction. The State Board of Education in California required that evolution should be taught "merely as a theory." Joining the list of anti-evolution States, Arkansas provided the peculiar distinction of the adoption of such a law by popular vote. The bill, in 1926, had passed the Arkansas lower house by a vote of one but had been squelched in the Senate. Submitted to a referendum two years later, it was added to Arkansas statutes. A New Yorker who had gone to Little Rock to protest publicly against endorsement of this measure was arrested as an atheist, fined $25, and, refusing to pay it, was jailed. The Arkansas law, like the same laws elsewhere, related to educational institutions supported wholly or in part by public funds. And since it forbade use of any book teaching man's derivation from a lower class of animals, Webster's dictionary and encyclopedias which did give that definition of evolution came under the ban.

Attacked as bigots, the sponsors of these laws might—had they the understanding—have well asked whether science itself was not essentially of the same stripe. In its time, flushed with its discoveries and researches, the body of science had become arrogant in its claims and all too certain of its conclusions. Already many really great scientists in different fields had discarded theories early acquired, and were demonstrating that perhaps the only reality was spiritual. But the mass of instructors of science were still teaching as absolute truths the partial facts, postulates and dogmas which they

[8] Ibid., May 24, 1926.

had learned by rote. Was there no alternative to the beliefs that man must either be descended from Adam or from animals? Based upon the old philosophy of India, the Theosophists had a very different explanation of man's origin. Yet if they had attempted to teach it in the public schools, would not the forces of materialistic evolution have sought to suppress it as intolerable error? Without meditating further on this aspect, the immediate question calling for answer is: Were the anti-evolution laws an impassible barrier to the intellectually acquisitive? Quite the contrary. Denied the right to acquaint themselves with outlawed books, the mentally curious manifested all the greater zeal in desiring to examine into the forbidden subject. Reports from States having such laws showed increased demand for evolutionist literature.

Again to the forefront of public attention came the Ku Klux Klan by reason of a series of scandals. One revolved around D. C. Stephenson who, as Grand Dragon of the Klan in Indiana, had been a conspicuous exemplification of its methods and power. A look at his career illustrates the type of men who became Klan functionaries. He had followed, in Texas and vicinity, a miscellany of occupations, including those of small-town editor and linotype operator. Then, under thirty years of age, he had gone to Indiana where he became a salesman of Klan memberships. Having a gift of persuasive talk he did wonderfully well in bringing in revenue.

His reward came in 1923 when he was appointed the head of the Klan in Indiana. At his beck, determined by venality as well as by preference, men were put into and thrust out of office. As the arbiter of political fortunes, he became arrogant and capricious. He quarreled with Imperial Wizard Evans, but over what differences was not known. Stephenson soon found that Evans was the master; out he had to go from the post of Grand Dragon. Evidently Stephenson had incurred an unslaked enmity which now busied itself with exploring his past life in which was a former wife who had divorced and remarried him. But it was his present life which proved his final undoing, and he himself supplied the occasion. An Indianapolis girl with whom he had been intimate was found murdered; he was convicted of the crime and sentenced to life imprisonment. Thereafter, he never failed to maintain that enemies had "framed" him, and this rancor contributed later to his making sensational revelations of political corruption in Indiana.

To what degree the effect of the Stephenson scandal hastened the exit from the Klan of many of its sub-officers and members could not be ascertained. Along with internal jarrings and squabbles it had its influence. The puzzling question of the disposition of revenues inclined many members to cease payment of dues and fees. One striking fact was patent. Some former Klan officers no longer had any reluctance to disclose the workings of the Invisible Empire.

A U. S. Senate investigation, in 1926, of moneys used in Senatorial primaries and elections afforded them the opportunity. A leading witness was Hugh P. Emmons; an evangelical minister, although never ordained, he had become Exalted Cyclops of the Klan in Indiana. In answer to questions put by Senator James A. Reed, chairman of the committee, he testified that from his knowledge of Klan activities it was trying to build a political machine to capture the country's political offices. Queried as to whether the Klan confined its efforts to members of the U. S. Senate, Emmons replied: "When we had a Grand Dragon by the name of Stephenson, he took everything from the mayors up." A confidential document sent forth by the Grand Dragon, Realm of Indiana, was handed in to the committee. This circular told how every candidate for U. S. Senator stood toward or against the Klan, and gave instructions to act accordingly. The same test, Emmons testified, was applied to candidates for judgeships, prosecuting attorneyships and to others seeking office.

With an air of innocence, Senator Reed asked regarding Imperial Wizard Evans: "By the way, what is he a doctor of, anyway? Medicine?" In a tone not devoid of scorn, Emmons replied: "No, he was a dentist; he had a little one-chair shop in Georgia." [He meant Dallas.] Ruefully reminiscent, Emmons added: "I thought he was a doctor of divinity when I joined the organization, and that is one of the things that had a lot of influence with me." Now the questioning turned to the inescapable subject of Klan revenue. What was the inpour? Well, Emmons testified, there was one source from the sale of robes on which Evans received a commission. As for annual income from dues, these reached, computed on a membership of 5,000,000 in the entire country, the total verging on to $7,000,000. And, as implied in Emmons' further testimony, the head office was mightily, impatiently concerned with promptly getting its large quota of the plethora of dues; if these were not paid in by any Klan organization, disciplinary action was swift in the taking away of its charter.[9] Other former Klan officers corroborated Emmons' testimony, particularly that relevant to the Klan's direct, peremptory interference in State Senatorial primaries and elections in Minnesota, Iowa and a tier of other States as well as Indiana.

In some States, including Texas, the anti-Klan forces had succeeded in passing laws prohibiting wearing of masks. Klan organizations in some States were actively moving to bring about the repeal of these laws. Terrorism in riots and nocturnal masked operations persisted. Previously Herrin, Illinois, had been the scene of a riot caused by Klansmen; and now, on April 12, 1926, the smoldering feud again broke out with volleys of shots taking a death toll of three Klansmen and an equal number of anti-Klansmen, besides a list of wounded; militia had to be summoned to restore order. In Alabama, the next year, resigning his Klan membership, Attorney-General McCall exposed Ku Klux Klan viciousness and brutality in mercilessly flogging victims. Appalled by outrages, two Southern judges defied Klan power by severely denouncing mob criminality. One of these jurists, Judge A. E. Gamble, addressing the Grand Jury in Crenshaw county, Alabama, on October 11, 1927, thus voiced his indignation: "People in this country have been taken from their homes and beaten, without a trial and without an opportunity to defend themselves. Most of this lawlessness has been perpetrated under cover of night. . . . There can be but one governing authority. One system is the courts of our State, the other is a body of masked men, responsible to no one, exercising their own power, crushing the weak without excuse. These two systems are in conflict, and if the courts are to govern, the other system must go, or else anarchy will pre-

[9] *Senatorial Campaign Expenditures, Hearings Before a Special Committee Investigating Expenditures in Senatorial Primary and General Elections,* U. S. Senate, 1926, Part 3, pp. 2032, 2043, 2063.

vail." At Covington, Louisiana, on a mere suppositious charge bruited about him, not only a professor but his wife and child had been driven from their home by a mob. Shocked by the circumstances and impressed by the widespread and unfavorable notoriety centering upon that locality, Judge Prentiss B. Carter urged to a special Grand Jury that mob law should not be tolerated.[10]

These were but some of the evidences of the outrages especially coming to public attention; in Georgia floggings by masked bands were commonplaces which there barely received notice. Continued lynchings of Negroes and the immunity of the mobs responsible in various parts of the South did excite much critical publicity in the rest of the country, but whenever a national anti-lynching law was proposed, great opposition came from the South on the ground of its violating the sacredness of State's rights. Yet entire attention should not be fixed upon Klan operations in the South or in small towns elsewhere. For instance, nearly 1,000 white-robed and hooded Klansmen, accompanied by 400 women relatives and friends, ventured to march in a 1927 Memorial Day parade, in Jamaica, New York City. This sight aroused the pugnacity of irate spectators and a riot resulted.

Already Ku Klux Klan membership was steadily decreasing. By the end of 1926 it seems to have dropped to slightly more than 2,000,000, and by the next year slumped to 321,-000. This by no means signified, as was soon unfortunately shown, the decline of bigotry. It merely denoted a certain disintegration of organization. During the years when Klan ranks magically rose to many millions a sizable proportion was composed of men fanatically and inseparably bound to it by voluntary fervor. A very much larger number, however, entered because it was the rage to do so, and this inrush had been accelerated by the suction of high-pressure salesmanship. Toward the Klan's purposes the attitude of this aggregation was one of assent but not so much so after a time as to overcome the painfully felt constant exaction of dues and fees. This was a sore point in all sections. Another consideration was the wearing away of the effects of novelty upon those tired of Klan trappings. Also, in the South, a segment of with-

<hr>

[10] Dispatch to *The New York Times*, October 12, 1927, which reported the action of both judges.

drawal was motivated by the example of influential Southern men who publicly renounced or condemned the Klan, and by the pronouncement of some veteran bodies there declaring the Klan a menace to America. In the North and West the recoil was now quickened by the responsiveness of many members to a general public sentiment greatly aroused everywhere over proved political crookedness and corruption as revealed by one who had stood high as a Klan leader.

Despairing of obtaining his release from prison, Stephenson, by July, 1927, was ready to unbosom the facts relating to the system of graft, bribery and trafficking in offices during his regime as Grand Dragon of Indiana. His testimony, backed by proof, caused the indictment of a number of high officials, one of whom was promptly convicted. Along with this exposure, Stephenson dealt with Klan manipulation of the courts. "How," he was asked, "did the Klan control the courts?" Answer: "By going into a campaign when a Judge was to be elected and offering him 5,000 votes—enough to elect him—if he would be guided by the wishes of the Klan." And, in a deposition, Stephenson told of Klan floggings, burnings, pillaging of Catholic churches, lynchings and numerous crimes. Then, pertaining to existent Klan leadership, he alleged that when it failed to break men to its will it trumped up evidence against them, often using women to entrap those proscribed. All of this came from an embittered man, brooding over his fate which he accounted that of a victim of persecution. Yet his charges in general coincided with the clear facts of the situation; no one was so rash as to attempt to disprove his main accusations.

Shrink as did Klan membership, bigotry still had its raucous mouthpieces. One of the loudest and most irrepressible was U. S. Senator Thomas J. Heflin, of Alabama, son of a country doctor who combined farming with that calling. Time and time again, in the Senate itself, this Senator would speak or rather rant for hours at a stretch attacking the Catholic Church and the Knights of Columbus. On February 17, 1927, he thus consumed three hours and ten minutes of the Senate's time and then announced his not being "half through," and assured his fellow Senators that he spoke "the language of nine-tenths of the people of Alabama." The Senate's rules forbade stopping his windy speeches in that body, but an appeal was made on that very day by Senator Wadsworth, of New York, to the National Press Club to have newspapers "squelch the religious poison which is being spilt in the Senate." On the next day, Heflin made another attack, hour after hour, assailing Catholics as "the most narrow-minded, intolerant, bigoted people in the United States" and as trying "to terrorize" himself and other American Senators "by showing how dangerous it is for any Senator to incur the displeasure of the Roman Catholic hierarchy." On Heflin went with his tissue of denunciations when, breaking in, Senator Phipps wearily asked him how long he intended to speak? "I think," answered Heflin, "I can finish in four hours," and he imperturbably proceeded. If a general reply was expected from Senator Bruce of Maryland, he contemptuously declined making one. "To do so," he said, "I should have to transport myself backward at least to the fifteenth or sixteenth century." [11]

Irrespective of matters under deliberation by the Senate, if any question came up which even remotely afforded him an opening to project his mania, Heflin would break out. He delivered in January another long harangue against the Catholic Church and the Knights of Columbus, which latter body, he alleged, had raised a fund of a million dollars for propaganda to bring about a war with Mexico, the Government of which had taken measures antagonistic to the Catholic Church. He represented the Roman Catholic "machine" as conspiring against free press and free speech. So he went on with his calumnies and falsehoods, and then gave the seal of his approval upon the Ku Klux Klan. He "endorsed many of the things the Ku Klux Klan stands for," and "it has some of the noblest principles that ever were embodied in any secret order."

Heflin was not allowed to go unrebuked. As to charges made by him that the Catholic Church or the Knights of Columbus had forged or inspired the forgery of certain documents relating to Mexico, Senator Robinson of Arkansas denounced it as unwarranted. A special Senate committee had investigated those documents, and not a word of testimony, said Senator Robinson, justified any of Heflin's assertions or

[11] *Congressional Record,* 69th Congress, 2d Session, Vol. 68, Part 4, pp. 4115-4146.

innuendoes. Senator Reed, chairman of the investigating committee, agreed with Robinson: "There was not one syllable of evidence that anything in this case was inspired by any religious sect or any religious group whatsoever." Notwithstanding these authoritative denials, Heflin repeated his assertions. Whereupon, in plain language not customary in the punctilious Senate, Robinson exploded: ". . . I have heard the Senator from Alabama a dozen times during the last year make what he calls his anti-Catholic speech. I have heard him denounce the Catholic Church and the Pope of Rome and the cardinal and the bishop and the priest and the nun until I am sick and tired of it as a Democrat." Came this dialogue, as further reported in the *Congressional Record:*

> Mr. Heflin. I would like to have the Senator make that speech in Arkansas.
> Mr. Robinson of Arkansas. I will make that speech in Arkansas, and I will make it in Alabama, too.
> Mr. Heflin. If you do they will tar and feather you.
> Mr. Robinson of Arkansas. Oh, yes. That shows the proscriptive spirit which dwells in the bosom of my friend from Alabama.[12]

Hitherto, editorials throughout the country had scored Heflin as a bigoted nuisance and a bore. Having a tough hide he did not mind these characterizations. But comments now made upon his threat to a fellow Senator did pierce his epidermis, since a possibility faced him of definite punitive action. A few days later Heflin—on January 23rd—sought to make it appear that the threat was just "fun or a facetious remark." On this day he made a two-hour speech on his usual lines. Senator after Senator walked out of the chamber until fewer than twenty members remained to the end. More of the same came from Heflin on February 7, 1928, a deluge of talk in which the only new thing was his quoting Chiniquy's book, published, as we have noted, decades previously. Chiniquy, it will be recalled, had represented the "Roman Catholic political machine" as setting out, through immigrant voters, to "capture" the large cities of the United States and then the Federal Government itself.[13] Heflin omitted the pivotal

[12] Ibid., 70th Congress, 1st Session, Vol. 69, Part 2, pp. 1649, 1654, 1656, 1660, 1661.
[13] Ibid., pp. 2613-2614.

matter of immigration, and took as granted that the alleged plan was still being engineered. None of the few Senators having the endurance to stay knew the contents of Chiniquy's book, and there was nobody to point out that, since his time, vast had been the influx of immigration and the Catholic population had increased to 16,000,000, yet there was no evidence that any such control had been achieved or even attempted.

Inexhaustibly in the following months Heflin's ravings—they could hardly be termed anything else—were loosed not only upon the overplagued Senate but upon the entire country through the newspapers. Alfred E. Smith, aspirant for the Democratic presidential nomination, Heflin asserted, "represented the crowning effort of the Roman Catholic hierarchy to gain control of the United States," and the Smith forces were inspiring "villainous and lying" reports about him, Heflin. In fact, no slight share of Heflin's gush of talk was devoted to fancied grievances concerning himself, of whose importance he had a superabundant opinion. A specimen is here selected: "The bold and brazen agents of Rome's political machine have invaded the Capitol with their attacks upon me. They sit in yonder press gallery, obeying orders to watch, misinterpret and slander me. I repeat, the agents of the Roman Catholic political machine of the State of Massachusetts have invaded my own State of Alabama with their impudent and insolent attacks upon me. . . ." [14]

Aside from intervening speeches, another tirade occupying more than three hours came from Heflin in the Senate, on May 8, 1928, against the Catholic hierarchy. This time no longer able to contain himself, Senator Bruce impaled Heflin. In newspapers Senator Bruce was reported as saying that Heflin's "abusive accusations are wholly the fictions of his own distempered and, I am beginning to believe, his almost deranged intellect." [15] Perhaps this was said, but, if so, was not formally recorded in the *Congressional Record*. Therein, Senator Bruce's rejoinder is thus given: "The only cross in which he [Heflin] is interested is the 'fiery cross' of the Ku Klux Klan which has been responsible during the last three years for no fewer than 700 floggings in the State of Alabama,

[14] Ibid., p. 2614.
[15] *The New York Times*, May 9, 1928.

some of old men, some of women and some of children."
Heflin ventured to say that it wasn't true.

Bruce retorted: "The truth would be in a bad way if the final test of truth was the ultimatum of the Senator from Alabama. . . . It is beyond the Senator's power to be accurate. I recollect that Judge Black once spoke of somebody or something as being 'marked by loose and lavish unveracity' and I never heard the Senator from Alabama make a speech in my life that was not marked by loose and lavish unveracity. . . . I should rather see a Catholic, if you please, nominated to the Presidency of the United States than any Protestant, because, in the Providence of God, the time has come when another solemn appeal should be made to the fidelity of the American people to the Federal Constitution, which, of course, bars sectarian distinctions of every sort so far as the political life of our country is concerned, and when every true American should be quick to set his foot upon the rising spirit of intolerance which has recently been such a disgraceful, not to say abnormal feature of our national life. . . ." And further making his remarks as pertinent to Heflin as senatorial courtesy permitted, Bruce deplored "that domain of narrow-mindedness, of bitterness, of rancor and of discord, in which the despicable bigot lives and has his being." [16]

Neither this castigation nor subsequent rebukes from Senator Borah, of Idaho, had the slightest effect upon Heflin, who continued his long screeches in the Senate—and elsewhere at meetings in various States. If the testimony of William N. Zumbrunn, chief counsel of the Kloncilium of the Ku Klux Klan, was accurate, Heflin was well paid for these speeches in a series of States. On May 31, 1928, Zumbrunn told the Senate Committee investigating campaign-fund expenditures of his having been informed, usually by high ranking officials of the State Klans, that Heflin received from $150 to $250 for each speech. Taking the witness stand, Heflin equivocally put forth the explanation that he was paid for "lecturing" and not for making speeches. At this hearing some proof was submitted from the Government Printing Office that Heflin had franked broadcast 556,600 copies of his Senate speeches denouncing the Catholic Church, Catho-

[16] *Congressional Record,* 70th Congress, 1st Session, Vol. 69, Part 8, pp. 8055-8057.

lic propaganda, as he termed it, and Alfred E. Smith. Nor was this the only distribution of Heflin's speeches. They were published as leaflets by the anti-Catholic publication, *The New Menace* (successor to the former weekly of that name) at Aurora, Missouri, and in that form were widely used in the Presidential campaign which now set in.

CHAPTER XXIII

CAMPAIGNING ON RELIGIOUS LINES

In an evident aim to win back such of the political hold as
the Ku Klux Klan had lost because of its odiousness as well
as to try stemming diminution of membership, Imperial Wizard Evans, on February 21, 1928, issued a revolutionary edict.
Henceforth the wearing by any Klansman of mask or visor as
part of his regalia was to be "unlawful." To Evans the use of
such a word seemed eminently proper, seeing that all members were pledged to absolute obedience to his orders. Further, a change of the organization's name was decreed; by
waving of a wand a body called the Knights of the Great Forest was magically created, and in this every Klansman was
automatically made a member.

True, the edict made a seeming relinquishment by disavowing political ambitions on the part of the Klan or its
members. But this posture was not taken seriously by the
legions of skeptics. In point of membership the Klan could
no longer command great direct political power. Down its
enrollment, in 1928, went to less than 150,000. But however
shorn its sway in political selection, it still had much potency
in influencing electoral action. If it could not manipulate
conventions, it could mold masses of voters by propaganda.
In this process it had achieved the active aid of a conjunction
of publications and organizations, all pouring forth attacks
on Catholics and Jews, but chiefly Catholics.

Sanctioned by the Klan, with Evans a steady and oracular
contributor, *The Kourier Magazine* of Atlanta, devoted the
bulk of its columns to lashing the Catholic Church, yet not
omitting thrusts at the "Hebrew menace." Although considerable, the circulation of this periodical was not comparable
to other publications engaged in the same business of fomenting religious hatred. Continuing its predecessor's make-

up, *The New Menace* boasted of its ranking as the leading anti-Catholic paper; it did not specify its circulation which, however, was consequential. Side by side with its title, *The Fellowship Forum,* of Washington, D. C., also a weekly, ran the claim "More Than a Million Readers," a result doubtless attained by counting a number of perusals for each copy circulated. Among its prized contributors were Franklin Ford whose radio attacks on Catholics and Jews placed him in the van of throaty bigots, and H. E. Woolever, editor of *The National Methodist Press. The Rail-Splitter,* published at Milan, Illinois, extolled itself as "the greatest anti-papal monthly published on the American continent," and as a force which the "Roman Catholic Church fears more than any other anti-papal publishing house." A North Carolina monthly called *The Yellow-Jacket* specialized, amongst its other performances, in exhuming and dressing afresh the old scare of a general slaughter of Protestant heretics once Rome fastened its clutch upon America.

Many more of varying degree were in the list of anti-Catholic publications, to catalogue which would be as superfluous as monotonous. Yet *The Protestant,* a monthly periodical in Washington, D. C., deserves explicit mention. High were its claims of its "patriotic" mission in seeking to preserve America from subjugation by the Jesuits, Knights of Columbus and other Catholic bodies. *The Protestant* cooperated with the American Protestant Alliance. So the comprehensive title seemed to imply a formidable union of Protestant members; as a matter of fact, although some Protestant clerics and laymen might approve its program, it in no sense represented Protestantism as a whole; it appears to have revolved around the figure of its General Secretary, William L. Anderson, a person of no enviable record. This organization was agitating for an amendment to the Federal Constitution, the practical effect of which would have been to bar from citizenship anyone acknowledging allegiance to the Pope. Such a position the Alliance—or rather Anderson—styled "militant, uncompromising patriotism." [1] Betaking to itself a distinctiveness in being superior to other anti-Catholic publications, *The Protestant* gave itself the special character of appealing to "thinkers." To support this statement

[1] *Allied Protestant American,* February, 1928.

it asserted that its contents were read in thousands of libraries.

In totality, the radius of influence of anti-Catholic publications was extensive. But that was only part of the propagandizing. Papers were ephemeral but books and tracts had a more permanent nature, and the publication offices in question made every effort to sell their output of these. "Bargain" prices were accompanied by sensational advertising, and that quantities of such productions reached and were retained by numbers of people was a clear enough fact.[2]

More than a year before the National Democratic Convention of 1928, an open letter from Charles C. Marshall had put certain questions to Alfred E. Smith appertaining to his candidacy for the nomination for President of the United States. Smith did not shield himself under the provision of the Constitution forbidding religious tests as qualification for office. Facing the issue he, as a Catholic, replied at length. He recognized no power in the institution of the Catholic Church to interfere with the operations of the Constitution of the United States or the enforcement of the law of the land. He believed in absolute freedom of conscience for all men, and in equality of all churches, all sects and all beliefs "as a matter of right and not of favor." He believed in the absolute separation of Church and State, and in the enforcement of the Constitution's provisions prohibiting Congress from enacting any law concerning an establishment of religion or preventing religion's free exercise. No tribunal of any church, he further set forth, had any power to make any decree contravening the country's laws; its latitude was confined to establishing the status of its own church communicants. He

---

[2] Ever the question may occur: What, at a particular time, was the substance of such books and tracts? Interest should not be left unsatisfied. "We will let the titles of the following books suggest their own contents," announced *The New Menace.* Two of its list of paper-bound volumes were *Crimes of the Popes* and *Convent Horrors,* and among its leaflets (selling variously from two to seven cents) were *Conquest of the United States, Popery in the Public Schools, Platform and Program of the R. C. Political Machine, Roman Oaths,* and *Heflin's Speeches.* The book department of *The Fellowship Forum* included (in addition to Watson's books previously mentioned herein) *House of Death and Gate of Hell,* in advertising which the public was urged to "help free 100,000 slaves from the aforesaid House," *Alien Rome* and *The Story of the Inquisition.* From the *Rail-Splitter* office came Edith Gorman's fifty-seven-year-old book *Convent Life Unveiled, Life of a Carmelite Nun or the Papal Blunder of Ages, The House of the Good Shepherd, A Revelation of Actual Practices in Vogue Behind the Prison Walls of the Catholic Slave Pens in America,* etc.

believed in the support of the public school as one of the foundations of American liberty, and in the right of every parent to choose whether his child should be educated in the public school or in a religious school supported by those of his own faith. He believed in the common brotherhood of man, and he fervently prayed "that never again in this land will any public servant be challenged because of the faith in which he has tried to walk humbly with his God." [3]

Smith stated his position so clearly on every point that the editor of the magazine publishing the discussion was moved to insert the comment that it had served its purpose. "Not in this campaign will whispering and innuendoes, shruggings and hunchings, usurp the place of reason and argument." Little or not at all did this optimistic editor imagine the terrific force of mad bigotry which was then whooping against Smith's nomination. At that very time anti-Catholic papers were stooping to make every conceivable kind of absurd charge against Smith, and the abnormal bigotry of several reached the fantastic height of stridently advocating the nomination for President—of whom? Of all persons, Heflin! Among the first proponents was "the thinker's organ" *The Protestant.* Close in order was *The New Menace;* this had conspicuously featured and effusively endorsed all of Heflin's speeches, and in the aim to present him "as the logical candidate" it apotheosized him as a notability having qualities and capacities outclassing those of every President since Abraham Lincoln.

The Ku Klux Klan (that name stuck and kept on sticking) was not the only organization powerless to prevent Smith's nomination. The Anti-Saloon League, a confederation equally fanatic in its way in bringing about laws prohibiting the making and sale of liquor, was intensely antagonistic to Smith who personally favored repeal of those laws. The excessively irrational and meddlesome opposition made by these bodies only the more militated to cause a reaction in Smith's favor among the fair-minded in the convention. Noting that in this Methodist and Baptist delegates joined with others of differing tenets in the nomination of Smith, some leading

[3] "Catholic and Patriot: Governor Smith Replies," *Atlantic Monthly,* May, 1927. Marshall's letter had been published in the previous issue of this magazine. The pith of both these articles, thus presented in the form of correspondence, was widely published in newspapers throughout the country. No one needed be in doubt as to Smith's stand.

Southern editors hailed the selection as a great victory over bigotry. "A Memorable Triumph for Religious Tolerance" was, for instance, the heading of an editorial written by the publisher of *The Montgomery* [Alabama] *Advertiser* and he confidently predicted: "The vaunted opposition to Smith in the South will soon fade away. . . ." He as well as some other broad-gauged Southern editors vastly misapprehended the extent of both overlying and underlying bigotry and did not estimate the methods to be used in its enhancement.

The individual votes of Baptist and Methodist delegates in the convention were no criterion of the stand of sects to which they belonged. In the North and West individual pastors might formally urge the defeat of Smith, as, for example, the Rev. I. M. Haldeman, of the First Baptist Church, Broadway and Seventy-ninth Street, New York City. "The ambition of the Romanists," he sermonized, "is to make America Catholic." The great issue at bottom, he said, was not prohibition but whether a Protestant or a Catholic should rule the country. He could veer from the main point to voice the complaint: "The Catholic churches are packed to the door, while Protestants are out driving or playing golf," while in the same breath that he denounced Romanism he extolled Protestantism as "the bulwark, defense and barrier against religious intolerance." Instance after instance of sermons similar in trend occurred in various Protestant churches in New York and other cities. In turn, such ministers were criticized by others for dragging the church into politics and inciting bigotry.

It was in the church-dominated South that the clerical opposition to Smith was concerted and consolidated as an organized crusade. Methodist bodies in some Northern sections opposed him on the ground, partial as it was, of his attitude toward prohibition, but in the South the demand by Baptist and Methodist churches and some Presbyterian groups for his defeat was, more or less openly, because of his Catholic faith as well. This, a mutual aim on the part of all, was the expressed determination, by keeping a Catholic from becoming President, to prevent the "Pope from governing America." As all of these organizations had tried to prevent Smith's nomination so now they were leagued to encompass his defeat. Quitting the Methodist church there, Brevard Nixon, a

Democratic leader at Charlotte, North Carolina, declared that the church had degenerated into "a political machine," and he named several of its bishops as proclaiming, in the name of the church, their stand for or against certain candidates. In fact, the widespread utilization, in the South, of pulpits for political ends was such a notorious scandal that, late in the campaign, the Baltimore Conference of the Methodist Episcopal Church, South, felt the need of taking remedial steps to allay scathing criticism from other parts of the country. Pulpits, it decreed by resolution, were not to be used for political purposes. But this debarment was no impediment to private activity by ministers.

Consultation of the regular newspapers of the time provides news reports of bigotry in action, but to get an adequate knowledge of its full scope and methods a scrutiny of wholly and distinctly anti-Catholic publications is necessary. Irrespective of which candidate they supported, the generality of daily newspapers editorially adhered to non-religious issues excepting comments on some definite occurrence warranting the deploring of bigotry or approval of some step in fighting it. This attitude was distorted by the anti-Catholic publications into one of subservience to the Catholic Church. To make it appear that they alone were unmuzzled these publications kept iterating such an assertion as this prominently displayed in *The Fellowship Forum:* "The subsidized daily press is afraid to print the truth—But here is one Newspaper [!!!] that has no apologies to make to a soul on earth for its patriotic Protestant policies." [4]

As the campaign warmed up, *The Fellowship Forum,* in a leading article, reminded its readers: "The political campaign now on in the United States to determine who shall be at the helm of the Government of the United States during the four years beginning next March 4th, is in large part a religious struggle. On the one hand is the Roman Catholic Church, seeking political power, while on the other are being arrayed the Protestant churches and all those citizens who believe in complete separation of Church and State." [5] Among other averments purporting to show the unison of Protestant churches was a representation published a little

---

[4] *The Fellowship Forum,* June 16, 1928, etc.
[5] Ibid., September 1, 1928.

later. *The Fellowship Forum,* using what it put forth as a statement in *The Presbyterian Monthly,* told how the membership of the Presbyterian Church, 1,962,288 strong (How were such minutely precise figures obtained?) had been called upon by a spokesman of its General Assembly "to work, pray and vote for the election of Herbert Hoover," the Republican candidate for President.[6]

Blackguardism had unfortunately not been absent in Presidential campaigns. But none had ever witnessed the depths of viciousness disgracing this campaign. Massed bigotry sated itself with piling vilification upon Smith, and unscrupulously used every means to besmirch and make him personally and religiously as well as politically the scoff of the country. Speaking in the name of Protestantism, the rabid anti-Catholic publications would have sacrificed anyone who did not treat it with all due respect, but not a mention was made of Catholicism without jeering at its rituals, enlarging on its ascribed design of conquest, and by more than implication branding it as the begetter of criminality. A long succession of Presidents of one or other of the Protestant sects had regularly gone to the church of their choice, but no one had presumed to distort this simple act of worship into a proof of subservience to ministers. A number of these Presidents had defied synodic opposition by appointing Catholics to high posts, including, as we have seen, Chief Justices of the Supreme Court of the United States. Now, merely because Smith was a devout Catholic, the alarmist cry was systematically made that the "Romanizing of the courts of the nation was the gravest danger in the election of Smith." [7]

Admixed with such tactics was the frenzied effort to fasten degradation upon Smith as nothing more than a besotted tool of the "rum forces." The adoption of the Liquor Prohibition Amendment to the Federal Constitution had by no means been unanimous, yet extremist Protestant organizations, holding America to be a Protestant country, eulogized it as distinctly a great Protestant reform. But under this "reform" tens of thousands of illicit stills and fermenters came into operation, prohibition investigators made vast numbers of arrests for transporting and selling liquor, organized gangs of

[6] Ibid., September 28, 1928.
[7] Ibid., September 1, 1928.

bootleggers and racketeers plied a lucrative business, a great crime wave was induced, and the list of killings of investigators and civilians was a long one. The cost to the Federal Government alone of attempted enforcement was annually very heavy. Already large sections of the public had begun to be both weary and disgusted at the obvious failure of both the Constitutional Amendment and its supporting statutes. Many signs prefigured the repeal of the Amendment and the connected laws. This event came a few years later. Ignoring the widespread violations and the general impotence of law's mandate, prohibition proponents assumed the situation to be ideal. Persisting in treating prohibition as a sacrosanct and immutable condition, they now, in 1928, used every ruse that malicious scurrility could devise to combine Smith's Catholicism with inevitable restoration of traffic in liquor.

A typical cartoon displayed in *The Fellowship Forum* was headed, "Will Dry Protestants of the South Put Their Worst Foe in the White House?" It depicted Smith as a ruffian driving a beer-laden truck on which was the placard: "Make America 100% Catholic Drunk and Illiterate." Running after the truck was a priest shouting to Smith: "Mr. President, allow me to suggest that I will receive your confession and advise you." Side by side with this cartoon was a leading article warning readers that the "hordes of satellites of the papal minds who are steering the Smith campaign" were spreading the idea that, as President, Smith would be powerless to weaken the Liquor Prohibition Amendment or nullify the national prohibition law. The article continued: "Intimidated and controlled newspapers and dispensers of papal goose-grease to unwary Protestants are playing up this deceptive propaganda under direction of the Jesuitical steering committee of the candidate of the Roman Catholic Church party. The plan is to lull to sleep as many Protestant and dry votes as possible between now and November 6th." [8]

Manifestly, it is not needful to encumber this narrative by further drawing upon copies of *The Fellowship Forum* before us. The excerpts given are the merest, but ample enough index to the bulk of its contents. Yet, because of their significant prognostications, mention of two more articles is all-essential. In general, the belief was fixed, even among sea-

[8] Ibid.

soned political and editorial wiseacres, that no matter who were the Democratic candidates or whatever their stripe, the South, in any and all circumstances, would as a whole, stick to its wonted course as a "Solid South" for the Democratic Party. Two months before the election *The Fellowship Forum* contained an article by the Rev. James A. Logsdon, of Searcy, Arkansas, predicting that the Smith ticket would not carry the "Solid South." He expatiated: "The writer has spoken in many counties of Arkansas, has traveled over much territory, has listened to many hundreds of conversations, has called for rising votes on many occasions, and has seen others do likewise," and he was convinced that any sureness of Democratic success in the Southland was an "illusive dream." In the same issue *The Fellowship Forum* advanced its own precognition: "Watch These States Rebuke Romanism." It named nine Southern States and grandiloquently went on: "These old rock-ribbed Anglo-Saxon aristocratic States of our country have always stood for the highest ideals of Americanism. They never have and never will stultify their conscience by voting for any man or group of men who represent a foreign potentate. This historic and glorious old Southland will never swallow the Pope of Rome. November 6, 1928, will witness a rebuke to the papacy that will be remembered through the ages. Keep your eyes on the South." [9]

Stigmatizing of Smith as a "Tammany candidate" was not confined to outright anti-Catholic publications; Republican newspapers freely used the term to discredit him as approved by Tammany Hall, so often a corrupt political machine. But it was in the South that the connotation was most vigorously put forward. Yet, as frequent disclosures showed, Tammany's periodic corruption had been more than matched by the continuous corruption of Republican machines elsewhere, and in New York City the situation was mitigated by the recurrent fact that at its worst Tammany had encountered an indignant and wholesome public opposition which was able to oust it from power. In the South, however, there was only one political machine which, continuously entrenched, tolerated no opposition whatever, and, festering in its immunity, presented a spectacle of sheer decadence. Moreover, as regarded Smith's affiliations, the only charge which could be

[9] Ibid.

brought—if it could be considered a charge—was that he was a Tammany product. This, rightly interpreted, reflected all the greater credit upon him, for previous to becoming Governor he had proved himself an official zealous for the public interest. As Governor he was an exceptionally capable and progressive executive, not the least in his understanding of social needs and in his effecting measures which conduced to the welfare of the many. While, let us say, the elements in the South reviling him boasted of what they called their "aristocratic States," Smith took pride in his lowly beginnings on the congested East Side, New York City; and the effects of that environment had a long influence in steadying his affection for the plain people and his realization of their condition.

The lines followed by *The New Menace* were similar to those of *The Fellowship Forum*. It linked "Liquor, Al Smith, Tammany and political Romanism," called upon all Protestant ministers to resist these, and characterized such of these ministers as refused as (1) "the pin-headed white-livered crowd; (2) the jealous or foolish . . . (3) the posing popularity-seeking who will betray their cause for a few pats on the back from a crowd that is looking for a chance to knife them." *The New Menace* called upon the entire body of Protestants to take advantage of the opportunity and "clinch for years, perhaps for a whole generation to come, some things that will make America safe for patriotism, Protestantism and prohibition." The American Protestant Alliance, this weekly further announced, was carrying on a radio campaign for its proposed Constitutional amendment; this had the support of *The New Menace, The Fellowship Forum* and other publications and that of church leaders "but mass meetings backed by the Protestant pastors are needed in every community." At this same time General Secretary Anderson of the American Protestant Alliance was exhibiting his caliber by describing Smith as "the darling of Tammany . . . brazen, blatant, blaring," and contrasting this with the "dignified, intelligent position" of the Republican candidate.[10]

There is no need of wading through a mass of muck to learn the further material embodied in successive issues of *The New Menace*. Still, before leaving this, one of its most

[10] *The New Menace*, October 13, 1928.

insistent bolts of propaganda requires attention. In utter ignorance of the real and full circumstances of Magna Charta, it sought to represent Catholics as traditionally opposed to liberty, and using the largest type at its command it burst out with this headline: "When the Pope Nullified England's Magna Charta. First Great Document of Liberty Was Declared Null and Void for All Catholics and of No Effect in the British Empire by Pope's Decree. That Which Is Good Roman Catholicism Is Anti-American. Pope Innocent Absolved British Subjects From Allegiance to the Crown and Set at Naught the First Great Charter of Liberty Wrung from a Tyrant King." [11] As thus presented, these one-sided assertions were widely accepted as the whole truth, whereas, (as we have earlier shown) the act of Pope Innocent had no such effect upon English Catholicism in vitiating the force and strict maintenance of Magna Charta.

The run of attacks in all of the other anti-Catholic publications was on the same low level, not stopping at patent lies. J. Pierpont Morgan was a well-known, conspicuous member of the Protestant Episcopal Church, but a *Rail-Splitter* appeal to voters transformed him into "the richest Catholic banker in the world who recently loaned the Pope $1,500,000," and to make a close papal connection, linked Smith as Morgan's friend. "This country," urged the abusive appeal, "is not ready for a president who was educated in the barrooms of Greenwich Village, graduated from the sidewalks of New York, and who knelt and kissed the hand of a scarlet cardinal fresh from the Vatican. . . . Smith will get the united wet and papal vote . . . in large measure the Jew and negro vote. . . . He will get the vote of the vice trust, the gamblers, the red-light and dope-ring vote. . . . He will get the vote of the Jew-Jesuit movie gang who want sex films and Sunday shows to coin millions through the corruption of youth. Smith is right now the most powerful political menace in America. Nothing but a heroic campaign will keep him right out of the White House and save America. . . ."

Perhaps the most decisive tactics of this "heroic campaign" were the circulation of anti-Catholic pamphlets, leaflets, handbills and cartoons, 10,000,000 of which, it was currently stated, were distributed weekly during the campaign. On

[11] Ibid., September 1, 1928.

their own account, the Ku Klux Klan and other organizations, it was reported, handed out large numbers. But accusations were not lacking that subsidies came from Republican forces. Whether or not these charges were based upon fact, we do not know. The variety of matter thus passed out was enormous, ranging from tracts on "amazing exposés of Papal Court infamies," convents and other Catholic institutions to personal abuse of Smith, and in the production of such pamphlets and leaflets individual pastors vied with anti-Catholic publication offices. A leaflet of four pages widely distributed presented "30 Reasons Why Protestants Should Be Sure to Vote for Alcohol Smith" if they wanted: "To contribute a boy to fill a drunkard's grave; to furnish a daughter to add to the Red Light District by the gin-fizz route," and more of the same *ad libitum*. On fair differences of opinion as to policies and on estimate of the qualifications of candidates there was much of a legitimate order to be said and room for honest criticism. But not one leaflet even entered into this phase.

The results of an investigation of pre-election conditions in Alabama, made by Grover C. Hall and detailed in editorial correspondence sent from Montgomery and published in *The New York Times,* described at length the methods of the anti-Catholic campaign. "The primary objection to Smith is his Catholicism. His wet views come second, his Tammany affiliation third. But it is hard to tell where one leaves off and the other begins." In speeches, campaign-committee pamphlets, newspaper advertising and editorials, attacks in the Ku Klux Klan organ in Birmingham, *The American Standard,* and by "mouth-to-ear" whispers the most bigoted assaults were made upon Smith. "Klan politicians and preachers in Methodist and Baptist pulpits are the chief purveyors of evil reports about Smith. Most of these are Democrats, some are Republicans." In some sections, Hall went on, the people were told that in the event of Smith's election the Pope would transfer his seat to America, dictate to the President, and the Cardinals would be quartered in the White House. How this would have been capable of housing them all was not explained, nor was the question ever asked; none of the listeners apparently had any idea of the White House dimensions. People were also told that Smith's election would result in alteration of the entire marriage system so as to legalize weddings by priests only, and all American schools would be forthwith "Romanized."

Two of the most persistent stump speakers were Senator Heflin and Dr. Bob Jones. As the most widely known Methodist evangelist in the South and owner of Bob Jones College, a Fundamentalist institution at Lynn Haven, Florida, adjacent to the Alabama line, Jones drew large audiences. He had already made 100 speeches in which he inflamed his hearers by telling them that in the Catholic view all children of non-Catholics were illegitimate, and he accompanied this assertion by other vehement imputations calculated to enkindle fear and anger. And to exhibit how much more he was appalled by the election of a Catholic as President than he was by liquor, he, a fiery prohibitionist, would repeatedly exclaim: "I'd rather see a saloon on every corner than a Catholic in the White House." Or he would make a variation applied to the same end by saying that he would rather see "a nigger President." Thoroughly ignorant voters did not have to be assured of more than one basic charge; Catholics were "idol worshippers" and "did not believe in Christ." [12] Such, here summarized, was the picture given by Hall, yet it does call for amplification. Throughout much of the South, as indeed other sections, among many of the so-called educated as well as among the illiterate, there was profound ignorance of what constituted Catholicism, and as a primitive belief the prejudice was strongly fixed that it was founded on idolatry.

The tactics outlined were supplemented by the widespread use of a forgery which, it was thought by the anti-Smith, or rather the anti-Catholic, forces, could not, as a seeming genuine document, fail to present Catholicism as a ghastly thing. Hall related how "the horrendous 'oath' of the Knights of Columbus is very popular with a certain class of anti-Smith agitators, especially country preachers who are Klansmen, many of whom have distributed copies of this 'oath' from their pulpits." To this account needs be added the fact that in the North and elsewhere as well as in the South, vast quantities of this forgery were circulated.

This alleged Fourth Degree "oath" as ascribed to the Knights of Columbus had been investigated and exposed in

[12] *The New York Times*, October 7, 1928.

1913 by a special Congressional committee. The inquiry arose from a contested election in which one of the candidates had circulated this "oath." The pledge therein purported to represent Knights of Columbus members as disowning allegiance to any Protestant or Liberal ruler, vowing eternal enmity to Protestants or Masons, and as engaging to carry on a relentless war, secretly or openly, against all heretics, Protestants and Masons, sparing neither age, sex or condition in extirpating them by the most horrible of methods from the earth. Even a cursory glance at the bloodthirsty terms of this "oath" was enough to stamp it as the crudely absurd contrivance of a disordered mind. Upon the findings of a group of high-degree Free Masons themselves, the Congressional committee, headed by a thirty-third degree Mason, decided to consider it and brand it for all time as a repellent concoction, "fake and libellous" and ever to be shunned as "spurious."[13] Naturally, in the circumstances, the Knights of Columbus took pains to publish the real oath. This pledge was effectively simple. It bound all members to support the Constitution of the United States and, in accordance, to perform conscientiously all duties as citizens in the interest of their country.[14]

Notwithstanding these facts, unscrupulous foes continued disseminating the imposture, and sought to give it full authority by citing it from the *Congressional Record* and trickily ignoring the condemnatory report made. Commonly the spurious "oath" was put out in the form of a handbill and conveniently passed from hand to hand, and, it seems, one of the most flagrant sources of its publication was located in Newark, New Jersey. According to a report made, on August 22, 1928, by Luke E. Hart, Supreme Advocate of the Knights of Columbus, millions of copies had been distributed throughout the country, particularly in the South, within the preceding three months. A radio station was also utilized by Catholic baiters to broadcast the bogus "oath." The Knights of Columbus offered a standing reward of $25,000 to anyone who could prove the "oath" to be a part of the order's ritual or obligation.

---

[13] *Congressional Record*, Vol. 49, part 4, pp. 3216-3221.
[14] Pamphlet, *Criminal Libels Against the Knights of Columbus Exposed.* Issued by the Knights of Columbus, New Haven, Connecticut.

Concluding that nothing short of criminal prosecution appeared sufficient to stop the circulation of the libel, the Knights of Columbus determined to take this action against such of the offenders as could be detected. Several were convicted. One was a Maplewood, New Jersey, pastor, publisher of an anti-Catholic magazine. At his trial, on January 15, 1929, he was asked: "Do you believe that members of the Knights of Columbus would take an oath to 'hang, burn, waste, boil, strangle and bury alive' Protestants and Masons?" "I do," he replied. "I believe the days of the Inquisition may return." He was fined $250. Of a number of cases in Georgia one was that of a woman who also in the campaign of 1928 had been caught red-handed. She was ordered to pay a fine of $500 or serve six months in jail. Her defence, too, in appealing the case was that the "oath" had been copied from the *Congressional Record*. Sweeping aside this plea, the Georgia Court of Appeals, in 1929, upheld her conviction; the special Congressional committee, presiding Judge Roscoe Luke pointed out, had, purely as a matter of record, incorporated the alleged oath in its report only to demonstrate its revolting nature and expose its utter falsity.

The results of the election showed a large break in the heretofore "Solid South." The popular vote in Florida, North Carolina, Tennessee, Texas and Virginia gave majorities for Hoover. Smith held the lead in Alabama by the slimmest majority. In the nation at large, the Republican Party's sweep was overwhelming; Hoover received 444 to Smith's 87 electoral votes. Essaying to analyze the cause, Republican newspapers widely attributed it to what was acclaimed as prevalent prosperity and the indisposition of voters to risk its impairment. Newspapers which had supported Smith thought that this argument had its strong influence upon Democratic voters. Generally in the North and West, and also in Southern newspaper editorials, the religious issue was either not mentioned or, if so, but passingly. One Southern newspaper, however, *The New Orleans Item,* was not blind to the great undertow of that issue in the South but also in other sections. "The idea," it said of Smith, "that he could have any certainty of the suffrages of States as West Virginia, Tennessee, Kentucky, Oklahoma and the like was illogical. For they are peopled by about the same proportion of citizens saturated with anti-Catholic prejudice. Those States have not really belonged to the 'Solid South' for a long time. The South is no longer solid at all."

If the Ku Klux Klan head or his satraps had any illusion that the effects of this election would revitalize the order and restore membership, they were vastly mistaken. The decline of membership was progressive—to 82,602 in 1929 and to 34,694 in 1930. The Klan successively reached lower levels, but it was by no means moribund in some States. From time to time indications of its activities came to public notice. In 1937 and later years its attacks were mainly directed against alleged Communists; some persons tarred and feathered a labor-union organizer, causing his death, and also there were floggings, but the Klan denied that, as an organization, it participated in these and other outrages. Nevertheless members had done so; in Georgia, at their trials, six men identified as belonging to the Klan had been convicted of flogging. When later an attempt was made to obtain their release from prison, Governor Talmadge of that State, agreeing with the opposition to clemency expressed by a large number of Atlanta ministers and other objectors, refused, on December 1, 1941, to pardon or parole the six. At a Klan open rally in July, 1941—the first of its kind in Charleston, South Carolina in twenty years—the Grand Dragon of the State, attempting to speak to an audience of 3,000, was booed and hissed, and tomatoes and ancient eggs were hurled at him. In Florida the Klan's robed members still parade, and in front of the lodge hall on meeting nights a burning cross is displayed.

Hiram W. Evans ceased to be Imperial Wizard; his place was taken by J. A. Colescott, of Atlanta. In his later years, Evans had professed by proclamation the sundering of the Klan from engaging in political activities; he had repudiated its anti-Catholic campaign, and likewise renounced its anti-Semitism, and the need of seeking white supremacy. He declared that he stood for the Klan acting within the law. Be all this as it may, he was implicated in other activities which brought him unpleasantly in trouble with the law.

He had become a dealer in emulsified asphalt, large quantities of which had been sold by him and associates to the State of Georgia. Under a provision of the Sherman Anti-

Trust Act, that State brought an action for treble damages against Evans, John W. Greer, purchasing agent for the Georgia Highway Board and against several companies. These, the State charged, had participated in a conspiracy to control the sale of emulsified asphalt. Through its Attorney-General, Georgia stated that, because of the excessive prices charged for the asphalt purchased, the State had been damaged to the amount of $128,027.13 and asked to recover thrice that sum, or some $384,000.

The Sherman Anti-Trust Act specified the damaged "person" as the one qualified to sue. When the case was argued before the lower Federal court, the defendants moved to dismiss it on the ground that the State of Georgia was not a "person" and therefore not entitled to bring such an action. Deciding that the State of Georgia was a sovereign, not a person, the court, on October 30, 1941, dismissed the suit, and in the following December denied a rehearing.[15] Therefore, when on January 24, 1941, the defendants, in the Federal Court at Atlanta, were haled for the transaction, they evidently were satisfied at escaping the treble damages, for they pleaded *nolo contendere* (no wish to contend) and were fined a total of $30,000, of which $15,000 was imposed upon Evans.

But as it turned out, the parties involved were not able to ground their partial immunity upon the construing of a single word. The State of Georgia carried its case to the Supreme Court of the United States. Surmounting technicalities, this, on April 27, 1942, reversed the opinion of the lower court. There was no reason, this final decision held, to believe that Congress "wanted to deprive a State, as a purchaser of commodities shipped in interstate commerce, of the civil remedy of treble damages which is available to other purchasers who suffer through violation of the Act."[16]

The State of Georgia did not rest with civil proceedings. Early in 1942 Evans, and also a former Governor and eighteen others were indicted, mainly on charges of conspiring to defraud the State. Charges against Evans included not only the asphalt deal; he was accused of collusion with State officials to obtain a contract to paint center lines on highways

[15] State of Georgia v. Evans et al., 123 *Federal Reporter, 2nd Series*, p. 57.
[16] 315 *United States Reports*.

at an excessive cost of $24,000. Furthermore, he was accused of making an unwarranted profit of approximately $11,000 on a State printing job. At Evans' trial, in the Superior Court, at Atlanta, in May, 1942, the asphalt contract loomed uppermost. A State engineer testified that an associate of Evans had sold sand asphalt to Georgia at double the price it was worth.[17] There were six weeks of edifying testimony; the State was aiming to show division of large into small orders so that higher prices could be charged, as a part of the imputed conspiracy. In a twenty-page unsworn statement to the jury, Evans made the plea that he was the victim of a political feud by means of which, he contended, it was planned to cause the political downfall of a co-defendant, former Governor Rivers. Evans hoped for an acquittal, but did not get it. Through three days the jury deliberated, half, it was said after the trial, for conviction. Finally, as no verdict was reached, Judge Moore ordered a mistrial. Solicitor General Boykin announced that he expected to give Evans a new trial at an early date.

Soliciting funds to continue the work until January 3, 1943, of the Committee Investigating un-American activities, its Chairman Representative Martin Dies, in Congress, on January 26, 1942, announced a forthcoming investigation of the Ku Klux Klan, and promised that it would be thorough "in every State in which the Ku Klux Klan is operating." This step was decided upon after the committee, behind closed doors, had heard the testimony of Colescott, who voluntarily presented himself and gave assurances of his co-operation.

It was only shortly after this—on February 28, 1942—that members of the Ku Klux Klan at Detroit engaged in what appeared to be a conspiracy to prevent sixty-five Negro families from moving, according to plans, into the Sojourner Truth Homes, a Government-backed project of the Detroit Housing Commission. More than 150 white pickets patrolled the site, the customary Klan fiery cross was burned, and by dawn the numbers of whites had swollen to nearly 1,200, many of whom were armed with knives, clubs, rifles and shotguns. Two truckloads of furnishings belonging to Negroes were destroyed; Negroes were stoned in trying to protect

[17] *The Atlanta Constitution*, May 12, 1942.

themselves; and there were a number of injuries. Three times unsuccessfully the police tried with tear gas to dispel the mob.

By a large majority—331 to 46—the House of Representatives voted on March 11, 1942, to extend the investigation of the Dies committee until 1943. On April 22, 1942, the House Accounts Committee granted the Dies committee an appropriation of $110,000, which sum was voted a week later by the House.

Up to this writing, there has been no reported investigation of the Klan by the Dies committee.

Chapter XXIV

HENRY FORD'S SEVEN YEARS' CALUMNIES AGAINST JEWS

PARALLEL to certain years of the Ku Klux Klan a centralized and intensive agitation was carried on exclusively against Jews by a publication owned and financed by one of the richest and most conspicuous of American industrialists. This was Henry Ford. Born, in 1863, on a farm near Greenfield, Michigan, he had been reared there until the age of fifteen, when he entered upon a job in a Detroit machine shop, and for many years thereafter was a mechanic in various concerns. The automobile had been invented in France and some cars exported to America, but their expensiveness made them available to the rich only. Seeing the automobile's field for general use, Ford harbored the idea of a product to be made by mass manufacturing methods and to be sold at a rate within the reach of the many. With eleven associates he organized the Ford Motor Company, in 1903, on a slim capital. The spirit of the times, demanding this new form of transportation, swept his company on to extraordinary success. In ten years alone, its assets increased to $250,000,000, and millions in dividends had been declared. By early in 1923 the company's assets were more than $536,000,000; it was producing 6,700 motor vehicles a day; and its revenues were between $8,000,000 and $10,000,000 a month. Sales and profits kept on cumulatively mounting; the Ford Motor Company greatly expanded its American plants and established large factories in some foreign countries.

Before about the year 1913 only sporadic mention of Ford was made in newspapers outside of Detroit. But when the realization burst upon the country at large of his phenomenal success and towering money wealth, multiplied by incessant accretions, he at once became the great cynosure. Newspapers, periodicals, magazines and biographical works vied in spreading accounts of his career. His opinion on all manner of subjects was solicited by editors, and treated as the words of an oracle. Thus fed on these deferences and eulogies, the public at large conceived Ford as a supereminent figure and as a fountain-head of practical knowledge and an apostle of worldly wisdom. The mechanic of extremely limited education was forgotten; only the ever-expanding multimillionaire filling the whole countryside with his automobiles was seen, and wherever a Ford car went thither it carried his name and blazoned his ubiquitous prestige.

However, his attributed grasp of practical affairs did not go long unshaken. The first noteworthy evidence of his almost childlike credulity came in 1915 when he was influenced to think that he, by the power of his money and the éclat of his name, could succeed in a maneuver to stop the wide-ranging First World War. Chartering a ship, he gathered on board a miscellany of educators, publicists and others and with them he sailed from New York, on October 4th of that year to Europe. The voyagers were persons of varying degrees of weight in their respective fields, all agreeing on their hatred of war but widely differing in theories and in the proposed steps to be taken. Ford's plan was that of having conferences in Europe to persuade the combatant Governments to cease hostilities. Leading American public men both derided and denounced the whole scheme as supine and visionary, and Ford and the delegation as ineffectuals who presumed that soft speeches could put a stop to a war determinable by force only. The experiment, of course, was foredoomed to be a fiasco, and it was made still more so by the wrangles on the way over between some of the party's members whose belligerent love of their own pet ideas outweighed their professional pacifism. In England the project was scoffed at as a delusion. The war continued for three more years.

Either too obtuse to be disconcerted by the immediate failure of this vaunted expedition or still fixed in the belief that lavish expenditures of money could accomplish any result, Ford set out to campaign against America's taking measures of preparedness for war. He later testified in court to his readiness to spend a million dollars to arouse public opinion for this object. A considerable portion of his propaganda distributed throughout the United States consisted of booklets and newspaper advertisements. That there was a clique conspiring to force President Woodrow Wilson into war was one of the main charges. Of course, Congress alone had power to declare war, but this vital Constitutional provision was not considered, if, indeed, it was known to Ford or his corps of writers, and if they did know the fact, it was shunted aside.

As an outgrowth of a suit for libel brought by Ford on September 8, 1916, against *The Chicago Tribune* for publishing an editorial "Is Ford an Anarchist?" Ford's irresponsibility in making charges was established by his own testimony. In the trial of that suit in a Michigan court nearly two years later, he was asked: "Do you know of anybody that was trying to drive the country into slaughter?" "I thought," he answered, "there were many people that were." Q. "Can you give us the name of one?" A. "No." Q. "And yet you made the statement in this book that there was a ring trying to impress the President and force him into war?" A. "I did say that, yes." Q. ". . . Do you mean to tell this jury that you had sent out advertisements printed broadcast all over the country, and you did not know what was in them?" A. "I sent out many statements to cause the people to think." Q. "You said you did not know that statement was in there?" A. "I have said that." The jury awarded Ford a contemptible six cents damages and costs; Michigan law provided only $50 costs.

Such exhibitions of utter heedlessness gave unmistakable evidence of the convolutions of Ford's mentality. Was he either abashed by his self-exposure or did he learn thereby not to repeat the same performance? Not in the least. For nearly a decade more he remained immune to lessons and irreclaimable in practice. By token of his wealth and industrial power he evidently arrogated to himself a special privileged position. He was not satisfied to stick to the production of automobiles, the one thing which he did know, but his publication plunged into a protracted campaign marked by the same recklessness on a more extended scale in attacking Jews.

What led him to do so? Perhaps acquired prejudices. Perhaps the influence of persuasive confidants. Perhaps the effect of the muddled condition in which continents found themselves after the war and the rising tendency to find a scapegoat in the Jews. Possibly the epidemic fear caused in many countries by the seizure of power in Russia by the Communists, or Bolshevists, as they were called. Viewed as a threat to the capitalist and social structure everywhere, this revolutionary new order was represented as the deed of Jews, although only a few of its principals were Jews, and they were not professing Jews.

Leaving aside speculation as to motive or combination of motives, one thing is certain: the continuity of Ford's attacks upon the Jews, beginning in 1920 and persistently carried on for seven years, stamped them as calculated and obstinately deliberate. The instrumentality was *The Dearborn Independent,* a weekly newspaper owned and published by Ford. In its heyday this publication boasted of a circulation of approximately 700,000. But the attacks were not confined to its pages. They were given permanence by the republication of the flow of articles in issues of paper-bound volumes which were widely distributed in America and elsewhere in English-speaking countries, and translations were brought out in the languages of various European countries and in other continents. Why, in America, at least, considerable sections of the people familiar with the widely published accounts of Ford's self-admitted untrustworthiness in making assertions should now give credence or even a hearing to his charges against Jews was no mystery. In this case every preconception which had been imbued uprose automatically and many were inclined to believe off-hand that what was now said of Jews must be true for no other reason than that they were Jews. In whatever way they thought Ford had been on the wrong tack in some other matters, he was on the right one in administering castigation to Jews.

The first volume, dated November, 1920, was a reprint of *The Dearborn Independent's* first twenty articles, and was entitled *The International Jew, the World's Problem.* The preface opened by assuming the baneful existence of a "Jewish Question." Exactly where this was resident or defined was not explained. Certainly, it was not located in the

Constitution of the United States, in the State Constitutions or in the statutes or institutions of the land. Under these, Jews had the inviolate right to be citizens or denizens and pursue their way on terms of religious and civil equality with their fellow beings. In singling out the Jews as an exotic people, Ford's editorial scribes brushed aside this basic fact as having no validity. Like the "Catholic Question" which, as we have abundantly seen, was spawned by bigots, the "Jewish Question" was sheer fabrication.

To brace this phantom, the preface brazenly went on to assert: "The Jewish Question has existed in the United States for a long time." This, at the start, was the beginning of a stream of allegations wholly belied by actualities, and if throughout the whole long-drawn series of articles there was any one thing their author or authors avoided, it was adherence to fact. As has been herein narrated, there were in Colonial times conditions which, by the same designative process, might have been styled the Quaker Question, the Puritan Question and the Catholic Question. But there was no "Jewish Question"; Jews were too few, too insignificant, and offered no challenge to established creeds. That deep prejudice of majorities against Jews was reflected in law was a fact, but not so much so as the same proscription applied in various places to Quakers or to Catholics or to other dissenters from the ruling creed. Had there been a "Jewish Question" after the formation of the United States, it inevitably would have been manifested in law. But save exceptional survivals of old concepts, there was not the remotest evidence of any such situation. On the contrary, as we have shown, founders of the Republic, in order to encourage immigration and development of agriculture, trade and commerce, made an express point of inviting people of all nationalities and religions, including, of course, Jews, assuring them that in America they would enjoy full religious as well as civil protection.

"There have been periods in our country," the preface had the hardihood to declare, "when it [the "Jewish Question"] has broken forth with a sullen sort of strength which presaged darker things to come." When was that time? Not in America's history. Minor rowdy outbreaks against Jews were occasionally not absent, but need we recapitulate that the repeated great organized movements were against Catholics? The blanket indictment which the preface now proceeded to make against Jews smacked strongly of that against Catholics by the Know-Nothings, the A. P. A. and the Ku Klux Klan. As witness: "Not only does the Jewish Question touch those matters that are common knowledge, such as financial and commercial control, usurpation of political power, monopoly of necessities, and autocratic direction of the very news that the American people read; but it reaches into the cultural region and so touches the very heart of American life." At this identical time anti-Catholic publications, as already noted, were accusing the Catholic hierarchy of controlling politics and the press. The same sweeping charge, switched by Ford's publication to the Jews, was equally groundless, but as professional Catholic baiters were ready to believe it about the "Romanists" so hostiles to Jews were likewise open to accepting it as true of Jews. Nor, as applied to Jews, was the charge without more sinister intent; seizure of control by "usurpation" was presented. This needless to say was a method foreign to Americans and, were it attempted, would have been quickly outlawed. But taking the preface at its word, had this "usurpation" been truth it would have implied gigantic strength on the part of a mere minority of 3,390,572 Jews, and corresponding ineptitude of the overwhelming majority of non-Jews in a total population of nearly 107,000,000 in the United States.

We linger upon that preface because it professed to give the reasons for publishing the attacks, and as an avowal of motives advanced for doing so has its preliminary proof of self-stultification. "The motive of this work is simply a desire to make facts known to the people. Other motives have, of course, been ascribed to it. But the motive of prejudice or any form of antagonism is hardly strong enough to support such an investigation as this." Following this smug self-exculpation, too glib for its own purposes, came a denunciation of the "International Jew and his satellites, as the conscious enemies of all that Anglo-Saxons mean by civilization." To deflect reproach branding Ford as a manufacturer of religious and social poison, the preface disclaimed that the articles proceeded "upon a false emotion of brotherhood and apology," and with bland self-satisfaction declared: "We confidently call the reader to witness that the tone of these articles is all that it should be."

Again and again in the preface came the claim that the substance of the articles was based upon "investigation." It is doubtful whether the world has ever seen volumes packed with more perversions of fact and outright falsities than these in question. Every article in the entire series bore the palpable impress of straining to make out a case against the Jews, and there was not the slightest scruple in the stringing together of myths, suppositions, innuendoes and falsehoods, all solemnly put forth as absolute facts. Obviously, considering the extended scope of those articles, we can do no more than select a few typical instances specifically proving how total lies were made to appear as standing truths.

The indictment in Article I was that by instinct the Jew was a trader and "the Jew is the only and original international capitalist."[1] Anyone with a smattering of history would have known of the great trading companies of the seventeenth and eighteenth centuries royally chartered to exploit the resources of North America, South America and the East and West Indies. The London Company, the Hudson Bay Company, the Dutch East India Company, the Dutch West India Company and John Law's Mississippi Company were but a few in the number, and there was not a Jew among the promoters and beneficiaries. In point of fact, the grantees were usually scions of royalty or largely titled noblemen.

For instance, the incorporators of the Hudson Bay Company were Prince Rupert, Count Palatine of the Rhine, Duke of Bavaria, Cumberland, etc.; the Duke of Albemarle; the Earl of Craven; Lord Arlington; Lord Ashley and others. The charter endowed the company with an exclusive monopoly of trade and commerce of all waters and lands adjacent to Hudson's Straits. Heading the South Sea Company was the Earl of Sunderland, who was at the same time Britain's Premier, and the Duke of Portland was heavily interested. All of the other companies likewise bristled with peers who, as favorites of kings, were easily able to get the most comprehensive charters endowing monopolies of trade

---

[1] *The Jew in Character and Business. The International Jew, the World's Problem*, The Dearborn Publishing Co., 1920, p. 15.

and commerce in particular areas of the world. The operations of several of these companies were attended by huge
stockjobbing frauds with general calamity ensuing. Among
the post-Revolutionary American trading merchants, sending
their ships all over the globe, there was not a Jew; the list
of individuals and firms, headed by John Jacob Astor, was
distinctly a roll call of Christian merchants.

And coming to the international industrial corporations
of more modern times we need only cite the Standard Oil
Company, the world-wide traffic of which made its head,
John D. Rockefeller, a billionaire and elevated his colleagues
high in the rank of multimillionaires. In this corporation as
well as most other corporations of international character
the officers, directors and chief large stockholders were non-
Jews. And, most pertinent of all the cases, Ford proved himself
a shining exemplar of outspreading trade internationalism,
grasping, as he ere long did, every opportunity to establish
his factories in one country after another and fattening on
great profits from divers peoples.

These were the plainest of facts, yet evidently because the
Jewish Guggenheim family, only following patterns long
since set by predecessor Christians, successfully launched
their international American Smelting and Refining Company; that fact, coupled with the sway of the Rothschilds and
a few other Jewish enterprises, loomed in the eyes of the
Ford propagandists as the proof of exclusive Jewish ascendancy. Consultation of the *Directory of Directors* or, even more
so, of the data given in such an authoritative book as John
Moody's *The Truth About the Trusts,* published in 1904,
would have shown the absurdity of this assertion as above
made. But suppose it wholly had been true? Had not Jews
the same right to engage in international dealings as anybody else—the same right to employ their initiative and ingenuity in any field they chose as Ford had in automobile
production? Who was he to disparage a people because, in
the essential of international trade, they might avail themselves of opportunities which no one else had the sagacity
to see?

However, further to place the Jew in the character of a
born trader, disdaining agricultural or menial work, Article
III ventured into giving what it termed "Jewish History in

the United States." When what is now New York City was
New Amsterdam, and Peter Stuyvesant was Director General
of New Netherland—later New York—Jews of Brazil, this
article related, found it necessary to emigrate because of a
disagreement between the Brazilians and the Dutch. They
sailed for New Amsterdam. The article refrained from saying how many there were, leaving the impression that it was
quite a sizable immigration of Jews who had acquired opulence in Brazil.   •

What were the facts as recorded in the official documents?
After Bahia, Brazil, was evacuated by the Dutch, a meager
twenty-three Jews "big and little" (adults and children)
sailed on the bark *St. Charles* for New Amsterdam. They
lacked sufficient funds to pay the full fare of the voyage, and
upon arriving at New Amsterdam, in 1654, the Court of
Burgomasters ordered their goods, "furniture" and other
things, sold to recoup the bark's master.[2] The twenty-three
had naturally gravitated to New Amsterdam because the
Dutch West India Company plied a regular trade between
there and Brazil. Six years before the first arrivals of Jews,
the Dutch West India Company, having virtual sovereignty
over New Netherland, complained that "agricultural laborers, who are conveyed thither at great expense to the Colonists, sooner or later apply themselves to trade and neglect
agriculture altogether."[3] Here we have the picture of non-
Jews, repudiating their contract, and turning traders. And it
was because of the dearth of agricultural labor thereby caused
that a plan was recommended to supply the deficiency. This
plan recommended that the tobacco, hides, furs, timber,
cotton and other wares exported by the Dutch West India
Company should be traded for slaves to be carried on the
return trip to New Amsterdam and used in New Netherland
for agricultural purposes.[4]

In telling how Stuyvesant ordered the Jews to leave—an

[2] *Records of New Amsterdam*, Vol. 1, pp. 240-241, 252. These were seven
volumes, transcripts of the handwritten minutes of the Court of Burgomasters, translated and published in 1897 under the authority of the City
of New York.
[3] *Report on the Affairs of the West India Company by the Company's
Commissioners of the Board of Accountants, January, 1648, Documents Relative to the Colonial History of the State of New York, Holland Documents*,
Vol. 1, p. 246.
[4] Ibid.

act revoked by the Dutch West India Company's directors—
the Ford article insinuated that the Jews were considered
undesirables by Stuyvesant, while it attributed to the company a partiality toward them because of their stockholdings.
As businessmen the directors had no feeling against Jews or
anybody else serving their ends, and as Holland had been a
refugee country for Jews who had fled from the second great
Spanish persecution, its rulers extended much toleration.
But Stuyvesant and the Dutch settlers of New Amsterdam
were the most extreme of bigots, unwilling to grant to Jews
even the moderate rights allowed in the parent country.
Prejudice and that alone accounted for unyielding discrimination against Jews in New Amsterdam. Not a single complaint is found in the records against the Jews either personally or in respect of practices.

The frequent complaints made by Stuyvesant and his
Council and by the Burgomasters were entirely against the
methods of Scottish merchants. "Many Scottish merchants
and small traders coming over in ships from Holland," read
a decree of September 18, 1648, "injure trade by their under-
selling and forthwith return to Europe with the profits.
Ordered, therefore, that all Scots and small traders be prohibited from doing business unless they remain here three
years and build a decent burgher's dwelling house."[5] This
law was either outwitted or circumvented; the Burgomasters
and Schepens, on January 22, 1657, found it necessary to
pass a resolution. This complained to Stuyvesant that the
number of Scottish pedlars coming by way of Holland was
daily increasing; they pocketed their profits and "go back
to Europe promptly"; their practices and trade were in violation of the rights granted to New Amsterdam by the Lords
Patroons; and request was made for a law prohibiting any
man from trading in New Amsterdam unless he were a City
Burgher.[6] Complying nine days later, Stuyvesant and Council recounted "the frequent complaints of the Burghery and
other inhabitants of this Province against the inland trading
and trafficking of the Scotsmen sailing hither and thither
even to the best trading places, taking the bread, as it were

[5] *Records of New Amsterdam*, Vol. 1, p. 10.
[6] Ibid., Vol. 2, p. 273.

out of the mouths of the good Burghery and resident in-habitants." Accordingly came a law requiring all arriving "Scotsmen and traders" to take out a license, costing twenty guilders, before conveying or selling their merchandise.[7]

This was the actual condition, yet the unoffending Jew was made the victim of the severest repression. To swindle a Jew was held a worthy performance; Lourens Van der Spiegel was haled, on October 2, 1668, before the Court of Burgomasters charged with making bran and meal and sell-ing the stuff as flour. His defence was that he had been authorized to "make the flour which he is to deliver the Jew on his account as coarse as he pleased, it being only for a *devilish Jew*." [8] Jacob Cohin Hendricus, a Jew, petitioned for leave to bake and sell bread in the city; without giving any reason, his application was refused.[9] Another Jew, Asser Levy, requested the New Amsterdam Court of Burgomasters to admit him as a Burgher; in the city of Amsterdam, Hol-land, he pointed out, Jews were Burghers, and he showed a certificate of his having been a Burgher there; moreover, in New Amsterdam he was "keeping watch and ward" like other Burghers. The Court of Burgomasters would not accede to his petition and referred him to the Director General and Council.[10]

The utter ignorance of the Ford writer was shown by the conclusions reached. No condemnation was made of the re-fusal of the authorities to allow Jews to enter useful occupa-tions and functions, but this very fact was transformed into the wild assertion that, barred from other sources of liveli-hood, Jews were driven "into foreign trade in which they were soon exercising all but a monopoly because of their European connections." Just how impoverished Jews, mostly herded in "Jews' Alley," four feet wide, could muster the funds to accomplish this feat was not considered. This omis-sion, however, does not matter. All of the foreign trade was at first entirely monopolized by the Dutch West India Com-pany, and then, in 1660, a measure of it was given to the City of New Amsterdam, but as a privilege only. This was

[7] Ibid., p. 287.
[8] Ibid., Vol. 6, p. 151. Italics in original.
[9] Ibid., Vol. 7, p. 154.
[10] Ibid.

done "to advance its [New Amsterdam's] prosperity." A stip-
ulation was added. All ships going from New Amsterdam
to France, Spain, Italy, the Caribbean Island and other
countries, whether touching at Amsterdam, Holland, or at
New Amsterdam, had to pay duties on sale of cargoes.[11]

Thus cooking up the fiction of Jewish trade monopoly,
the Ford publication proceeded to prop it with this com-
panion absurdity: "Unwittingly, old Peter Stuyvesant compelled the Jews to make New York the principal port of
America. . . ." Not then nor until long afterward was New
York the chief port, unless it was largely for pirate ships, the
captains of which, often in collusion with officials and leading merchants, there disposed of their booty.[12] Philadelphia
and Boston often outranked New York in the flow of regular
commerce. Even considerably after the English conquest of
New York, Jews were prohibited from entering both retail
and wholesale business. By an ordinance of New York City's
Common Council, on September 12, 1685, on the petition
of Saul Browne to grant Jews the right to do business, permission to go into the retail trade was refused, but, evidently
with the aim of building up the city's commerce, the Common Council decided that Jews could sell "by wholesale if
the Governor think fit to permit the same."[13] Jews could
not legally even worship according to their faith. They had
petitioned Governor Dongan for liberty to do so; he had referred their petition to New York City's Mayor and Common
Council. "They returned their opinions thereupon, that no
public worship is tolerated by the Assembly, but those that
profess faith in Christ, and therefore the Jews' worship not
to be allowed."[14]

The Ford publication made the case appear that even in
Stuyvesant's time Jewish mercantile influence overlorded
business in New York City. How many Jews were there?
Governor Dongan's report, in 1686, gave an indication of the
slight number. "Here be," he wrote, "not many of the
Church of England; few Roman Catholics; abundance of
Quakers preachers men and women especially; singing

[11] Ibid., Vol. 1, p. 45.
[12] See the History of the Great American Fortunes for details. Some of the
early fortunes were largely acquired by such transactions.
[13] Minutes of the Common Council of New York, 1675-1696, Vol. 1, p. 169.
[14] Ibid.

Quakers; ranting Quakers; Sabbatarians; anti-Sabbatarians; some Anabaptists; some Jews." [15]

In dealing with this era, the Ford writer, contradicting his own assertions as to Jewish trade monopoly, set forth the recourses to which the Jew was driven. Excluded from regular branches of business, he had to turn scavenger in picking up old rags, or dealing in cast-off clothes, or other such out-of-the-way lines. More by way of innuendo than anything else this course was presented by the Ford writer as an example of "Jewish resourcefulness." The implication was that the Jew would descend to any means, however low, to wrest a living, and, from the basest start, would use his adroitness to attain success. But the real and tragic point was characteristically ignored. Namely, that the bigotry against Jews, solidified into repressive laws, left them no choice; their resort to narrow opportunities, regarded with contempt by their oppressors, was far less an example of Jewish "resourcefulness" than it was a shameful proof of an inhumanity loading them with onerous discriminations.

From the most unpromising beginnings some Jews, by dint of industriously attending to their obscure traffic, self-denial and conserving their resources, did get money together. And the Earl of Bellomont, Captain-General of New York and Massachusetts Bay, was both thankful and relieved that they did so. In a communication, on October 17, 1700, to the Lords of Trade, at London, he related his difficulties in procuring funds to pay the soldiers weekly. "The merchants in this town . . . combined together to traverse me all they could. At first, they lowered the exchange of money considerably, and what is worse they will now advance no money at all on my bills; so that, were it not for one Dutch merchant and two or three Jews that let me have the money, I should have been undone. This at once shows the wickedness of these people, and the necessity of returning the soldiers' pay in trade, that we may not be at the mercy of these merchants." [16] Who, then, were the skinflints?

[15] *Documents Relative to the Colonial History of the State of New York, London Documents*, Vol. 3, p. 415.

[16] Ibid., Vol. 4, p. 720. In another matter Bellomont recorded his appreciation of Jewish help. His special mission in America was to suppress piracy. Among the goods seized on a pirate ship was a bag supposedly containing jewels. "This," Bellomont reported, "was opened before myself and the

In perverse imagination that Ford writer could see Jews in earliest times almost as financial conquerors of New York City. But let us get to actualities. Jews were not infrequently harried by rowdies often of the well-to-do official class. One such outrage was indignantly related by Governor George Clinton, in a letter sent from New York City on February 17, 1749, to a Mr. Catherwood. He told how a small mob, headed by Oliver Delancey, brother of the Chief Justice of the Province, had blacked their faces and otherwise disguised themselves. They then went to the house of a Jewish couple who in Holland had means but were now poor. All of the windows were shivered, the door broke open, the house was entered, and the party "pulled and tore everything to pieces, and then swore they would lie with the woman, which put the man and woman to great fright." What later happened? "The Jew was advised to go to Mr. Murray, the Attorney, for his opinion, who took a fee and advised him to make it up, as the persons were related to the principal people of the town, Mr. Chambers advised the like and told him he would be ruined if he proceeded against them, and Mr. Smith advised the same. This shows you that notwithstanding Mr. Delancey is under a persecution by the Crown he goes on in his riotous manner, bidding defiance to everybody, as no lawyer will undertake to prosecute him, being afraid of the Chief Justice's power."[17]

Of the numerous other assertions in that Ford article, "Jewish History in the United States," we necessarily have to pass by many, but will advert to one more. After the American Revolution, this read, the instinct of the Jews seemed to make them aware that New York, as the chief port of America, "was to be their principal paradise of gain. And so it has proved." If Jews had such a prescience it was more than had George Washington who was of the opinion that Baltimore would remain and rank as America's leading port.[18] It was not until after the Erie Canal, begun in 1817,

Council, where I had ordered a Jew [Symon Bonane] in this town to be present, he understanding jewels well. At first sight we thought there had been $10,000 worth, but we soon found they were counterfeit. . . ." Ibid., p. 512.

[17] Ibid., Vol. 6, p. 471.

[18] So Richard Parkinson wrote that George Washington told him. An English "gentleman farmer," Parkinson had a farm estate for three years near Baltimore. Returning to England, he wrote two volumes *A Tour in*

was well under way that the future of New York City as America's great port loomed in sight, and it was not Jews but such a personage as Chancellor Kent who foresaw that city's consequent and rapid development. New York City, he predicted in 1821, was "destined to become the future London of America" and a "great manufacturing as well as commercial" center.[19] The city then had a population of 123,000. After the completion, in 1825, of the Erie Canal, extending 350 miles from the Hudson River at Albany to Lake Erie at Buffalo, New York City bounded forward as America's preeminent port and emporium.

To apply the same minute test of historical fact and authentic knowledge to the 746 pages of equally reckless assertions in *The Dearborn Independent* volumes would require infinite space. Embodying another series of articles, Vol. 2 was entitled *Jewish Activities in the United States,* and still another series was republished in Vol. 3 *Jewish Influences in*

America in 1798, 1799 and 1800 Exhibiting Society and Manners and a Particular Account of the American System of Agriculture. These volumes were published in London, in 1805. He asserted (Vol. 1, p. 78) that, Washington had declared to him, although New York would "always maintain an eminent commercial rank," yet Baltimore, as a port city, and Washington as a Federal city, would be the "risingnest towns," ultimately great places of trade because the produce from the western country would come to these two places via the Susquehanna and the Potomac rivers. With eyes fixed upon the great land speculative companies (see *The History of the Supreme Court of the United States* for full examples), Parkinson showed his animus against both Americans and Jews by asserting (Vol. 2, p. 652) that Americans were such sharp traders that Jews could not do well there. Parkinson's volumes abounded with misjudgment and gall, as for instance his writing that he never "saw any land worth having in America." Yet at the time George Washington doubtless did make the statement regarding Baltimore and the City of Washington. A few years later, it may be passingly mentioned, many members of Congress were complaining of primitive conditions in the City of Washington, and some were urging a return to Philadelphia. On February 3, 1809, Representative Gardener said of the City of Washington: "This place is not fit to be the seat of a great and powerful empire, and could never become so. . . . You have scarcely been able to form a village, capable of accommodating the members of Congress. Yet gentlemen talked of *this city* . . . Yes, sir, a *city* which for eight years has baffled all the liberality, all the profuseness of government. How long are we to go on through *dirt and mire* before we are able to perceive that it can never be a city?" Representative Sloan derided the site of the capital. "What is there here? Two stately edifices on the hill. Yonder we see a few scattered houses. It is said that when it is all built upon, it will be warm and pleasant. But can that low ground ever be built upon? It is impossible. On this hill we are exposed to the most violent winds from every point. Last year we were driven out of our hall by the breaking of our windows. It seems that heaven and earth are against our continuing here." Etc., etc. (*The American Register or General Repository of History, Politics and Science,* 1809, Vol. 5, pp. 45, 67, 69.)

[19] *Report of the Proceedings and Debates of the* [New York Constitutional] *Convention of 1821,* p. 222.

American Life. The nefarious drift and evil purport of all of the incorporated articles may be judged by the specimens already here presented. Yet before dealing with one more of the assertions—the biggest lie of all—we have to note the audacious brag in the Preface to Vol. 2: "The articles thus far printed remain unanswered. They have been denounced and misrepresented but not answered." This was a stark falsehood. Aside from the fact that it was impossible to misrepresent such articles, the most infamous and preposterous of all of the libels therein contained had been thoroughly exposed. And, as we shall duly see, the most effective answer to the entirety of vilifications had to come finally from no less a person than Ford himself.

CHAPTER XXV

1. THE PROTOCOLS 2. FORD'S RETRACTION

THE chief instigation used by the Ford publications, both periodical and book, to excite fear of Jews and feeling against them was a weird set of alleged documents to which was given the title *The Protocols of the Wise Men of Zion*. As differentiated from the meaning, that of preliminary memorandum, used in diplomacy, protocol here was used to signify a permanent record. Devoting article after article to these *Protocols,* the Ford publications accepted them, without suspicion or investigation, as genuine and as full proof of Jews plotting "the most comprehensive program for world subjugation that has ever come to public knowledge." Profusely citing from the *Protocols,* those publications based upon them a voluminous series of conclusions purporting to show a world-wide Jewish conspiracy to overturn civilization and establish Jewish supremacy.

From where was this startling accusation derived? All that Ford's staff knew was: "It came by way of *Russia.* It was incorporated in a Russian book published about 1905 by a Professor Nilus, who attempted to interpret the *Protocols* by events then going on in Russia. . . . The internal evidence makes it clear that the *Protocols* were not written by a Russian, nor originally in the Russian language, nor under the influence of Russian conditions. But they found their way into Russia and were first published there. They have been found by diplomatic officers in manuscript in all parts of the world. Wherever Jewish power is able to do so, it has suppressed them, sometimes under the supreme penalty."[1]

The Ford who had spent great sums on his "Peace Ship," his anti-preparedness campaign and in other ways, could see no necessity for disbursing the small sum needed to trace

[1] *The International Jew, the World's Problem,* p. 94.

down the source of the Nilus book or even to inquire who "Professor [Sergius] Nilus" was. As a matter of fact, Russian standard reference books and encyclopedias did not even mention his name; one noted Russian publicist described him as a raving monk, and another familiar identified him as an employee of the Okrana, or Russian secret police department connected with the Greek Orthodox Church.[2]

Nor did Ford publications even attempt to describe what were the events then going on in Russia when Nilus' book was published. An elucidation of these events has the most significant connection. When, after the Russo-Japanese war, revolutionists sought to overthrow Czardom, a new organization to maintain it was formed. Called the "Union of the Russian People" or the "Black Hundred," this Czaristic body blamed Russia's defeat and its woes on the Jews, and, under tacit approval from Czar Nicholas II himself, engaged in those methodical massacres, called pogroms, of Jewish men, women and children. Count Sergius Witte, Russia's Premier, was no Jew, but because he prevailed upon the Czar to grant some semblance of a Constitution—the best that Witte could obtain—he was branded by the "Black Hundred" as a Jew, and an effort was made to assassinate him. Two Jewish members of the Duma, or council having some faint powers of a Parliament, were murdered in cold blood. These were some of the conditions prevalent in Russia when Nilus' book, catering to rampageous Jew-phobia, appeared.

Outside of Russia Nilus' book attracted little or no attention until after the First World War. In 1910 a translation was published in Germany. Then, when an attempt was made to instill violent anti-Semitism in England, a translation entitled *The Jewish Peril; Protocols of the Wise Men of Zion,* was published in that country. Anyone halfway conversant with Jewish history would have known that there never had been or was any such organization of Jews as the Elders of Zion, the Wise Men of Zion or any similar conclave. But, as in Germany, the book found a sufficient num-

---

[2] A recognized authority on Russia and Russian literature as well as on Jewish affairs, Herman Bernstein took pains to find out what he could about Nilus. See his *The History of a Lie,* exposing *The Protocols of the Wise Men of Zion,* pp. 9-11.

ber of readers to warrant a second edition in England in 1920, and successive later editions there.

Realizing that certain passages in Nilus' prologue and epilogue to his book would prove too staggering even to the most acquiescent credulity and divulge its pro-autocracy propaganda, editors of the *Protocols* in England and elsewhere deliberately omitted those tell-tale utterances. In the copy of the original in the British Museum, Nilus professed to have obtained the *Protocols* from a man who since had died. He, it was related, gave the assurance that it was "an accurate translation of the authentic documents stolen by a woman from one of the most powerful and sacred directors of Free Masonry, after one of the secret meetings of the initiates in France, the present nest of the Free Mason's sect. This manuscript under the general title *Protocols of Meetings of the Wise Men of Zion* I now call to the attention of all who wish to see or hear. . . ." At length, the omitted portions went on to connect Free Masonry and Jews as the sources of the world's evils. The Jews had "covered the whole of Europe with a network of Masonic lies," and, in preserving the symbol of the temple of Solomon, had poisoned peoples by scientific theories, and contributed to the decline of the Christian spirit. The Sanhedrin (which since antiquity had not existed) was now represented as an omnipotent body; abetted by Masons it had shown its "significance and strength" in the French Revolution, and was still conspiring to help out English capitalism to exploit the world. All of this was declared a "new manifestation of Satan." While, on the one hand, declaring that the "God-Anointed Tsar" was the only force which could save Russia, Nilus, on the other, pointed to the Jews as embodying the great antithesis of autocracy. Thus he did so: "The history of the Rothschilds shows that the whole republican era of France is due to Zion and that not a single one of those elected to office has to this time ever done what he promised to do if the demands of his electors did not coincide with the plans of the government of Zion."[3]

When *The Jewish Plot* was first published in England,

---

[3] The verbatim translation of the many passages thus omitted from English and American translations of Nilus' book were given in full in Ibid., pp. 42-44.

the *Times,* of London, favored it with what was virtually editorial approval masquerading as a book review. In "some features of the would-be Jewish program" the *Times* writer thought he descried an "uncanny resemblance to situations and events now developing under our eyes." Further, that "some of the passages assume the aspect of fulfilled prophecies unless one is inclined to attribute the prescience of the 'Elders of Zion' to the fact that they are really the hidden instigators of these events." The perturbation here evidenced was because of the stupendous fright of Britain's possessing class over Communism in Russia, and the legend, as heretofore stated, that Jews had planned and executed that terrific coup. *The Morning Post,* of London, purveying to the smug educated class, now published a series of seventeen articles under the title of *The Causes of World Unrest.* What were they? Well, according to the theme of the articles, they were the fell work of a "Formidable Sect" which was basically the Jews who were united in a subterranean conspiracy with the Free Masons, and the Bolshevist or Communist revolution was designated as a Jewish movement to affect fulfillment of the *Protocols.*

Whereupon Lucien Wolf, an eminent English scholar, the author of many works, wrote articles which were published in *The Manchester Guardian, The Spectator* and *The Daily Telegraph.* In these articles he showed convincingly that the *Protocols* were a forgery. These articles were published both in London and New York, as a book.[4] In the Preface, dated London, November, 1920, Wolf wrote that he confessed to a feeling of shame in having to write at all about the subject. "That reputable newspapers in this country should be seeking to transplant here the seeds of Prussian anti-Semitism, and that they should employ for this purpose devices so questionable and a literature so dramatically silly, cannot but cause a sense of humiliation to any self-respecting Englishman. It is for this reason that I have strictly limited myself to an examination of the specific charges formulated by these publications. I cannot bring myself to believe that it is necessary to deal with them on a larger scale."

But it was the *Times,* of London, itself now which also

[4] *The Myth of the Jewish Menace in World Affairs or the Truth About the Forged Protocols of the Elders of Zion.* The Macmillan Company, New York, 1921.

and incontestably proved the *Protocols* a "string of clumsy plagiarisms." Herman Bernstein had cited a number of German novels as the progenitors of Nilus' book. Although the twelve tribes of Israel had totally vanished 2,500 years before, the author of these fictions depicted the representatives of all as holding a midnight meeting in a Prague cemetery and plotting world domination.[5] But the real main source of Nilus' book, the *Times* showed in detail, was a book written in 1865 by a certain Maurice Joly, a Parisian lawyer and publicist. The Constantinople correspondent of the *Times* had received information putting him on the trail of Joly's book. To find a copy, however, was extremely difficult. A few European scholars had a tradition of its contents but it had disappeared from circulation long since, and in the libraries of most of the capitals of Europe it could not be found. Its rarity was explainable by the fact that, aimed at the regime of Napoleon III, all available copies had been seized and confiscated, and, on April 28, 1865, Joly was sentenced by the Tribunal of Sena to fifteen months imprisonment and fined 200 francs for inciting contempt for the Government. The *Times* related how its Constantinople correspondent had managed to get hold of a copy of Joly's book which he forwarded to the editors, and a search among the special books in the British Museum exhumed a copy there. Published in Brussels, Joly's book was entitled *Dialogues aux enfers entre Machiavel et Montesquieu, ou la Politique de Machiavel au siècle XIX par un Contemporain* (*Dialogues in Hell between Machiavelli and Montesquieu, or Machiavelli's Policies in the XIXth Century by a Contemporary*).

Convinced by a thorough comparison of the *Protocols* with Joly's book of the obviousness of the *Protocols* having

---

[5] This was one of a series of novels published in Berlin, in 1866-1870, and written by Herman Goedsche, a German, using the pseudonym "Sir John Retcliffe" to convey the impression that the anti-Semitism filling his books emanated from English sources. Bernstein cited *Meyer's Konversations Lexicon* (Sixth Edition, 1904, Vol. 8, p. 77), as recording that Goedsche had been employed in the postal service, but, implicated in the Waldorf forgery case, had to quit postal work in 1849. Thereafter, under various names, mainly that of Retcliffe, he took to fiction. A Russian translation of the particular enormity above mentioned was published at St. Petersburg, in 1872, by the Association "Obschestvenaya Polza" under the title *The Jewish Cemetery in Prague and the Council of the Twelve Tribes of Israel*. Bernstein gave a facsimile of the title page of this Russian edition, and a translation of its vital contents. *The History of a Lie*, etc., pp. 13-31.

been forged, the *Times,* of London, presented the evidence in three articles on August 16, 17 and 18, 1921. The authenticity of the *Protocols,* said the *Times* "foreword to the articles," had been frequently attacked and many arguments have been adduced that they are a forgery but now "for the first time . . . the conclusive proof" was set forth circumstantially. Giving many parallels of passages from both books, the *Times* showed the deadly sameness of the points and language appropriated by Nilus and adapted to his anti-Semitic purposes. The one question which could not, of course, be explained, was where or how Nilus obtained a copy of Joly's book, but that he drew from that book was incontrovertible. After spreading the evidence in detail, the *Times* stated these conclusions as inescapable:

"1. The *Protocols* are largely a paraphrase of the book here provisionally called the *Geneva Dialogues.*

"2. They were designed to foster the belief among Russian conservatives, and especially in Court circles, that the prime cause of discontent among the politically minded elements in Russia was not the repressive policy of the bureaucracy, but a world-wide Jewish conspiracy. . . .

"3. The *Protocols* were paraphrased very hastily and carelessly. . . ." [6]

Complete in itself, so far as the Nilus forgery went, the account in the *Times,* of London, did not, however, give recognition to the fact that forgery of documents to incriminate people of a particular religious belief or order had long been and remained an occupation. In no small sense one of the most sinister and lasting of these productions, a precursor of the *Protocols,* was the notorious *Monita Secreta (Secret Instructions)* represented as having been issued by the Superiors of the Society of Jesus, instructing subordinates to put into constant practice Machiavelli's devious and unscrupulous policies. The concoctor of the *Monita Secreta* seems established as one Zaworoski, a Polish ex-priest who, for cause, was expelled from the Society in 1614. And although cautious, analytic enemies of Jesuits were extremely doubtful of the genuineness of such a production, neverthe-

---

[6] Fortunately for convenience of reference, the *Times,* of London, published these articles as a pamphlet: *The Truth About the Protocols. A Literary Forgery.* The conclusions above stated are on pp. 20, 21. *The New York Times* republished the articles.

less it then had and continued to have its hold upon the credulous not only outside the Catholic Church, but upon some within the fold. Apart from other like forgeries perpetrated before Ford's time, there were plenty, as we have noted, contemporaneous with him—forged oaths of prelates and priests and, flush with his career and publications, that unspeakably vicious Knights of Columbus oath forgery.

Pamphlets issued by American Jewish committees exposed in detail the spuriousness of the *Protocols*.[7] Meantime, did successive exposures make any impression upon Ford and his scribes? None. Realizing that they had to make some acknowledgment of the rising and widespread denunciations, they, who had already treated the *Protocols* as beyond question, now hedged in this pusillanimous way: "It will be time enough to take up the authenticity of the *Protocols* when the parallel between them and the activities of the Jewish leaders is shown." [8] And, months after the exposure in the *Times,* followed by *The New York Times,* a third Ford volume, in lauding *The Dearborn Independent* articles, kept harping on the "Jewish Question," accompanied by brazen self-glorifying testimonials. Facts, it said, "constitute the strength of the articles." It went on: "The facts are provable; they are not disprovable. . . . With regard to matter discussed in these volumes, there are too many observers of the Jews to permit misstatements to pass. This also constitutes the dilemma of the self-appointed defenders of the Jews; they may abuse *The Dearborn Independent* but they cannot disprove the facts. They do not make even an impressive denial of them. . . ." [9] Arthur Brisbane was one of the numerous editors who expressed his indignation at the Ford attacks. *The Dearborn Independent's* long reply could, in effect, be boiled down to this gratuitous and supercilious fling: "Of course, Mr. Brisbane has not studied the [Jewish] Question."

Irrespective of the flood of falsities degrading the whole series of articles, the most ordinary rule of fair dealing ur-

[7] For instance, *An Address by the American Jewish Committee and Nine Allied Organizations* and *The Poison Pen* by the Anti-Defamation League which had been organized, in 1913, by the Independent Order of B'nai B'rith to combat and abate defamation and discrimination.

[8] Preface to Vol. 2, *Jewish Activities in the United States,* The Dearborn Publishing Company.

[9] Preface to Vol. 3, *Jewish Influences in American Life,* Ibid.

gently called for an acknowledgment of grave error in foisting the *Protocols* as a reality. Deep mischief enough had already been done, and the circumstances demanded prompt admission. But in the very act of unremittingly accusing all Jews of underhand ways and shady dealings, the Ford publications betrayed a want of the first principle of decency. Year after year passed but they did not give the slightest attention to the fact that the forgery of the *Protocols* had been definitely proved.

Not until 1927 did Ford find himself in an entanglement which brought him to account. The belated steps he now took nominally seemed of a voluntary kind, but were actually the result of being summoned as a defendant in the courts. As we have seen, he, jealous of his own standing, had been quick to take action in a case wherein *he* complained of having been libeled, but he had allowed in his publications the rearing of a mountain of libels against Jews and he had not stirred. A simple order from him would have stopped the revilement. And he, too, whose publications continuously slurred Jews as avaricious, loomed as the possessor of a vast hoard of money. In 1926, the Ford Motor Company, owned by him, had a *cash* balance estimated at from $300,-000,000 to $350,000,000, and it was growing at the reckoned rate of $1,000,000 a day.[10] Gigantic had been and still were the dividends declared. He, also, whose publications had posted the Jew as the "only and original international capitalist" more and more evinced his own universality in that character. Before the First World War he had bought land in England as a site for a factory. Now his long-prejected aim for international scope soon matured. Through the Ford Motor Company, Ltd., of England, as a holding corporation, subsidiary companies were established in France, Belgium, Germany, Holland, Spain, Denmark, Sweden, Finland, Italy and Turkey. In addition, Ford products were marketed and distributed in great parts of Asia and Africa. He, as an individual and not as a corporate entity, was the mammoth personification of international capitalism, and there was nothing to indicate that he did not enjoy supreme felicity in thus bestriding the world.

[10] *Wall Street Journal*, September 21, 1926. The authority for this statement was the president of one of the leading national banks in Detroit.

The master of all of this outstanding wealth and far-reaching power had remained aloof to denunciations of Jew-baiting. But when he found himself confronted with trials of libel suits he was constrained to take another posture. He had, of course, the means to engage an array of skilled lawyers, and he did so. One suit, for $1,0000,000 damages, by Aaron Sapiro, leader of large agricultural movements, came to trial in March, 1927. The complaint charged defamation of character in a series of articles published in *The Dearborn Independent*. One of these articles, it was recited, accused Sapiro of being a participant in "a conspiracy of Jewish bankers who seek to control the food markets of the world." Sapiro's complaint further cited this passage from *The Dearborn Independent*: "This whole Kahn-Baruch-Lasker-Rosenwald-Sapiro program is carefully planned to turn over to an organized international interest the entire agricultural interest of the Republic. . . . Between the lines one reads the story of the Jewish Communist movement in America, which seeks to make the United States what it has already made of Russia."

To attribute Communist designs to a banker such as Otto Kahn, or to Julius Rosenwald, head of a great mail order house, or to the others named was a manifest travesty. A demand presented by Sapiro for retraction had been ignored. When now asked whether he and Ford ever had any discussion regarding *The Dearborn Independent's* policy, William J. Cameron, editor of that publication, testified: "Mr. Ford used to drop in occasionally and chat quite frequently." Q. "Did you and Mr. Ford ever have disagreement in regard to policy?" "Yes, and we would give reasons." This showed that Ford was not unaware of lines followed in his weekly. But when Cameron was asked to give instances, he was barred by the objections of Ford's counsel, sustained by the court, from mentioning any instances connected with the anti-Semitic campaign. Ford, so Cameron testified, gave him free rein, and the views expressed in the publication were his own, not Ford's. A few days later Cameron admitted having put before Ford himself Sapiro's demand for a retraction, and that Ford had refused to pass upon it saying: "You are the editor; be sure of your facts." On April 21, 1927, Ford obtained a mistrial on the ground of a Detroit newspaper interviewing a juror.

Shortly came a set of events which precluded a resumption of the trial. Also, a little later, Ford averted the trial of a libel suit brought by Herman Bernstein. Likely enough, as was believed, in retaliation for his exposure of the *Protocols*, Bernstein had been attacked in *The Dearborn Independent* as the person who, on the Peace Ship, had furnished Ford with the information upon which the assaults in the Ford publication were based. Bernstein sued for $200,000 damages. Reversing his many years of hermetic silence concerning the anti-Jewish campaign in his publications, Ford now came forward in the role of a profuse apologist.

First, in a letter, on June 30, 1927, to Earl J. Davis, of Detroit, Ford made an omnibus apology to Jews in general. This letter, as well as the other correspondence involved, is, as a historical record, well worth giving *in extenso*. A mere condensation of Ford's apologies would fail to give a literal idea of the manner in which he approached his complete retraction. Ford's letter to Davis was released in New York City for public information through Arthur Brisbane, published in all newspapers, and a copy sent to Louis Marshall, president of the American Jewish Committee. Ford's signed statement read:

For some time past I have given consideration to the series of articles concerning Jews which since 1920 have appeared in *The Dearborn Independent*. Some of them have been reprinted in pamphlet form under the title *The International Jew*. Although both publications are my property, it goes without saying that in the multitude of my activities it has been impossible for me to devote my personal attention to their management or to keep informed as to their contents. It has therefore inevitably followed that the conduct and policies of these publications had to be delegated to men whom I placed in charge of them and upon whom I relied implicitly.

To my great regret I have learned that Jews generally, and particularly those of this country, not only resent these publications as promoting anti-Semitism, but regard me as their enemy. Trusted friends with whom I have conferred recently have assured me in all sincerity that in their opinion the character of the charges and insinuations made against the Jews, both individually and collectively, contained in many of the articles which have been circulated periodically in *The Dearborn Independent* and have been reprinted in the pamphlets mentioned, justifies the righteous indignation entertained by Jews everywhere toward me because of the mental anguish occasioned by the unprovoked reflections made upon them.

This has led me to direct my personal attention to this subject in order to ascertain the exact nature of these articles. As a result of this survey I confess that I am deeply mortified that this journal which is intended to be constructive and not destructive, has been made the medium for resurrecting exploded fictions, for giving currency to the so-called *Protocols of the Wise Men of Zion*, which have been demonstrated, as I learn, to be gross forgeries, and for contending that the Jews have been engaged in a conspiracy to control the capital and the industries of the world, besides laying at their door many offenses against decency, public order and good morals.

Had I appreciated even the general nature, to say nothing of the details, of these utterances, I would have forbidden their circulation without a moment's hesitation, because I am fully aware of the virtues of the Jewish people as a whole, of what they and their ancestors have done for civilization and for mankind toward the development of commerce and industry, of their sobriety and diligence, their benevolence and their unselfish interest in the public welfare.

Of course there are black sheep in every flock, as there are among men of all races, creeds and nationalities who are at times evildoers. It is wrong, however, to judge a people by a few individuals, and I therefore join in condemning unreservedly all wholesale denunciations and attacks.

Those who know me can bear witness that it is not in my nature to inflict insult upon and to occasion pain to anybody, and that it has been my effort to free myself from prejudice. Because of that I frankly confess that I have been greatly shocked as a result of my study and examination of the files of *The Dearborn Independent* and of the pamphlets entitled *The International Jew*.

I deem it to be my duty as an honorable man to make amends for the wrong done to the Jews as fellow-men and brothers, by asking their forgiveness for the harm I have unintentionally committed, by retracting so far as lies within my power the offensive charges laid at their door by these publications, and by giving them the unqualified assurance that henceforth they may look to me for friendship and goodwill.

Finally, let me add that this statement is made on my own initiative and wholly in the interest of right and justice and in accordance with what I regard as my solemn duty as a man and as a citizen.

According to a dispatch from Detroit, William J. Cameron expressed great surprise at learning of Ford's announcement to "discontinue permanently all articles hostile to the Jewish people." Cameron was quoted as saying that he could not believe this; and that he did not think that Ford would make public such a statement without first consulting him, as editor; and that he would "get in touch" with Ford to find out whether it was all true.[11] He soon learned.

Accepting Ford's apology, Louis Marshall wrote to Ford:

I am in receipt of your letter to Mr. Earl J. Davis, accompanied by your statement regarding the long series of vituperative articles which, since May, 1920, has appeared in *The Dearborn Independent* and which contains the most violent attacks upon the Jews. You now declare that after an examination of those articles you feel shocked and mortified because of the harm which they have done, and you ask for forgiveness.

For twenty centuries we Jews have been accustomed to forgive insults and injuries, persecution and intolerance, hoping that we might behold the day when brotherhood and goodwill would be universal. We had fondly hoped that in this blessed republic, with its glorious Constitution and just laws, it would be impossible to encounter the hatred and rancor to which our brethren have been and still are subjected in other lands. We could not at first credit the information that *The Dearborn Independent* had permitted itself to be made the vehicle for disseminating exploded falsehoods and the vilest concoctions of vicious minds, invented by adventurers who had barely found asylum here when they attempted to introduce the exotic growths of anti-Semitism.

Happily such excrescences could not flourish on American soil. Happily the enlightened press of this country treated them with contempt and as unworthy of notice. But we Jews none the less suffered the anguish of tortured memories, the nightmares of a horrible past, and the sorrow that, in spite of the progress of civilization, there were those who stood ready to misunderstand us. What seemed most mysterious was the fact that you whom we have never wronged and whom we looked upon as a kindly man, should have lent yourself to such a campaign of vilification, apparently carried on with your sanction.

The statement which you have sent me gives us assurance of your retraction of the offensive charges, of your proposed change of policies in the conduct of *The Dearborn Independent,* of your future friendship and goodwill, of your desire to make amends and what is to be expected from any man of honor, you couple these assurances with a request for pardon. So far as my influence can further that end, it will be exerted, simply because there flows in my veins the blood of ancestors who were inured to sufferings and nevertheless remained steadfast in their trust in God. Referring to the teachings of the Sermon on the Mount, Israel Zangwill once said that we Jews are after all the only Christians. He might have added that it is because essentially the spirit of forgiveness is a Jewish trait.

It is my sincere hope that never again shall such a recrudescence of ancient superstition manifest itself upon our horizon.

But while extending forgiveness, Louis Marshall was too discerning not to see the evil consequences which inevitably would be the aftermath of the Ford publications' long campaign. Noting the tendency of many Jews to rebound to unstinted praise of Ford for what they considered his "handsome apology," he, in a statement, warned them against exaggerating Ford's retraction into a finality. "Ford," he said, "has done much damage to Jewry, especially to Jewish communities in Eastern Europe. His recantation will in a manner right the wrong and we can be satisfied with that." [12]

---

[12] *The New York Times,* July 14, 1927. Nor did Ford's retraction dispel continuing calumnies against Jews in America. Falling in with the feeling built up against them, the anti-Catholic publication, *The American Standard,* linked the "Israelitic Americans and Romanist Americans" as having undertaken a campaign "to eliminate the Bible from the American public school." Also "Jew-Jesuit motion-picture producers persist in making the screen a

As, however, events a few years later tragically proved, Marshall greatly underestimated the imminent results. For as we shall see, it was not in Eastern Europe but in Germany that a maniacally cruel persecution of Jews set in and swept over great parts of Europe. And Ford's publications had no inconsiderable share in the incitations used.

Although graciously taking Ford's excuse of unfamiliarity with the contents of his publication at its word, many editorials in leading newspapers could not refrain from voicing expressions tantamount to doubts. "Nobody but Mr. Ford," said one editorial, "could be ignorant of a major policy of his own publication. Nobody but Mr. Ford could be unaware of the national and international repercussions of this policy of anti-Semitism. Nobody but Mr. Ford could say that he did not 'appreciate even the general nature, to say nothing of the details, of these utterances' by his own editor." [13] More to the point was another type of editorial of which the following was an example: ". . . He phrases his statement as if his attention had 'recently' been drawn to the grievous wrong which he had done. The fact is, of course, that for several years, he has had the matter brought to his notice, both privately and publicly. Till now he has remained unyielding. . . ." And with well-founded although not full apprehension of future effects the editorial declared that Ford's apology "will not at once undo the damage which his violent and unfounded attacks have caused." [14]

Herman Bernstein did, in fact, publish the irrefutable evidence that, seven years before Ford's retraction, he had personally called Ford's attention to the pernicious results of *The Dearborn Independent* campaign. He made public a

school for teaching seduction." This and much more from *The American Standard* was, in 1928, reprinted by the *Rail-Splitter Press* as a pamphlet entitled *Rome and Jewry Fighting the Bible in the Public Schools.* The newspapers published accounts of Jewish internes hazed in a Brooklyn hospital, and of the limitation of Jewish students in one of America's oldest universities. The ancient ritual-murder canard turned up in Massena, New York, in 1928, when a rabbi was suspected because a child had temporarily disappeared; an official investigation showed the absurdity of the charge; the mayor of Massena apologized for having made a serious error of judgment in seeming to lend countenance to the charge; and the Permanent Committee on Better Understanding Between Christians and Jews denounced the accusation as "an abhorrent fiction, calculated to transplant into American minds a long-refuted medieval libel that has been the cause of untold suffering and repeated acts of bloodshed in the Old World."
[13] *New York Herald Tribune,* July 9, 1927.
[14] *The New York Times,* July 9, 1927.

telegram which he had sent to Ford on July 16, 1920, and the Dearborn Publishing Company's stiff reply. This accused Bernstein of "biased judgment."

Yet, in his retraction to Sapiro, Ford iterated the self extenuation of his lack of acquaintance with the matter in *The Dearborn Independent*. Announcing that Sapiro's suit for libel had been "terminated satisfactorily to all parties," Ford's retractive statement, on July 16, 1927, opened by saying that the assertions made about Sapiro had been "accepted at their face value," by the Dearborn Publishing Company The statement went on:

> It has since been found that inaccuracies of fact were present in the articles and that erroneous conclusions were drawn. As a result of this, Mr. Sapiro may have been injured and reflections cast upon him unjustly. Such statements as may have reflected upon Mr. Sapiro's honor or integrity, impugned his motives, or challenged the propriety of his personal or professional actions are withdrawn. Likewise, the charge that there was a Jewish ring which sought to exploit the American farmer through cooperative associations is withdrawn.
>
> Mr. Henry Ford did not participate personally in the publication of the articles and has no personal knowledge of what was said in them. He, of course, deprecates greatly that any facts that were published in a periodical so closely connected with his name in the minds of the public should be untrue . . .[15]

To Herman Bernstein, Ford, on July 23, 1927, wrote this apology:

> You are, of course, familiar with the context of the public retraction and apology for the articles appearing in *The Dearborn Independent* that I have made and had spread broadcast. I sincerely regret any harm that may have been occasioned to the people of that great race, and am anxious to make whatever amends possible.
>
> I take this occasion to retract and apologize for those parts of the article that appeared in *The Dearborn Independent* concerning you and for the alleged interview with me assailing you that was published in that paper.

[15] This statement was published in *The Dearborn Independent,* July 30 1927.

It was not intended in that article to imply that any of the matters concerning the Jews appearing in *The Dearborn Independent* were based upon information furnished by you. You have at no time said anything that would justify such an inference.

In the next paragraphs Ford stated that through the explanations made to him by his counsel through Samuel Untermeyer, Bernstein's counsel, he had been brought to realize the damage done. He recognized the expense to which Bernstein, who could ill afford it, had been put "by the protracted litigation to vindicate the good name of the Jewish people and your own reputation against the charges contained in the articles." Although, Ford agreed, "no mere money damage will make good the harm done you," yet he offered to pay the legal expenses incurred by Bernstein. Ford's letter of apology to Bernstein continued:

I am informed through your counsel that the articles in *The Dearborn Independent* have been translated into many languages and distributed throughout many countries of the world in book form under the title of *The International Jew*. Neither I nor *The Dearborn Independent*, so far as I know, have had anything to do with the translations, publications or distribution, and am not only willing but anxious to actively co-operate with you that the volumes shall be withdrawn and destroyed. . . .

Notwithstanding Ford's disavowal, the fact remained that a German publisher claimed having received rights to publish *The International Jew*, and it was Ford himself who revoked those rights. Anti-Semitic publishers and agitators in Europe had continued to deny the authenticity of Ford's signature to his retraction. At the annual meeting, on November 13, 1927, of the American Jewish Committee, Louis Marshall made public a letter written by Ford, on November 1, 1927, to Theador Fritsch, then leader of the German anti-Semites, translator of the book into German, and owner of a publishing house (Hammer Verlag) which issued the translation. Ford's letter notified Fritsch of his having made the retraction which had been given the fullest publicity. Ford went on: "I am informed through the public prints that you are still publishing and circulating these pamphlets in various European countries in a number of foreign languages using my name in connection therewith and asserting that the publication rights have not been withdrawn. In order that there may be no misunderstanding as to my wishes in this regard you are accordingly notified that whatever rights you have or claim to publish *The International Jew* anywhere or in any language whatsoever are hereby revoked and terminated, and that the publication, sale or distribution of *The International Jew,* and the use of the name of Henry Ford or of the Dearborn Publishing Company in connection therewith, by you or by any person or claiming under you or acting by your authority as agent, licensee or otherwise, are hereby forbidden." [16] Despite this explicit notice, various agencies in European countries kept on circulating the book and suppressing the fact of Ford's retraction.

After the settlement of Bernstein's suit, Samuel Untermeyer issued a statement summing up the effects of the anti-Jewish campaigns by the Ford publications. All of the articles lumped together in foreign countries under the title *The International Jew* had been "translated into almost every known language and distributed all over the world." They "contained the most colossal lies and forgeries concerning the Jews and their history ever known to have been gathered together."

Untermeyer's statement proceeded:

And yet they were believed the world over. Wherever I went on my recent tour of the world, even into the most remote corners of the earth, in every country, city and hamlet, the Ford cars were to be found. Wherever there was a Ford car there was a Ford agency not far away, and wherever there was a Ford agency these vile libelous books in the language of the country were to be found. They, coupled with the magic name of Ford, have done more

---

[16] This communication was published in the newspapers, and a full reprinting given in *The History of a Lie,* 1928 edit., p. 72. A most able lawyer and a courageous and skilled investigator, Untermeyer had performed a particularly notable public service as counsel for the House of Representatives Committee on Banking and Currency in searchingly bringing forth the facts as to the ramifications of interlocking large banks, their control of great industrial corporations, and the accompanying stockjobbing and other plundering. See *Report of Committee to Investigate the Concentration of Control of Money and Credit,* 1913.

than could be undone in a century to sow, spread and ripen the poisonous seeds of anti-Semitism and race hatred. These articles are so fantastic and so naive in their incredible fantasy that they read like the work of a lunatic, and but for the authority of the Ford name they would have never seen the light of day and would have been quite harmless if they had. With that name they spread like wildfire and became the Bible of every anti-Semite. . . .[17]

Had Untermeyer, let us say, refreshed his memory on the course of bigotry he would have recalled that no lie is ever so fantastic that it does not muster its legion or legions of avid believers. Ford did not create but he enormously enlarged the receptive audience. Down in the abysmal depths of prejudice the substance of many of the lies to which his publications gave modernized form had lodged for centuries. But aside from this observation, a most cogent question projects itself: Did Ford dispense with the services of William J. Cameron? To this day Cameron remains the principal Ford spokesman on the radio and in printed addresses.

Fourteen and a half years after his retraction came another formal statement from Henry Ford deploring anti-Semitism and all other kinds of bigotry. No one could find grounds for impugning this declaration as not being entirely voluntary; anti-Semitic publications which had twisted his repudiation of the *Protocols* as due to "Jewish pressure" might repeat the same charge in this case but it would be even more absurdly untenable. One reason for Ford's now taking the action that he did was publicly explained by Harry H. Bennett, chief of the Ford Motor Company's personnel department. On Bennett's invitation, the national director of the Anti-Defamation League of B'nai B'rith had called at the Ford office in Detroit. To him Bennett stated that Ford was "highly indignant" over the charges of anti-Semitism leveled at him through the interval of years and more recently with renewed intensity. Ford's own written reason, and a timely one, was that now America was at war, unity of all citizens was a supreme necessity. Toward winning this war, the Ford Motor Company, it should be added,

[17] Published at the time, a pamphlet *Henry Ford's Retraction and Apology to the Jews*, confined itself to a reproduction of the retraction, the correspondence between Henry Ford, Louis Marshall and Herman Bernstein, and the settlement of Sapiro's and Bernstein's libel suits. Untermeyer's statement is included, pp. 5 and 6.

was applying all of its great efforts and resources in producing war equipment. On January 7, 1942, Henry Ford wrote a letter to Sigmund Livingston, founder and national chairman of the Anti-Defamation League. This letter was given national publicity, and here deserves full reproduction. It read:

In our present national and international emergency, I consider it of importance that I clarify some general misconceptions concerning my attitude toward my fellow citizens of Jewish faith. I do not subscribe to or support, directly or indirectly, any agitation which would promote antagonism against my Jewish fellow citizens. I consider that the hate mongering prevalent for some time against the Jew is of distinct disservice to our country, and to the peace and welfare of humanity.

At the time of the retraction by me of certain publications concerning the Jewish people, in pursuance of which I ceased the publication of *The Dearborn Independent,* I destroyed copies of literature prepared by certain persons connected with its publication. Since that time I have given no permission or sanction to anyone to use my name as sponsoring any such publication, or being the accredited agent thereof.

I am convinced that there is no greater dereliction among the Jews than there is among any other class of citizens. I am convinced, further, that agitation for the creation of hate against the Jew or any other racial or religious group, has been utilized to divide our American community and to weaken our national unity.

I strongly urge all my fellow citizens to give no aid to any movement whose purpose is to arouse hatred against any group. It is my sincere hope that now in this country and throughout the world, when this war is finished and peace once more established, hatred of the Jew, commonly known as anti-semitism, and hatred against any other racial or religious group, shall cease for all time.

To withhold credit from Ford for his entirely altered views and for his well-meaning exhortations would indeed be churlish. And yet, to repeat, he would have proved his sincerity more conclusively had he dismissed the employee designated as the responsible editor of his publication which had poured forth its flood of anti-Semitism. By retaining this aide all through the intervening years he did give the impression that he was not so deeply concerned as to rid himself of the individual who stood forth in the public mind as his chief scribe. This might have been popular misjudgment of motives but the connection was such as to lead to widespread questioning of Ford's actual sentiments. In this case Ford's possible attachment or devotion to an employee who had long been in his service should have been counteracted by recognition of the need of complete severance of relations demanded by the occasion.

As a whilom publisher of anti-Semitic revilement, Ford had been on a different footing from most other leading agitators against Jews. Their campaigns were largely calculated exploitation for pelf, sheer rackets, not disassociated from the side aim for notoriety. The animus which Ford's publications had diffused was based, not upon desire for personal gain or for any other ulterior purpose, but solely upon the stimulus of bigotry.

This is why the letter just quoted was now lamentably defective. Having done vast harm by the issuance of lies against Jews and having, in time, come more and more to realize and regret his mistake, Ford had reached an age when he could well have made an instructive confession for the benefit of all concerned. In his plants, he could have pointed out, he had taken no decisive step until by careful study and successful experiment he had learned the full principles and mastered the processes. But assaults upon Jews as a whole were rashly undertaken without any attempt to learn the facts. Yet the vehicles turned out by his works were, so to speak, things of the moment, while despite his retraction, the lies were, as we shall continue to see, converted into durabilities having wide, persistent and fatal influence. Ford would have done a memorable service to the cause of truth had he held himself up as a powerful example and warning to agitative successors to inform themselves of their subject first before conducting outbreaks of bigotry.

However, within the range of his vision, Ford was determined in taking steps to stop the publication of anti-Semitic literature as attributed to him and as associated with his name. On January 31, 1942, Ford's attorney, I. A. Capizzi, made public the fact that, through him, Ford had threatened the Ku Klux Klan with legal action if it did not cease the publication of such literature. The notification, on January 25, 1942, to Imperial Wizard Colescott asked that the Klan "desist from further publication and circulation" of *The International Jew* and also of any reprints of other articles relating to this subject matter which had appeared in *The Dearborn Independent*. The manner in which this reprint had been presented to the public, Attorney Capizzi said, "amounts to a deliberate and intentional misrepresentation." And he amplified: "It is a malicious attempt to mislead the public into believing these articles were, and still are, Mr. Ford's opinions and sentiments; whereas, as you well know, Mr. Ford retracted these articles in 1928 [1927] and at that time disclaimed them as being an expression of his views and sentiments."

At the same time, through Attorney Capizzi, Ford asked the Mexican Government to co-operate in the suppression of similar anti-Semitic literature which purported to name Ford as the author. Capizzi's letter to Miguel Aleman, Secretario Gobernacion, expressed the belief that distribution of the pamphlet in Mexico City and Pueblo "is the pernicious work of the German Propaganda Department attempting to undermine the esteem which the Mexican public has for the United States Government. Any intimation that Mr. Ford was the author of the anti-Semitic pamphlets is a gross misrepresentation. Any assistance which your office can render in effecting the cessation of this harmful exhibition of deceit and misrepresentation will be greatly appreciated."

Interviewed at Atlanta, Colescott made the lame explanation that the Klan had withdrawn the pamphlet in question from circulation on the day war was declared, which was in December, 1941. Immediately upon this event, Colescott said, the Klan had withheld from circulation "all our pamphlets of a controversial nature." The question of why the objectionable pamphlet had been circulated so long before America's entry into the war was left unanswered.

Chapter XXVI

ON THE NAZI PATTERN

Since 1920 there had been in America a movement embracing a unity of some leading Catholics, Protestants and Jews, striving by means of writing, lectures and radio addresses to combat bigotry and promote a better religious understanding. No doubt, this endeavor had some effect in counteracting the venom of anti-Catholic campaigns and in neutralizing that of the Ford and other publications against Jews. But, in the case of the Jews, how much was the actual effect? Reporting early in November, 1930, the executive committee of the American Jewish Committee declared that it had received very few complaints of *overt* evidences of anti-Semitic prejudice in the United States. But that the manifestations were taking a more effective if less violent course was denoted by the steps taken at the same time by the committee. It announced its co-operation with other Jewish bodies to make a study of discrimination, especially by larger corporations, against Jews seeking employment. A year and a half later, Dr. I. M. Rubinow, an authority on social-industrial conditions and international secretary of the B'nai B'rith, gave more positive findings. Addressing the annual convention of the National Conference of the Jewish Social Service, at Philadelphia, he described existent racial discriminations. These had not been applicable to government service because that employment was largely recruited under civil-service regulations. But in the professional field, he stated, the most searching inquiries were made as to the social, religious, racial and nationality status of applicants for jobs, and there it was that discrimination against Jewish applicants was most frequent. In important branches of office and clerical work "the door to the Jew is almost absolutely closed." [1]

Expressions of satisfaction over the absence of any overt movement against Jews was altogether premature and soon to be dissipated. By "overt" was probably meant the concrete action of organized movements. But at that very time the introduction of these was being fostered by emissaries from Germany whence the stimulus to Jew-baiting now came, and these imported products were supplemented by natively led organizations.

In either open or threateningly latent form, anti-Semitism had long been rife in Germany. That country had been a hotbed of rabid animus against Jews, and in medieval times the scene of persecutions and massacres. The first Crusaders near the close of the eleventh century, signalized their start to Jerusalem by pillaging and slaughtering many thousands of Jews in Mentz, Spires, Worms and other cities; such Jews as survived owed their rescue to the humanity of the bishops of those cities who opened their palaces as asylums.[2] This was only one of a long line of anti-Jewish excesses. Throughout the centuries lurked deep, dark prejudice against the Jews, and although gradually Germany's rulers in modern times allowed Jews to enter finance and business and to exert themselves in the arts, sciences and other professions, the underlying feeling against them ever remained. During periods it might be quiescent but it was a state full of foreboding, with the pent-up fury ready to burst forth on the slightest fancied provocation. To all the nursed prejudices and traditional calumnies was added the bureaucratic caste hatred of Jewish liberalism.

Never, from ancient times, renowned for admitting any fault in themselves, the Teutons could now find a convenient and numerically helpless scapegoat in the Jews. The financial crisis of 1873 ruined many a German family or individual. Great was their gratification at being cleared of any suspicion of their own folly or other failing by seeing the blame cast upon the Jews. In his book then published, the translated title of which was *The Victory of Judaism over Germany,*

---

[1] The vital points of Dr. Rubinow's address were published in *The New York Times,* May 16, 1923.
[2] Gibbon, *Decline and Fall of the Roman Empire,* Vol. 6, 31-32.

one William Marr, an obscure Hamburg journalist, conjured up every possible charge he could invent against the Jews as the perpetrators of the crash. That book had an enormous appeal and left an indelible impression. Presumably set in motion by Bismarck's deft handiwork, a furious anti-Semitic wave, late in 1879, overspread Germany, and Marr's book, which, as gospel, had gone into many editions, ran to nine more. Assisted by the German historian, Trietske, there was formed, in Berlin and Dresden, in October, 1879, an Anti-Semitic League. Its leader long was Adolph Stoecker, a preacher at the German Imperial Court.

This, in brief, was some of the prelude leading to the time when Adolf Hitler came forward with his diabolical agitation against the Jews. Varied are the accounts of his early career; he, it was said, had been an ordinary paper-hanger, and after he had catapulted himself into power, the story, evidently to enhance his reputed gifts, was spread that he had nourished ambition to be an artist or architect. During the First World War he had served as a corporal in the Austrian Army. Sullen over its defeat in that conflict, Germany was riper than ever for a convulsive attack upon the Jews as responsible for its woes. Hitler proved himself the impressive spokesman. He united in himself all the cruel bigotry of Torquemada with the rough hysterical eloquence of Peter the Hermit. His book *Mein Kampf (My Struggle)*, written in 1924, disclosed many proofs of his acute monomania as well as his justification of mendacity. "Thus the Jew today," read one passage, "is the great instigator of the complete destruction of Germany. Wherever in the world we read attacks on Germany, they are manufactured by Jews, just as in peacetime and during the war the Jewish stock exchanges and the Marxist press fanned hate against Germany according to plan, until State after State gave up its neutrality." As a whole, the German people, themselves monomaniacal on the subject of Jews, greedily devoured Hitler's tirades. The fact that Hitler, in the same book, openly preached the need of lying did not one jot discredit with his widening audiences any of his assertions. In speech after speech, highly theatrical, Hitler iterated and reiterated his denunciations of Jews as the crafty enemies of Germany and German civilization.

As the pre-war census of Germany showed, that country contained slightly above 500,000 native Jews. There were also some numbers of Eastern European Jews, fugitives from pogroms. This in Germany's total population of 68,000,000. Now was seen the spectacle of the German people, while extolling itself as the "master race," gobbling Hitler's frantic accusations that the fraction of its Jewish population had been able to wreak its undoing. Yet before the war not a single Jew functioned in the German Diplomatic Service, nor on the German General Staff, and in the Imperial German Government there was not a Jew. Of the relatively slight Jewish population, 96,000 had served in the German Army; almost four-fifths of these in front-line trenches; and more than 12,000 Jewish soldiers had died for Germany.

One of the many falsehoods lavishly used by Hitler was that of grossly misrepresenting the number of Jewish office holders after the overthrow of the Imperial Government and, under its successor, the Republic. His assertions that nearly half or more of those occupying Government posts were Jews greatly contributed toward augmenting seething anti-Jewish rancor. Hitler's accessories manufactured lists, which were widely distributed, purporting to give the names of these alleged officials. A scrutiny made by competent investigators proved that nearly three-fourths of the names compiled were those of one or the other of three categories. The names were largely fictitious or they were not those of Jews or they comprised some persons of Jewish descent. From the installation of the Republic to early in 1933, there had officiated nineteen successive Cabinets. These had counted more than 250 members, among which there had been only five Jews. During the half dozen years preceding 1933 no Jew had held tenure either in the cabinets of the Central Government or in the administration of the various States. Likewise not a Jew figured among the number of provincial governors or in the management of bank, railway and other such agencies. Dispassionate inquiry would have shown that of nearly 500 officials in consequential Government positions, only the slim proportion of fifteen were Jews or of Jewish lineage. Both the Reichstag and the Prussian Diet contained but the most negligible sprinkling of Jews or men of Jewish descent; in a roll call of many hundreds of members they could not have been reckoned even a handful. Nonetheless, such was the popular avidity to believe anything incriminating Jews as the nation's incubus that Hitler's magnification was gulped down as the infallible proof of Jews overrunning the Government.

In another important respect Hitler presented himself as the one savior who could rescue Germany from the grip of the Jews. After the First World War Germany was faced with growing financial, industrial and economic pressure. This reached a catastrophic crisis in September, 1923. Vast inflation caused the paper mark to sink to utter worthlessness, and there was widespread unemployment and grinding despair. For years this pall of unemployment continued, and Hitler, using every demagogic resort of craft, took full advantage of the opportunity to press his program. Making the most plausible promises of how he would restore Germany's greatness he coupled two propositions as all-requisite. Germany's sad plight, he put forth, was due to the Jews during and after the war. Germany, a martial nation, had to recover its standing and lost integrity by force of arms, and Jews, as a non-military people and pacifists, were its enemies. Also, employment would be found for those of "pure Germanic blood" by driving out the Jews from positions, professions and business. Multitudes were swayed by Hitler's declamations appealing at once to their bigotry, swollen pride of nationality, and hopes of a dawning millenium in a Germany freed from all Jewish contact or influence.

The fairly long existence of the Social-Democratic Party in Germany and the large vote it had polled had made the name Socialist much of a household familiar. Appropriating it, Hitler and his group formed a party called the National Socialist Party, abbreviated into Nazi, and adopted a salute and the swastika as their emblem. "None but those of German blood, whatever their creed," declared the Nazi constitution, "may be members of the nation. No Jew, therefore, may be a member of the nation." Feder, one of the inspirers of the Nazi movement, stated this as an unalterably guiding principle: "Every National Socialist is an anti-Semite; the German Reich shall be a home for Germans, not for Jews . . . who have no Fatherland called Germany." To make clear the cleavage between Germans and Jews, the Nazi leaders exploited a grotesque fiction. In the days of Jewish, Grecian and Roman civilization, the Teutonic tribes, of which there were seventy, subsisted in a condition of near savagery. Now the Germans were vaunted as a special and distinctive race of "Aryans," and all others, particularly Jews, were branded as of the debased blood of "non-Aryans."

Before Hitler's incumbency as dictator in Germany, the Nazis had sent agents to the United States to create organizations designed to instill Nazi propaganda. It was in this period that an organization called the Teutonia Society was formed in America.[3] After his election, in 1933, as Chancellor of Germany, Hitler immediately put into operation a series of the most repressive laws against Jews. "Non-Aryan descent," it was decreed, "means descent from non-Aryan, and especially Jewish parents or grandparents, even though only one of the parents or grandparents was of the Jewish religion." But the reservation as to religion was of no weight; the test applied to Jews was that of blood descent, in other words that of race. As a result of intermarriage with Christians, numbers of persons having a Jewish ancestor were reared in the Protestant or Catholic faith, yet they were put in the same classification of outcasts as either nominal or orthodox Jews. Their crime was that of having Jewish blood.

Never had the world known so frightful a persecution as was now methodically waged against Jews. Persecutions in olden Spain had been severe enough. But there Jews had the option of conversion to Catholicism and remaining in full possession of rights, or if they persisted in their beliefs they were haled before the hooded tribunal and at least accorded a trial, although this was often only a semblance. The Hitler regime summarily condemned all of the proscribed without trial. As it developed against Protestant and Catholic recalcitrants, Free Masons, Christian Scientists, trade unionists and other elements, the Nazi program was not the outcome of a monomania as in the case of the Jews; it proceeded from a set determination to allow no creed other than its own, which it announced the only one ordained to the German people.

[3] *Investigation of Nazi and Other Propaganda,* House of Representatives, 74th Congress, 1st Session, *Report No. 153.* February 15, 1935. Representative John W. McCormack, of Massachusetts, was chairman of this committee. The testimony taken was voluminous.

In all cases, however, whether or not Jews were the victims, conversion of property was the prized and common aim of the ring of Nazi leaders. Before their advent to power almost all of the Nazi chieftains had been compressed in extremely moderate financial circumstances or floundering in debt. Viewing the subsequent ascent of many of those leaders to great wealth and resplendency, a premeditative motive seems to become quite obvious. Persecution offered a facile and fertile means of spoliation. This undoubtedly was no afterthought, but a course calculated beforehand. In the prospect of taking to themselves such coveted businesses or estates as were owned by Jews, Hitler's deputy leaders saw dazzling opportunities for self-aggrandizement, and, as events proved, they avidly grasped these. No bar would exist to prevent glut of brigandage.

The first drastic set of laws promulgated by the Nazis excluded Jews or "non-Aryans" from many occupations, professions and offices. While seeking to assure the world that it was committing no atrocities, the Hitler regime, with Satanical calculation, was enforcing measures the import of which was to starve to death cumulative numbers of Jews by depriving them of any opportunity to earn a living. The scum of Germany embodied in Hitler and his associates could now vent its low instincts upon some of the world's most eminent scientists, physicians, musicians, artists, writers and others all high in the realm of culture. They were condemned along with the mass of other Jews or Christians of part Jewish descent. If less distinguished, many of these had contributed their variegated share in promoting Germany's interests by enhancing the professions. As for Jews having large business enterprises they knew their turn would duly come.

Terror-stricken at the prospect, many of the proscribed who were alert or able enough to do so began to quit Germany, and a continuing exodus set in. Still other Jews, hopeless and disgusted, found a speedy exit from their despair in suicide. In Germany the Jew or consanguineous Jew was not even accorded the elementary rights of a human being. He whose Hebrew ancestors had attained a high degree of development when the Germanic tribes domiciled themselves in dugouts covered with dung,[4] was now not even given a trace of the consideration which Germans gave their swine. Aimed at first at the Jew's economic extinction, the barbarous code put in force was successively extended to strip him of every right. It is far from exaggeration to describe the entire Nazi structure, from bottom to top, as that of an indivisible gangsterdom. The helpless Jews became the victims of a vile, hate-infested gutter populace which, aided by Storm Troops, overlooked no effort to humiliate, boycott, maltreat and loot Jews, and often destroy synagogues. And, upon trumped-up charges, numbers of Jews were herded in foul concentration camps, and there treated with indignities and unbelievable inhumanity by ruffianly guards who well knew that this brutality was expected and sanctioned by the high authorities.

The reading of Hitler's book was made compulsory, and as an adjunct of confirming his grounds for outlawing of Jews, the circulation of Ford's *The International Jew* was zealously pushed. Ford stood high in the estimation of Hitler who, a few years later, on Ford's seventy-fifth birthday, presented him with a medal of the Grand Order of the Great Eagle of Germany. Happily only one of two Americans so far abasing themselves as to accept such a testimonial from Hitler, Ford, despite the most scathing criticism in America, persisted in retaining the decoration. From many parts of the world came the severest denunciation of anti-Jewish terrorism in Germany. Fixing attention upon the United States we note indignant mass meetings and processions; fiery editorials in a great number of newspapers throughout the country; in May, 1933, a strong resolution of protest signed by 1,200 Christian clergymen; sturdy protests by bar associations, and, on June 10, 1933, speech after speech in the U. S. Senate flaying the barbarities of Hitler and his herd. Citing Hitler's declaration in *Mein Kampf,* "When I defend myself against the Jews I fight for the work of the Lord," Senator Joseph T. Robinson, Democratic leader, showed

---

[4] See contemporary description in Tacitus' *A Treatise on the Situation, Manners and People of Germany.* Having been there and closely observed what he saw, Tacitus was familiar with conditions. Usually the Teutons were at war with other peoples or with themselves; war was their occupation and glory. In the winter they retreated to these dugouts in which they also concealed their booty to render it safe from invaders.

how that "work" had resulted against those of Jewish blood in cruelty "which has startled and shocked the world." Senators David I. Walsh, Royal S. Copeland, Jesse H. Metcalfe and Millard F. Tydings all expressed their abhorrence in the same vigorous strain.[5]

Confronted with such evidences of American sentiment, the Nazi regime decided to redouble or treble efforts to imbue America with its Jew-baiting and other of its destructive so-called "philosophy." In the United States were more than 20,000,000 persons of German birth or descent, and the plan afoot was to try to make American-German organizations the great centers of Nazi propaganda. The Teutonia Society was now reorganized under the enticing name of, first, the Friends of Germany, then, the Friends of New Germany. One Heinz Spanknoebel, an alien who had entered the United States with the claim of being a clergyman, "usurped"[6] the leadership of this body. "One of his first activities," reported the McCormack committee, "was to take over, by intimidation and without compensation, a small newspaper in New York, published by the German Legion, which paper he largely financed by subsidies under the guise of advertisements granted him by the German steamship lines as well as the German railways."[7] Then, gaining access to the Stahlhelm, a German veteran organization, Spanknoebel at once set out to domineer it, but to his surprise came into collision with some members unwilling to stomach him or his policy. He succeeded, however, in causing these opponents to withdraw. "By devious methods" he next wormed his way into control of the United German Societies of New York, composed of delegates from many German-American organizations. His methods and aims precipitated a serious breach in the membership but he, nevertheless, stood in arbitrary control. "As a result of such efforts," the McCormack committee reported, "Spanknoebel exerted tremendous influence on the various organizations, most of which had been in existence for decades in the United States." Consisting mostly of aliens, locals or units of

[5] *Congressional Record,* 73rd Congress, 1st Session, pp. 5538-5540.
[6] *Investigation of Nazi and Other Propaganda,* House of Representatives, 74th Congress, 1st Session, *Document No. 153,* 1935, p. 4.
[7] Ibid.

the Friends of New Germany, directly and indirectly aided by certain diplomatic representatives of the Hitler Government in the United States, were established in many American cities.[8]

Indicted, in the fall of 1933, by a Federal Grand Jury in New York for failing to register as the agent of a foreign country, Spanknoebel became a fugitive from justice. His successors were various. First came Fritz Gissibl, an alien; then Reinhold Walter, an American citizen; after him, Hubert Schnuch, a naturalized citizen and a college graduate. "This committee," the report went on, "found indisputable evidence to show that certain German consuls in this country, with all of the appurtenances of diplomatic immunity, violated the pledge and proprieties of diplomatic status and engaged in vicious and un-American propaganda activities, paying for it in cash, in the hope that it could not be traced." One of these transactions went straight into the German Embassy. For reports on public and political questions in the United States, relayed to the Hitler Government through the I. G. Farben Industrie, Ivy Lee's publicity firm received $25,000, and other such agencies and concerns were paid various sums.

The Nazi forces in the United States had ample funds to engage in widespread pro-Hitler campaigns and incitations against Jews. The McCormack committee reported: "Gigantic mass meetings were held, literature of the vilest kind was disseminated, and short-wave radio was added to the effort. . . . Orders were issued in Germany and transmitted to the United States ordering certain lines of conduct in connection with this movement. German steamship lines not only brought over propaganda but transported back and forth certain American citizens without cost, for the purpose of having them write and speak favorably of the German nation." Through a subsidiary organization, the Friends of New Germany established summer camps. There not a word of American history or principles was taught even to children of American citizens of German extraction, let alone those of aliens. On the contrary the swastika was

[8] Ibid., p. 5.
[9] Ibid., p. 6.

rampantly displayed, the Nazi salute ceremoniously given, and all of the Nazi formulas and catchwords instilled.[10]

The McCormack committee's report also described how, in the two years which its investigation covered, America had "been flooded with propaganda material dealing with the Treaty of Versailles and also extensively devoted to defamatory statements, the purpose of which was to create racial and religious hatred in the United States." The author and publisher of this propaganda was Otto H. Vollbehr, a German citizen—if, indeed, anybody in Hitler's enslaved Germany could be termed a citizen. Vollbehr was a dealer in rare books, and although he had done his most profitable business in the United States, coming here on trips through thirty-five years, more recently on an immigration visa, he had never seen the fitness of taking out first citizenship papers. From the United States Government he had received, in all, the sum of $1,500,000, in the sale of collections of rare books and incunabula. German, however, he remained, and now he was steeped in Nazism. The bulk of his funds, he testified, were in Germany. Not all, however. He admitted having disbursed many thousands of dollars of his money to circularize propaganda which he styled "memoranda." Also he admitted supplying Americans with material for lectures and articles to present a pro-Nazi point of view. Saying that he did not intend to return to Germany for some time, Vollbehr promised to desist in propaganda activities. But, the committee reported, he, within ten days, left for Germany and later returned to America, continuing those activities.[11]

What, in addition to the frightful persecutions of the Jews, were some of the other conditions in that Hitlerized Germany in behalf of which Nazi agents were trying to create an approbative opinion in America? The German Evangelical Church, in which twenty-nine independent Lutheran church organizations had been unified, was suppressed, to be replaced in 1934, by a mockery which the Nazis were pleased to call their National Synod. When Lutheran pastors and congregations passively resisted, the Hitler Government forbade public discussion, effaced

[10] Ibid., pp. 6-7.
[11] Ibid., p. 8.

church periodicals, seized church funds, suspended pastors, and to crown its rigor, placed 700 of those pastors under arrest or rushed them to concentration camps. Catholic bishops in Germany had formally condemned the sway of hatred and persecution which, in many directions, was being carried on. The iron hand of the Nazis soon began to descend upon Catholics. Upon the ground of their violating money-exchange regulations, many Catholic orders of monks and nuns in Germany were raided by the police, and Nazi courts expeditiously declared several monks and seven nuns guilty and sentenced them to terms of imprisonment. The Nazi campaign against Catholic organizations, in fact against Christianity itself, was only beginning.

Long so self-reliant and self-protective, the trade unions were dismembered, and the remnant reduced to a mere serf of the Hitler regime. This process was accompanied by the murder of recalcitrant trade-union leaders. And, not to mention many other enormities, there came that more sensational slaughterous purge to crush what Hitler viewed as incipient revolt by groups which had been his own partisans but now differed from him as to policies. Flying, on January 30, 1934, from Berlin to Munich, Hitler supervised the deadly work there. Captain Roehm, Chief of Staff of the Storm Troops, Karl Ernst; head of the Berlin Nazi body called "Brown Shirts," and various others were shot down in cold blood, and after this carnage Hitler vaunted himself as a defender of morality by accusing some of the victims as having been addicted to homosexuality! Simultaneously in Berlin, Göring's squad of special police and bullies called Storm Troops battered into the home of General von Schleicher, and making the pretext that he and his wife were "resisting arrest," shot and killed both. These were but a few of the slain. Justifying the act before the Reichstag, some months later, Hitler stated seventy-seven as the number killed in the "purge." But the horror included more than actual killings; several thousand men had been tried by court martial, and some 3,000 others imprisoned in the Dachau concentration camp. Subsequently, assuming the role of a magnanimous victor, Hitler decreed a general amnesty for all minor offenders, which meant those who had done nothing more than incautiously make some slight criticism.

Two later investigations, one a New York legislative, the other a Congressional, gave both further details of the career of the Friends of New Germany and full accounts of that of its successor. On May 7, 1937, the New York Legislature adopted a resolution for the appointment of a joint committee to investigate the administration and enforcement of law. Of this committee Senator John J. McNaboe was chairman. According to its report, the name of the last head of the Friends of New Germany was spelled Griebl, and that, under indictment for spying activities, he fled to Germany. Some of his henchmen were convicted under the same indictment. "The Friends of New Germany," the McNaboe committee reported, "chiefly through the stupidity of its leaders, brought a great deal of unfavorable publicity upon the organization. Mass meetings were held with uniformed storm troopers, and Jews and Catholics were called even more vile names than those now used. Many of the meetings ended in riot and bloodshed, and as a result, a reorganization came about, and the German-American Bund came into existence with explicit instructions from Germany to carry on propaganda without antagonizing the whole country." [12]

At the head of the Bund was one Fritz Kuhn, endowing himself with the title of Bundesfuehrer in imitation of that of Fuehrer or leader applied to Hitler in Germany. Born in Munich, in 1896, Kuhn had served in the German army in the First World War as a lieutenant of a machine-gun detachment and had been wounded. After that war he had studied chemistry and had, as an active participant, joined the Nazis in 1921. He went, in 1924, to Mexico, and from there entered the United States in 1926. According to Kuhn's own testimony the Bund had been founded in 1933, after Hitler came into power. At any rate, by 1936 it was in vigorous operation in many American cities and was constantly expanding.

The reports of the two investigative committees just named throw full light upon Kuhn's and the Bund's activ-

---

[12] History and Organization of the German-American Bund, State of New York, Report of Joint Legislative Committee, 1939. Legislative Document No. 98, p. 303.

ities, and the findings of both committees were substantially the same. And before both Kuhn was haled as a witness. The Bund developed three major divisions in the United States —the Eastern, the Midwestern and the Far Western. Each of these was under the direction of a division leader taking orders from Kuhn. He was also the head of the O.D. (*Ordnungs Dienst*), Bund uniformed members mimicking the Storm Troopers in Germany. Questioned as to the reason for the O.D., Kuhn tried to make out that its purpose was to protect Bund meetings. This answer evoked ironical quizzing, and after squirming in evasive replies, Kuhn finally admitted that every time a request had been made for police protection the authorities had provided it.[13] "The O.D.," reported the McNaboe committee, "is neither more nor less than a private army, being trained to serve not America nor the democracy for which it stands but a foreign dictator." [14] One paragraph of a Bund circular stated these as the Bund purposes and objects: "To unite with all Americans defending the Aryan Culture and Code of Ethics upon which this nation was founded, helping to build a great American Movement of Liberation under the Swastika, the common Symbol of the Defenders of Aryan Nationalism against the Bolshevik Scourge." Queried as to whether this coincided with the guarantees of freedom of speech and worship in the Constitution of the United States and the Bill of Rights, Kuhn replied that it "absolutely coincided." [15] In his testimony Kuhn, in the presence of a committee which knew the facts, had the audacity to parrot the preposterous assertions current in Germany. Communists and financiers, he declared, were Jews; he rated Lenin as a Jew; J. P. Morgan as having Jewish blood; Kuhn, Loeb & Co. as controlling the Democratic, and the Warburgs the Republican Party. The real figure of Jewish office holders in the United States was less than one per cent; Kuhn represented that with only three per cent of Jews in America's population "60 per cent of the Government is Jewish." [16] Such was some of the evidence showing from its start the Bund's dominant

[13] Ibid., p. 304.
[14] Ibid.
[15] Ibid., p. 1363.
[16] Ibid., p. 1371.

anti-Jewish fanaticism as well as its leader's total ignorance.[17]

Stripping away subterfuges, the McNaboe committee reported that the Bund operated all over the country not merely to bring members into its own fold "but also to give impetus to many other organizations which, though nominally anti-Communist, are actually anti-Semitic, and to a lesser degree, anti-Catholic."[18] On the one hand, the Bund was the parent of many other organizations such as the Freuenschaft composed of wives and daughters of Bund members; the German-American Youth Movement embracing children up to the age of eighteen; and the Prospective Citizens League. The Bund, on the other, often co-operated with nativist or quasi-nativist anti-Jewish organizations among which were the Christian Front, the Christian Mobilizers, the Social Justice Society, the Silver Shirts, the Industrial Defense Associates, the Knights of the White Camellia and the like.[19]

[17] Or could it be designated as merely that? The tactics of anti-Semitic organizations in America followed those of the Nazi regime in seeking to label as Jewish many conspicuous men elsewhere and thus trying to cement in the general mind the impression of Jewish control of politics, finance and other fields. In Germany J. P. Morgan's name was twisted into having originally been Morgenstern and his firm, although all members were Christian, was depicted as a Jewish house. General Dawes was declared a "full-blooded Jew." Even President Franklin D. Roosevelt did not escape this process of deliberate falsification; he was referred to as "Rosenfeld" with all the implications it conveyed. The foul depths reached by the official Nazi press was particularly evidenced in their attacks, in March, 1937, upon Mayor Fiorello H. La Guardia, of New York City. At a luncheon of the Women's Division of the American Jewish Congress he had approved the idea for a building dedicated to freedom of thought and he added a suggestion. He would, he said, "have a chamber of horrors, and as a climax I'd have a figure of that brown-shirted fanatic who is now menacing the peace of the world." In language that even the most vulgar of American newspapers would not stoop to use, official German newspapers berated him for having dared to criticize Hitler, who, they demanded, must be treated with courtesy. Much of the comment in those newspapers was of such a vile nature as to be unprintable in an American publication, but some of the invectives in *Der Angriff*, organ of Propaganda Minister Goebbels, were reproduced. The climax of "insulting Germany" it snarled, "was before a thousand Jewish women, whom he fetched in from the streets," and La Guardia, one of the greatest of New York's Mayors, was called a "Jewish lout" and "chief gangster of the town." The German Ambassador had the effrontery to protest against La Guardia's remark. The reply of Secretary of State Hull was a clear notification that if objections could be taken to reprobations in America, there was equal ground for taking the same stand toward those in Germany. Mayor La Guardia stood by what he had said, and regretted that his mother had only a slight infusion of Jewish blood, for, he observed, "it is not enough to boast of."

[18] *Legislative Document No. 98*, p. 306. Also, *House Report No. 1476*, p. 16.

[19] Ibid., also *Investigation of Un-American Activities in the United States*, 76th Congress, 3rd Session, *House Report No. 1476*, p. 16. This report was signed by Chairman Martin Dies and all of the other members (Joe Starnes,

"In 1936," the Dies committee reported, "Fritz Kuhn, accompanied by a large delegation of Bund members, went to Germany for the ostensible purpose of visiting the Olympic games. The group paraded in the uniform of the Orderly Division (Storm Troops) and the parade was reviewed by Adolf Hitler. Following the parade, Fritz Kuhn and the officials of the German-American Bund were received by the German Fuehrer, at which time they presented him with a golden book containing autographs of the Bund leaders, and delivered to him a contribution of $3,000 for the German winter relief fund. This money had been solicited from Bund members, some of whom, according to Kuhn's testimony, were unemployed and on relief.

". . . The December 10, 1936, issue of the official Bund newspaper carried an article concerning a speech which Kuhn made in San Francisco following his return from Germany. According to the article, Kuhn stated in his speech that Chancellor Hitler advised him, 'Go back and carry on your fight.' "[20]

All during this time drastic mandates of law, to which Storm Troop and mob violence were superadded, had spread increased devastation among Jews in Germany. Almost shorn of all visible property a certain number of Jews were able to effect their own escape from Germany. Many of the great number of fugitives, wholly or partly of Jewish blood,[21] who had already left were, however, impecunious, and it was only by the funds collected by Jewish relief organizations elsewhere, principally in America, that their way to other countries was paid. A considerable quota of exiles found refuge in the United States, while the wanderings of others in the attempt to locate a haven in other parts of the world were often marked by frustration and tragic circumstances. As for Jews remaining in Germany, 80,000 to 90,000, it was estimated, had by now been arrested for the crime of being

Joseph E. Casey, Jerry Voorhis, John J. Dempsey, N. M. Mason and J. Parnell Thomas).

[20] *House Report No. 1476*, 76th Congress, 3d Session, Ibid.

[21] In a report made public, on September 4, 1937, by the American Jewish Joint Distribution Committee, New York City, the data, compiled from the registers of refugee organizations in various parts of the world, showed that 125,000 persons had fled Germany since 1933. Of that number between 13,000 and 15,000 were non-Jews. This committee gathered and expended large sums for relief work among Jews in many countries.

Jewish and cast, for varying periods, into the putrescence of concentration camps. Bands of Nazi roughs swaggered through Jewish neighborhoods terrorizing the inhabitants. On one occasion the cafés and restaurants of the fashionable Kurfuerstendam section of Berlin were raided by Nazi ruffians and all recognizable Jews were driven to the street and there mauled and beaten.

Fiercer and fiercer became the persecution. Pope Pius XI solemnly protested against the whole artificial and inhuman doctrine of "racism" advanced by the Nazis as their justification. But neither the Pope's declaration nor outcries elsewhere had the remotest effect upon calloused Hitler and his cohorts. Year after year the wave of studied cruelties and the looting and ravage went on unchecked. A climax unparalleled in modern times was reached in November, 1938. Frenzied over the persecution of Jews, Herschel Grynzspan, a seventeen-year-old Polish Jew, the son of a German-born Polish emigrant, shot and killed, on November 7th, Ernst vom Rath, third secretary of the German Embassy in Paris. Upon hearing of this, mobs everywhere in Germany, as if by common action or by issued order, broke out to inflict retaliation upon all Jews for the act of a single Jew. For three days and nights the raging mobs sated themselves with plunder, arson and the spread of desolation. By dusk of November 10th there was not a remaining synagogue or any other distinctive Jewish place which had not been damaged, wrecked or burned.

This general visitation of vandalism brought forth, it need hardly be said, a manifesto of approval from Hitler's government. Propaganda Minister Joseph Goebbels extolled the infamy as "the justified and understandable anger of the German people over the cowardly Jewish murder of a German diplomat in Paris." And hitting upon the event as a convenient pretext for exacting at a stroke more loot from such Jews in Germany as still retained property, or to prove the German capacity for colossal revenge, the Hitler Government levied a fine of 1,000,000,000 Reichsmarks (say nearly $500,000,000) collectively upon all Jews in Germany.

From America came expressions of the profoundest amazement and indignation. "The news of the last few days from Germany," declared President Franklin D. Roosevelt, "has shocked public opinion in the United States. . . . I myself could scarcely believe that such things could occur in a twentieth-century civilization." The American Ambassador at Berlin was instructed to return home and give his report. News accounts of the event were confirmed in all their nakedness. Along with President Roosevelt's condemnation came stronger utterances in America from leading public men and from Protestant and Catholic clergymen and editors who were not bound, of course, by the excessive circumspection that the President had to use. Here, they deplored, was a wolfish persecution which, not stopping at seeking to blot out a whole people and subjecting it meanwhile to famishment, pillage and incendiarism, mulcted all of that people for the solitary deed of an enraged boy.

Such Jews as could do so increased frantic efforts to get away from Germany. Laden with German-Jewish refugees, the steamship *St. Louis* sought a friendly port in the Americas. But the quota in the United States was exhausted, some South American countries refused entrance to refugees, and the *St. Louis* docked at Cuba. There, on June 12, 1939, the Cuban Government, falling back upon its laws and justifying itself by its economic condition, refused to allow landing of the refugees and ordered the ship to leave. Attempts by American Jewish organizations to dissuade the Cuban Government from its course were unsuccessful, and thirteen days later the *St. Louis* had to sail back to Antwerp from whence some refugees managed to get into Britain or French provinces.

Why, it may be asked, is this outline of some indicative conditions in Hitlerized Germany inserted here? Because it was from the Nazi Government, responsible for those conditions, that the German-American Bund took its course and its orders. The Dies committee reported: "Testimony before the committee, both from friendly and hostile witnesses, established conclusively that the German-American Bund receives its inspiration, program and direction through the various propaganda organizations which have been set up by that [Nazi] Government and which function under the control and supervision of the Nazi Ministry of Propaganda and Enlightenment." Further, "It was established that the program and the activities of the German-American

Bund were similar to Nazi organizations in Germany and in other countries. The Bund makes frequent use of material emanating from Nazi propaganda sources. . . ."[22] But this imported anti-Jewish propaganda had a wider distributive agency than the Bund. Some of the leaders of the nativist anti-Semitic organizations, Kuhn testified, had addressed meetings sponsored by the Bund. In turn, he related, Bund representatives frequently made speeches at meetings held under the auspices of one or the other of these organizations. "It was also established that the Bund co-operated with some of these organizations and their leaders by exchanging literature and publications with them and by publishing material emanating from them in the official organ of the Bund. Numerous articles have appeared in the Bund newspaper expressing approval of the activities of the organization already mentioned. The literature put out by the various groups and individuals is distributed and sold at the Bund camps, meetings and gatherings."[23] Also evidence taken indicated "that Nazi propaganda agencies, through officials of the German Government in the United States, have attempted to propagandize educational institutions in this country."[24]

Early in the Nazi movement Hitler had avowed his scorn for Christianity. Teaching, as it did, precepts of mercy, he scoffed at it as effeminate and altogether incompatible with his war plans which called for, in his scheme, a virile German people insusceptible to ethics and compassion. Moreover, he had no place for a power independent of the all-penetrative dictatorial State he aimed to create.

The concerted move to dispose of Christianity did not come until after the Jews had been crushed, or well-nigh so. Then to damn Christianity in the eyes of a people already crazed against Jews, Nazi writers set about railing against it as nothing more than a Jewish product. "Jewish-Oriental-Christian philosophy," "Jewish-Christ creed," "Jewish Christianity"—these were some of the favorite terms. Headed

[22] *House Report No. 1476*, p. 15.
[23] Ibid., pp. 16-17. The standard "literature" in Bund camps, the Committee reported, were Hitler's *Mein Kampf*; books by Julius Streicher, one of the most ferocious of Nazi Jew-baiters; Father Charles E. Coughlin's publication *Social Justice*, and Silver Shirt William Dudley Pelley's publication *Liberation* and his booklets.
[24] Ibid., p. 17.

by General Erich Ludendorff, the Tannenburg League,
functioning as a neo-pagan, anti-Semitic, anti-Christian organization, ran its own publishing house. Supplementing
its numerous treatises against Judaism, it published others
against Free Masonry, Catholicism and "other supernatural
powers inimical to the Reich." A host of books otherwise
issued in Germany ridiculed Christian concepts. To the
question it asked, "Did Jesus ever live?" one book replied,
"We say No." This book derided New Testament ethics as
fit only for "morons and idiots." Another book declared
Christianity "a Utopia born of the true Jewish spirit, to
destroy the peoples and turn them into will-less slaves." Pronouncing Christianity "debasing," a third book disavowed
the God of the Bible as "never congenial to the German."
And so on through the whole gamut of the concurrence of
such books.[25]

Simultaneously came the German Faith Movement, the
Messiah of which was Hitler himself. Idealization of Hitler
had been drilled into the German people. Now was sprung.
a move to attribute supermundane powers to this stubby-
mustached individual as the elect of heaven and earth. In
ancient Rome Emperors were deified but usually this flattering formality came after their death. The ardor of some
Nazi principals led them to apotheosize Hitler during his
lifetime and at a time when in many parts of the world he
was denounced as anti-Christ and cursed as one of the greatest monsters ever scourging mankind. "Hitler is a new, a
greater, a more powerful Jesus Christ. Our God, our Pope,
is Adolf Hitler." So rhapsodized Nazi leader Binve. And

---

[25] The inquiring reader may find adequate translations of many of these
books in Stanley High's *Watchman, What of the Night? Can Christianity
Survive? A Compilation of Original German Documents.* Mr. High commented: "It should be noted that while the Nazis have pressed their contention that the writings of many protagonists of the new paganism are but personal and not official declarations, the fact remains that no answers to them
are permitted by radio or press."

Subsequently the number of such books was increased by an anonymous
book entitled *Gott und Volk (God and the People).* It contained an outline
of a "new religious order" to supplant Catholic and Protestant churches with
a "national German faith." To break with Christianity, this book urged,
would be an honor. Stating that hundreds of thousands of copies had been
spread, Catholic bishops, in a letter read from all pulpits in Germany, indignantly refused to make the proposed choice of substituting Germany as
"our holy land" and "our religion" for Christ. The bishops' letter warned
the faithful: "The existence of Christianity and the Church in Germany is
at stake." Dispatch from Berlin, *The New York Times,* December 1, 1941.

not to be outdone in ecstatic homage, Propaganda Minister Goebbels, in an address at Berlin, instructed the regimented German nation: "Our leader becomes the intermediary between his people and the throne of God. . . . Everything which our Leader utters is religion in its highest sense, in its deepest sense, and in its deepest and most hidden meaning."

The *Osservatore Romano,* organ of the Vatican, on September 15, 1937, reported that the penetration of the new Nordic paganism was constantly progressing in Germany, "and the official representatives of the Nazi Party, far from opposing this penetration, encourage it." The anti-Christian movement in that country was "sowing seeds of hatred and vilification." A pastoral letter signed by the German Cardinals and read from all Catholic pulpits in Germany, on August 28, 1938, charged undiminished persecutions of religion and slurs on the Pope. Soon came the time when the Nazis ordered the evacuation of more than a dozen monasteries of the Benedictine Order in Germany. With the Nazi occupation of Austria, in 1938, came riots against Cardinal Innitzer's palace and the commission of other outrages. Severe restrictions placed upon Catholic education led the Catholic bishops in what was now Austrian Germany to issue a pastoral letter of protest. The next Nazi step in due course was to spoliate and close Austrian monasteries and convents, noteworthy for their material riches and intellectual contents. Save for a few who succeeded in fleeing abroad, the inmates were driven into concentration camps and kept there.

Nazi troops had barely entered Austria before the Hitler Government announced that its anti-Semitic laws would be applied to Austria. From March to June, 1938, both Jews and Catholics, but Jews most predominantly, were the victims of outbreaks of terrorism abetted by the Nazi uniformed bullies in the shape of Storm Troops. Catholic organizations were raided and plundered, and many affluent Catholic opponents of Nazism were arrested and their property seized. "In Austria overnight," wrote a correspondent on the spot (he had to go to London to send his wireless accounts), "Vienna's 290,000 Jews were made free game for mobs, despoiled of their property, deprived of police protection, ejected from employment and barred from sources of relief. The frontiers were hermetically sealed against their escape." Refined Jewish men and women were manhandled by mobs, and the by now familiar pattern of gross indignities and indecencies were practiced upon Jews of every age and condition, all with official sanction.[26]

Inflexibly over all were Nazi decrees ordering the systematic economic eradication of Jews; not one should henceforth have any opportunity of earning a living. Expressions of the most intense indignation came from America and some other countries. But Nazi organs in Germany and Austria exulted as much over the abject misery of Jews as they did over the vast amount of booty bagged. Following its seizure of Czechoslovakia, the Nazi regime extended its repressions of Jews there as it later did, as we shall see, in other subjugated countries, and waves of suicides of Jews were an accompaniment. An ally of Germany and imitating its performances, Italy early gratified the Nazis by action against Jews, the beginning of a series of rigorous decrees which inevitably caused great disruption among resident Jews. More of these calamitous conditions will be treated later.

During the time when the swath of Nazi persecutions had swept over some European countries and was imminent in others, the German-American Bund was seeking to engender in America the same hate which had already caused brutal excesses in great parts of Europe. "They," reported the McNaboe committee describing the Bund, "have distributed thousands of pamphlets designed to convince not only the German-Americans of this country that this country is Jew-dominated. . . . The foreign and inimical doctrine of racial superiority and concomitant hatred and persecutions of the Jews and other racial minorities is an importation from a foreign dictatorship, and, as such, antagonistic to the principles of our government as guaranteed by the Constitution."[27]

Inasmuch as the German-American Bund's membership

[26] See detailed accounts of G. E. R. Gedye and other *New York Times* correspondents published in that newspaper on April 3, 25, 27, 28 and May 23, 1938.

[27] *Report of the* [State of New York] *Joint Legislative Committee*, etc. Document No. *98*, p. 298.

rolls were kept secret or destroyed, investigating committees
could not learn the authentic number of its members. In his
testimony before the Dies committee, Kuhn placed the roster
at about 20,000 to 25,000, with a radius of enlisted sympathizers "three or four times that number." This might have
been an expansive claim, and in view of the Department of
Justice investigation which, in 1937, placed the membership
at 6,500, it doubtless was so.

Nevertheless, membership was by no means the measure-
ment of the Bund's drawing power in some big cities, where
it proved it could summon large picked audiences. To show
this as well as to expose the character of its meetings, the
McNaboe committee incorporated in its report a vivid account of a Bund mass meeting held in Madison Square
Garden, New York City, on the night of February 20, 1939.
During the previous year or more the Bund, with all due
publicity flourishes, had professed undergoing a metamor-
phosis. Americanism and nothing but that was henceforth
to be its theme and goal. One of its moves had been to dis-
card the black breeches and riding boots of the Nazi Elite
Guards, and substitute a uniform which, Kuhn announced,
was modeled on the American Legion's. Opportunely came
a handy disclaimer from the Nazi regime in Berlin that it
did not endorse the Bund. To sever in the general public
mind the fixed conviction that the Bund was a Nazi annex
was now the simulated policy. In September, 1938, the German title of the official Bund newspaper had been supplanted by the English title *The Free American,* to which,
however, a German sub-title was attached. No longer, was
Kuhn's assurance, would the German national flag be displayed at Bund public meetings; at these the American flag
would proudly wave.

The German-American Bund's unchanged nature was
blatantly attested by its Madison Square Garden mass
meeting. Ostensibly held in honor of George Washington's
birthday, this meeting was advertised as a patriotic demonstration. "Dynamic" speeches—a characterization well understood by the initiated—were promised. Under no illu-
sions as to Bund intentions, city authorities would not
allow use of the auditorium until the Bund agreed not to

conduct any anti-Semitic propaganda there. Still wary of the Bund's word and to provide against expected trouble, the municipal officials stationed platoons of police on the blocks surrounding the place and a squad inside the hall. In the streets throngs of angry Communists, anti-Fascists and other elements hostile to the Bund were massed, but the police kept order. Fully 19,000 Bund adherents jammed Madison Square Garden. This was ostentatiously decorated with a large portrait of George Washington and an array of flags. The committee's account went on to relate:

The flags, however, were not all American flags. Just as prominent but more in evidence, were flags so well known to the American public and the whole world as the emblem of Nazi Germany, the hated swastika. Inside the hall there seemed to be two kinds of officials—one the familiar policeman, the other much like the Storm Troopers of Germany, the "O.D's or *Ordnungs Dienst.*" The brown shirt was replaced by a gray with Sam Browne belts, arm bands and American Legion trousers. It seemed as though a private army had taken over a small portion of New York City. So-called ushers, the O.D's paraded up and down the hall with long searchlights in their hands which could easily maim or kill. Huge banners were placed about the Garden with the following propaganda: "Wake Up America," "Smash Jewish Communism," "Stop Jewish Domination of Christian America," and perhaps the most startling banner of them all contained the following: "1,000,000 Bund Members By 1940."

The promise of no anti-Semitic speeches "was violated by every speaker." President Franklin D. Roosevelt "was described as Franklin D. Rosenfeld." Also, "Loud cheers greeted the names of Mussolini and Hitler, and American democracy was cudgelled and derided. The expulsion of the Jews and Jewish Communism was the main topic of the evening . . ."[28]

But Kuhn's sway as the Bund's National Fuehrer was drawing to an inglorious close. On November 29, 1939, he was convicted in New York City of larceny of Bund funds

[28] Ibid., pp. 227-228.

and of forgery, and off he was sent to serve two and a half to five years in Clinton prison. Hard did he, as Convict No. 26,558, try to get out on parole, but the New York State Parole Board, on June 18, 1941, adjudging him "a hazard to the public peace and security," unanimously declined to grant release. The New York Legislature had passed an act, the effect of which was to forbid the use of uniformed "O.D.'s" at meetings. Kuhn's successor was one Gerhard Wilhelm Kunze, formerly a chauffeur in Philadelphia. Fast and faster the Bund encountered decisive public hostility. Great was the surprise of Bund officials in 1940, at court proceedings against them based upon a law enacted by New Jersey, in 1935, prohibiting the incitation of racial or religious hatred by persons making speeches or permitting them. (From their conviction and sentences as offenders, the Bund group, invoking the unconstitutionality of the law, appealed to the New Jersey Supreme Court. This, on December 5, 1941, ruling that although the speeches made were revoltingly "not welcome to the ear of any good citizen," reversed the convictions on the ground of that particular law's unconstitutionality. The jurists on that bench took the stand that to make a speaker amenable to criminal law, his utterances must be such as to present a clear and present danger to the State, and, it was held, the speeches were not of that character.)

Public anger was much accentuated when, in August, 1940, contingents of the Ku Klux Klan joined with the German-American Bundsmen in what was barefacedly flaunted as an "Americanism" meeting at the Bund's 205-acre Camp Nordland, at Andover, New Jersey. Throughout the night a Klan forty-foot fiery cross blazed; in consort Bund swastikas and other of its paraphernalia were in profuse display, and from loud-speaker apparatus belched the raucous notes of Nazi marching songs. New Jersey's store of tolerance was exhausted. By authority of a legislative act, the officials of that State, in June, 1941, took effective steps to end, as a standing public nuisance, the career of Camp Nordland. Citizens there as elsewhere were greatly relieved at the closing of this rendezvous, detested as much for its Bund gatherings as for its being converted into a center, in the heart of an American community, for the innoculation of youth with Nazi doctrines and ways.[29] Florida enacted a statute outlawing Bund activities, and from other sections came evidences of a determination either to wield the power of efficacious ostracism or to invoke that of stern law.

Although its own standing in the general public mind had from the beginning been dubious, the German-American Bund, whether in surly resolution or in lumpish obtuseness, had cherished the idea that it could somehow swing American public opinion and action. On May 24, 1941, the Dies committee publicized the fact that it had come upon documents pledging the Bund and urging all others concerned "to eradicate the Red Jewish pestilence in America." But, the committee rejoiced, the plan to launch a first-rate Nazi movement in the United States had been thoroughly discredited by the effective exposés of the Bund's connections, composition, methods and aims.

Discredited, yes, but by no means dispersed. Defiant of all exposures, insulated from American ideology, doggedly set upon pursuing its course, the German-American Bund, although much depleted, kept its framework as an organization. In boastful strain, *The Free American,* on September 11, 1941, reported as a delectable event: "The German-American Bund met in National Convention in Chicago with a full attendance of delegates." What "full" signified was not explained. Characteristically, the bulk of the account bearing upon this convention was devoted to whining over the tribulations that the Bund claimed to have experienced. No word of disapproval of the catastrophic Nazi persecutions of Jews and others had, of course, come from the Bund. Measures thus far taken against the Bund could in no sense be interpreted as persecution; they were neces-

---

[29] The German-American Bund's youth leader, or *Landesfuehrer,* was one Theodore Dinkelacher, classing himself as a mechanical engineer. His duty, he grandly testified, was to teach "all youth has to know." Upon questioning he disclosed his qualifications. He did not know the name of the Vice President of the United States. Queried further, he first thought Morgenthau (Henry M. Morgenthau, Jr., U. S. Secretary of the Treasury) was U. S. Secretary of State; then he ventured the name of Perkins (Miss Frances E. Perkins, U. S. Secretary of Labor) as head of the Department of State. A minority, that of Jews, Dinkelacher asserted, "rules the country." Asked to substantiate that statement, he replied, "Look at the names of the people who rule and control." Informed that President Franklin D. Roosevelt was not a Jew, Dinkelacher, apparently implying Jewish control of the nation's Chief Executive, answered, "But he doesn't hold the job." *Report of the* [State of New York] *Joint Legislative Committee, Document No. 98,* pp. 1405-1407.

sary and legitimate against a Nazified organization violating every precept of American life and law by sowing racial hatred. But in *The Free American* these measures were tearfully represented as vindictive hounding. Thus did the Bund publication bemoan: "Feeling that the Bund has been persistently persecuted and that its enemies were employing every foul expedient to discredit this outspoken German-American organization, the spirit of the delegates was that of a people who are determined to defend the rights not only of the Bund but of all American citizens of German blood. . . . It has been possible, from 1917 down, to overwhelm the German element with suffering, deprivation and discrimination, but the free spirit of the German-Americans has not been broken. . . ." Upon this squealing, habitual enough in the case of that organization, no comment is necessary. But as an illuminative fact, a finding emphasized by the investigating committees solicits prime notice. Neither the Bund nor its propaganda had made any headway among the great mass of citizens of German birth or descent. These remained stonily aloof or such as were importuned refused to participate in a movement obnoxious to them personally and contravening the ways and principles of America treasured as their homeland.

Under its hybrid name, *The Free American and Deutscher Weckruf und Beobachter,* punctuating its comments with sneers at Jews, kept sputtering along until a few days after the declaration of war, on December 11, 1941, between the United States and Germany. Then U. S. Treasury agents took sole possession of the offices occupied jointly and interconnectedly by that publication, by the German-American Business League and by the German-American Bund.

Action against foreign-born Bund members individually, especially those of the German-American Bund, was announced on March 25, 1942, by U. S. Attorney-General Francis Biddle who declared that thirty or forty petitions for denaturalization of such persons as were disloyal to the U. S. Government would be presented to the Federal courts. The plan in view was to void the citizenship of those in the list. Attorney-General Biddle, in an interview, read quotations from Bund-member letters or statements. "No matter how many citizenship papers were in the closet," affirmed one of these, all Germans were still members of a Pan-German movement. "No one can force us to give our souls to America" and "become mongrels," defiantly asserted another. A third boast was that "the term German is higher than German-American citizen." At the same time came a declaration from the Department of Justice that, upon his release from Sing Sing prison, Fritz Kuhn would be interned as an enemy alien if the Federal court approved a denaturalization petition to be filed against him in New York City. Early in April, 1942, sixty-four German ex-soldiers, all aliens and members of the Kyffhaeuser Bund, a veterans' organization, were arrested by the Federal Bureau of Investigation in New York City; quantities of ammunition and printed propaganda were seized; other naturalized members of this particular Bund, although not arrested, faced denaturalization proceedings. Such was public feeling against Bundists that four former members of the German-American Bund, long holding important positions in a large New Jersey gasworks, were dismissed by the concern from their jobs.

Kunze, whose whereabouts were now unknown and who no longer officiated as head of the German-American Bund was, with several others, indicted by the Federal Grand Jury, at Hartford, Connecticut, on June 10, 1942, on the charge of having been a member of a spy ring furnishing military information to Germany and Japan.

Overlapping somewhat the point of chronology, this is the natural, appropriate place for a brief narration of the further course of the German-American Bund. Its campaign against Jews was only part of its members' plans to aid the Nazi cause in every possible treasonable way. As a blind, testimony revealed, an organization edict provided that all "service rooms" were to contain a picture of George Washington, but side by side with this was to be hung a portrait of Hitler. The deadly purposes of Bund influence was luridly shown by the detection and quick arrest by the Federal Bureau of Investigation in June, 1942, of two groups of saboteurs, all of whom had been members of the German American Bund, had been infiltrated with its doctrines and had returned to Germany where they were given special education in sabotage. They had secretly landed on the

American coast, carrying cases of powerful explosives and nearly $150,000 in cash, with instructions to blow up certain highly essential plants and to cause panic in large cities. Tried by a military court, six of these terrorists were promptly executed, and two sentenced to serve long terms in prison.

After the United States had been attacked, the Government proceeded with great energy against the German-American Bund. The story of the series of prosecutions is a long one; many local leaders and members were convicted, and the citizenship rights under which some had pretended to act were cancelled. Apparently defunct, the German-American Bund had still been the covert center of the most seditious activities. Suffice it for the purpose here to refer to the fate of former national Bund leader Kunze. Identified in Mexico, he had been taken to Hartford, Connecticut, to stand trial with a group for conspiracy in sending military secrets to Germany and Japan. One of the group had already admitted guilt; a five-year sentence was his portion; another, a clergyman, was found guilty and was consigned to ten years in prison; and Kunze, confessed conspirator, received a sentence of fifteen years in prison. Others of the group pleaded guilty.

With two dozen associates Kunze was later put on trial in the Federal court in New York City charged with fomenting resistance to military service in violation of the Selective Service Act. With such obduracy did the Bund persist in its intent to keep going that Kunze was heard by a witness to say that the Bund would continue even by subterfuges as seeming to be a singing, hiking or even knitting concern. This testimony was given by a Government witness who had joined the Bund for the purpose of getting information. Kunze and his fellow Bundists were convicted, and on October 22, 1942, they were all given the maximum penalty, each receiving a sentence of five years in prison. This was in addition to prison sentences Kunze and a Chicago Bund leader had already incurred.

CHAPTER XXVII

HITLER'S ADVENT THE SIGNAL

WHILE cluttered with its alien trappings the German-American Bund had steadily nauseated the American public, other organizations of native label had, as already incidentally mentioned, been active in fomenting hatred against Jews. Presenting themselves to the public as American sponsored, these organizations took advantage of what seemed to be their native cast to exploit themselves as wholly of American composition. Yet the striking feature of nearly all was their bursting into existence coincidentally with Hitler's acquiring dominion over Germany. In his book, *The Door to Revelation,* William Dudley Pelley related how instantaneously he launched the Silver Shirt Legion of America on January 31, 1933, the day after Hitler took power. Nor did Pelley omit saying in that same book how, in taking that step, he esteemed himself as having the qualifications of an American Hitler. Mushroom-like, many other organizations sprang up over night. The McCormack committee wasted no words in attributing nice motives. Bluntly and significantly it reported of numerous of these organizations: "Investigation disclosed that many are in reality the breeding places of racial and religious intolerance, and their financial statements show them petty rackets."[1]

Under this characterization of mercenary aims were specifically grouped several bodies. One, pretentiously calling itself the Order of '76, seemed by its name to rally to itself Americans of old descent or traditional principles, but it was a skeleton affair which could not actually record more than 146 members. Also enumerated was an organization having the pompous name of The American Vigilante In-

---

[1] *Investigation of Nazi and Other Propaganda,* House of Representatives, 74th Congress, 1st Session, February 15, 1935, *Report No. 153,* p. 11.

telligence Federation. This largely resolved itself into the person of Harry A. Jung who joined in himself the status of founder, promoter and honorary general manager. To what net result? The McCormack committee related: "Testimony of his secretary showed that a solicitor had been paid 40 per cent of all money he collected as his fee, and that nationally-known organizations and individuals had contributed. The committee finds the contributors had no knowledge of the purposes for which the money was used. Miss Peterson's testimony showed that Harry A. Jung and the A.V.I.F. had published great masses of literature tending to incite racial and religious intolerance." There was a multitude of other such organizations "created and operated for the financial welfare of those who guide them and who do not hesitate to stoop to racial and religious intolerance in order to achieve their selfish purposes." Among the organizations which had passed the incipient stage, the committee noted, was the Silver Shirt Legion of America.[2]

Reporting four years later the result of its extended investigation, the Dies committee set forth that with Hitler's advent to power hundreds of anti-Jewish organizations had bounded into existence in America. "Many of the anti-racial organizations that have come under our scrutiny were created for the pecuniary and selfish aggrandizement of the crackpots whose offspring they are. . . . The only thing that kept them from being welded into a cohesive group . . . is the fact that they cannot agree on who should be the Fuehrer, and, equally as important, their source of individual revenue would be cut off." After the McCormack committee's exposure of many as rackets, there had been some lessening of their activities. Nevertheless the Dies committee enumerated approximately 135 individuals and groups propagandizing such hatred had been brought to its attention. Of fifty-four organizations personally checked by this committee "not more than 25 per cent can be considered bona fide," presumably those not in the sheer money-seeking class. "The other 75 per cent are pure rackets or letter-head organizations created for the sole purpose of enriching their leaders."[3]

[2] Ibid., pp. 11-12.
[3] *Investigation of Un-American Activities*, House of Representatives, 76th

The Dies committee took pains to point out the meretricious nature of numbers of the so-called organizations and the veneer with which they covered themselves. Many were little more than a name and an address; in some instances one individual would create and be the self-designed "dictator" of several such groups at the same time; and the allurements "patriotic," "Christian," and "American," were frequently used in the names of such schemes as bait to attract followers. "Needless to say, the use of these words by such organizations is a gross misrepresentation and entirely inconsistent with the actual purpose for which the organizations stand."[4] Obviously, those purposes were the capitalization of racial and religious hatred.

Directly borrowing its name as a paraphrase of the brown-shirted Nazis, the Silver Shirt Legion of America did not resort to disguise. And such was a prevalent spirit of stark imitation of the Nazi example manifested in what were supposed to be American terms that the Dies committee was constrained to report: "Probably the largest, best financed and best publicized of such groups is the Silver Shirt Legion of America."[5]

What, is the arising question, was its founder's background? Tackling the varied accounts, both those in *Who's Who in America* and in Pelley's own weekly, it is hard to harmonize discrepancies. One account gave his birth at Lynn, Massachusetts, in 1885, another as happening in 1890. In a biography published under his own supervision, he was declared the only son of a Methodist clergyman; a few lines later he was represented as having, at the age of seventeen, left the Lynn public schools to enter paper manufacturing with his father in Northern New York. No astonishment need be expressed at the claim that before he was twenty-one years old Pelley had made a fortune of $75,000. For that was only one of his large claims. According to *Who's Who in America* he had worked on various small-town newspapers and had written miscellaneous books of

Congress, 1st Session, (January 3, 1939) *House Report No. 2*, p. 117. The effort to intensify feeling against Jews because of race so far overleaped the regular bounds, in the case of one of the anti-Semitic groups, that it made a special anti-Semitic campaign among Negroes. Ibid.
[4] Ibid., *House Report No. 1476*, p. 19.
[5] Ibid., p. 20.

fiction. This fact became transposed into this high-flown eulogy: "By the time of the World War he had made a national name as one of the highest-paid writers in America, being attached to the contributing staff of the *American Magazine*."[6] Testifying at a later date before the Dies committee he did not elucidate just what was his magazine connection, but he did state that his salary from that publication was $1,500.[7] In one of his books Pelley wrote gorgeously of his accomplishments: ". . . Two hundred and twenty published narratives—fiction enough to fill thirty volumes of the ordinary novel length—was my record in the period when I made my living by popular writing. I had mastered my craft and knew it. There were four different text books on the American short story containing specimens of my work acclaimed as examples of dramatic construction so perfect that college students must analyze them as part of their courses in English." Yet all of his boasted large income as a writer and his self-accredited artistry did not save him from the need of entering the ruck of trade. He had sold some of his fiction to a Hollywood motion-picture concern, and tarried in California in 1927, 1928 and 1929 to engage in the real-estate business. There also he was president of a restaurant chain called the Brief Meal Corporation, which was all too brief; it folded up in failure.

Upon which, in 1930, Pelley gravitated to New York, and in spiritualism found a new line of activity. Writing and lecturing on the subject he attracted to himself a considerable following the cultivation of which he did not neglect. Encouraged in what seemed a most promising field he hied himself to Asheville, North Carolina, and on February 7, 1931, established the Galahad Press, from which he drew a salary of $100 a week.[8] "For years," reported the McCormack committee, "Pelley, according to testimony, had been writing on metaphysical [psychical] subjects, with nine out of ten of his followers being women who gave him and from whom he borrowed varying sums of money, in one case receiving bonds valued at $14,000." Upon establishing his Silver Shirt Legion of America, headquarters at Asheville,

[6] *Pelley's Weekly*, February 12, 1936.
[7] *House Report No. 1476*, Vol. 12, p. 7281.
[8] Robert B. Barker, Investigator for the Dies committee explored Pelley's career fully. See his testimony, Ibid., Vol. 6, pp. 4186-4187.

he told persons who later testified to the fact that the idea was copied from Germany. Immediately, reported the Mc-Cormack committee, his prolific writing changed from its dissertations on psychic matters into violent, vitriolic and scurrilous attacks upon certain religious groups.[9] These targets were Jews—not some, but all Jews. Overtures, further reported this committee, were made to Nazi groups and Nazi leaders in America, and, as his "foreign adjutant," Pelley attached to himself Paul Lilienfeld who helped make contacts with German steamship-line officials by whom he was employed. Pelley's weekly publication became the organ of the Silver Shirts. "Another and more vicious weekly was started in Oklahoma where State authorities told them to 'get out.' "[10] And although the Silver Shirt Legion of America had not yet complied with the requirement of incorporation, chapters or branches sprang into being in a number of States—twelve in all, by the spring of 1934, according to Pelley's testimony. When, on March 17, 1934, the Silver Shirt Legion of America was incorporated, its structure was so devised that no member had a right to vote, and powers of self-perpetuating dictator were vested in Pelley.[11]

Some months previously Pelley's Galahad Press had plunged into insolvency. Documentary evidence showed this to have been caused by the diversion of more than $100,000 in funds to other accounts. This sum was derived by his organization from the sale of anti-Jewish "literature," from Silver Shirt membership dues and from other sources. Of the more than $100,000, there had been deposited $29,497 in Pelley's personal account in the Franklin National Bank, Washington, D. C., and $81,366.97 had been deposited in two Asheville banks to the credit of the Foundation for Christian Economics, a dummy corporation set up by Pelley.[12] Court evidence showed that on January 19, 1934, Pelley, from Hollywood, California, wired Harry F. Sieber, one of his associates at Asheville, to destroy all records of the Galahad Press.[13] On May 1, 1934, the Galahad Press

[9] *House Report No. 153*, p. 11.
[10] Ibid.
[11] Ibid.
[12] *House Report No. 1476*, p. 20.
[13] Ibid.

was adjudged bankrupt with losses of more than $13,000 to the preferred stockholders and $20,000 to the creditors.[14]

At this point a "Dear Friend" circular letter sent broadcast by Pelley from Asheville, on September 13, 1934, invites germane attention. Pelley wrote: "I have a fairly thick skin but now and then I get a letter that makes me wince. Diatribes and defamations I can stand, but this week a man up in New York wrote me: 'It seems every time I open any mail from you or your organization, it turns out to be a new demand for money.'" Waxing hot, Pelley invidiously implied persecution by asserting that he was not complaining of what "Jewish intrigue" had done to his headquarters or organization. But he was "mightily concerned that there may be scores of others who feel like my New York correspondent but do not want to express themselves."

When revenue sources were endangered, well might Pelley have been perturbed. To show his heroic work for a cause he therefore contrasted the hardships he had undergone with a later success which had been shattered by Jewish enemies. "I started this national weekly five years bygone on a lone $10 banknote of my own and $40 borrowed from a friend. When the aforesaid intrigue resulted in our headquarters being smashed or closed the financial turnover was better than $50,000 a year, all based on either magazine or book sales or donations." Now, he went on, to prevent stoppage of his work, he had to solicit donations. Then resorting to a common device of forestalling objections by self-reference to a current charge, he continued: "I have been vilified from coast to coast by the radical Jewish press, with innuendoes spread that I was nothing but a racketeer who had lined his own pockets handsomely from capitalizing on people's religious sympathies. . . . If I wanted to stop this work tomorrow and return to private pursuits, I could command the same $25,000 a year which I was earning in 1929 when I voluntarily relinquished private earnings in order to give my whole time and talents to this Higher Calling."[15]

---

[14] Ibid.

[15] A copy of this edifying letter is inserted in Vol. 1 of *Pelley's (The Silver Shirt) Weekly* in the New York Public Library. For a time at first this publication was called the name here given. In 1936 the title was changed to

Now turning to the testimony of Robert B. Barker, here is what that special investigator for the Dies committee plucked from the records: The common stockholders (of Galahad Press) were Pelley and two women in his office. The preferred stockholders were fifteen persons of whom ten were women, "and some of them very prominent and well-to-do and interested in spiritualism and psychic matters. . . . They lost the preferred stock . . ."[16]

Pelley's Skyland Press took the place of the defunct Galahad Press. From the mass of anti-Jewish "literature" contained either in Pelley's publications or published as pamphlets, we need only give some characteristic specimens. On September 5, 1934, came forth "The New Emancipation Proclamation—The Silver Shirt Platform." Signed by Pelley as National Commander of the Silver Shirts of America, it presented a plan for disposing of Jews. Based upon the fiction of Jews filling a disproportionate amount of offices, the section under the head of "The Jew" declared: "We contract to impose racial quotas on the political and economic structure, observing rigorously in effect that no racial factions shall be allowed further occupancy of public or professional office in excess of the ratio of its blood-members to the remaining sum total of all the races completing the composition of the body politic." Under the section "Deportation of Aliens" this was the program advanced: "We shall expeditiously appoint Alien Registration Day throughout the public domain [sic] in which all persons of Hebrew blood or extraction, or all persons not native born or completely naturalized, shall be required under penalty of confiscation of their goods and a term of imprisonment, to register their nationalities, countries of birth, and dates and manner of their entries to this country. It shall be punishable by confiscation of goods and a term of imprisonment for any Hebrew to give a false or adopted Gentile name to secrete the evidence of Jewish extraction, at the time of such

Pelley's Weekly. Before the Dies committee Pelley confirmed earlier testimony that from individuals, whom he named, in American cities he had received for his agitational work contributions some of which ranged from about $10,000 to $20,000, and a $5,000 loan from a Kansas and Texas "goatgland doctor" which loan, so Pelley testified on February 10, 1940, had not been repaid.
[16] _House Report No. 1476,_ Vol. 6, p. 4200.

registration or at any time in future, and legislative change of name shall not excuse such Hebrew from such registration."

Once more was trotted out the old absurdity which anti-Catholic movements had applied to Catholics indiscriminately, that they formed a solid political voting power. This time the Jewish people, both American born and otherwise, were likewise described in the Silver Shirt Platform. To prevent this alleged cohesion as "a nation" all Jews were to be relegated permanently to the inferior position of Resident Aliens deprived of civil rights unless, was one condition, they "forswear forever such Jewish allegiance." Moreover, if any Jew was apprehended in future "giving moral or financial support to Jewish nationalism operative in this country," he was to be criminally prosecuted for sedition. In the very act of demanding repression of Jews on race grounds, the Silver Shirt Platform, declaring America a "Christian Democracy," concluded: "We are pledged to respect and sustain the sanctity of the Christian Ideal . . . to deify Patriotism and pride of race." But in America, outgrowth of all races, the platform inferentially ejected Jews by its refusing to "recognize the license of no race or racial group to undermine national unity. . . ." [17]

Week after week and year after year Pelley's publications continued their savage attacks upon Jews. In Hitler's Germany, as elsewhere later, one specious justification for pillaging Jews of property was that it had been acquired by chicanery. This, an old pretext, was joined with the groundless accusation of their owning the mass of the country's wealth. Pelley's tirades followed these and similar Nazi lines. "When," one of his editorials stated, "95 per cent of this nation's wealth is concentrated in the hands of 5 per cent of its population, and when, in addition, that 5 per cent is mostly comprised of one race of people that insolently and arrogantly strives to use its golden hoard to bring in a political and social autocracy, history had shown that something fearful happens. Equally is this true when such a racial clique is brainless enough to go about openly sneering at the victimized 95 per cent: 'We have got your money and what are you going to do about it?' " and parroting another

Nazi croak about Jewish "arrogance," the article went on: "It is the arrogant and increasingly domineering attitude of the average Jew in the average Main Street in the nation today that is going to direct the fire of retribution at his race in general. . . . The Christian public sees Jews everywhere in authoritative positions on our Relief Committees, it sees Jews everywhere in authoritative positions in our finance and commerce. The preponderance is too menacing, says the Christian public . . ."[18]

Such a charge is wearisomely familiar to us. We have seen how anti-Catholic movements shrieked the same of Catholics, and it had no more basis relating to Jews than it had pertaining to Catholics. The most cursory study of U. S. Treasury *Statistics of Income* on the persons or families in whom or in which control of great industrial and financial power was centered would have shown the great predominance of non-Jews. Nor did such a condition change. Pursuant to a resolution of Congress, in 1938, a select committee was authorized to make a complete investigation, under the auspices of the Securities and Exchange Commission, of the concentration of economic power. Issued by the Temporary National Economic Committee, of which U. S. Senator Joseph C. O'Mahoney was chairman, this voluminous report did not, of course, enter into religious or racial connotations. But the well-known non-Jewish character of families in stockholding ascendancy in 200 of America's largest industrial corporations disposed of the canard of Jewish business autocracy. Thirteen families, including the Ford, duPont, Rockefeller, Mellon, McCormick, Hartford, Harkness, Duke, Pew, Pitcairn, Clark, Reynolds and Kress held (as of December 31, 1937) an ascertained total of $2,700,574,000 of stock. This, it was explained, represented only part of the wealth of these families; many had other investments, particularly in large financial corporations not covered by the study, and also investments in corporate bonds, tax-exempt securities and real estate, and cash deposits in banks.[19]

"The Jews have the money," blared Pelley, "but the

[18] Ibid., September 12, 1934.
[19] *Investigation of Concentration of Economic Power*, Temporary National Economic Committee, 1940. *Monograph No. 29*, p. 116.

Gentiles have the numbers," and predicting trouble he declared, "It will be a fine thing in that hour not to be a Jew." [20] In a succeeding issue he shifted to other grounds. The Jew, threatened one of his editorials, had provoked destruction by "his insolence and ethics" [sic]. He amplified: "The Silver Shirts have suddenly come upon the scene with certain prescriptions for society's convalescence." Then, unmindful of his just previously having assailed Jews as the capitalistic 5 per cent of population controlling America's wealth, he now represented them as a "radical and revolutionary faction" of which the whole nation should take cognizance. The Silver Shirts and their leaders "have perceived in the ethics and strategies of the megalomaniac Jew a menace to the social peace and welfare." Fancying himself already a dictator, Pelley, with stroke of pen or touch of typewriter, summarily read Jews out as being no part of the American nation. Having performed this legerdemain, he now urged his reconstructed American nation to shackle that "Jewish faction . . . so that honest men can function." Rushing into prophecy, he proclaimed: "Within another year the entire United States will have awakened to the fact that the Jewish problem takes precedence over all other problems begging public attention. . . ." [21]

Pelley soon had to face his own problem which was none other than the heavy hand of the law. Early in 1935 he and an aide were convicted of violating North Carolina's "Blue Sky" statute in having sold stock of the Galahad enterprises without registration and authorization and by fraudulent representation. Pelley was fined $1,719.50 and received a jail sentence which was suspended on condition of his probation on continuous good behavior for five years after February 18, 1935.[22] Did he fulfill this stipulation? We shall a little later have occasion to see.

Under the vigilance of law, Pelley nevertheless persisted in retaining a brassy front and obtruding himself in still greater degree. In the very next year—1936—he came forth to stage a creation which he called the Christian Party. So far this existed as a mere individual promotion with no pros-

[20] *Pelley's (The Silver Shirt) Weekly*, September 12, 1934.
[21] Ibid., October 3, 1934.
[22] *House Report No. 153*, p. 11, and *House Report No. 1476*, p. 20.

pects of its becoming a serious movement. Yet Pelley at once hailed it as a consummation. "We Americans," he whooped in his introductory announcement, "now have a Political Party that is openly and fearlessly anti-Jewish. The newly organized Christian Party gives us our opportunity to register effective protests at the way in which Jews are taking over our industries, our property and our money." And again jumbling capitalism and Communism as one and the same, he went on in this strain: "To put the Christian Party in control at the next Presidential election means the smashing of Jewish Communism in the United States and the disenfranchising of the Jew from further political and economic mischief." Pelley, however, could not avoid equally panegyrizing something else than the Christian Party, which something else was his transcendent Self. Not suffering anyone to be unaware that he was the great redoubtable procreator, he appended a long eulogy carrying a photo of himself. Telling of the entry of this new Party, the eulogy thus presented Pelley as responding hero-like to a popular call: "But along with this epochal announcement goes the demand on the part of the unenlightened for further particulars about the man who is making the Christian Party a deadly reality." In like vein: "The man who suddenly and dauntlessly made the Christian Party a power in the impoverished United States is William Dudley Pelley, Commander of the Silver Legion, and a pioneer in the strictly American movement to smash the megalomaniac clutch of apostate Jewry on our Christian institutions." [23]

Although not exactly abortive, the Christian Party was little removed from that status. Pelley, of course, ran as its candidate for President of the United States, and in a Western State particularly the platform on which he stood demanded urgent restrictions upon Jews. They should, it was proposed, be forbidden to hold property "except under the condition that Japan imposes on Occidentals," and should be required to obtain licenses to engage in business or the professions. The scattered vote cast for the Christian Party was so altogether negligible that almanac compilers of election returns did not take the trouble to give it notice. Appertaining to the platform just mentioned, Pelley, on Feb-

[23] *Pelley's Weekly*, February 12, 1936.

ruary 8, 1940, testified before the Dies committee that he still endorsed it "100 per cent." "If," asked Representative Casey of the committee, "the Silver Shirts had achieved their aim would you have become the head of the Government?" "Probably," replied Pelley. "And would you have put into effect Hitler's policy toward the Jews?" "I probably would, sir."

However slight the Christian Party's vote, Pelley felt himself able to represent the Silver Shirts as having, by 1939, organizations in twenty-two States. By that year also, the testimony of special investigator Barker brought out, Pelley headed a variety of organizations, including the Silver Shirts, the Pelley Publishers, *Pelley's Weekly*, the magazine *Liberation*, the Skyland Press and others. The only one of these incorporated organizations maintaining a bank account was the Skyland Press. It was this concern which published pamphlets and other propaganda comprehending sixty separate pieces among which were *The Cause of Anti-Semitism in the United States* and nasty aspersions upon President Franklin D. Roosevelt and some members of his Cabinet. According further to Barker's testimony, Pelley now owned in Asheville an $80,000 building housing his own printing plant. Besides revenue from other sources he had, it was proved, received considerable sums in donations. As to which inflow the Dies committee reported: "A careful investigation of Pelley's bank accounts and books and [of] the records of the Post Office at Asheville has established the fact that thousands of dollars in funds coming into Pelley's hands from his organization and publishing house now known as the Skyland Press, have been disposed of in a way so devious as to defy accounting." [24] The committee further related how, on September 2, 1939, as a result of false testimony before it in the previous month "a paid secret agent of Pelley's was indicted by a Grand Jury in the District of Columbia for perjury committed by said agent in his efforts to secure employment as an investigator with the committee." [25] Making a mighty gesture, Pelley, on the very next day, sued six members of the committee and an investigator for $3,150,000 damages, "but," the committee nonchalantly

[24] *House Report No. 1476*, p. 21.
[25] Ibid., p. 20.

observed "it is believed that this suit will, like numerous suits filed by Pelley in the past, be dismissed on motion." [26]

A little more than a month later a juridical action and scathing denunciation confronted Pelley. Judge Zeb Nettles of the Superior Court of Buncombe County, North Carolina, directed the court clerk to issue a capias for Pelley's arrest to show cause why his parole should not be revoked. The Dies committee quoted Judge Nettles as making this statement in open court: "It is not those from without that we must watch, but those so-called saviors of mankind who are preaching doctrines deadly to American institutions. This defendant who is moving in our midst seeking to further the cause of Nazism with himself as the dictator, seeking to destroy justice and liberty, and abolish all laws—living under the very protection of that law—he is seeking to overthrow and undermine our system of government. . . . He is a menace to our society. . . . For three weeks I sat here in this very courtroom and helped to unravel a course of crooked dealing, thievery and stealing sufficient to damn any man, much less this contemptible seeker after notoriety, W. D. Pelley, so-called and self-styled leader of the Silver Shirts—convicted felon—not even a citizen. A Buncombe County jury says he is not, yet he would be our dictator and would tell our country what to do." [27] Seized, on February 10, 1940, after having been a witness before the Dies committee, Pelley was denounced then and there by Representative Starnes of Alabama, the committee's acting chairman, for fulsomely praising Hitler and his dictatorial policies; for defending and advocating vigilantism; and for urging the segregation of certain American citizens.

After citing Judge Nettles' remarks, the Dies committee gave these as its findings: "From the documentary evidence and testimony before the committee concerning the activities of Pelley, the conclusion that he is a racketeer engaged in mulcting thousands of dollars annually from his fanatical and misled followers and credulous people all over the United States, Canada and in certain foreign countries, is inescapable. Pelley provides the typical case, but his methods differ little from others in the same field." [28]

[26] Ibid., p. 21.
[27] Ibid.   [28] Ibid.

So deep an impression did this abhorrent type of racketeering make upon the Dies committee that it felt the need of extra emphasis upon the widespread condition. "The committee's evidence shows that virtually all these organizations and individuals [investigated] make the common use of racial and religious hatred to enlist members and secure financial support." And again: "It is clear from the testimony received that many of the organizations were set up primarily for the purpose of selling religious and racial hatred, and that their leaders are nothing more than racketeers." [29]

The committee was likewise appalled by the enormous mass of anti-Jewish propaganda published and distributed. Relevantly the committee could have pointed out the possible or probable evil ultimate effect of the dissemination of this poison. Organizations of the character described may and do have a transient existence but their published matter sinks into many a receptive mind there to abide long after the perpetrators responsible have disappeared and their malodorous methods have been forgotten. And so long as the pamphlets and books issued remain extant in homes or in circulation their power of renewing prejudice or instigating future movements of hate subsists. In previous chapters we have evidenced how the bias of two leaders of anti-Catholic movements had been shaped in youth by just such propaganda which in their adult years asserted itself in aggressive action.

An indication of the vast amount of anti-Jewish defamations set afloat was furnished by Special Investigator Barker's testimony which dealt with the Pelley establishments. Barker's tabulation covered only part of the time these had been spewing pamphlets and other "literature." In the nineteen months ending July 31, 1938, Barker estimated, three and a half tons of such matter had been sent out in large bulk express shipments alone; most of it went to the Western Mountain States and to the Pacific Coast. A conservative estimate of the whole of such material distributed in one way or another by the Pelley concerns, Barker testified, would be 1,000,000 pieces a year. In its report the committee gave this general summation: "The groups and indi-

[29] Ibid., p. 22.

viduals engaged in this particular type of activity have turned out an almost unprecedented volume of literature of the most vicious kind with which they have flooded the United States in their efforts to secure supporters." Their efforts, the committee added, were "ably supplemented" by a mass of matter sent to them by foreign propaganda agencies in Germany and elsewhere." [30] Long resisting extradition, Pelley finally surrendered on October 24, 1941, to the Buncombe County, North Carolina, authorities. Pelley had shifted some of his activities to Noblesville, Indiana; a dispatch from that place on December 14, 1941, stated that *The Roll Call,* an anti-Semitic periodical published by him there for more than a year, had been suspended indefinitely.

Meanwhile Pelley was placed in North Carolina under a $10,000 bond for surety. He now had to face the consequences of his failing to observe the conditions of his suspended sentence in 1935. Before Judge F. Don Phillips, in the Superior Court, at Asheville, the Pelley case was given a full hearing, in the course of which the prosecution submitted correspondence between Pelley Publishers and alleged Nazi and Fascist agencies and individuals in Germany, Italy and England. Ordering Pelley to be placed in the county jail at once to ensure his appearance in court when sentence was passed, Judge Phillips was reported as saying: "That is the only way I can be sure he will be here." On January ·20, 1942, Judge Phillips sentenced Pelley to two to three years in prison, with the sentence of one to two years inflicted in 1935 to run concurrently.

Free while an appeal was being taken by him to the North Carolina Supreme Court, Pelley did not escape further proceedings. Dividing much of his time between Asheville and Noblesville, he published at the latter place *The Galilean,* successor to *The Roll Call.* Ironically enough his publishing house was named the Fellowship Press. Late in March, 1942, *The Galilean* was suspended when the Post Office Department declared recent issues were "non-mailable." On April 4, 1942, Pelley was arrested by Department of Justice agents while staying at the home of George B. Fisher, at Darien, Connecticut. Before the Dies committee in 1940, testimony had shown that, in a period of eighteen months, Fisher had

[30] Ibid.

given $20,000 to Pelley's Silver Shirts. Under orders from
U. S. Attorney General Biddle, conducting a campaign
against sedition, Department of Justice agents accused Pelley of having violated the Espionage Act by having in *The
Galilean* made false statements purported to interfere with
the success of the United States' military and naval forces
and thereby promote the success of its enemies. For conviction for this offence, the statute provides a maximum penalty
of not more than $10,000 fine, or imprisonment for not more
than twenty years or both. Pelley was held in $15,000 bail,
which he made no effort to obtain, and, waiving extradition,
was sped to stand trial at Indianapolis.

Upon arriving there, Pelley, in an interview at the marshal's office, manifested his characteristic exhibitionism. In
the interval, until lodged in jail, he "expanded statements of
his philosophies and smoked cigarettes in chain fashion."
He "willingly posed for photographs, amiably answered
most questions, and skilfully parried others." Now that his
periodicals were suspended, he still, he announced, published de-luxe metaphysical books which, however, were not
"authored by myself." [31] Complaining of discrimination in
the making of sedition charges against himself, he asserted
that he had done no more than Father Coughlin and various
commentators whom he named. What was his view of Hitler? Oblivious or indifferent to the mockery which his estimate would arouse, he regarded Hitler as trying to "set up a
United States of Europe to do away with tariff barriers and
racial prejudices." No, Pelley conceded, he would not treat
what he called the "Jewish problem" in America as it was
handled in Germany. But apparently or presumably having
somewhere in mind the ghettos established in Europe under
Hitlerian domination, Pelley proposed this as his remedy:
"The happier solution would be to have one city in each
State for Jews. Let them live there and run it and have their
own culture." A week later, Pelley was able to provide the
$15,000 cash bond required and was released from Marion
County jail. On June 9, 1942, Pelley and two of his associates
in the operation of the Fellowship Press, also the latter as a
corporation, were indicted by a Federal Grand Jury at Indianapolis for violating the anti-sedition statutes. This ac-

[31] *The Indianapolis Star*, April 6, 1942.

tion was based upon assertions in *The Galilean*. One of which the Government, with good reason, cited as "false and untrue" was this published in the issue of December 22, 1941: "We have, by every act and deed performable, aggressively solicited war with the Axis." Various counts charged Pelley and associates with having, while the United States was at war, printed reports and statements designed to interfere with the military and naval forces, with fomenting insubordination and obstructing recruiting.

The Supreme Court of North Carolina had, on June 24, 1942, affirmed the sentence which the Buncombe County court had passed upon Pelley. This conviction did not interfere with his trial for sedition a little later at Indianapolis. In opening the case, the Federal attorney branded Pelley as an enemy of the nation, and a Government analyst produced a digest of the Axis propaganda themes which Pelley had harped upon in his publication. The President of the United States was vilified, Great Britain was denounced, Nazi Germany praised, and as for the United States and the world they were "menaced by Communists, Jews and plutocrats." In fact, Pelley had represented the President as their pawn. The jury convicted Pelley, and on August 12, 1942, he was sentenced to serve fifteen years in prison; one of his associates to five years; and a fine of $5,000 was levied against the Fellowship Press.

Chapter XXVIII

BIRDS OF A FEATHER

AMONG the anti-Jewish organizations investigated by the Dies committee was the Knights of the White Camellia. In an earlier chapter we have brought out that this was one of the bodies allied with the Ku Klux Klan after the Civil War. Formed then by ex-Confederate officers, its head was General Bedford Forrest, and its concern was wholly that of maintaining the ascendency of the white race. Falling in with the epidemical movements against Jews sequential to Hitler's dominion, George E. Deatherage and a handful of other descendants of the original members resuscitated the Knights of the White Camellia, and in 1935 obtained a West Virginia charter of incorporation. Headquarters were in Deatherage's home at St. Albans in that State.

Despite the paucity of its first members, this newly fledged organization, within a few years, made the huge claim—at least for public effect—of its having 100,000 members.[1] Over this imputed array stood Deatherage with the florid title of Hon. Grand Commander. Yet when put upon the witness stand by the Dies committee on May 23, 1939, Deatherage declined to divulge the memberships lists, holding that he was under oath to his organization not to do so. Professing the aim of his organization as that of joining in a world-wide drive against "Jewish Communism," he, like so many others of his ilk, showed a ridiculous ignorance of Communism. This, he testified, "all over the world is hooked up with Jewish finance." He had, he further testified, discussed with Major General George Van Horn Moseley, U. S. A. (retired), the possibility of organizing an all-embracing national movement to combat "Jewish Communism." What, Deatherage was asked, did the General mean by concentrating

[1] See figures furnished to *The World Almanac*, 1941, p. 568.

on Jews? He meant, Deatherage stated, "a minority clique at the top of Jewry in which are identified the international bankers, the very same thing which has torn Europe upside down." [2] Deatherage was confronted with an article of his entitled "Will America Be Jewry's Waterloo?" which had been distributed by the World Service Organization from Erfurt, Germany. He had, he testified, only a hazy recollection of this document, but he did admit sending to that Nazi bureau ten copies of the Knights of the White Camellia publications.[3]

Installing himself as president, Deatherage had whiffed into being an embryonic organization to which he gave the comprehensive and imposing name of the American Nationalist Confederation. His object, he explained, was to unite in this all the various groups having the same aims. In the summer of 1938 he issued a call for a coalition of Christian organizations to meet at Kansas City, Missouri, on August 20th of that year. At this conference Deatherage loomed high in self-importance, and to show the extraordinary forces there represented he made vastly elastic claims. The organizations present, he asserted, had a membership of more than a million. This, the Dies committee later reported, "was found to be a terrific exaggeration." Urging the assemblage to operate in spectacular fashion, Deatherage advocated the adoption of the fiery swastika as its emblem. For, he argued, just as the Ku Klux Klan had been brought into greater effectiveness by the burning of the fiery cross, so this new formidable group would bring terror and fear into the hearts of many by burning a fiery swastika.[4]

Who were the elements to be intimidated by this proposed display? The Jew-baiters in attendance well knew, but Deatherage's mouthpiece, the American Nationalist Confederation, kept on spouting the policy to be followed. Thus a bulletin sent out by that self-styled organization mapped the course: "Fascism is defined as a patriotic revolt (much as the White Russians) against Jewocracy (alias democracy) and a return to statesmanship. Fascist (or patriotic rule) insists upon the duty of co-operation." [5] But if there was any

[2] *House Report No. 1476*, p. 3462.
[3] Ibid., pp. 3493-3495.
[4] *House Report No. 2*, p. 118.
[5] *House Report No. 1476*, Vol. 5, p. 3526. The claptrap of such pronounce-

one thing in which the motley groups visioned in the projected fusion could not co-operate it was in aligning themselves in a single organization. In another similar attempt, it will be recalled, the Dies committee had pointed out the reasons, and in this case it felt impelled to do so again. Since control of each group was vested in one domineering man or woman these autocrats could not efface themselves to make way for a supreme head to direct all of the groups. There was a further impassable barrier. In the event of a merger each group would have to stand the unthinkable fate of shutting off its intake of revenue.[6] The breakdown of Deatherage's aspirant plan left the American Nationalist Confederation as little more than a bare name; for as he later conceded in his testimony, it did not contrive to rise above the mere plane of a "letter-head" organization. So slight was the response of other bodies to it that Deatherage could not, as he testified, make more than "half-hearted contacts" with them. Such were his relations with Pelley's Silver Shirt Legion, the Militant Christian Patriots of Los Angeles, the National Gentile League,[7] the American Rangers and sundry other of such groups. With individuals carrying on campaigns much along his chosen lines Deatherage kept in touch. Among these was the obtrusive Rev. Gerald B. Winrod. Although he never had, he testified, dealings with the Rev. Charles E. Coughlin, Detroit priest, he lauded Coughlin's publication *Social Justice* as doing excellent work.

Before dealing with Winrod, it is advisable to present the sequel to Deatherage's activities. Early in America's war with Japan, Germany and Italy, Kenneth G. Crawford of the New

ments was evidenced by the fact, among other facts, that the term "White Russians" had become well-nigh obsolescent. It had been applied, after Czarism's overthrow, to supporters of that regime seeking to restore its rule. Some adventurers, cloaking their anti-Semitism under show of opposition to Communism, still paraded the term.

[6] *House Report No. 2*, p. 118.

[7] Only a few days after Deatherage testified, Secretary of the Interior Ickes, on May 29, 1939, refused permission to the National Gentile League, the headquarters of which were in Washington, D. C., to hold a three-day "Gentile rally" in the Sylvan Theater on the Washington Monument Grounds. The theater, Secretary Ickes tartly informed the applicants, belonged to all of the people of the United States, regardless of race, color or creed. According to its own statements, Ickes pointed out, the National Gentile League was "designed to foster, if not create, race prejudice against another group of American citizens." Under the slogan "Gentile supremacy vs. Communist slavery," the National Gentile League made an appeal to "Vote Gentile, buy Gentile."

York City daily newspaper *PM*, had discovered the fact that Deatherage, no longer head of the Knights of the White Camellia and the American Nationalist Federation, was working in a responsible engineering post for private contractors on a $30,000,000 expansion project at the Norfolk Naval Base. *PM* ran articles on Deatherage's career and testimony in its issues of February 15 to 20, 1942. The Dies committee at once communicated with Frank Knox, Secretary of the Navy, placing its records at the disposal of the Naval Intelligence Service. On February 23, 1942, after a prompt investigation, Secretary Knox, invoking the provisions of an article in the contract, held Deatherage to be "undesirable to have access to the work and/or materials of the Navy Department," and ordered his removal from his position on further naval work. However, it was reported, he was later employed as an engineer in the Army ordnance works. And now back to Winrod.

Trailing after Thomas E. Watson's methods, Winrod attacked both Jews and Catholics, bearing harder upon Jews, and also including Negroes in the range of his antagonism. Differing from Watson, he stretched his program of assault to comprise Protestant organizations and Free Masons. Inasmuch as no biography of him is contained in *Who's Who* or in any other ascertainable source, we shall have to glean such particulars of his early life as can be obtained from current newspaper accounts. In young manhood his father was a barkeeper; his mother was interested in Bible society work; and probably because of her influence, Winrod, Sr., graduated from serving liquor to becoming an evangelist in Wichita, Kansas. There Gerald was born; the date is given as 1898. Reflecting home environment, he flowered in his adolescence into a preacher. That later Gerald B. Winrod held the degree of Doctor of Divinity did not signify his having taken any regular theological course. This degree was accommodatingly conferred upon him, in 1935, by a California Baptist Seminary, and was primarily grounded upon his ascribed leadership in Christian journalism as editor of *The Defender Magazine*. This at the precise time when that publication was pre-eminently engaged in venting religious and racial hatred. Such were his services as "a distinguished minister of the Gospel"—a tribute also recorded in awarding the degree. He never, it seems, was attached to any pastorate, holding himself outside the orbit of any denomination. Various depictions of his early career agreed in representing it as one of modest if not straitened financial circumstances, dependent upon such collections as he was able to take up at his evangelical meetings.

However this might have been, he was in a position by 1925 to establish *The Defender Magazine*. At that period, it will be recalled, the contest of Fundamentalism vs. Modernism was sensationally in the limelight. Accordingly Winrod's publication foamed for Fundamentalism. He announced plans for a State-wide campaign for the passage of a law by Kansas prohibiting teaching of the theory of evolution in its public schools. But the excitement over this question wore away, and Winrod found a new outlet in the rising agitation against Communism and in connecting that economic system with the drift of the newly installed Administration of President Franklin D. Roosevelt. Winrod claimed that in all of his important undertakings he was under Divine direction, and pinnacled himself as gifted with prophetic powers.

In a screed written by him soon after President Roosevelt took office he attacked the New Deal and the President's so-called Brain Trust. He dealt seriatim with the members of this, darkly stressing the fact that three advisers were Jews. The Gog of the prophet Ezekiel he identified as Soviet Russia. In view of the present world conditions and of the great war assistance America is giving to Russia, Winrod's certitude in prophesying has its ironical interest. "Every genuinely informed student of eschatology," he wrote, "knows that Gog will eventually make war with the nations of the Western world. For this reason it is asinine to think of the United States entering upon a permanent merger of interests with Russia. Every effort in that direction will come to an ultimate end of uselessness." [8] Communism, Winrod declared in this pamphlet, was being subtly introduced and it must be eradicated from America. "The Christian element of our citizenry must be stirred out of its lethargy. . . . The time has come when America *must* be

---

[8] *Communism and the Brain Trust*, p. 23. Upon its publication by the Defender Publishers, Wichita, Kansas, in 1933, a sale of 36,000 was already claimed in this pamphlet.

visited by a great spiritual awakening, or our doom is sealed!" To avert this he proposed a general sending of letters to the President protesting against "the dictatorship which is evidently being created in Washington, contrary to our Constitution." Winrod also urged protests against the recognition by the United States of the Soviet Russian Government.

Briskly from the press of the Defender Publishers came forth ten volumes advertised in his magazine as *Gerald B. Winrod's Prophetic Books.* That 104,000 copies had been sold was the claim in April, 1934, in his magazine which importuned: "Make sure to read the entire series. They interpret current history in the light of Bible prophecy." And now what is encountered? All fair-minded Americans had supposed that Henry Ford's retraction had excluded further possibility, in the United States, at any rate, of any exploitation of the *Protocols* forgeries. One of Winrod's books, invidiously entitled *The Hidden Hand,* was thus advertised: "Many of the world's greatest thinkers believe that civilization is in the grip of an international conspiracy designed to overthrow all Gentile governments. This book discusses the *Protocols* from the angle of prophecy." [9]

So here the *Protocols* were disinterred to do their mephitic work. But how could Ford's complete retraction be disposed of? Winrod bridged the difficulty in this way: *"Dearborn Independent* articles. So many requests have been received for the exposure that appeared in Mr. Henry Ford's magazine a few years ago (before powerful Jews intimidated him) that Wichita Headquarters has secured a few copies of the volume published in England that contains the principle articles. The manner in which developments, during those intervening years, have confirmed these articles is one of the most amazing paradoxes of the present generation. The price of the book is $1.50." [10] Trusting Winrod's valuation of himself as an emissary of God, not a single follower questioned his word by asking him to disclose the names of some or all of those "powerful Jews."

In later issues of Winrod's magazine the *Protocols* were much featured. One leading article by him was entitled

[9] *The Defender Magazine,* April, 1934.
[10] Ibid.

"Israel's False Messianic Ideal. Latest Information on the *Protocols.*" This heroized Sergius A. Nilus as "the man who tried to save Russia from Antichrist."

In 1935 Winrod went to Germany—a not inexpensive trip, but he did not lack the funds. The result of that visit was shown, upon his return, in his ecstatic enthusiasm over Hitler. Winrod could see in the Democratic President Franklin D. Roosevelt only a fast maturing dictator, but he could not discern any autocracy in the all-absolute Hitler. In an article, "What I Saw in Germany," Winrod started by attacking Jews as mainly responsible for the French Revolution and for Communism. Then he dived into the subject in hand, which was nothing more or less than lauding Hitler as the supernal regenerator, the saintly soul who had purified a Germany defiled by Jewish immorality.

In the straining to multiply counts against Jews, one of the traditional charges in successive anti-Semitic outbreaks was to single them out as contaminators in the moral realm as well as despoilers in the business field. Refutation of this canard is not necessary, but, nonetheless, a brief survey of some realities is not supererogative. As attested by laws passed or other punitive measures taken, the codes of many a country showed the existence of gross indecency on the stage and otherwise in times when, by no stretch of bias, could the participants be classed as Jews. It is only facing an historic truism to remind ourselves that ever, from the most ancient times, vice has been resident in all races, peoples and countries. In this common respect the "Aryan" Germans did not lag. Not to go further back, scandals of sexual perversions in the upper castes in Germany broke into public attention before the First World War. As for regular prostitution in established brothels the German Government had long legalized it by a system of strict supervision which compelled all women inmates to be registered and medically examined. Every German city had its supply of brothels.[11] But outside of these was a swarm of floating prostitutes the extent of which was estimated at three times that of the registered. And such was the prevalence of extra-marital relations that the number of mistresses was supposed to be

[11] Statistics of registered prostitutes in 1900 showed 4500 in Berlin, 1021 in Breslau, 250 in Dresden, 733 in Hamburg, 500 in Cologne, 294 in Leipsic, 60 in Munich, etc.

considerably higher than the whole number of prostitutes. A law enacted in 1900 authorizing the police to send all prostitutes under the age of eighteen to an institution had, it was stated, some effect in reducing the number of women plying the traffic.

Consequences of the demoralization ensuing from the First World War and of the disproportion of men to women were felt in the various war-torn European countries. But the sequel was markedly evidenced in defeated Germany. Children born out of wedlock were a not uncommon occurrence, and bent upon the goal of replenishment of the population for draft of future soldiers, the German militarist cabal did not look with disfavor upon births under any conditions.

Chorusing Nazi calumnies, Winrod attributed the entire previous conditions of vice in Germany to Jewish origin and promotion. Winrod represented Hitler as appalled by Jewish licentiousness. In Germany, after the First World War "one of the first things that disgusted Hitler was that he discovered that centers of vice, nudist colonies, the filthy screen and stage as well as the poison literature, to be *under control and direction of an organization of Jews* who, for money, were willing to tear down the Gentile morals of the nation. The women saw the tide of mass immorality sweeping their country and organized to give defiant opposition to every form of unbridled lust. About this time Adolf Hitler appeared on the scene making a dynamic appeal to popular imagination. By degrees he won the confidence of the women and succeeded in enlisting their support behind his movement. They *came to him like an avalanche because his political philosophy provided for the* upbuilding of the moral standards of the nation . . ." [12] This of the man who in *Mein Kampf* and otherwise had proclaimed to the world his contempt for scruples and consistently followed that unprincipled course.

Not long after Winrod was putting the entire blame upon Jews in Germany for immoral conditions there, the Nazi press was virulently attacking Catholicism for the same responsibility. Forth, along the old trite lines, came a book *Kloster Leben (Life in the Cloister)* purporting to give a

[12] *The Defender Magazine*, March 15, 1935. Italics in the original.

picture of licentiousness in German convents and monasteries. Meanwhile, Nazi newspapers were descanting on the same charges, the fury of which increased when the Pope refused to comply with a Nazi Government demand to reprimand Cardinal Mundelein, of Chicago, for having referred to Hitler as "an Austrian paperhanger and a poor one at that." Such was the scandalously offensive language of Nazi organs in attacking the Catholic Church that the Vatican was moved to remonstrate.

Winrod's approval of the Nazis and his slur upon Jews as "Christ killers" were interlarded with articles reviling the Catholic Church and Jesuits in particular. The Catholic Church was "the harlot of the Bible." Jesuits were "correctly called the secret service department of the Pope." [13] Under the heading "Jesuits Oppose Constitution" came an enlargement upon Nazi mendacity which contented itself with 'the charge that Jews ran the American Government. Winrod's magazine expanded that charge. "Many observers," it averred, "believe that Jews and Jesuits are charting the course for the Roosevelt Administration." To which was added: "The Jesuit Order has many crimes against various governments to its credit." [sic] [14] Among the contributed articles was a croak by the Rev. S. L. Testa. "One scholar," he wrote, shrouding the identity of that putative authority, "has found that 75 per cent of the rites and ceremonies of the Roman Catholic Church are of pagan origin." [15] These extracts are only a very few of the long series of wildcat writings by Winrod and others in his publications. Apt occasion will presently arise to cite more of the output.

To how many readers was *The Defender Magazine* an acceptable diet? Conspicuously on the cover of that publication, issue of April, 1934, a circulation of 50,000 was claimed; in the September, 1935, issue, more than 70,000. A year later, 94,000 circulation was the number asserted.[16] For a time Winrod also published a periodical which, reflecting his self-accredited capacity as a seer, was suggestively named

[13] Ibid., August, 1935.
[14] Ibid., September, 1935.
[15] Ibid., February, 1936.
[16] N. W. Ayer & Sons' *Directory of Newspapers and Periodicals*, the most authoritative source for circulation statistics, refrained in the 1936 edition, p. 339, from giving any figures for *The Defender Magazine*.

The Revealer. Comprising a mass of books, tracts and pamphlets, Winrod's total manufacture of propaganda was great; up to this time the number of anti-Jewish pamphlets alone verged—if claims made are to be accepted—upon a circulation of nearly 100,000. The absorbers of his published matter were mainly the hidebound folk vegetating in small towns and rural sections, and the scope of influence embraced many States. Along with his publishing activities, Winrod exhibited, as an itinerant preacher, his evangelistic trait. Traveling distances throughout the country, he, in cities and towns, held "revivalist" meetings at which audiences were induced to lash themselves into hysteria. Craving the widest possible outlet, he made much use of the radio. To attach to himself a large sustentative group he formed the Defenders of the Christian Faith. These did not reach the solidity of a regular organization; they were nothing more than a roll of names on Winrod's mailing list, and neither dues were required nor membership cards issued. The sacred duty implicit in the Defenders of the Christian Faith was to exert themselves to forward the sale of Winrod's "literature" and not to be remiss in subscriptions or contributions.

From the Winrod headquarters there came, in the Presidential campaign of 1936, a string of assertions which even the most rabid Nazi commentator on American personages could not outstrip. Starting with President Franklin D. Roosevelt and going down the list, leading members of his Administration were lumped in the category of Jews, and all proponents of New Deal social security and other progressive measures were accused of being in secret league with "international Jewry that is seeking to dominate the Christian World." In the case of President Roosevelt there was concocted an elaborate chart purporting to demonstrate that his ancestors were all Jews. It was probably at this time that the President replied to a letter asking him if he were a Jew: "No, I'm not, but if I were I'd be proud of it."

Maintaining that he was doing God's work, Winrod, in the next year, sought to influence Congress as well as public opinion against President Roosevelt's plan for a reorganization of the Supreme Court of the United States. In a letter addressed "Dear Christian Friend," sent to members of Congress and mailed generally he held up the specter of the President's evolving into an "absolute dictator." Asking for 500,000 protests to pour in upon Washington, Winrod's letter, combining smugness with pious pretension, declared: *"The Defender Magazine* has the largest and most select group of Protestant readers in the United States. . . . There are indications that God has brought us together for just such a specific work at this particular time." Reading Winrod's letter in the U. S. Senate, on March 1, 1937, Senator Joseph T. Robinson commented: "It sounds like one of the old appeals from the Ku Klux Klan of years gone by. It is a deliberate effort to influence unfairly the minds of Senators and Representatives and to distort public opinion concerning the question at issue." [17] In a radio answer from Mexico, Winrod denied Senator Robinson's charge, and boasted that he "could get word to 20,000 pastors of churches of all denominations who are with me in this fight for democracy, and three-fourths of them will take this fight into the pulpit Sunday if I think it necessary." [18]

Early in 1937 Winrod had embarked upon a project which he thought would make him a national fashioner of rural thought touching events in Washington. There he established the Capitol News and Feature Service to supply his interpretation to country newspapers. The venture proved a failure and soon passed away. His ambitions in no wise discouraged, Winrod, in 1938, set out to gain, in the Kansas primary, the Republican nomination for U. S. Senator. A group of Kansas ministers demanded that he withdraw his candidacy, and evidently anticipating that he would make smooth professions to the voters, issued a pamphlet giving the evidence of his indiscriminate bigotry by incorporating photostatic copies of articles in the Winrod publications. One article thus shown charged Postmaster-General Farley with trying to subjugate the United States to Rome. "Being a Roman Catholic," the slur went on, "his first allegiance is to the temporal ruler of the Vatican, a certain Mr. Pious." Other photostatic copies reproduced Winrod calumnies against Jews and Free Masons, and an assault upon the Federal Council of Churches as a "Protestant papacy." The

[17] *Congressional Record,* 75th Congress, 1st Session, p. 1658.
[18] *The New York Times,* March 3, 1937.

pamphlet could have enlarged upon Winrod's vilification of all Protestant organizations and periodicals condemning his bigotry; in his *Defender Magazine* they were aspersed either as "fronts" for Jewry, or for "Jewish Communism." Winrod had attacked organized labor. In a protest, the National Association for the Advancement of Colored People had charged that Winrod had labeled it a Communistic organization. Winrod's nomination, the ministerial pamphlet further declared, would be disastrous to the Republican Party. "If Winrod is not a Fascist and Nazi, why does his *Defender* read like a directory of pro-Nazi and pro-Fascist groups in America, carrying the advertising and announcements of those organizations?"

Winrod's electioneering methods were a spectacle. He was now thirty-nine years old, paunchy, bald and self-complacent in vociferating piety. Traversing Kansas with a sound-amplifier-equipped truck, he would open his meetings with the strains of "Onward Christian Soldiers," and he would invite the rurals: "Come on up, come on up and shake my hand, shake the hand of a Christian and a man of God." At both these meetings and in his radio talks he sought to persuade the voters that he was not the bigot which his publications seemed to demonstrate. No, was his assurance, he was a man of gentle tolerance for everybody and everything except the New Deal. He so succeeded in impressing responsive rustics that the betting on his chances was decidedly in his favor.

The liberal-minded of every kind in Kansas were alarmed. William Allen White, noted and outspoken editor of the *Gazette* at Emporia, in that State, and a nationally known author, had shown his courage in opposing the Ku Klux Klan, in 1924, when both Republicans and Democrats in Kansas straddled the issue. Now White wrote a long advertisement which he ran in his own paper, and at his expense placed in other Kansas papers. This advertisement denounced Winrod for his use and sale of the spurious *Protocols,* for his reviling of Jews, and for his attacks upon Catholics, Negroes, leading Protestant bodies and organized labor. "To nominate him," White remonstrated, "we must defend his position as a peddler of racial and religious hatred—the Nazi position, in short." White's plea was followed by a formal statement from John D. Hamilton, himself a Kansan, and now chairman of the Republican National Committee, at Washington, D. C. Telling how in his public life in Kansas, in 1924-1928, he himself had been opposed by the Ku Klux Klan, Hamilton's statement went on: "Once again intolerance has raised its head in the midst of our political picture, and the voters of our State cannot avoid the issue whether they will or no. . . . We have all been shocked by the manifestations of intolerance going on in the world elsewhere, and we should be more than shocked at its appearance on our very doorstep and therefore doubly vigilant. . . . I certainly would not vote for anyone who had dedicated himself to a course of intolerance such as has Mr. Winrod." Hamilton asked Kansas voters to consider the possible disastrous effects which his nomination would have upon the entire Republican Party.

Answering Hamilton over the radio Winrod produced his story. He had been told, he said, that a million dollars would be available from Eastern sources to try to consummate his defeat, "which money is now being unloaded in Kansas." [19] Another version of his remarks was that attacks upon him were being financed by a slush fund poured into Kansas by Communists and other enemies.[20] Considering that in Kansas $15,000 spent in a primary campaign was regarded as a large sum, Winrod's imputations were derided by well-informed Kansans as an effort to appear important. Judged by Kansas standards his own expenses were not slight. Toward the final phase of the campaign the tactics of his many campaign workers centered upon exalting him as a martyr in a holy cause.

In a contest of four candidates, Winrod slumped to third place, although the sizable vote he received was disquieting to all elements opposing bigotry. Of progressive views, former Governor Clyde M. Reed, of Parsons, Kansas, emerged from the primary vote as victor. The grudge borne by Winrod against William Allen White was all the more edged when, later in the same year, White enrolled himself in a Journalists' Fund to aid Grynzspan, and announced the formation of a Provisional Committee Against Anti-Semitism.

[19] Ibid., July 23, 1938.
[20] New York Post, July 29, 1938.

Winrod lost no opportunity to spill his splenetic ire, reaching some years later such a crescendo of abuse and untruth
as: "William Allen White, the well-known literary clown
who pulls chestnuts out of the fire for international Jewry in
Kansas politics." [21]

During the months when Winrod was seeking to inject
himself into the U. S. Senate, another trial was made to
amalgamate all of the many anti-Jewish organizations and
propaganda agencies. Getting wind of this move, the Descendants of the American Revolution, issued from their
New York City headquarters, on July 2, 1938, a warning.
There was a design, this announced, to merge organizations
masquerading as ultra-patriotic into a "patriotic" confederation. All really patriotic bodies were urged publicly to reject
membership in a coalition promoted and inspired by such
proponents of hatred and intolerance as Moseley, Kuhn,
Winrod, Deatherage, Pelley, Robert Edmondson, James
True, Gerald Smith, Henry Allen and others.[22]

The actual account of this attempt was disclosed by Allen's testimony before the Dies committee. Allen had been a
former Silver Shirt Legion functionary, then organizer of
the American White Guard. Mrs. Louise Fry, otherwise
Paquita Louise de Shishmaroff, at the time, was head of the
Militant Christian Patriots. The Dies committee report described her as the "mysterious international figure who has
since fled the country." She, Allen testified, had financed an
extensive trip he made throughout the United States. Allen
did not know the source of the money she had given him.
He visited Winrod, Deatherage, Kuhn, True, publisher of
the so-styled *Industrial Control Reports* at Washington,
D. C., and Edmondson whose *Economic Service* was another
floodgate of anti-Jewish pamphlets and weekly letters. Un-
fruitful was a talk Allen had with Ku Kluxer Hiram W.
Evans who, Allen testified, said he "was not interested in the
idea."

Nominally anti-Communist, the convention was held in
August, 1938, at the German-American Bund's headquarters
at Los Angeles. The participants were more minor than
major figures in anti-Jewish movements. Present were Ken-

[21] *The Defender Magazine*, August, 1941.
[22] *The New York Times*, July 3, 1938.

neth Alexander, Southern California leader of the Silver Shirt Legion; J. H. Peyton, of the American Rangers; Charles B. Hudson, of Omaha, Nebraska, organizer and leader of America Awake; Mrs. Fry; and a nondescript lot of representatives of Italian, Russian and other anti-Semitic organizations. On the convention's tables was spread "literature" issued by the German-American Bund, Pelley, Deatherage, Mrs. Fry and Edmondson. Itself largely occupied with probing into Communist activities in America, the Dies committee could detect no trace of the convention's pretended aim of gathering to oppose Communism. The fact was clear to it, reported this committee, "that this convention was in no sense an anti-Communist convention, but rather another of the series of attempts to unite some of the various forces of intolerance, racial hatred, Nazism and Fascism to achieve greater influence in the United States. This effort, like others of the kind, yielded no apparent results." [23]

[23] Report No. 1476, pp. 17-18.

CHAPTER XXIX

ANTI-SEMITISM VIA FATHER COUGHLIN

UNLIKE similar movements emanating from Protestant bigots, there came, in the summer of 1938, a priest-led agitation
against Jews. It by no means represented the Catholic
Church's attitude or had its endorsement. It was the individual promotion of Father Coughlin who had already managed to make himself known to great numbers of people by
several years of radio discourse on banking institutions,
Communism and the New Deal. Of Irish lineage he was the
son of a workingman who was born in Indiana and who in
maturity had obtained a job as sexton of the cathedral at
Hamilton, Ontario. Educated in a parochial school there,
and later taking a course in the University of Toronto,
Charles E. Coughlin then studied for the priesthood, was
ordained, served in that capacity in Ontario, and was transferred to the Detroit diocese.

With his assignment to the Royal Oak parish, in Michigan, in 1926, he commenced his series of radio addresses.
These at first were of a discursive nature without any particular character. Nevertheless, impressed by a priest thus
talking to them over the ubiquitous radio, hosts of Catholics wrote letters of approval to him. Thus furnished with an
index to the support that he could command, Coughlin set
out to obtain funds for his project of building the Shrine of
the Little Flower, and in its name organized the Radio
League. The bill for his weekly expense of broadcasting was
large, but the multitude of letters, many enclosing contributions for the new shrine or to help defray radio costs,
stimulated Coughlin to widen his radio outlet.

In the 1932-1935 period he commingled high praise of
the New Deal with denunciations of financiers and capitalistic exploitation, presently turning his attention to con-

demnations of Communism. Veering, in 1936, from President Franklin D. Roosevelt's New Deal measures, he made bitter personal attacks upon the President and, at the same time, indulged in outright political activities by supporting in the Presidential election, a third-party ticket headed by Representative William Lemke. Coughlin publicly avowed that if he could not swing at least 9,000,000 voters to Lemke, he would "quit broadcasting educational talks on economics and politics."

Coughlin's political polemics and his inveighings against President Roosevelt caused serious concern at the Vatican and among American Catholic prelates. There was a hint of possible disciplinary action. For having, in a speech, called President Roosevelt a "liar," Coughlin found it advisable to make public an apology he had written.[1] The *Osservatore Romano*, which indicated the Vatican's opinions, repeatedly criticized Coughlin's course as all the more improper because it came from a priest. Despite which, Coughlin persisted in his personal attacks upon President Roosevelt whom he was quoted as describing as "anti-God," and in the same speech as having advocated the use of force "when an upstart dictator in the United States succeeds in making a one-party government and when the ballot is useless." For this attributed suggestion of revolution, Coughlin was publicly and severely rebuked by Archbishop John T. McNicholas, of Cincinnati.[2] Two months later, at the prompting of Bishop Gallagher, of Detroit, his immediate superior, Coughlin made a public apology for having called President Roosevelt a "scab President."[3] In a total popular vote of 45,646,817, Lemke's vote was 882,479. Coughlin now announced that "in the best interests of all of the people" he was withdrawing from all radio activity.

Instead, however, of taking such a step, he increased the number of his radio stations. Holding Jews responsible for existing woes, he now began a campaign against them, under cover of attacking them as Communists. Auxiliary to his radio harangues was his weekly paper *Social Justice*, founded in 1936. This publication attained an immense circulation accelerated by a multitude of fanatical devotees who, armed

---

[1] Dispatch from Detroit, *The New York Times*, July 24, 1936.
[2] *The New York Times*, September 26, 1936.
[3] Ibid., November 1, 1936.

with copies, stood at crowded centers in many cities and importuned passers-by. Adroitly courting the support of what were termed the "underprivileged classes" and at the same time playing upon prejudice aroused against Jews, Coughlin combined a number of designs in a full-page "appeal" in his organ. A Christian Front, this urged, was needed to force industrial capitalism to yield to labor a fair share of its wealth. Such an organization was also required "to curb the Molochs of international finance." The proposed Christian Front would "never compromise with Communism, Fascism, Nazism or any other movement tending to destroy representative Government." Having thus in the "appeal" posited himself as an arch champion of democracy, Coughlin came to the direct instigation: "A Christian Front which will not fear to be called 'anti-Semitic' because it knows the term 'anti-Semitic' is only another pet phrase of castigation in Communism's glossary of attacks." [4]

In brazen despite of the *Protocols* having been exploded as a fraud, Coughlin set out to utilize them as ammunition. Article after article was signed by him in his priestly character as "Father Coughlin." In an introductory onslaught he made this representation: ". . . The book *The Protocols of the Meetings of the Learned Elders of Zion* is preeminently a Communist program to destroy Christian civilization. The best rebuttal which the modern leaders of Zion can offer to the authenticity of the *Protocols* is to institute a vigorous campaign against Communism." [5] A week later, in

[4] *Social Justice*, July 25, 1938. Passingly, it may be remarked of Coughlin, that he was said—although with what basis we do not know—to possess one of the most comprehensive anti-Semitic libraries in the world.

[5] Ibid., July 18, 1938. The persistent use of *The Protocols of the Elders of Zion* convinced a group of American professors, much later, that it was anew needful to investigate and report upon this "document." Heading the group was Dr. John Shelton Curtiss, author-historian, and the study was published, on May 6, 1942, by the Columbia University Press. Thirteen leading historian-professors concurred in Dr. Curtiss' findings which were based largely upon an examination of French and Russian writings from which, as heretofore set forth, the plagiarism was taken. The investigation, Dr. Curtiss' conclusions declared, showed that the *Protocols* established "beyond doubt the fact that they are rank and pernicious forgeries." In addition to proofs of this long before published, as we have previously noted, by the *Times*, of London, and by other authorities, Dr. Curtiss expressed the view that certain passages in the *Protocols* were more appropriate to the world of a later date than to the world of 1897 when that "document" was supposed to have been discovered. Also, Dr. Curtiss questioned whether alleged Zion leaders would have been so foolhardy as to write their imputed plans, and, he concluded, the *Protocols* were merely what their drafters assumed to be the Jewish character.

an article, "The Protocols of Zion," Coughlin resumed his attack, this time accompanying it with a box note by the "editors." Apparently to meet derisive criticisms that the exploitation of the *Protocols* was nothing but the impudent revival of a hoax, the "editors" claimed that they expressed no opinion as to the validity of the *Procotols*. "But," they sinuously went on, "we cannot ignore the news value of their strikingly prophetic nature . . . the *Protocols*—either by coincidence or design—call the turn on events transpiring many decades after their alleged authorship. Is this accident or plot?"

Dealing with the age-long persecution of Jews, Coughlin, in his article, gave a conglomeration of explanations which inferentially were advanced as justifications. "The reasons for their being persecuted are many. Their ancestors crucified Christ, as the Gospels assert." Here we break in to note the commonplace historical fact that long before Christ's advent prejudice against Jews was manifested by their enslavement in ancient Egypt, and their attempted extinction by Haman in Persia in the fifth century B.C. Jewish refusal to worship pagan gods was converted by the Roman historian Tacitus into a declaration against "the horrid superstitions of the Jews." To resume with Coughlin: "They [the Jews] steadfastly maintained that they were the chosen people, which claim offended the intelligence of all other peoples." At this very time the Germans were, as we have seen, placing themselves on the apex of humans as *the* master and incomparable race, and Coughlin's propaganda against Jews was not much removed from that used in Germany. For he went on with this sweeping arraignment of Jews: "Their nationality was internationalism in its final analysis; and finally they became identified with the gold hoarders and wealth concentrators of the world. It is true that the titles of 'money bags' and 'gold calfers' have been identified with Jews because from time immemorial they were expert at hoarding gold and lending money at interest—yes, lending gold receipts at interest which were not backed by real gold." Then giving them the weight of his priestly authority, Coughlin printed quotations from Protocols No. 20 and No. 21, advising readers to consider them carefully.[6]

[6] Ibid., July 25, 1938.

Two premises here arrest attention. Accepting Coughlin's appraisement of himself as having expert knowledge of finance and economics, his legion of uninformed hearers and readers believed the stuff he ladled out. His adherents were not intelligent Catholics but those of meager education, stunted understanding, highly credulous and totally unacquainted with the outstanding facts of American financial history, not to speak of that of other countries.

Decades before Jews had undertaken the business of banking, the operations of the monopolistic Bank of the United States, headed by Nicholas Biddle, were a national scandal. Not to mention further scandals of banking practices we come to the exhaustive investigation made by a Congressional (Pujo) committee in 1912. Of the five foremost banking institutions in which the control of money and credit in the United States was concentrated, only one was Jewish.[7] Certainly, even the most grasping Jewish banker could not have exceeded the record of George F. Baker's First National Bank of New York. As to this the evidence showed, the Pujo committee reported: "From 1889 to 1901 dividends were paid at the rate of 100 per cent per annum on a capital stock of $500,000. In 1901 there was a dividend of $10,750,-000—2,150 per cent—$9,500,000 of which was declared for the purpose of increasing the capital stock to $10,000,000." On this inflated stock dividends, from 1902 to 1912, varied from 20 to 38 per cent, reaching in one year—1908—126 per cent.[8] Little wonder that this first George F. Baker—a son was of the same name—could leave an estate valued at $73,209,683.

In 1933 another searching set of disclosures was supplied, as the result of its investigation, by the U. S. Senate Committee on Banking and Currency. Evidence showed the far-reaching ramifications of interests centered in the firm of J. P. Morgan & Co., and its affiliate, Drexel & Co. Members of these concerns were directors of eighty-nine banks and corporations, with total assets of $20,000,000,000. Morgan

[7] This was Kuhn, Loeb & Co. The other banking houses in the group were J. P. Morgan & Co.; First National Bank of New York; National City Bank of New York; Lee, Higginson & Co., of Boston and New York; Kidder, Peabody & Co., of Boston and New York. See *Report of the Committee to Investigate the Concentration of Control of Money and Credit*, February 28, 1913, p. 56.
[8] Ibid., pp. 66-67.

partners were directors in these companies: fifteen bank and trusts, ten railroads, thirteen public utility holding or operating, thirty-eight industrial, six insurance, and seventeen miscellaneous holding companies. Such were the interlocking corporate relationships of but one of the large banking houses, others of which likewise had their widespreading tentacles.[9] A separate survey of the National City Bank of New York, for example, showed that it held forty-one directorships in other banks, 104 in miscellaneous companies; forty-four in insurance companies, 102 in manufacturing companies, twenty-nine in transportation companies, 115 in public-utility corporations.

The plethora of evidence before the Senate committee showed in detail the unscrupulous transactions and insatiable greed of some of the foremost bankers. Nearly all of these, it is not irrelevant to remark, considering the point in question, were Christians, and not a few were privately animated by anti-Semitic bias. Dealing with these "many bankers," the Senate committee in its summary related how they had promoted or allied themselves with great stock-jobbing schemes to ensnare and loot the public. In all too restrained a way the committee thus described the orgy of plundering: "Personages upon whom the public relied for the guardianship of funds did not regard their position as impregnated with trust, but rather as a means for personal gain. These custodians of funds gambled and speculated for their own account in the stock of the banking institutions which they dominated; participated in speculative transactions in the capital stock of their banking institutions that directly conflicted with the interests of those institutions they were paid [high salaries] to serve; participated and were the beneficiaries of pool operations [in the Stock Exchange]; bestowed benefits of 'preferred lists' [in awarding stock at low prices] upon individuals who were in a position to aid and abet their plans"—and committed many other specified malefactions. Having pocketed their booty, these bankers "resorted to devious means to avoid the payment of their just Government taxes." [10]

[9] *Stock Exchange Practices, Hearings before the U. S. Senate Committee on Banking and Currency*, 1933, Part 2, pp. 904-907, *et seq.*
[10] Ibid., p. 186.

These excerpts are a mere fragment of the total findings in the Senate committee's report, but they give a tolerably sufficient picture of conditions. Coughlin could hardly have been unaware of the revelations or of the particular bankers incriminated, so wide and constant was the publicity given to the hearings. Nor could he have been ignorant of the fact that it was the practices thus exposed which led to the passage of drastic regulatory laws. Furthermore, as pertained to wealth concentration in another field, on February 20, 1931, the report of Walter M. Strawn, special counsel to the House of Representatives Committee on Interstate and Foreign Commerce, showed how America's railroad mileage was controlled by a few powerful families, all Christian. By ownership of large blocks of stock, fifteen major groups held mastery over 210,000 miles or nearly 85 per cent of railroad lines. High in the beneficiary families were the Vanderbilt, Harriman, Whitney, Widener, Baker, Jr., Harkness, Arthur Curtiss James, and Fahnestock.

While, à la Nazi, Coughlin was singling Jews exclusively as avaricious for wealth, Nazi leaders were swooping upon opportunities in Germany, Austria and elsewhere and demonstrating their gluttony for riches and splendor by turning up as owners of "liquidated" Jewish and other expropriated businesses and estates. From time to time uncontradicted accounts in American publications gave an insight into the matchless rapacity of this band of Nazi upstarts. The verification of these accounts was seen in the way in which Göring, Goebbels, Himmler and confederates transmuted themselves into moguls of wealth, variously possessing important businesses or taking over mansions, city estates, villas or castles in which they blazoned in palatial style. Göring became a leading banker and branched out as a plutocrat having a share in dozens of factories. Especially, numbers of Jewish businessmen, dispossessed and disfranchised, now had to endure the grim sight of their oppressors and calumniators installing themselves as successors and gorging on the spoils.

Supplementing the frequent accounts of the high-pressure acquisitiveness of Nazi deputy leaders, there later came a series of confirmatory details from a noted German who was in a particularly advantageous situation to observe. This was Fritz Thyssen, Germany's steel magnate. He had helped finance the Nazi movement in its preliminary stages, and carefully noted its course after its attaining power. Later he was repelled by its excesses and was proscribed. He had to flee, but before the Nazi secret police managed to seize him at Cannes, France, and spirit him away to a fate unknown, he had written a book which was published in the United States.[11]

Besides vesting in themselves Jewish and other properties, Hitler's deputy leaders battened upon other sources of revenue which patently came under the head of systematic blackmail and graft. Necessarily, having iron control of every channel of publicity in their dominions, they succeeded there in concealing their devious operations from general knowledge. Nevertheless, outside of Germany came rumors of high Nazi officials smuggling vast sums out of that country and causing them to be deposited in American and other banks. It remained for this to be proved, as it was, in a trial in the Federal Court, in New York City, on January 10, 1941. The proceeding was a criminal action against one Lee Lane, whose real name was Isidore Lazarus, for passport frauds. Of Rumanian birth, he had come to America in 1900, where later for some years he pursued a life of crime, served prison terms, and returned to Europe in 1923. This was the type of Jew that high-ranking members of the Nazi Government did not hesitate to employ as their intermediary. As tallied from information gathered by an unnamed foreign agency, by the U. S. Department of State, and by other investigators, the transactions, as Assistant U. S. Attorney Richard J. Burke informed the court, were conducted on these lines: Before they left Germany such refugees as had scraped cash together were persuaded by Lazarus to turn it over to him. He, meantime, had made with Göring, Goebbels and other Nazi functionaries arrangements by which the refugees, upon reaching other countries, would receive only a small part of their cash, the remainder being deposited to the credit of the Nazi officials concerned. Judging from Burke's explanation of the disposition of these

[11] As a vivid and contemporaneous historical document, throwing much light upon Nazi banditry, Thyssen's book, *I Paid Hitler*, deserves wide reading.

funds, some portion was used for propaganda and espionage in various countries. Lazarus maintained that the money was for the personal use of those officials. He was sentenced to two years in prison and a fine of $2,500.[12] The testimony in this case furnished a definite glimpse into the multifarious ways by which Nazi chieftains had been and were hugely enriching themselves.[13] No means of exaction was left untapped.

In all of this particular predacity Hitler was not personally involved, but his lack of participation did not by any means imply lack of awareness of what his aides were doing. He was already on the summit of wealth from the ceaseless deluge of revenues brought by the stupendous sale of his book and increasingly from his publishing monopoly. According to the "Literary Supplement" of the *Times*, of London, Hitler was actually sole owner of the Zentral Verlag. Having absorbed its competitors, this business reached the point where it published all Nazi party books and periodicals, controlled almost all news bureaus and owned most advertising agencies. An estimate set forth by the foregoing "Literary Supplement," early in 1942, placed the Zentral Verlag's annual turnover at $280,000,000, and its yearly net profit was computed at between $28,000,000 and $40,000,000. Hitler well knew how to combine amassing of personal wealth with power, and the pertinent question occurs: as dictator, he was assuredly a mighty privileged character above the reach of all law, and as such what taxation did he, or his all-embracing publishing house, pay at a time when Germany and the peoples of conquered countries were loaded down with yokes of taxation?

[12] See full account in the *The New York Times*, January 11, 1941.
[13] Having married into a rich family, Joachim von Ribbentrop, Nazi Foreign Minister, was the one Nazi official who had not been poor when his party came into power. This fact, however, according to specific accusation from several sources, did not preclude his clutching more riches. In a German program to which it invited his attention, the British Broadcasting Corporation, on August 2, 1941, reiterated previously published statements that he had smuggled 38,960,000 marks out of Germany, and related how, when Gustav von Remitz (a nephew of Fritz Thyssen) had refused to sell his Salzburg castle to von Ribbentrop, Remitz was sent to a concentration camp where his death (Thyssen openly charged from assassination) soon happened. Ribbentrop then became owner of the castle. These radio accusations, with accompanying trenchant comments on Ribbentrop's career and methods, were widely published, and no denial was forthcoming.

Coughlin resorted to many acrobatics of explanation seeking to justify his constant flaunting of the *Protocols*. Above all of his windings and wrigglings stood out the fact that he was determined to make capital out of those counterfeits. Faced by the reality that they were such, he, in one of his many signed articles, circumvented this vital point by assuming that there must be a connection between them and a condition he imagined. "Although," he insinuatingly wrote, "Nilus gave no proof for the authenticity of the work and although Jews at various conventions have repudiated the *Protocols* as a forgery, nevertheless a correspondence between the prophecy contained in this book and its fulfillment is too glaring to be set aside or obscured." The implication here was that the exposé came from Jews as interested parties, whereas, as we have shown, it came first from the *Times,* of London. "However," Coughlin's article further asserted, "The authors of *The Protocols of the Wise Men of Zion* did outline a plot and this plot has, in part, been carried out in our own day—a plot against Christian civilization." [14] Hence, the inference was to be drawn, the "plot" must have come from Jews.

Again, while further quoting the *Protocols,* he took shelter behind the disclaimer: "At the outset we may repeat emphatically that we are not concerned with the authenticity of the *Protocols* attributed to the Wise Men of Zion." None the less he was bent upon publishing and advertising the contents of those same *Protocols,* the validity of which he could not affirm. What were his objects in doing so?

Presenting himself as a crusader against injustice, economic wrongs and an alien social system, he explained his purpose as threefold. He sought to have all peoples know that tyranny, oppression and poverty were "the result of planning, for the most part, by men who hate and detest the Christian principle of brotherhood and the Christian economics of plenitude."

The knowing reader could aptly have asked just when, during the many centuries of dominant Christian religion in large parts of the world, those principles had been transmitted into action? Doubtless because of scathing criticism, Coughlin, in itemizing his second object, did a balancing

[14] *Social Justice,* August 1, 1938.

act. Having an opportune awakening to the existence of Christian financial buccaneers, he seemed to endow himself with a quality of fairness by "encouraging the mass of Jews to join with us in opposing the Jew money changers as well as the Gentile money changers." And he, who only shortly before had urged the formation of an anti-Semitic Christian Front (which soon materialized as a wide-flung Jew-baiting organization), put forth his third object. As if to suggest that Jews were the passive or active supporters of Communism, Coughlin insolently "invited the Jews to become militant, together with the Gentiles, against the spread of Communism with as much vigor as they oppose Fascism or any other foreign 'ism'." [15]

At this time responsible Catholic publications were severely denouncing Coughlin's course, and at least one, *The Catholic Herald,* made analagous reference to the results of just such propaganda in Germany and Austria. Feelingly telling of "the great and revolting persecutions of Jews" in those countries, an editorial in that publication declared: ". . . For anti-Semitism the Catholic has less excuse than anyone else. One has but to read the writings of a man like Streicher to realize to what depths this anti-Semite passion can drag a man. That any Christian should come within range of such a bestial attitude to his fellow man is a monstrous thing." The editorial proceeded to make a demarcation. Seeking to ward off dangers which might come from "the Jewish mentality" in either acquiring wealth control or displaying itself in revolutionary doctrines, or in both ways, was one thing. "It is quite a different thing to persecute the race as such, to make life miserable for all Jews because they are Jews, to hound them out of a country without making any provision for them, to attribute all evils to Jewish origins, and, above all, for Catholics to forget that Jews are our brothers, who, even when they are acting against the truth, specially benefit under Our Lord's prayer, 'Father, forgive them, for they know not what they do'." Scouting Coughlin's use of the *Protocols, The Observer,* official organ of the diocese of Rockford, Illinois, stated: "Crazy forgeries like the *Protocols* will not in the end hurt the Jews."

[15] Ibid., August 8, 1938.

Considering that he had to make some reply to such criticisms, Coughlin now performed another gyration. Called to account, he admitted that the vast majority of Jews were "guiltless of the social sin of exploitation and concentration of wealth." Of what, then, were Jews guilty? He advanced this indictment: "Nevertheless, because Jews reject Christ, it is impossible for them to accept his doctrine of spiritual brotherhood in the light in which Christians accept it," [16] and of which Father Coughlin essayed to stand forth as the unrivalled expounder and exemplar, seeing that soon his organ made this unqualified announcement: "The only unbiased source of truth is Father Coughlin." [17]

Over his own signature, Coughlin, in an article "The Fifth Protocol," evaded the crucial point by taking cover under this notification: "I emphasize once more that I am not interested in the authenticity of the *Protocols*. I am interested in their factuality." [18] Presuming on the witlessness of his readers as well as on his own sacerdotal standing, Coughlin boldly plunged into casuistry. Then, to bolster the claim that he gave the other side a hearing, his organ went through the form of allowing an answer in "The Truth About the Protocols," by Philip Slomovitz, editor of *The Detroit Jewish Journal*. Slomovitz set forth the reminder that their fraudulent character had been positively proved; they were an outrageous anti-Semitic forgery, and no tie could be made between these falsities and Communism; additionally that Jews were essentially anti-Communist was a fact.[19] Again eluding the matter of the *Protocols'* genuineness, came, a week later, an article having the same title by one signing himself "Ben Marcin, Social Justice Writer." Protecting himself, he acknowledged having been *warned by Father Coughlin to avoid any effort to prove the authenticity of the* Protocols because no one is interested in the identity of the author, whereas everyone is interested in the contents of the book written by the unknown author." [20] To give credibility to his consecutive attacks upon Jews "Ben Marcin" made claim of being a Jew. But, in his exten-

[16] Ibid., August 22, 1938.
[17] Ibid., November 14, 1938.
[18] Ibid., August 29, 1938.
[19] Ibid., September 26, 1938.
[20] Ibid., October 3, 1938. Italics in the original.

sive investigation later of the activities of Coughlin and *Social Justice,* John L. Spivak could find no trace of any "Ben Marcin," and had to dismiss him as non-existent.[21]

There is no need of giving further examples of Coughlin's tergiversations of propaganda. Admissions wrested from him were counteracted by a network of recurrent animadversions upon Jews. It was the repetition and totality of these which sank into the dim minds of his supine following, too many of whom were already soaked with bigotry. When, on the most manifest grounds of salutary public policy, one large radio broadcasting company refused to renew its contract with Coughlin, and another large company declined to make a contract with him, his organ construed these rebuffs as the work of Jews. These, was now the representation, controlled big broadcasting companies, as they did banking and much else. In effect Coughlin was thus posed as a victim of Jewish power and suppression. Implicitly believing this to be so, many of his followers replied with more contributions enabling him to establish his own ramification of stations reaching large parts of America. Because Coughlin was a priest, large numbers of his adherents assumed that he spoke and wrote in the name and behoof of the Catholic Church. Puzzled by the omission of Coughlin's immediate superior, the bishop of the diocese, to institute disciplinary steps, other persons raised the question of whether Coughlin actually had the Church's backing.

Cardinal Mundelein, of Chicago, was moved to clarify the precise situation. His statement, issued on December 11, 1938, and read over a nation-wide radio broadcast by Vicar-General and Bishop Sheil of Chicago, disseminated this information: "His Eminence, George, Cardinal Mundelein, of Chicago, having been importuned by news commentators and correspondents from every section of the country in reference to the broadcasts of Father Coughlin, of Detroit, makes the following statement: 'As an American citizen, Father Coughlin has the right to express his personal views

---

[21] Spivak wrote that he had "a complete list of all payments made for articles and no payments ever were made to 'Ben Marcin'." According to Spivak the articles purporting to be "Marcin's" were written by E. Perrin Schwartz editor and Joseph Patrick Wright, one of the staff of *Social Justice.* Spivak's series were entitled, "Charles E. Coughlin, a Documented Exposé." The article in which he thus disposed of "Marcin" was published in *The New Masses,* December 5, 1939.

on current events, but he is not authorized to speak for the Catholic Church, nor does he represent the doctrines or sentiments of the Church.' " [22]

Apparently, this notification did not detach from Coughlin many of his special following, which, looking up to him as a priest, accepted anything he said as having sufficient weight of itself. How large was that following? Reporting on the organizations it did investigate, the Dies committee concluded that, on the evidence before it, "not over 1,000,-000 people in the United States can be said to have been seriously affected" by the un-American activities of such bodies.[23] But the Dies committee had not investigated Coughlin's propaganda mill nor did it inquire into the developing Christian Front and the Christian Mobilizers. For an estimate of the number of Coughlin's radio auditors we have to depend upon a survey made by the Institute of Public Opinion and issued early in January, 1939. According to this estimate, fully 3,500,000 persons listened to Coughlin every Sunday, and it was judged that two-thirds of that number were in accord with the tenor of his addresses. Moreover, the same survey found, Coughlin's followers were mostly in the stratum of low incomes. Whether or not Coughlin's *Social Justice* had the circulation of 1,000,-000 copies attributed to it cannot be affirmed, but its circulation was such as to place it in the rank of the foremost anti-Semitic publications in the United States. Many of its readers were undoubtedly inclusive in the aggregation of his radio hearers. Along with these propaganda agencies went the publication of anti-Semitic books and pamphlets, the sale of which was regularly boosted in *Social Justice*.

The continuing sources of Coughlin's radio fund were described in an appeal in that publication. "Many readers of *Social Justice*," this conjoined plea and complaint said, ". . . have pledged themselves to contribute $1 or $2 per month to the Broadcasting Fund. Many of the pledgers have carefully kept up their monthly allowance. . . . Many have fallen behind, one, two, three and four months in their remittances." Such as could not afford to contribute should not strive to do so, "for Father Coughlin's broadcasts are calculated to bring about conditions which would permanently relieve these persons." Having held out this alluring prospect, the appeal solicited: "On the other hand, those who can afford to keep up their pledges should do so, so that the only nationwide, truth-telling voice in America might not be stilled. Take stock friends. Bring your pledges down to date by remitting what is in arrears. The Broadcasting Fund needs it more than ever before. It is not much to pay for continuing the fight for liberty in the United States. How about it?" [24] A week afterward, in (of all things) decrying "Red" influence and money as behind the revival of the Ku Klux Klan in South Carolina and New Jersey, Coughlin's organ commented that the Klan was, for a time, a good racket, and a new "crop of suckers are [sic] ripe for a trimming." [25] Assuredly, Coughlin was in a choice position to know.

As the upshot of his investigation, set forth in a series of six articles, beginning November 21, 1930, Spivak stated that by the end of 1937, from contributed money, Coughlin's Radio League had assets of more than $190,000, and no liabilities, and that this was only part of the cash or property acquired. The intake, in 1938, Spivak further stated, reached almost half a million dollars.[26] That Coughlin's radio expense was, near the close of 1939, almost $10,000 a week was openly admitted by his organ in an appeal for a $200,000 radio fund.[27]

More definite figures were given by Miss Alberta Ward, a bookkeeper for the Radio League of the Little Flower, at an Unemployment Compensation Commission hearing at Detroit, Michigan, on March 11, 1942. The Radio League of the Little Flower was appealing from a commission ruling that it was not a charitable organization and therefore was liable as owing the State accumulated payroll taxes. Employees of the Radio League, once numbering twenty, had been refused unemployment benefits because it did not pay the taxes. The Radio League, Miss Ward testified, had since its organization, paid over to Coughlin's parish a total

[24] Social Justice, November 20, 1939.
[25] Ibid., November 29, 1939.
[26] The New Masses, January 2, 1940.
[27] Social Justice, December 18, 1939.

of $1,458,658. Specifying some years, the League's income, Miss Ward stated in testimony, was $404,469 in 1937; $574,416 in 1938; went down to $102,254 in 1939; and further declined to $82,283 in 1940 the last year recorded. As the president of the Radio League of the Little Flower, Coughlin's salary, according to Miss Ward's testimony, was extremely modest. He received $2,600 in 1936 and 1937, in addition to loans of $5,443 in 1936; $2,000 in 1938 and $2,100 in 1939. The Radio League, it was brought out, was the backer of the Social Justice Publishing Company. In 1936 an investment of $1,000 was made; subsequently the books showed Radio League loans of $83,009 and $145,902 to the publishing firm.[28]

At the second hearing, it may be added, there came a turnabout. Coughlin's Radio League of the Little Flower had maintained that it was a charitable, non-profit organization, not subject to law. The league, the commission's referee decided, was amenable to the unemployment tax. At first, the attorney for the league appealed from this finding, but later asked leave to withdraw the appeal indicating an admission that the league was an employer. But the commission's referee was not satisfied. He, on May 12, 1942, denied the application for the appeal's withdrawal, and stated that the figures submitted by the league did not furnish an adequate basis to enable the commission to ascertain the nature of the league's financial activities. The hearings, it was ordered, should be resumed.

Among much other data regarding the man whom he dubbed "Silver Charlie Coughlin" (evidently referring to a published hint of alleged deals in silver), Spivak gave documents showing that while Coughlin, on the radio, was denouncing stock-market gambling as "shooting craps with other people's money," he himself was taking a whirl at the stock market.[29] If Spivak's specific accusations were untrue, Coughlin should have found it easy to disprove them. Instead of any attempt at refutation Coughlin's organ ran a long article and an editorial reviling Spivak as "a smearer."[30] And in a later issue, Coughlin asserted: "There is not a fact

[28] *The Detroit Free Press*, March 12, 1942.
[29] *The New Masses*, December 5, 1939.
[30] *Social Justice*, November 13, 1939.

in the whole Spivak series." [31] Spivak wrote to Coughlin inviting him, if that were so, to sue for libel, and in fact, pressing him to bring such a suit. "I should," Spivak assured Coughlin, "very much like to see you take the stand and explain your various financial and other manipulations—if you can explain them." [32] Coughlin did not comply.

Coughlin's procession of assertions in both radio fulminations and articles were replete with garbling of citations and with outright misstatements. Jewish organizations did not allow his misrepresentations to go unexposed. The General Jewish Council, composed of the American Jewish Committee, the American Jewish Congress, the B'nai B'rith and the Jewish Labor Committee, published, in 1939, a conclusive pamphlet[33] showing the great and inexcusable gap between Coughlin's assertions and the facts of record. In the frontispiece of the pamphlet was pertinently spread this incisive comment made by Alfred E. Smith and reported in *The New York Times,* November 29, 1933: "When a man presumes to address so great a number of listeners as Father Coughlin reaches, particularly if he be a priest, he assumes the responsibility of not misleading them by false statements or poisoning their judgments with baseless slanders. From boyhood I was taught that a Catholic priest was under the divine injunction to 'teach all nations' the word of God. That includes the divine Commandment, 'Thou shalt not bear false witness against thy neighbor.'"

Communism, as the outward subject of Coughlin's attack, was the lever he used against the Jews. He contended: (1) Communism was the fructification of Jewish endeavor; (2) that it was to prevent the introduction of Communism by Jews that Nazism came into power in Germany; (3) that there was an international Jewish conspiracy to foist Communism everywhere.

Repeatedly to prop his postulate, Coughlin mouthed what he passed off as "evidences." One of the most glaring of his methods was, in a radio speech, on November 20, 1938, his purporting to quote from an article in *The American Hebrew,* September 10, 1920. He twisted that article as

[31] Ibid., December 4, 1939.
[32] *The New Masses,* December 12, 1939.
[33] *Father Coughlin; His "Facts" and Arguments.*

saying: "The achievement, the Russian-Jewish Revolution destined to figure in history as the overwhelming result of the World War, was largely the outcome of Jewish thinking, of Jewish discontent, of Jewish effort to reconstruct." The General Jewish Council's pamphlet gave a reproduction of the article in question. The indictment against both government and finance, the article declared, lay in their joint rejection of the Golden Rule. The modern revolt was "a continued phase of the unrest that formulated through Jewish lips the Sermon on the Mount." *The American Hebrew* article went on: "The workings of this unrest are seen in the events that have accomplished, since the fateful year 1914, a task that looms far larger than the French Revolution —the annihilation of the most firmly entrenched, the most selfish and most reckless autocratic system in the world, Russian Czarism. That achievement, destined to figure as the overshadowing result of the World War, was largely the outcome of Jewish thinking, of Jewish discontent, of Jewish effort to reconstruction . . ." [34] The article was written by Suetozar Tonjoroff, who was not a Jew.

Independently making a search, by a comparison of Coughlin's assertion with the particular copy of *The American Hebrew,* Rev. William C. Kernan, Rector of Trinity Episcopal Church at Bayonne, New Jersey, delivered his findings in an address there, on December 4, 1938. The article, he said, stated exactly the opposite of what Coughlin made it appear to say; the article's plain meaning was that it was the overthrow of Czardom which was largely the consequence of Jewish resistance and action, and the Kerensky Revolution which extinguished Czarism was (as every well-informed person knew) one which preceded the Bolshevik or Communist Revolution. [35] Now resident in America, Alexander Kerensky took occasion to point out that, at the time of the Revolution headed by him, all important classes favored deposition of the Czar, and the part taken by the Jews was not of exceptional prominence. [36] Even the high aristocracy, we may add, was indignant at the pernicious influence wielded in the Czar's family by the

[34] Ibid. Facsimile of *The American Hebrew* article on p. 9.
[35] Ibid., pp. 10-11, giving Rev. Kernan's address.
[36] *The New York Times,* November 29, 1938.

infamous Rasputin who was finally beguiled into the mansion of a prince and there murdered.

Based upon documentary proofs, the General Jewish Council's pamphlet, showed point by point, the falsity of Coughlin's palaver that Communism in Russia was financed by Jewish, especially American Jewish bankers. By its nature such a charge was as absurd as would be the imputed harmonizing of fire and water. But well aware that his votaries were of a species to accept his word, Coughlin arrogated to himself the license to make assertions suiting his purpose. First, over the radio, on November 30, 1938, he professed to have a copy of a 1919 British official *White Paper* which he averred, named Kuhn, Loeb & Co., as among the participants in financing the Russian Communist Revolution. This so-called *White Paper* was not, as represented, a secret but a public British document entitled *A Collection of Reports on Bolshevism in Russia,* and copies were accessible in all important public libraries. Examination of the document's contents revealed that nowhere throughout its pages was there any mention of Kuhn, Loeb & Co. Challengings of Coughlin's assertions led him a week later to take another tack. Now he quoted from a book written by Dennis Fahey, of Ireland, as his authority for saying that Kuhn, Loeb & Co., were named in an American Secret Service report. That firm issued a public statement categorically denying that it ever had any relations, financial or other, with any Government in Russia, whether Czarist, Kerensky or Communist. "A letter," the statement said in part, "was recently addressed by one of the partners of this firm to Father Coughlin, following the first appearance of these charges in his magazine, calling attention to their falsity. Father Coughlin has, nevertheless, elected to disregard the facts and had repeated his misstatements in his last two broadcasts."

There was, of course, no such agency as an American Secret Service. The only governmental body of that kind was the U. S. Secret Service, a division of the Treasury Department. In response to inquiries by several newspapermen regarding Coughlin's assertions, Frank J. Wilson, Chief of the U. S. Secret Service, gave out, on November 28, 1938, a statement for general publication. The extract that Coughlin attributed to Fahey whom he described as a Professor of Philosophy at Dublin, purported, Chief Wilson's statement said, to be a quotation from a document printed, in 1920, by *Documentation Catholique* of Paris. This publication ascribed responsibility for the assertions as to the financing of the Bolshevik Revolution of 1917 to the "American Secret Service." Chief Wilson's statement told how an exhaustive investigation of U. S. Secret Service records had been made. Also questionings of members of the service from 1916 to 1920. "They know," his statement concluded, "of no such investigation or report as that which Father Coughlin discussed, and it is quite certain that no such report was ever made by the United States Secret Service."

Coughlin glided to another position. He began: "Once more, then, I refer to the British *White Paper* which contains documentary evidence received from the Secret Service." This "cannot be brushed aside by idle denials." He had, so he said, telephoned to Fahey who assured him that a safeguarded original copy of the *White Paper* did contain the reference from "Section 8." There was no such section. The only number 8 in the document was a page containing a report on the imprisonment and death of the Czar's family. There was not the slightest mention of Jewish banking houses in the entire document from which Coughlin had purported to quote at length.[37]

But it was an eminent American Catholic scholar and educator who probed deeper into the sources of Coughlin's assertions. This was Monsignor John A. Ryan, at this time professor of sociology in the Catholic University, Washington, D. C. His findings were published in his penetrative article in a Catholic magazine.[38] Mgr. Ryan began by telling how, in his radio address on November 20, 1938, Coughlin at the outset, had expressed deep sympathy for the Jews of Germany, and had then sought to look into and give the reasons for Nazism's deep hostility to Jews. "His explanation," Mgr. Ryan commented, "was stated in such terms as to suggest that the Jews in Germany deserved, to a considerable extent, the cruel injuries which they have suffered

[37] The complete exposé of Coughlin's assertions, together with facsimile reproductions of documents, was set forth in *Father Coughlin; His "Facts" and Arguments*, pp. 11-17.
[38] "Anti-Semitism in the Air," *The Commonweal*, December 20, 1938.

at the hands of the Nazis. The majority of his hearers undoubtedly concluded that 'the Jews had it coming to them.' " [39] A more judicious and telling exposition of Coughlin's tactics could not have been made.

Coughlin had flourished a list of names of twenty-five men prominent in the Soviet government. Of these Coughlin specified twenty-four as "atheistic Jews." What were the sources of this list? In reverse order, this collection of names came from priest Fahey who, in turn, had taken it from *The Patriot*, a weekly paper published in London. Typical extracts from that periodical Mgr. Ryan stated, showed it to be "definitely anti-Semitic." Fairly, in the same category, he wrote, could be put Fahey's book *The Mystical Body of Christ in the Modern World*, steadily recommended by Coughlin on the cover of *Social Justice*. Where, asked Mgr. Ryan, did *The Patriot* get the list? As its authority it fell back upon the *Documentation Catholique* of March 26, 1920. This Mgr. Ryan discounted as a "publication whose statements, of course, have not the authority of the Church." Again, in turn, what was the purported authority given by that French periodical? It claimed to have taken the list from an alleged report of the American Secret Service to the French Commissioner.

There we have a maze of fiction completely exposed. But Mgr. Ryan did not stop at doing this valuable service. "Probably Coughlin's worst misrepresentation," he declared, was his *American Hebrew* distortion. Ryan showed how, in the act of seeming to quote from Fahey's book, Coughlin ascribed to it an expression as to "Lenin's quasi Cabinet." No phrase of this kind was in Fahey's book. This was only one of Coughlin's inaccuracies in his handling of that volume. Imputations in Coughlin's *Social Justice* were often at variance with the plain facts. For example, it placed as among Jewish leaders of the German Communist movement Friedrich Ebert, who had been president of Germany. As a matter of easily ascertainable knowledge, Ebert's heritage was that of an old Catholic family in Baden, and far from having the slightest connection with either Jewry or

---

[39] Among the Catholic publications denouncing the persecution of the Jews in Germany and elsewhere *The Catholic World* magazine was especially persistent; its editorial comments were most ably written.

Communism, he was viewed with great enmity by the Communist Party.[40]

"Of course," Mgr. Ryan set forth, "no person, banker, Jew or anyone else, need be ashamed of helping to overthrow the Government of the Czar as it existed in the spring of 1917." But so far as concerned Coughlin's assumption that Jewish banking houses helped finance the expulsion of the Kerensky Government by the Bolshevists and Communists nearly six months later, it "has been denied by the New York banking houses as well as by Kerensky, and it remains without substantial support anywhere else."

[40] George N. Shuster, then Contributing Editor of *The Commonweal*, took Coughlin to task for this "almost grotesque error." See Shuster's article "The Jew and Two Revolutions" in that magazine, December 30, 1938.

Chapter XXX

CHRISTIAN FRONTERS AND MOBILIZERS

In reproof of Coughlin's broadcast of November 27, 1938, Monsignor Ryan wrote that the net effect of the new material injected into it "was to arouse further ill-feeling against Jewish people in America and to discourage feelings of sympathy for the Jews in Germany." He pointedly added: "It would seem that the enormous cruelties inflicted upon the Jewish people in Germany, no matter what offences have been committed by a small number of Jewish individuals, ought to move every Christian heart to pity, and ought to prevent any Christian from saying anything which would make their lot harder to bear." And having a keen cognition of a future probability, Mgr. Ryan warned his fellow Catholics: "It has been urged that Catholics in particular ought to refrain from encouraging this campaign of anti-Semitism for fear that the same psychology will be used against them when the next anti-Catholic movement gets under way. The first two Commandments provide an infinitely higher motive and an immeasurably more effective one. From every point of view Catholics should refrain from fostering by speech, action or by silence anti-Semitism in the United States." [1]

Such condemnations did not prevail upon Coughlin to discontinue or even alter his course. This, too, notwithstanding the cumulatively disquieting fact that in the year 1939 and in later years persecution of Jews leaped to even more ferocious extremes in Germany and in many other European countries which it had now subjugated. Altogether the concomitance of these persecutions formed a mesh of inhumanly staggering proportions and a historic iniquity of prime magnitude. Inasmuch as Mussolini, Italy's dictator,

[1] *The Commonweal*, December 20, 1938.

was nothing more than an echóing satellite of Hitler, he further proved his truckling in 1939, 1940 and 1941 by substantially taking more Nazi laws against Jews as his copybook and adding them to those already decreed in Italy. In the large group of countries occupied by the Nazis this standardized anti-Jewish code was ingrafted by sheer force of domination. However these superimposed laws might vary from the German in minor ways, they were equally designed to reduce Jews to penury, squalor and helplessness.

Even more. In the pattern of those Nazi laws which were thus transferred to other lands was the cold-blooded, thinly disguised aim to inflict, so far as feasible, the death agonies of a race by measures that indirectly but effectively were calculated to produce widespread extinction.[2] And not waiting for this result which was sure to come from privation and disease, the Nazis exulted in placing what they considered a brand upon the living Jews. By decree all persons of Jewish blood in Germany, Bohemia and Moravia were ordered not to fail to attest their racial identity by having sewed on the outer garment a large yellow and black star carrying the inscription *Jude* (Jew). But with this measure, the relentless Nazis did not remain satisfied, as was afterward shown by a supplementary Berlin decree, that of April 7, 1942. Enlarging what they considered the ignominy such Jews as remained had to bear, this law required all Jewish inhabitants to display the Star of David on the doors of their dwellings. A law compelling wearing of the Star of David was at once imposed upon Jews in Poland when after September, 1939, the German army battered its way to conquest over

[2] Witness some of the Nazi laws serving as models to be adopted elsewhere and the baleful consequences which were self-evident: No Jew could appear in the streets of any German city after 6 o'clock in the evening, and from Friday night until Monday morning had to remain indoors or face punitive arrest. The food card supplied to Jews was a travesty; not until after 1 o'clock in the afternoon could it be presented, and by that time all the available eatables had been preempted by "Aryans." No card allowing purchase of clothing was granted to any Jew; even buying of thread for mending was prohibited. To have shoes repaired, the Jew had to surrender his soap card for a year. The outcome was that many Jewish men, women and children rather than be seen in tatters or nakedness had to shut themselves permanently in their habitations in localized neighborhoods. Yet there, however, in winter's rigors, they were invited to freeze to death, since no Jew could legally buy coal for heating premises. Like other anti-Jewish measures, this law was so sternly enforced that coal was denied even to the Jewish hospital in Berlin; during a major operation, Jewish doctors had to get such heat as they could by burning alcohol.

much of Poland. Not the least hideous of many other typical Nazi laws bearing upon and enslaving Jews of Poland was the establishment of walled-in ghettos where Jews were left to languish in despair and rot away.[3] In fact, as reliable

[3] In the Warsaw ghetto 530,000 Jews were herded. Imprisoned, they did not have the fare provided to convicts in regular prisons. Food allowance to each ghetto inmate was sixty grams of bread, about one quarter of a pound, and the same amount of potatoes a day. Obviously because of this undernourishment, the death rate was great, quickly reaching the ghastly figure of 5,000 a month. Conditions of filth brought on epidemics of typhus. From this cause alone, correspondents telephoned from Berne, Switzerland, and from Stockholm, Sweden, to *The New York Times*, on January 6, 1942, related, deaths in the Warsaw ghetto ran from an estimated 300 to 400 a day. Having no means to pay burial expenses, ghetto Jews had to put their dead in the streets, where police collected the corpses. Mortality from these and other causes in the Lodz ghetto, in which 150,000 Jews were confined, was commensurately high. The total imprisoned in Warsaw, Lodz, Lwow, Bialystock, Wilne, Cracow and Lublin ghettos was estimated at about 1,100,000. In Warsaw, ten Jews were publicly executed for leaving the walls of the ghetto without permission. From the ghettos in Poland typhus spread into a half dozen other European countries. Mostly a Catholic country Poland had long maltreated and oppressed Jews. But the Nazi conquerors were also venting their fury upon the Catholic Church there. In his recently published factual book (*The Persecution of the Catholic Church in German-Occupied Poland*) Cardinal Hlond felt justified in writing that never in its long existence had "the Catholic Church in Poland suffered such persecution and torments as at present under German occupation." Now with a confraternity of feeling for Jews, such sympathetic Catholics as could evade Nazi vigilance smuggled food into the ghettos. Nevertheless, such were the inroads of malnutrition that the number of Jews monthly dying of starvation and disease in Warsaw rose to 10,000 by March, 1942, according to figures furnished by Dr. Henry Shoskes, former general manager of the Central Co-operative Bank in Warsaw, and now chairman of the International Committee for Co-operative Reconstruction. If present conditions in Poland continued for a series of years, Dr. Shoskes reported, Polish Jews were doomed to annihilation.

In Holland, where the Nazis set about carving a ghetto in the city of Amsterdam, bands of young Jews fiercely resisted the military authorities. Many of these Jews were killed or wounded; of hundreds of others arrested and sent to a concentration camp in Austria, the larger number soon died from the effect of conditions there.

Rumania, as we have seen, was never noted for lenity to Jews; now under Nazi motion it expeditiously proved its anti-Semitism by penning Jews in ghettos and confiscating their property. The Rumanian Under-Secretary of State announced on March 6, 1942, that 2,000 Jewish and foreign concerns with a total capital of more than 20,000,000,000 lei had been placed under State control. In a desperate attempt to find relief from pogroms, 760 Rumanian Jews, men, women and children, in December, 1941, boarded the small, decaying, totally unseaworthy *Struma* which with great difficulty contrived to reach Istanbul hoping to get to Palestine. The long-awaited permission to enter that country was refused, the ship was ordered out of Turkish territory, and towed by a tug, it soon when reaching open water capsized during the night. All but two of the 760 were drowned. In the British Parliament, on March 10, 1942, Lord Davies denounced the action of the Palestine administration in not admitting the refugees as "a stupid, callous, inhuman act, the only reason for which was to curry favor with the Arab recalcitrants." Lord Wedgwood likened the *Struma* to the Black Hole of Calcutta, and declared that the root of the trouble in Palestine was: "The administration does not like Jews. All the excuses are those of the pro-Arab, pro-Italian clique.

reports indicated, the Germans did not stop at this slow, lingering process but often resorted to wholesale slaughter of Jews. More than 100,000 Jews, it was declared, were slain in Latvia, Estonia and Lithuania alone, and when the Nazi armies invaded Russia they further glutted their murderous hatred by killing a number stated as exceeding twice that many Jews in the Western Russian regions.

These are merely the most fugitive references to the frightful persecutions of Jews—persecutions repeated in varying ways in one Nazi-overpowered country after another. Even to outline the multiplicity of decrees and the resultant monstrosities would necessitate the drag of a very long chapter. But to show how in this bedlamish time the most prized traditions of some countries were turned upside down, the cases of Holland and France offered sickening evidence. So long an asylum for Jews harried in other lands as well as for political refugees, Holland had seemed a secure place for its long-resident Jews as well as a safe goal for the 30,000 Jews who had fled thither from Germany and Austria. Now all Jews in Holland encountered a Nazi outpour of repressive decrees. The same was the fell situation in France —that France which, since the French Revolution, had held streamingly aloft its motto, "Liberty, Equality, Fraternity." What a descent was now seen! Both in the large and most populous domain of France occupied by the heel-clicking German troops and in that portion plus the French colonies ruled by the supine Vichy Government headed by Marshal Petain, a swarm of seemingly endless anti-Jewish measures was progressively put in force. Nor should those against Free Masons be left unmentioned. But the far more destructive effect fell upon Jews. As in so many other countries mastered or cowed by the Nazis, no means was left unused to beggar and strangulate Jews. It was the same repetitiously wretched story of taking away their property and businesses,

We have had twenty-two years of this policy of continuous bias against Jews." An indignation mass meeting was held in New York City on March 12, 1942, by the American Emergency Committee for Zionist Affairs.

In Hungary, Slovakia, Yugoslavia and Bulgaria persecution of Jews continued in a state of fury, according to the findings of S. B. Jacobson, chief representative for two years of the American Joint Jewish Distribution Committee in the Balkans area. In a detailed statement, on March 13, 1942, he related the conditions, based on the German model, including internment camps, forced labor camps, deportations, ghettos in Slovakia, and the deliberate starvation of Jews, many of whom were driven to suicide.

forbidding their engaging in occupations, trades and professions, stripping them of all civic rights and otherwise enveloping them in woe and degradation. And inevitably the time came when in occupied France the French police enforced German requirements compelling Jews to wear Star of David armbands.[4]

Most of these conditions were in process when Coughlin was declaiming, and received the widest publicity in America, yet he and others of his ilk were bent upon stirring up the same hate which had caused such terrors in most of Europe. Aside from the authenticity of the official decrees themselves and of the continuous and undenied accounts written by correspondents, the flood of refugees which had poured from the scenes of persecution was of itself proof of the calamities undergone or from which escape was made. Not to include the hundreds of thousands of Jews who had gone to Palestine, and hosts seeking haven in other hemispheres, nearly 40,000 Jewish refugees had come to America from 1933 to 1940. There were, in 1939, about 20,000 Christian refugees who, likewise under the immigration quota law, had been able to gain admittance to the United States. Having some Jewish ancestor many were classified by Nazi law as "non-Aryan"; others were entirely of Christian lineage or were Christian "Aryans" proscribed for their liberal principles.[5] Thousands of Catholic refugees were able to find safety in America. Some of these were so-called "Aryan" Catholics who were either banished from Germany or hastened to quit because of their prominence in the Catho-

---

[4] A more adequate account of the cruelties inflicted upon Jews is necessitated by a sketch of a later atrocity. In September, 1942, the Vichy regime promulgated measures to turn over the large number of refugee Jews to Germany. This caused a wave of suicides among many Jews affected. In vigorous protest against the "revolting and fiendish" Vichy action, U. S. Secretary of State Hull denounced "the delivery of these unhappy people to enemies who have announced and in considerable measure executed their intention to enslave, maltreat and eventually exterminate them under conditions of the most extreme cruelty."

By this time the exterminating process had reached ghastly proportions. From reports obtained from reliable sources, spokesmen for the World Jewish Congress charged that in the various Nazi-occupied countries more than 1,000,000 Jews had been murdered by one method or another in three years. Although this seems a large figure, other estimates placed the number slaughtered at much more.

[5] Pamphlet, *Report of American Committee for Christian Refugees*, p. 5. This committee was formed in 1935 when the persecutions in Germany disclosed that the problem was Christian as well as Jewish.

lic Action organization outlawed by Hitler. Most of the incoming Catholics were converts from Judaism, or married to Jews, or remotely back to the fourth degree, were descendants of mixed marriages between Jews and Catholics.[6]

If Coughlin refused to be impressed by the catastrophic results of the spirit of bigotry against Jews abroad, and in a lesser although sad enough degree against unpliant Protestants, he, as a priest, it might have been supposed, would at least have bethought himself of the enormities against those of his own faith in Germany, Austria and other countries now incorporated in what was called "Greater Germany." We have hitherto made fleeting reference to this aspect, but some further picture of the conditions as recorded by a committee of American Catholic prelates will not be here superfluous. This committee composed of Archbishop Stritch, of Milwaukee, Archbishop Rummel, of New Orleans, Bishop Noll of Fort Wayne and Bishop Auxiliary Donahue, of New York, reported:

> . . . It is clear that during the seven years of the Nazi regime there has been carried on a systematic campaign against the [Catholic] Church in which her ideals have been ridiculed, her dogmas and institutions mocked, her priests defamed and her religious bishops branded as arch enemies of the German people. Religious communities and individuals, including lay leaders, have been terrorized, property confiscated, or in some instances bought or rented for ridiculously low sums, while the courts and police have given little or no protection. Equally shocking are the reports of sacrileges committed during the past year. Statues and crucifixes have been mutilated, destroyed or removed from wayside shrines, often thrown into rivers and gutters. . . . It is a known fact that Catholic leaders of the clergy and laity have been frequently molested and assaulted on the streets, ordered out of their homes on the shortest possible notice and deprived of their property by confiscation.

As for confiscation of distinctively Catholic Church property, including edifices, buildings, libraries, art collections and other kinds summarily seized in Germany, Austria and

[6] Pamphlet, *Report of the Committee for Catholic Refugees from Germany, from January 1, 1937 to September 30, 1939*, p. 8.

Czechoslovakia, the estimated value, by September, 1939, "approximated several billion marks." In the case of many other Catholic properties which were not overtly confiscated "they have been actually taxed to such an extent that they have been forfeited to the State." Upon the slightest pretext "convents, schools and even universities have been closed and the communities in charge imprisoned." Some 20,000 schools, "formerly rated as Catholic, have been transformed into State schools . . . in which the atmosphere is decidedly un-Christian." And in the Catholic section of "Greater Germany," Catholic sensibilities were flouted by Nazi-organized and sponsored "mock parades ridiculing Catholic customs and institutions." [7]

These manifestations of how, once aroused to frenzy,

[7] Ibid., pp. 6-8. The extremes to which this "veritable war against Christianity" was being waged by the Nazi regime was later set forth in a communication sent to the Vatican by Cardinal von Faulhaber. An outline of the contents of this indictment was somehow smuggled out past Italian censorship, and, reaching Berne, was made public to the world on May 9, 1942. Persecution had driven the Catholic and Protestant churches into an accord of opposition to the Nazi anti-Christian espionage and maltreatment. Speaking for the Catholic Church, Cardinal von Faulhaber was reported as describing how, as an anticipatory step, to prevent the reading from pulpits of certain episcopal documents, bishops and priests were peremptorily arrested. Faithful Catholics and the Church were subjected to "moral blackmail" in being forced to yield greater amounts in money and property to the Nazi rulers than was required of unbelievers. Intensified propaganda was carried on among poorer members to induce them to disavow the Church, and violence was often administered to those refusing. Publication of religious text books and other kinds of church publications was prohibited. Church sacred articles, including ritual vessels, were summarily seized "for the good of the country and the prosecution of the war." These were some of the conditions. The question now, the Cardinal stated, was one of life or death for Christianity, since in its blind rage against religion, the Nazi "faith" did not or could not distinguish between Protestantism and Catholicism.

A long pastoral letter issued later by the German bishops of the Catholic Church reviewed the situation. "For years a war has raged in our Fatherland against Christianity and the Church, and has never been conducted with such bitterness . . . Catholic priests are banned from their dioceses and homes and . . . are being punished with expulsion from the country or internment in a concentration camp without court procedure. . . . Catholic orders have been expelled from schools almost entirely. . . . A large part of their property and their institutions has been taken away from them and many are destined to perish because of the law prohibiting able-bodied men to work for them. Not only the Church refectories for students have been largely destroyed or taken from the administration of the Church authorities, but even seminaries for priests have been confiscated. . . . Even places of worship have been confiscated and desecrated. . . . Catholic priests and laymen are . . . secretly suspected, nay, publicly branded as traitors and national enemies just because they stand up for the freedom of the Church and the truth of the Catholic faith. . . . We emphasize that before the authorities we not only stand up for religious and clerical rights but likewise for the human rights bestowed by God on mankind. . . ."

bigotry becomes an undiscriminating scourge, striking at one today, another tomorrow, were lost on Coughlin. The combination of bigotry and wholesale plundering of victims in Germany was one of both voracity and accelerated velocity. This was again soon seen in the suppression of the Christian Science Church as "hostile to the German State," and the confiscation of that church's property. It was in such an appallingly evil time, when every precept of religion and reason should have counseled the strongest discouragement of bigotry, that, swayed by Coughlin's influence, a rabid anti-Jewish organization took shape. Simultaneously came another body of the same character which could have traced its impulse to the like source.

While habitually, as we shall see, Coughlin opportunistically sought to evade responsibility, his incitations were numerously recorded in his mouthpiece *Social Justice*. In addition to the appeal (cited in a previous chapter herein) for an openly avowed anti-Semitic Christian Front, that publication, to give such an organization substance, advocated its inception by the formation of platoons. The response first came in Brooklyn, New York City, where a unit was started by a group of Coughlin's followers; his organ lauded their step as "the patriotic action of thirty-six Christian men in Brooklyn." Units were rapidly organized in other cities. In a radio address Coughlin praised "the heroism and zeal of the Christian Front in those areas where its work has already borne fruit." [8] Soon thereafter, in another radio address, Coughlin, mouthing the specious claim that the Christian Front was wholly a foe of Communism, gave a jubilant assurance. "The Christian Front," said he, "is no longer a dream; it is a reality in America, a reality that grows stronger." In this address he again revealed his characteristic deviousness. Deftly he mingled profession of piety and humility with subtle suggestions that on proper occasion force should be met with force. Christian Front spokesmen, he sleekly advised, should model their speeches after the Sermon on the Mount.

But well knowing that underneath the more superficial opposition of his followers to Communism was the deep-seated enmity to Jews that he himself had so largely in-

[8] *Social Justice*, July 24, 1939.

flamed, he, without specifically committing himself, gave this cryptical advice: Any ideologies aimed at Christianity's destruction or at private property or national culture should be resisted, for, he proclaimed, "Christianity does not teach that the mystical body of Christ shall submit to the mystical body of Satan." [9] What the word ideologies meant not many of Coughlin's undeveloped listeners knew. However, steeped in his propaganda, they could piece together the evident import of his remarks. His doting audience assumed that it was the Jews, of course, who aimed at Christianity's overthrow. Had not the *Protocols,* as used by Coughlin's organ, made out what was taken to be a clear case? And that large part of Coughlin's hearers and readers responsive to his assertions and pleas had been led to believe by his propaganda that Communism was a Jewish product, threatening to the holding of private property no less than to American cultural standards.

If cornered, Coughlin could slide out of any accusation of having openly said this, since his finesse was that of implication and indirection, taking care not to expose himself by a bluntness which would be brought home to him. But he, so fertile in denials and disclaimers when his purpose was suited, could not elude the fact that his *Social Justice* joyously hailed the Christian Front's growth. In its issue of July 31, 1939, that organ lauded the Christian Front as "the inevitable counteraction to Communism" and as "a protector of Christianity and Americanism." Then, indulging in soaring expectations, the *Social Justice* article predicted a Christian Front membership of 5,000,000 by 1940.

All during this time Christian Front speakers were not concerned with Communism, but endeavored to excite street audiences against Jews. This was particularly a notorious condition in New York City against the Jewish population of which the Christian Front concentrated its main efforts. In this ranting campaign the Christian Front was abetted by an offshoot calling themselves Christian Mobilizers.

The violence of the language used was attested in many a court proceeding following arrests of offenders. Typical of such harangues were the expressions used by two men convicted of making anti-Semitic instigations at a meeting in

[9] *Ibid.*, August 14, 1939.

Columbus Circle, New York City. One of these men had shouted that he "wished to see Jewish blood flow all over America." The other had screeched that he "would like to see every Jew in the United States hanged," and that if he "got $100,000 from Hitler" he would "show the damned Jews." In the effort to forestall jail punishment, these men went on a five-day hunger strike. Unimpressed by this ruse, Magistrate Henry H. Curran, in the West Side Court, on September 25, 1939, sentenced each to serve seventy-five days in the workhouse, and denounced the movements which had brought the men to such a state of hatred. "We should remember," said Magistrate Curran, "that the founder of Christianity, Jesus Christ, was a Jew. These people who call themselves the Christian Front and Christian Mobilizers are dragging Christianity through the dust. They do not speak for Christianity." [10]

Mayor La Guardia, of New York City, had instructed the Police Department to take action "as to the Christian Front street meetings and other meetings held by similar hatred-breeding and discriminatory groups . . . which abused the sacred privilege of free speech to incite violence." Evidence collected by the police resulted in 233 arrests in New York City, in 1939. Supplementing street meetings was the not uncommon sight of "Coughlinite" boys flitting through subway cars. Carrying bundles of *Social Justice* they urged passengers to buy copies, and often were followed by a group of men and women shouting "Buy Christian only! Save America! Down with the Jews! Read *Social Justice!* Do not buy from Jews!" More stealthy was the work of a crew giving itself the name of the American Gentile Youth Movement. On train windows it surreptitiously pasted a black placard on which was inscribed in white letters: "Hitler failed. He let them live. To have peace and prosperity each Nation must kill their own Jews. When the last hour for the Jew in America strikes there will be no Passover. Jews, America is your last mile!"

Because, it said, approximately 90 per cent of the membership of groups federated in the Christian Front was Catholic, an appeal was sent to Archbishop Spellman, of New York City, to state the position of the Catholic hier-

[10] *The New York Times*, September 26, 1939.

archy regarding that organization. This appeal was made in an open letter signed by twenty-two editors and members of the non-sectarian magazine *Equality* and was also published in the October, 1939, issue of that periodical. This open letter contained the warning that "the hate-rousing and anti-Semitic activities" of the Christian Front following the leadership of Father Coughlin might "eventually culminate in a violent, bloody rioting such as the city has never known." Analyzing Christian Front membership, the open letter stated: "Most of the members regard Father Coughlin as their personal leader, and refer to themselves as Coughlinites. Except for a small group of rowdy adventurers, most of them are sincere, well-meaning citizens misled by the hymns of hate emanating weekly from Royal Oak and almost nightly from the rostrums of Father Coughlin's representatives in New York." Another factor, it was pointed out, tending to give an impression of the identification of Coughlin's and. Christian Front activities with the Catholic Church in New York City was support of the Christian Front by certain priests in that city. Continued silence about the official attitude of the Catholic Church in New York City, Archbishop Spellman was told, "will be interpreted as implicit sanction of the Christian Front in this city." Since, however, as we have related, Cardinal Mundelein had already made it clear that Coughlin spoke and wrote purely on his own initiative, any statement from Archbishop Spellman would not have elucidated that fact further. The question seems to have been whether Archbishop Spellman could take condemnatory action against the Christian Front which was not exclusively Catholic nor any part of the Catholic Church organization.

From the Brooklyn Church and Mission Federation, representing virtually every Protestant congregation in that borough of New York City, came a more telling denunciation of the Christian Front. Unlike the above open letter it did not adopt any palliative mode of distinguishing the rowdy Christian Fronters from the mass of members whose mental plane was the same and whose inbred hatred of Jews could easily lead to bellicose explosions. Whether professional or latent rowdies, the membership as a whole was permeated by the mob spirit. The occasion for the Brooklyn

Church and Mission Federation's statement was in consequence of its learning that the Christian Front "is strenuously endeavoring to increase its forces by inviting Protestants into its membership." Cautioning Protestants against receptiveness to such overtures, the statement condemned prejudicing of race against race, and further declared: "No organization or groups of individuals fostering such evil propaganda which has resulted in numerous acts of violence in our city has the moral right to call itself Christian." And in doing so, the Christian Front was "guilty of practicing inexcusable hypocrisy."[11] At an annual meeting of the Social Service Commission of the Protestant Episcopal Diocese of Long Island, on January 18, 1940, Representative Jerry Voorhis, a member of the Dies committee, delivered an address. After which he was asked what the committee intending doing "about Father Coughlin." This was a well-understood criticism that Coughlin personally had been spared, which was the fact. Explaining that he could not speak for the committee, Voorhis replied: "I would certainly think that an investigation of organizations like the Christian Front should be pushed much harder than it has been and wherever it leads there the committee should go."[12] Meanwhile, *Social Justice* had been banned in Canada.

Having the endorsement of many leading Christians, an American League to Combat Anti-Semitism was formed. Pioneering a "Stop Coughlin" movement, it issued pamphlets, booklets, circulars and news releases denouncing Coughlin for what he was, exposing propaganda aimed to inspire hatred of the Jewish people, and encouraging the holding of good-will meetings between Christians and Jews in communities infested by anti-Semitic organizations. At this time seventeen members of the Christian Front were under arrest in Brooklyn charged with conspiring to bring about successive revolutions with the ulterior aim of having the Christian Front take over the Government of the United States. Notified of these arrests, Coughlin, in Detroit, told the Associated Press that he "roundly disavowed" the "specific" Christian Front group implicated. But, enlarging the ground for his approval of the Christian Front, he said

[11] Ibid., November 16, 1939.
[12] Ibid., January 19, 1940.

that he had always advocated the need of such an organization to combat Nazism and Communism. This chameleonic claim concerning Nazism was surely a piece of gratuitous information refuted by the course of his own organ.[13]

Coincidently, in a leading editorial, the Catholic magazine *The Commonweal* severely criticized Coughlin. Dealing with the arrest of the seventeen men it said: ". . . These men were members of the Christian Front, a hazy organization claiming to be devoted to Christianity and the American Way and inimical to Communism and atheism. But the Christian Front idea of Christian society and the American way is very strange. So are its ideas of proper political, economic and social action. Destruction of the Jews was one of these. 'Direct action,' street. demonstrations, control of the gutters—bombs and rifles and setting up a dictator by force are some more." The editorial stated that Father Coughlin, *The Brooklyn Tablet, Social Justice* and their many abettors and sympathizers must bear the direct responsibility for the plight of these young men. Coughlin was further accused of "eely writing" in seemingly advocating peaceful methods while at the same time presenting an alternative way and supplying a clue to his real meaning by saying, " 'Call this inflammatory, if you will. It is inflammatory. . . .' But Father Coughlin says he had nothing to do with it . . ."

Before another of their statements was published in the February, 1940, issue of *Equality,* the editors of that magazine had released it for advance newspaper use. This statement, or rather, appeal, requested Catholic prelates in cities where the Christian Front had most intrenched itself to

[13] Instance *Social Justice* publishing, over Coughlin's signature, on December 5, 1938, an article entitled "Background for Persecution." Comparison showed that this article, save for slight change here and there, was a parallel of Goebbels' speech alleging butchery of opponents by Jewish Communists in various countries in prior years, and giving this as a reason for Nazi persecution of Jews. To shift responsibility for the Nazi system of shooting hostages in mass, the Goebbels speech charged Jewish Communists with its introduction. This typical and persistent Nazi barbarity of hostage murder was thus denounced by President Franklin D. Roosevelt on October 25, 1941: "The practice of executing scores of innocent hostages in reprisal for isolated attacks on Germans in countries temporarily under the Nazi heel revolts a world already inured to suffering and brutality. Civilized peoples long ago adopted the basic principle that no man should be punished for the deed of another. Unable to apprehend the persons involved in these attacks, the Nazis characteristically slaughter fifty or a hundred persons. . . ." The Nazis, it should be added, systematically used the subterfuge of describing these victims as "Judeo-Communists."

take action against Coughlin. The U. S. Attorney General and the chief of the Federal Bureau of Investigation were asked "to go below the surface of the activities already uncovered and specifically to investigate the connection of Father Coughlin with the Christian Front." If the aforesaid prelates saw no ground for their taking proceedings, Catholic ecclesiastics and laymen joined with Protestants and Jews in combating anti-Semitism, as did distinctively Catholic organizations such, for instance, as the Catholic Lay Apostle Guild.

Coughlin was agile in vaulting from one position to another. "While I do not belong to any unit of the Christian Front," said a statement he, on January 21, 1940, gave out for publication, "nevertheless I do not disassociate myself from that movement. I reaffirm every word which I have said in advocating its formation." [14] He soon took another tack. With measureless effrontery, an editorial in his organ eight days later, set out to place this construction upon the rising wrath at him and the Christian Front: "We repeat with emphasis that there is a serious anti-Christian persecution in this country. Why should we hope to escape it?" Avowing that "we don't hold a brief for anybody charged with sedition against the Government," the editorial, in extra heavy type, announced: "but neither are we running out on the fine body of Christians who make up the membership of the Christian Front. . . . We retract no word of encouragement we have uttered for the need of a Christian Front in this country—consecrated men and women imbued with the love of Christ and the love of their country . . ." [15] Yet in another statement he fortified himself with what he could assert was a positive disclaimer. He was not, this set forth, either the sponsor or organizer of the Christian Front. "As a clergyman I do not find it compatible to identify myself with any movement in any way whatsoever. I must act in no other capacity toward you than as a friend and a counsellor whose privilege it is to address you in your homes each Sunday." This, as we shall see, in the case of another organization, was not the only disavowal Coughlin felt impelled to make.

[14] Ibid., January 22, 1940.
[15] Social Justice, January 29, 1940.

Addressing the New York Society, Order of the Founders and Patriots of America, at the annual dinner at the Hotel Biltmore, New York City, on January 26, 1940, Representative J. Parnell Thomas, of New Jersey, a member of the Dies committee, said that most of the un-American organizations in the United States were no more than "financial rackets." He specified the Christian Front, the Christian Mobilizers, the Bund and the Silver Shirts as race and religion hate-fostering organizations which should not be tolerated by decent Americans.[16]

At the trial of the accused Christian Fronters the testimony, on April 5, 1940, of a leading witness indicated that, judging from data given to him, the Christian Front's membership was already 300,000 and was "growing by leaps and bounds." Whether or not this figure could be accepted as authentic was a question. According to the same witness' further testimony, he had been instructed that the Christian Front had been formed to "eradicate the Jews," and he was told that 45 per cent of its membership was Irish, and the balance Italians and Germans. A Christian Front leader had held out to this witness for emulation the example of Hitler's success with a few early followers. As outlined by the prosecution, the alleged plot, back of opposition to Communism, was to train leaders, and "the ultimate idea was to incite Jews to riot and then have a revolution and a counter revolution." That the defendants were fanatically, belligerently anti-Jewish was not open to question. But that they were actually guilty of any such fantastic plot as was charged to overthrow the Government was not proved to the satisfaction of the jury, especially as some of the testimony on the stand regarding National Guard officer accomplices was effectively challenged. After a protracted trial the jury disagreed on the conspiracy charge against many of the defendants and others were acquitted or the charges dismissed.

There was a continuing series of denunciations of Coughlin and the Christian Front. A body of 273 Protestant clergymen and religious leaders in New York City issued a call to American citizens to join the Christian church in standing "implacably against the sin of religious hatred in any of its forms." The call went on: "With deep concern we have noted the rise within our city of organizations which to every observation exist merely and mainly to foster anti-Semitism. Some of these have had the blasphemous effrontery to represent themselves as Christian—for instance, the 'Christian Front' and the 'Christian Mobilizers.' . . . We take this additional means of disavowing the use of the word 'Christian' in association with any organization for a propaganda of hatred. . . ."

Without debate, the Social Service Commission of the New York East Conference of the Methodist Church adopted on May 18, 1940, an annual report scoring religious bigotry. Such of "our Roman Catholic brethren, both clergy and laity, who have repudiated Father Coughlin's fascistic and anti-Semitic activities" were commended. Professor Samuel L. Hamilton of New York University, chairman of the commission, presented the report, one section of which, however, was critical of the Catholic hierarchy "from whom no word of disavowal has come at those who have blasphemed the name of Christ by making it synonymous with hatred for the Jew." The report further declared: "We have witnessed the alarming growth of a new, vicious, anti-Semitic, anti-democratic movement in the United States. The center and inspiration of this new drive is the Rev. Charles E. Coughlin and his storm-troop organization, the so-called Christian Front. This is not the usual 'polite anti-Semitism' to which we have become more or less accustomed in the United States; it is a militant, hate-breeding drive, not alone against the Jews, but against the labor unions and our democratic form of government." But because of its breeding hatred for the Jew and because it was predominantly Catholic, "the Christian Front well merits the title of 'Catholic Klan.' "[17]

From various other sources came condemnation of Coughlin and the Christian Front. Not mincing words, an article in the magazine *Dynamic America* thus summed its campaign: "*Dynamic America* has done much to unmask the Royal Oak demagogue by warning honest money reformers to give Coughlin a wide berth and by pointing out the essential reactionary features of his program. Few decent

[17] Ibid., May 19, 1940.

Americans, whether Catholics, Protestants or Jews can understand how it is that the great Catholic Church tolerates this venomous creature in its midst. For years now this 'man of God' has stood before the microphones, in the relative seclusion and security of his church, spewing out his Nazi-Fascist lies, poisoning the minds of his moronic listeners and inciting purple-faced goons to organize so-called 'Christian Fronts' to destroy our democratic institutions in the 'Franco way' to use his own language." [18]

The particular denunciation of Coughlin which, however, naturally received national publicity was that by Wendell L. Willkie, the Republican Party's nominee, in 1940, for President of the United States. Long before he or anyone else had thought of his being thus selected, he had appealed to all of the American people to exercise tolerance in not allowing any infringement of religious liberty. He considered "anti-Semitism in America as a possible criminal movement, and every anti-Semite as a possible traitor to America." Over the radio and otherwise, he had strongly condemned race hatred, bigotry and Hitlerism. Obviously Coughlin did not like this stand but he liked less the candidacy of President Franklin D. Roosevelt now nominated for the third term.

After Willkie's speech accepting the nomination, *Social Justice* highly praised that speech and came out in support of Willkie's candidacy. Upon reading the *Social Justice* article, Willkie, on August 27, 1940, prepared a statement. "I am not interested," this said, "in the support of anybody who stands for any form of prejudice as to anybody's race or religion, or who is in support of any foreign economic or political philosophy in this country." Then referring in direct terms to Coughlin, Willkie added: "If I understand what his beliefs are, I am not only not interested in his support—I don't want it. If I understand correctly, he is opposed to certain people because of their race or religion. I have no place in my philosophy for such beliefs. There is no hedge clause about that. I want to make it completely and absolutely clear. I don't have to be President of the

United States but I do have to make my beliefs clear, that is, in order to live with myself. I am not interested in being President of the United States to compromise with my fundamental beliefs."

Injecting itself into this campaign, in New York City, the simulacrum of a political organization sonorously calling itself the American Destiny Party flared forth with its anti-Jewish fomentations. Its candidate for Congressman was one Joseph E. McWilliams, also a leader of the Christian Mobilizers. In a speech in the Yorkville district, considerably populated by Germans, he opposed Willkie's candidacy. Hearing of this, Willkie expressed his gratification; he did not want the support of any movements seeking "to put any part of our population under any prejudice because of their race or religion." McWilliams was defeated but the effect of his speeches outlasted the election. Upon complaints that (sometimes accompanied by fighting among his audiences) he had incited hatred against Jews, he was convicted on a disorderly conduct charge and sentenced to seventy-five days in the workhouse. The Appellate Court granted him a retrial. Convicted a second time, he was released on parole upon promising to cease his public tirades against Jews. Incorrigible, he continued doing so. Testimony in court showed that he described President Franklin D. Roosevelt as a "Jew king," charged Jews and Communists with controlling Washington and Wall Street and further declared, "The Jews are the real power in this country." The Court remanded him to serve the remainder of his workhouse term. Dismissing a writ of habeas corpus in his behalf, Supreme Court Justice Ernest H. Hammer declined to consider the offence as other than a plain and despicable one likely to arouse animosity and conflict. "Making this a *cause célèbre* seems to give the relator undue proportion and stature in the courts and press, and tortures the simple offence of disorderly conduct into a trial involving the gravest and yet most delicate question of freedom of speech, particularly in respect to race and religion."

So far as any imputed connection of his with the Christian Mobilizers or McWilliams was concerned, Coughlin had already provided himself with a disavowal. This action on his part coincided with the time when the German-American

Bund had become widely detested and the slightest approval of it was suspect. From Mrs. Mary S. Reilly, Bronx, New York City, Coughlin had received a check for $128, the proceeds of a dance sponsored by the Christian Mobilizers. In returning the check, Coughlin wrote: "We know that at least 90 per cent of those who belong to the Christian Mobilizers are good people and friends of social justice. Unfortunately, the followers have been led by Mr. McWilliams into an alliance with the [German-American] Bund, which no one can gainsay is an un-American organization." Acceptance of the check would put himself, Coughlin went on, in the untenable position of being tied up with the Christian Mobilizers and thence with the Nazi Bund: "McWilliams has not repudiated the Bund, nor followed advice I constantly gave in *Social Justice* to all organizations I considered American and Christian."[19]

Here, again, with vast egotism, Coughlin asserted his role as supreme judge of what was American and Christian. Rarely, upon the American scene, had appeared a man replete with such unblushing pretension. All the while, as the conference of the Council Against Intolerance later reported, the spirit of bigotry had ground deep into schools, permeating many classrooms as well as communities. Among thinking Christians, as set forth in the report of Dr. Everett R. Clinchy, director of the wide-working National Conference of Christians and Jews, there was well-grounded apprehension that "anti-Semitism leads on to anti-Christianism." And Americans were "becoming increasingly aware that anti-Semitism is an instrument in the 'Trojan horse' tactics to divide a people so they may be rendered impotent in the face of attack."

[19] *Social Justice*, November 13, 1939.

Chapter XXXI

"WE WANT LINDBERGH"

COUGHLIN abandoned his radio campaign in September, 1940, but *Social Justice* continued, likewise the Christian Front. Formal ownership of *Social Justice* was now vested in Coughlin's father and mother. The intermingled Jew-hating, pro-Nazi elements found in Charles A. Lindbergh a new oracle who, while not entirely displacing Coughlin, subordinated him as a rallying pivot. Single-handed, Lindbergh in 1927, had adventurously piloted his monoplane across the Atlantic Ocean from New York to Paris, which feat at once raised him to international fame. Upon his return to America he was greeted with enthusiastic ovations, showered with distinctions and elevated to the dizzy rank of a national hero. President Coolidge conferred upon him the honor of appointment in the U. S. Army Air Corps Reserve.

For one reason or another, Lindbergh's popularity in the ensuing years somewhat declined, and he definitely forfeited the respect of many Americans when, on October 19, 1938, he accepted at Berlin, from Field Marshal Göring, as Hitler's representative, the Order of Merit of the German Eagle. One of the many instances of American criticism of Lindbergh's action on this occasion was contained in an address on November 27, 1938, by Professor Clyde R. Miller, of New York, director of the Institute for Propaganda Analysis. Specifying German decorations received by Henry Ford and Lindbergh as examples of "effective propaganda," Professor Miller explained the reason: "By acceptance of such decorations, Ford and Lindbergh express approval of the Nazi Government, whether they know it or not. Equally effective counter-propaganda would be for Ford and Lindbergh to return the decorations, saying that they do not care to be honored by a Government which persecutes Jews and Christians."[1] Nevertheless, all that Lindbergh said or did still was accorded conspicuous newspaper publicity, and imagining this a proof of his undiminished importance and influence, the groups in America favoring Nazism either for itself or for its outlawing of Jews, clustered around Lindbergh's personality to trade on the great attention it was assumed he could command.

Although unvaryingly in speech after speech Hitler had unleashed his monomania by holding the machinations of Jews responsible for the war he had planned and provoked, Lindbergh at first made no attack upon Jews. His stand was that of an isolationist aiming to keep America out of the war, and toward this end he was one of the principals of an organization calling itself the America First Committee, leaders of which also comprised two United States Senators and a rather widely known writer. As many a realist pointed out and as the circumstances indubitably portended, the choice of whether it would stay out of the war was not America's; when Hitler decided to attack America he would not fail to do so, and we all know that this turned out to be the inevitable fact. Persisting in their delusion, Lindbergh and associates propagandized it on a national scale.

These exertions precisely suited all of those whose opposition to Jews made them partial to the Nazi regime and its methods. Hoping for Hitler's ultimate success, they did not want America to prepare itself by arming. Indicative of how hatred of Jews and praise of Nazism were made synonymous were, for example, typical utterances in Winrod's anti-Semitic publication. Said one of these: "Every conceivable form of propaganda is being used to inflame the passions and fan the emotions of the American people. With Jewry shaping the foreign policies of the United States Government, the objective is obvious—namely *total war* for our country to help save the tottering structure of international Jewish banking."[2] In a previous number was an article by Dr. Oswald J. Smith, of Toronto, Canada. Professedly based upon an extensive and just-completed European tour, his article related how Nazism and Fascism stood for "life, happiness and prosperity; Bolshevism for death, misery and

[1] *The New York Times*, November 28, 1938.
[2] *The Defender Magazine*, April, 1941.

starvation; all three are repugnant to British and American ideals, but when it comes to a choice between them there can be no hesitation."[3]

Even though Lindbergh had not yet expressed anti-Jewish sentiments, his program was construed by his followers as designed to foil ascribed Jewish endeavors to have America enter the war against Hitler. Lindbergh's course was one giving bigoted organizations, subversive of America's principles and interests, the opportunity to regard him as their eminent standard bearer. Not a mere abstraction, this fervor for him was demonstrated at mass meetings and uproariously by street gatherings. One of a number of flagrant instances was brought prominently to public attention by a two-column advertisement in heavy type in the form of a letter addressed to Mayor La Guardia and Police Commissioner Valentine, of New York City, by the Committee, Fight for Freedom, Inc.[4] Of this body U. S. Senator Carter Glass was chairman and Mrs. Calvin Coolidge vice-chairman. The letter-advertisement read:

Friday night a group of pro-Nazi hoodlums—German-American Bundists, so-called "Christian" Mobilizers and "Christian" Frontists—attacked an orderly meeting of Fight for Freedom at 59th Street and Lexington Avenue. These Storm Troopers tried to push two young women off the platform. They tried to overturn a car. In disciplined formation they charged the crowd shouting, "We want Hitler; We Want Lindbergh." Similar tactics were used in Germany when the Nazis seized power. . . . We have been informed that the Nazis will try—in carrying on their battle against America—to break up other gatherings. They must not be permitted to do so. There must be adequate police protection. . . .

Why, it may be wondered, was this lacking? One explanation may have been afforded by the result of an investigation ordered by Mayor La Guardia; 407 members of the

[3] Ibid., March, 1941. It was in this same year that, in an address to the International Labor Organization's delegates, President Roosevelt declared: "Nazi Germany . . . has imported about 2,000,000 foreign civilian laborers. They have changed the occupied countries into great slave areas for the Nazi rulers. And at this moment Berlin is the principal slavemarket of all the world."

[4] *The New York Times*, June 22, 1941.

New York police department had joined the Christian Front. Both along with and independently of such street assemblages in cities, men and women distributed pamphlets and leaflets reviling Jews.

In a speech in New York City, Secretary of the Interior Ickes bitterly criticized Lindbergh for retaining the Hitler decoration, and asked the audience whether anyone had ever heard Lindbergh speak in behalf of democracy. There was a chorus of Noes. Sarcastically referring to Lindbergh's saying, when interviewed for his stand on a question, that he would have to give it thought before replying, Ickes more than implied that Lindbergh was waiting until he got his cue from Berlin. Stung to reply, Lindbergh protested that this was not so, and when assailed for his isolationist views by the President, who compared him to the "copperheads" of the Civil War era, resigned his commission as Colonel in the Army Air Corps Reserve.

It was at an America First rally, at Des Moines, Iowa, on September 11, 1941, that Lindbergh charged Jewish, British and Roosevelt administration groups with seeking to press America into war. This meeting was only partially pro-Lindbergh, as was shown by the mixed cheers and boos when he appeared before the crowd estimated at 7,500, and his address was frequently interrupted by cheers for President Roosevelt. Lindbergh's emphasis was upon the opposition of Jews to the Nazi Government as if they pre-eminently were the group bent upon its overthrow and maneuvering to accomplish it by enlisting America's aid. For what reason? "The persecution they suffered in Germany would be sufficient to make them bitter enemies of any race." In numerous editorials from time to time Lindbergh had been condemned as an ignorant young man. He now so again proved himself. He did not seem to know that in the First World War, a decade and a half, of course, before the great persecutions of Jews in Germany, Jews in America and in the allied countries were active in combating German militarism, aggression and schemes of conquest. And now, in unison with many other nationalities and races Jews were resistant to the entire Nazi plans to foist their enslaving "New Order" upon as much of the rest of the world as could be done by force and terrorism.

Evidently, to acquit himself of making too one-sided an indictment of Jews, Lindbergh proffered this mitigation: "No person with a sense of the dignity of mankind can condone the persecution of the Jewish race in Germany." This was only repeating what many another had already said, and he could not well put himself in the position of justifying an epochal, horrifying persecution. But this concession on Lindbergh's part was merely interpolated. On he speedily went to hold a threat before Jews. "Instead of agitating for war, the Jewish groups in this country should oppose it in every possible way, for they will be among the first to feel its full consequences." What these would be he did not elucidate. But as, in the same speech, he declared that England could not win the war, he presumably had one of two eventualities in mind—either in the outcome of Germany's victory, Jews in America would have to bear the blame for misleading to be attributed to them, or Germany would find ways, in Nazi mode, of making reprisals. Then Lindbergh passed to the hackneyed legend of Jewish power in America. "Their [the Jews'] greatest danger to this country lies in the large ownership and influence in our motion pictures, our press, our radio and our Government."[5]

Lindbergh seemed to be unaware of the alacrity with

---

[5] In this parroting of charges, Lindbergh left a void in not rounding out wonted anti-Semitic practice of assailing Jewish financiers. U. S. Senator Wheeler, a colleague on America First Committee, had not been so remiss. While, in a speech in the Senate on February 28, 1941, Wheeler professed abhorring bigotry, he, in the act of denouncing political control by a financial oligarchy, produced a list of bankers which, as arranged by him, was predominantly Jewish. (*Congressional Record*, 77th Congress, 1st Session, p. 1555.) Some other members of Congress followed the same or a similar line. But it took a tragic event in the lobby of Congress itself to bring one of such attacks sharply to the attention of the American people. Representative John E. Rankin, of Mississippi, asserted that "Wall Street and a little group of our international Jewish brethren are still attempting to harass the President and Congress of the United States into plunging us into the European war unprepared." Indignantly replying, Representative Edelstein, of New York, on June 14, 1941, denounced such talk "as the play and work of those people who want to demagogue." Representative Edelstein went on: "The fact of the matter is that the number of Jewish bankers in the United States is infinitesimal. It is also a fact that the meeting which took place yesterday on the steps of the Sub-Treasury was entirely controlled by persons other than Jewish bankers. I deplore the idea that any time anything happens, whether it be for a war policy or against a war policy, men in this House and outside this House attempt to use the Jews as their scapegoat. I say it is unfair and I say it is un-American. . . ." Five minutes after making this speech, Representative Edelstein collapsed and died of heart failure. Ibid., p. 4838.

which the Hitler regime at this very time was recouping itself in money and goods for the vast outlay by Germany of an estimated $36,000,000,000 in its seven years of feverish war preparations. Its tentacles omitting nothing, it plundered all Jewish property and by superfine pillage of all peoples in conquered countries, Nazidom, it was reckoned, had paid itself back the entire amount. Although in the aggregate the sums looted from Jews were admittedly large, no precise computation is obtainable. And all during their raping of conquered lands the Germans were using part of the enormous levies exacted for occupation costs in transferring to themselves, at their own figures, such properties as could not be seized outright or confiscated.

Finally, Lindbergh solemnly delivered this warning, or more properly, prediction: "If any of these groups—the British, the Jewish, or the Administration—stops agitating for war, I believe there will be little danger of our involvement." Need it be said that nearly thirteen months later came the answer to that silly prophecy when, carrying out a pact with its confederate Germany, Japan treacherously attacked American territory, and Germany and Italy declared war on the United States?

Anti-Jewish organizations, groups and individuals were elated at Lindbergh's coming into the open with his accusations. Editors in Germany, Italy and Spain lavishly approved his speech. But plaudits from such sources were drowned by the torrent of denunciations in America. At the White House, Stephen Early, President Roosevelt's secretary, made this trenchant comment: "You have seen the outpouring of Berlin in the last few days. You saw Lindbergh's statement last night. I think there is a striking similarity between the two." [6] Finding some justification for those who felt that Lindbergh nourished sympathies with Fascism, the Committee to Defend America issued a statement which read: "One of the cruelest and most used methods of the Nazis is to lay blame for misfortune on the shoulders of the Jewish people and whip up hatred against them. In the United States this is one of the most deplored of all the atrocious Nazi practices. Nothing is more repugnant to American ideals than anti-Semitism, which is a car-

[6] *The New York Times*, September 13, 1941.

dinal principle of Nazi-Fascism. Mr. Lindbergh may say that 'no person with a sense of the dignity of mankind can condone the persecution of the Jewish race in Germany.' But he should know that this persecution was brought about in Germany by exactly the kind of thing that he said at Des Moines."[7] This was assuming a degree of knowledge which Lindbergh never evinced he possessed; he had skyrocketed to renown wholly on his daring prowess as an airplane navigator, and not in the least on general attainments. His was but one more of the frequent cases whereby men having acquired great wealth or celebrity felt qualified to discourse on almost any subject.

Most biting were comments made by F. H. Peter Cusick, executive secretary of the Committee, Fight for Freedom. "Mr. Lindbergh's prestige," said he tartly, "has descended even more quickly than Hitler's dive bombers about which he talks so admiringly. Americans know that Mr. Lindbergh lied when he said that British and Jews were foremost among the groups advocating war. As a matter of fact, every survey reveals that it is in the South and Southwest that interventionist sentiment is strongest. In these sections there is the smallest Jewish or foreign population."[8] Which was so. But to charge Lindbergh with lying was no doubt misplaced; he simply was uninformed and jumped at preferred conclusions without apparently trying to learn the facts. Soon after his speech, a cross-section poll, in forty-eight States, by Gallup's American Institute of Public Opinion, showed that only one person in sixteen mentioned Jews as seeking to involve America in war.

---

[7] As the Nazi expectation of a "conqueror's early peace" vanished and Germany's losses mounted and its hardships increased, the Nazi regime, to distract attention from its own miscalculations, resorted still more frantically to intensifying hatred of Jews as Germany's "implacable enemy." Two months after Lindbergh's speech, Propaganda Minister Goebbels, in an article in *Das Reich,* the Propaganda Ministry's weekly publication, gave a long set of instructions to the German people on the inflexible attitude to be observed toward Jews. He listed ten points. Among them: "There is no difference among Jews. Every Jew is the sworn enemy of the German people. The Jews have no right to pose among us as equals. . . . They are to be silenced not only because they are fundamentally wrong, but because they are Jews and have no voice in the community. Jews contrived and brought on this war. With it they want to destroy the German Reich and our people. . . . They are suffering no injustice in the treatment we bestow on them. They more than earned it." Berlin dispatch to *The New York Times,* November 13, 1941.

[8] *The New York Times,* September 13, 1941.

Scoring Lindbergh for his "open appeal to anti-Semitism as a political principle," Kenneth Leslie, editor of *The Protestant Digest,* probably referred to Coughlinite and other prior movements in pointing out that anti-Semitism in America "has been assiduously cultivated in preparation for this Des Moines zero hour" which "climaxes a whole series of prepared positions."[9] Francis E. McMahon, associate professor of philosophy at Notre Dame University and vice-president of the Catholic Association for International Peace, challenged Lindbergh to a debate on the subject of America's foreign policy. "Fully aware of your influence upon many of my fellow Catholics," Professor McMahon telegraphed, "I cannot remain silent while you foment the spread of anti-Semitism at a moment when the Jewish people sustain one of the supreme agonies of their history. . . . My conscience leaves me no course save to challenge you to defend your prejudices, errors and sophisms in the public forum against me."[10] Lindbergh did not assent. In a public statement, Lewis W. Douglas, former U. S. Director of the Budget, and chairman of the policy group of the Committee to Defend America, said: "Anti-Semitism, implied in Colonel Lindbergh's speech, is one of the characteristics of Nazism wherever it has stuck up its ugly head," and it was to prevent Nazism in America that patriotic citizens, believing Hitler must be defeated, had formed the committee.[11] George Gordon Battle made public a telegram from William Allen White characterizing Lindbergh's Des Moines speech as "moral treason" and "unkind, unneighborly, dishonest words." "Shame on you, Charles Lindbergh," the telegram read on, "for injecting the Nazi race issue into American politics. Why was it necessary to defame an honest, patriotic cause by the indefensible injection of Hitler's anti-Semitism into the issue?"[12]

A joint statement by the American Jewish Committee and the Jewish Labor Committee denounced the "unsupported and unsupportable charge impugning the patriotism of Americans of Jewish faith"; the interests of American Jews and those of America were "one and indivisible"; and Lind-

[9] Ibid.
[10] Ibid., September 15, 1941.
[11] Ibid., September 14, 1941.
[12] Ibid., September 19, 1941.

bergh's speech was "only another example of the now familiar tactics to divide countries by stirring up religious and racial hatreds and setting group against group."[13] Brandishing a copy of Hitler's *Mein Kampf* in Congress, Representative Luther Patrick, of Alabama, on September 18, 1941, read aloud some of it and exclaimed, "It sounds like a paragraph of Lindbergh's, does it not?" Unsparingly, Representative Patrick deflated Lindbergh. "We hailed him as a hero. Mr. Lindbergh, however, has turned sour on the United States. . . . Yet this man puts himself up as a leader of a nation, but only after the infusion of some kind of doctrine he got somewhere outside of the United States. Any barber is his equal and any justice of the peace is his superior on matters of legislative knowledge and activity, or in statesmanship. . . . Now Lindbergh even tracks him [Hitler] so closely that he says we are being pulled into the war by the seat of the pants by President Roosevelt and the Jews.[14] The lower branch of the Texas Legislature adopted a resolution advising Lindbergh to stay away from Texas.

From coast to coast the press, editorially and otherwise, teemed with denunciations of Lindbergh. Various State members withdrew from the America First Committee which, however, as a central body, remained intact. Facing the avalanche of condemnations, it now sought to absolve itself by the audacious move of fixing responsibility for the anti-Semitic war-cry upon its adversaries. Its statement, issued on September 4, 1941, neither denied nor disowned Lindbergh's assertions; it crassly declared: "We deplore the injection of the race issue into the discussion of war and peace. It is the interventionists who have done this."

This paltry attempt at shirking was of itself a confession that Lindbergh's attack upon Jews had to be discountenanced for policy's sake, if for nothing else. In a casual, off-hand way individuals had happened upon the term "race issue," but this committee used it formally as if Jewish citizens were persons singularly apart from the rest of Americans. Judged by adherence to American principles and equalitarian standards, the great majority of Jews were in-

[13] Ibid.
[14] *Congressional Record*, 77th Congress, 1st Session, pp. 7680-7681.

disputably more American than the American First Committee, the course of which, as tested by Lindbergh's speech, was the antithesis of American standards of freedom. And all Jews were as much a vested integral of the population as any other segment. Pertaining to Americanism measured by residence in the United States and long attachment to it, there was apt point in the observation made by Rabbi Louis I. Newman of New York City. He spiritedly asked: "How dare any friend of Nazi Germany, whether he have a medal from Göring or not, whose forefathers came to this country later than the Jews, assert, like Haman of old, that Jews have special interests and opinions contrary to the welfare of the nation?" But refutation was really unnecessary; in taking over the Nazi "race issue" dogma, the America First Committee obviously belied the name under which it chose to pass.

Four days after this distraught committee had put out its statement, *The Protestant Digest* made public a declaration signed in the meantime by 700 leading Protestant clergymen and churchmen throughout the United States. Since the Lindbergh speech, this declaration proclaimed, "the most important political opposition to the Government has apparently decided to make anti-Semitism one of its major tactics, following identically the Hitler technique in Germany." The 700 called upon Christianity's spokesmen to preach and otherwise wage war against the "moral disease" of anti-Semitism which, in addition to its other evil features, was pronounced anti-Christianity.

Apparently Nicholas Murray Butler, president of Columbia University, looked upon the Lindbergh outburst as a sensational renewal of anti-Semitism. Although in an address at that university, on October 7, 1941, he did not mention Lindbergh's name, the relevancy was clear in his warning freshmen to beware of anti-Semitic persecution which had been "violently and publicly revived in this country within the last few weeks or months." The notion that all of a particular descent or faith could be lumped as of one mind in their public attitude was ridiculed by Dr. Butler "as a grotesque departure from fact." As for the charge of the Jewish population trying to jockey America into war, that was "absolutely contrary to every known fact." Yet, if repeated long enough, such a charge would be believed by "a certain large number of the population."[15] The same, Dr. Butler could have added, was the effect of repetitions of previous charges against Jews, although the extent of the number of people affected could only be conjectured. "We cannot," Dr. Butler urged, "protest too vigorously and too strongly against that sort of thing. It may be the Ku Klux Klan persecuting the Catholics; it may be the anti-Semites persecuting the Jews; but persecution on racial and religious grounds has absolutely no place in a nation given over to liberty which calls itself a democracy."[16]

Lindbergh retired into silence, but Hitler was still giving for German and world consumption his ding-dong against Jews as conspirators and war plotters. Years before this particular time, Hitler had said that he didn't care whether the *Protocols* were spurious; he had obtained from them valuable ideas which he would use.[17] Now he especially and seasonably availed himself of the myth so widely exploited as fact by these concoctions. Upon declaring war upon the United States, Hitler, in his speech to the Reichstag, on December 11, 1941, reeled out this explanation of the causes of world turmoil: "We know, of course, that the eternal Jew is behind all this. Roosevelt himself may not realize it, but then that only shows his limitations. Indeed, we all know the intention of the Jews to rule all civilized States in Europe and America . . ." A few days later, in his Bill of Rights Day radio address, President Franklin D. Roosevelt effectively designated the Nazi rulers. They were a "small clique of ambitious and unscrupulous politicians; political and moral tigers"; their entire program and goal "was nothing more than the overthrow throughout the earth of the great revolution of human liberty, of which our American Bill of Rights is the mother charter."

That contemplated destruction also comprised the entire

[15] A personal note: When a member of my family entered the U. S. Selective Service as a volunteer in 1941, he not infrequently heard some conscripts grumble: "The Jews got us into this."

[16] *The New York Times*, October 8, 1941.

[17] So Herman Rauschning tells us in his book *The Voice of Destruction*, p. 238. Rauschning reminded Hitler that the *"Protocols* were a manifest forgery." Hitler replied: "He didn't care two straws whether the story was historically true." Naturally in line with his total and admitted lack of scruples in everything else, Hitler could be expected to take this his accustomed amoral view.

annihilation of religious freedom. In a Navy Day radio address, on October 27, 1941, President Roosevelt had announced that the U. S. Government possessed a Hitler Government document containing a plan to abolish all existing religions, of whatever nature, confiscate remaining property, and set up an international Nazi church, with *Mein Kampf* replacing the Bible. Nazi vilification of President Roosevelt came as a matter of course. "Cowardly jackal," "tool of international Jewry" were two of many specimens. But President Roosevelt's statements were fully confirmed, early in the next year, by the Nazi release for publication of a thirty-one-point program for a "religion of National Socialism." Drafted by Dr. Alfred Rosenberg, Reich Minister for the East and one of the members of the Nazi select inner circle, this plan called for the abolition of the Bible and the substitution of *Mein Kampf* as furnishing the "ethnic morals under which Germans must live." Every ecclesiastical sacrament was to be abolished; marriage was to require merely the marital ceremony of the couple laying hands on a sword and vowing fidelity to each other; parents of a new-born babe were to take an oath that they were "proved descendants of the Aryan race" and would bring up the child "in the German spirit for the German people."

Pope Pius XII had denounced the undermining of Christian culture's foundation as "black paganism." This elaborate Nazi plan went far toward that atavistic end, but temporizingly stopped short at one point. It did accommodatingly allow God an omnipresent place in the universe. German men and women were bidden "to recognize God and his eternal work." But what institution was to reflect and interpret God's work? Such a need was provided for by one F. M. Schmidt, a Nazi administrator, in a pamphlet issued in mid-January, 1942, to the Hitler Youth. Away, wrote he, with the "theory of humanitarianism of the Christian Church"; henceforth the Church must be dispensed with "as mediator between God and man; it must be the nation" fulfilling that function. By nation he meant the German State which, of course, was centered in Hitler who, at the same time, either endowed himself or was endowed with god-like qualities. Intended to apply primarily to Germany, these plans, was the expectation, would be extended to conquered countries and to colonies if Hitler's schemes of conquest succeeded. The fixing of such plans into absolute law hinged upon the finality of Hitler's approval which, at this writing, so far as is known, has not officially been forthcoming. However, since Church influence in Germany had already been shattered, the youth, indoctrinated with the new "Aryan" credo, were bumptiously able to avow it without sanction of formal decree.

With Japan's perfidious and surprise attack on Pearl Harbor, Hawaii, on December 7, 1941, at the very time when Japanese envoys were in Washington ostensibly engaged in peaceful negotiations, all differences in America instantaneously vanished. The war, Lindbergh declared, had to be met "as united Americans regardless of our attitude in the past." The same stand was taken by his fellow members of the America First Committee which promptly disbanded. Volunteering his services to the Government, Lindbergh was assigned, in a civilian capacity, to do research for the War Department. When, late in March, 1942, Lindbergh, as a luncheon guest of Henry Ford, was taken on an inspection tour of the Willow Run bomber plant of the Ford Motor Company, his host offered him a position in the plant's engineering department. Consulting the Department of War at Washington as to whether it had objections, Lindbergh found that it had none, and a little later went to work at aeronautical and engineering research in the plant.

At about the same time, *The Florida Catholic,* a weekly published at St. Augustine, and the diocesan organ of Bishop Joseph P. Hurley, severely denounced "that un-American paper misnamed *Social Justice*"[18] for its activities as it affected the war. Condemning this "Axis-minded magazine," the editor of *The Florida Catholic* waxed highly indignant that *Social Justice* should be regarded by anybody as Catholic merely because it had been founded and carried on by Father Coughlin. *"Social Justice,"* the editorial said, "is not a Catholic paper. It does not reflect Catholic views. It does not acknowledge or obey any Catholic authority. Indeed, it has on occasions made bitter attacks on those authorities."

---

[18] In comment in other publications, *Social Justice* was described as having a wide circulation. Ayer's *Directory of Newspapers and Periodicals* for 1942 (p. 457) gave no figures.

And the editorial thus stigmatized *Social Justice:* "Despite its mock concern for the welfare of our country, despite its peculiar brand of piety, the magazine is both unpatriotic and un-Christian."

In a statement Coughlin had denied proprietorship of *Social Justice* which he could now avow his parents owned. On April 3, 1942, the Catholic Archdiocese of Detroit disavowed any connection or responsibility, directly or indirectly, for that weekly. A statement by the Right Rev. Edward J. Hickey, chancellor of the archdiocese, was published in an editorial headed "An Authoritative Confirmation" in *The Michigan Catholic.* Referring to the emphatic disclaimer of some Catholic papers in America that *Social Justice* was not a Catholic paper, the editorial said: "We had thought that this was clear to all our readers." Receipt of some inquiries, however, had led to the request to the Archdiocesan Chancery for authoritative confirmation on this point. Monsignor Hickey's reply pointed out that, by definition, a Catholic paper was one published under sanction of proper church authority. *"Social Justice,"* he continued, "is not under such supervision and is, therefore, not a Catholic paper. Moreover, for nearly two years back—since Father Coughlin's latest withdrawal from responsibility for *Social Justice* with the issue of May 27, 1940—no priest of this diocese has asked or received permission to contribute to *Social Justice,* and no priest of this diocese has been authorized to associate himself in any capacity with its publication or circulation, or to the knowledge of this office, has accordingly done so. . . ."

Many indignant or angry complaints about the character of *Social Justice* had been sent to Washington, but a specific crusade was launched by *PM.* This New York City newspaper ran scathing editorial denunciations of Coughlin and *Social Justice,* nor was it the only paper to brand that organ as "filthy." One *PM* editorial, on April 6, 1942, declined to consider Coughlin solely in his capacity as priest. It said: "We have no issue with any spiritual leader in his pulpit. . . . When Father Coughlin steps down from his pulpit, leaves his church and goes to sit at his editorial conferences, he ceases to be *Father* Coughlin and he becomes—we blush to say it—one of us journalists." *PM* assembled evidence of comments in *Social Justice* which, it pointed out, might have their deleterious effect upon the loyalty of workers in America's war factories or unduly influence sentiments of men going into its armed forces, notably those of youths of Catholic upbringing. A coupon which was a petition to U. S. Attorney General Biddle calling for action was published in *PM*. Readers were requested, if they approved, to sign and send it to Washington, which an estimated 43,000 did.

Of strong liberal convictions, while firmly believing in retention of free speech and free press, the Attorney General, at the same time, could not consider temporizing with charges of sedition. Consistent with the facts and the law he made an investigation. The results were set forth in an exhaustive letter he sent to Postmaster General Frank C. Walker. Pointing out that the Espionage Act had been upheld by the courts, he went on:

> Before considering specific violations of the Espionage Act by *Social Justice* I should like to call your attention to certain facts bearing upon the question of "intent." This publication has engaged over a period of time in a sustained and systematic attack on certain of our activities directly related to the war effort, as well as upon public morale generally. Furthermore, a study of ten major themes which have been broadcast by our enemies since December 7, 1941, as reported by the Foreign Broadcast Monitoring Service of the Federal Communications Commission, shows a close relation of material contained in *Social Justice* to those themes during approximately the same period. This parallelism has existed in a series of items and in repeated issues in which these themes are reproduced.

Giving examples, U. S. Attorney General Biddle's letter continued:

> The themes played upon by *Social Justice* since our entry into the war, at which time the statute came into operation, are in the main but a continuation and development of those appearing over a long period of time prior to December 7th. In fact, a striking similarity between this publication and Axis propaganda appeared as early as the issue of December, 1938, in which whole portions of a

speech made on September 13, 1935, by Propaganda Minister Goebbels, were published in *Social Justice* as an original article with but few words changed here and there and with no crediting or other identification of the source.

Some of the themes emphasized both by *Social Justice* and by enemy propaganda are: Pride in the achievements of the Axis powers and sympathy with their aims; disparagement of the intentions and motives of Great Britain and the United States; blame for the war on international bankers and their control of or influence in the present national administration and in the governments of the Allies; creation of racial hatreds and distrust; constant and frequent attacks upon the war policies of the present Government; and doubt as to the ability of the United States to win this war.

What in a single instance might be excused as careless overstatement may by constant repetition become evidence of a deliberate and intentional distortion of the truth—the more so when one considers the probable effect of such publication upon persons in the armed services of the United States and those not yet inducted but subject to induction or enlistment. It would appear to be a reasonable assumption that *Social Justice,* with an estimated circulation of 200,000, must reach such persons and that the statements used must have their intended effect.

In addition to quotations from *Social Justice* already submitted to Postmaster General Walker, U. S. Attorney General Biddle now sent more "made since our entry into the war, as a few of the many statements establishing in my opinion that the necessary elements constituting a violation of the Espionage Act are present and that denial of second-class mailing privilege is proper." Simultaneously, the U. S. Attorney General ordered an inquiry by a Federal Grand Jury to find out, among other phases, who really owned *Social Justice,* who did the editing and who was its guiding influence.

Pending further inquiry which would grant the publisher of *Social Justice* a hearing to show cause why that publication should not be permanently excluded from second-class mailing privileges, Postmaster General Walker, on April 14, 1942, issued an order barring the particular issue from such transportation. A few days later came a typical development. The Grand Jury at Washington had already issued subpoenas, and Coughlin, in a press statement issued at Royal Oak, made a significant announcement. Although, he declared, he had repeatedly avowed that he neither edited, published nor owned *Social Justice,* it was not necessary for the Grand Jury to determine who was responsible for the publication. ". . . I do here and now publicly state," Coughlin's admission said, "that I, Father Charles E. Coughlin, pastor of the Shrine of the Little Flower, alone am responsible for and do control the magazine, its policies and contents. This sole responsibility and control over the policy-making and content of the magazine I have exercised personally and officially by my effective moral and spiritual influence and direction over the editors, publishers and owners of *Social Justice.*"

Soon after Coughlin's statement, the Chancery of the Roman Catholic Archdiocese of Detroit released a highly informative copy of a letter written by Coughlin on May 16, 1940, to Archbishop Edward Mooney. In that letter Coughlin had assured Archbishop Mooney: "I will not be responsible for *Social Justice* magazine beyond the issue of the date of May 27, 1940." Coughlin added in that letter: "Already, I have informed Social Justice Publishing Corp. of my decision through the medium of a copy of this letter."

Following Postmaster General Walker's order, the Railway Express Agency refused to accept copies of *Social Justice* for shipment, but means were found to distribute the immediate issue. Its peddling and hawking on the streets and sale in news and book stores in the German section in Yorkville aroused particular indignation in New York City. There, on April 17, 1942, members of the American Labor Party in the City Council introduced a prohibitory ordinance. This aimed, under penalty of not exceeding six months in jail or fine up to $500 or both, to forbid the sale of any publication inciting religious hatred or interfering with the nation's war aims. In explaining the need of such a law one of its advocates in the City Council said: "The mere barring of such papers from the mails is an indefinite measure. The papers may still be shipped to various localities and distributed on the streets or house to house. The apparently inexhaustible resources of these anti-democrats make it possible to continue their anti-American action despite the banishment from the mails."

In a letter to U. S. Attorney General Biddle, the executive secretary of the Civil Rights Federation, in behalf of 300 Michigan organizations, having a claimed membership of more than 500,000 devoted to defense of civil liberties, approved his action against *Social Justice*. This magazine, the letter said, had "spread the poisonous doctrines of disunity, race and religious hatred, and surrender to aggressive fascism at home and abroad." It had, the letter went on, inspired bands of Christian Front storm troopers to co-operate with Nazi groups in acts of violence and terrorism. The International Labor Defense sent an open letter to Biddle congratulating him on the steps he had taken.

Coughlin, however, seemed obdurately bent upon pursuing his course, and in a spirit of defiance he challenged Biddle to give him an opportunity "to defend the property of *Social Justice*." An advance proof of an editorial to appear in that publication on April 27, 1942, handed to reporters affirmed the purpose to keep on publication ·until, was the reservation, "prohibited by some legally constituted authority." But, came the militant assurance, if the owners lost the "legal battle," then "we will observe the order literally."

Despite breathing of big words, there was no battle, and any intention of contesting the evidence placed before the postal officials evaporated. First, Postmaster General Walker found that, although the April 27th issue of *Social Justice* had changed its tone in some respects, yet there remained the obnoxious essentials "containing statements clearly within the prohibitions of the Espionage Act." A sustained and systematic attack was continued, the Postmaster General declared, on certain of America's war activities and policies. Specifying these attacks—which were a repetition of those which the U. S. Attorney General had already pointed out in detail—the Postmaster General told how they emphasized enemy propaganda themes and sought to affect the general public morale in America. Copies of this issue, the Postmaster General ruled, on April 25, 1942, were non-mailable.

Then came the hearing, on May 4, 1942, to determine why *Social Justice* should not be permanently denied second-class mailing. Notwithstanding his vaunts, neither Coughlin nor any representative chose to appear in defence. In the absence of this, the Postmaster General issued a standing order barring *Social Justice* from second-class use of the mail. At the same time, as if to make the relinquishment seem voluntary, a letter was received by the Postmaster General from E. Perrin Schwartz, styling himself president and editor of the *Social Justice* outfit, stating that the publication of the paper would be discontinued. By telegram Coughlin notified the Postmaster General that he endorsed Schwartz's stand in abandoning the second-class mailing opportunities.

After the hearing was concluded, Joseph Goldstein, a former New York City magistrate, found opportunity to voice a request for proceedings by the Department of Justice against *Social Justice* for a threat that, in the event of the paper being forced to discontinue publication, action detrimental to the Jews in America would be the result. The threat to which reference was made was doubtless one, in a recent issue of *Social Justice*, which warned: "The worst possible injustice that *Social Justice* could do to the Jews of America would be to discontinue publication of its own volition, seizing this opportunity to blame the Jews for our retirement. Were we to succumb to such a satanic temptation, the pogroms which crimsoned the soil of Europe would rank as a poor second to what would occur on the streets of New York."

In Detroit, Archbishop Mooney promptly expressed himself as gratified at the outcome of the Postoffice Department's disposition of the case against *Social Justice*. Numerous were the comments of satisfaction throughout the nation at large upon the exit of this reprehensible publication. Reasonably and naturally, *PM* broke forth in exultation. He had been told by responsible men, its editor Ralph Ingersoll wrote, that nothing could be done about Coughlin because his "hold on the ignorant and superstitious was too strong." Well, the purgation, so far as it concerned the Postoffice, *was* done, and now there remained the action of the Grand Jury on the Attorney General's definite charges of sedition.

Coughlin, however, escaped indictment. But the Federal Grand Jury, on July 23, 1942, did indict twenty-eight persons as seditionists, including many of the Jew-baiters whose careers we have already set forth. The Grand Jury gave a list of their numerous publications, and the organizations through which they operated. The indictment additionally charged that these persons would even make use of the *Congressional Record* to publish matter designed to obstruct and defeat national defence.

No such repeated campaigns as had been carried on against Jews could have failed to leave their varying imprint upon a host of minds. The National Conference of Christians and Jews, which had facilities for estimating prejudicial currents and undercurrents, judged this to be the case. With a realization of the task ahead, it, early in 1942, launched an educational campaign designed to reach 25,000,000 Protestant adults and children in America and combat prejudice. The basic plan was that of, through various means and channels, giving Protestants a better understanding of the background and beliefs of the people of other faiths. The hope was expressed that Catholics and Jews would undertake a similar work of enlightenment. The annual meeting of Catholic Bishops of the United States, at Washington, D. C., had embodied this pronouncement in its resolutions: "We cannot too strongly condemn the inhuman treatment to which the Jewish people have been subjected in many countries."

But although to a partial degree, Protestants, Catholics and Jews might or could be brought to co-operative effort in the aim to dispel prejudices against one another, there seems to have been no thought of overcoming those spread by an organization of ultra-religious zealots, fanatically truculent, calling themselves Jehovah's Witnesses. These bitterly assailed beliefs of Protestants, Catholics and Jews alike.

Founded in 1876, by Pastor Charles E. Russell, of Pittsburgh, the International Bible Students' Association, generally called Russellites, postulated its creed upon Biblical prophecies, mainly those of the Old Testament. These prophecies, it was maintained, revealed God's purposes in controlling the world's destinies, and all that other religions taught was an adulteration of His Word. To know what was in store for peoples it was only necessary to study and adhere to the prophecies. And as God had ordained a theocratic government for the rule of peoples, mundane governments were mere passing affairs, entitled to no respect and certainly no reverence. Opposition to war was a vital tenet of Jehovah's Witnesses.

Upon Russell's death, in 1916, Joseph Franklin Rutherford, who had been his legal adviser, became head of the movement which thereafter adopted the name Jehovah's Witnesses, so called because by attesting God's word and recognizing His will, as thus preached, members sanctified themselves as living witnesses. The infliction of Judgment Day, the return of old prophets and of Christ, and the ushering in of the Kingdom of God to redeem the sinful earth were sanguinely predicted. Recruited from a class of poorly circumstanced men and women, sunk in inferiority and obscurity, joiners of this movement thereby acquired a high sense of self-importance and superiority of standing. In the ardor of their roving missionary spirit they insisted upon thrusting themselves, their preachments and attacks, willy-nilly upon individuals, householders and neighborhoods. Their methods were often roughly intrusive and sometimes violent. Aside from cases coming up in the courts[19] the action of communities in various parts of America in running out of town these undesired characters was not unfamiliar.

Yet the organization of Jehovah's Witnesses thrived to

[19] One recent instance was a Jehovah Witness minister killing a deputy sheriff in Maine, in 1940, for refusing to listen to a phonograph record of the sect's teachings; the murderer was sentenced to life imprisonment at hard labor. In New Haven, Connecticut, on April 26, 1936, a father and his two sons, both of the latter in their late teens, yet all claiming to be ordained ministers of Jehovah's Witnesses, called from house to house in a thickly populated neighborhood 90 per cent of the residents of which were Catholic. Along with a bag of books and pamphlets they carried a portable phonograph which was set to playing a long attack upon the Catholic Church. This, among other abuses, was described as one of "fraud and deception" and as operating "the greatest racket ever employed amongst men and robs the people of their money. . . ." The trio was arrested and convicted of soliciting money without official approval and for shocking religious sensibilities. The case was taken to the Supreme Court of the United States which, on May 20, 1940, decided that the particular Connecticut law invoked was unconstitutional in restraining liberty by exercising a "censorship of religion." The conviction was accordingly reversed. Cantwell v. Connecticut, 310 *United States Reports*, p. 296. In a more current case, that affecting Walter Chaplinsky, a member of Jehovah's Witnesses, who was sentenced to six months in jail for abusing a Rochester, New Hampshire, police officer, the Supreme Court of the United States, on March 9, 1942, unanimously sustained the New Hampshire law. The court decided that "insulting" or "fighting words," among other objectionable expressions, did not come within the Constitutional provisions safeguarding freedom of speech.

such an extent that it maintained an eight-story printing plant at Brooklyn, New York, which published great numbers of books and booklets in many languages. Also, this organization operated an assembly plant capable of producing tens of thousands of portable phonographs, records and amplifying apparatus to be used in automobiles or trucks. If we accept the big claims made by the organization spokesmen, millions of booklets and books, at attractively low prices, had been annually distributed mainly by the persistent efforts of missionary canvassers calling from door to door. By the same claims, the total circulation, for all the years up to 1940, was several hundred millions of pamphlets and books; should persons approached be acquiescent but unable to pay, leaflets were freely given to them.

Unlike the crude and often ill-tempered speech of many of his followers, Rutherford spoke over the radio in a soft, urbane tone and his diction was unexceptionable. At the average price of 70 cents, an estimated 145,000 phonograph records of his lectures were yearly sold. In anticipation of the return of King David to earth, so Rutherford gave out, he had built at San Diego, in 1933, a twenty-room mansion as a fitting residence for the royal returner. In that mansion Rutherford lived and there, on January 10, 1942, he died. He had claimed a following of 2,000,000 in thirty-six different countries, but these figures were undoubtedly an exuberant computation. In the United States the number of militant and participant Jehovah's Witnesses perhaps did not reach more than 40,000 to 50,000, shifting from time to time, while circumjacent to this band were probably some hundreds of thousands of passive supporters who could hardly be classed as outright adherents yet all of whom were reckoned as followers.

Evidences of the deep-seated feeling incited by the various movements against Jews were seen in the steady advertisements of a number of important employment agencies which specified Christians only as eligible for the professional positions open. But the practice was even more flagrant in a list of corporations having large war contracts. Although skilled and manual workers were urgently needed, these corporations excluded both Jew and Negro. This discrimination was established, after public hearings and a study of the records, by President Franklin D. Roosevelt's Committee on Fair Employment Practice. Of this, Dr. Malcolm S. MacLean, president of Hampton Institute, was chairman. Ten industrial concerns, all in the Chicago and Milwaukee areas, were ordered by this committee, on April 11, 1942, to cease exclusion of available workers because of their race or religion. Failure to comply, it was pointed out, might be construed by the Government as violation of contract. The companies in question, the committee charged, had refused to employ Negroes or Jews, or both, chiefly Negroes; they had given instruction to public or private employment agencies asking for white or Christian workers exclusively. Moreover, that they had advertised in newspapers for workers specifying "Gentile," "Protestant," or "white," and if perchance any other than these were employed in the plants, they were refused opportunity for promotion in accordance with their qualifications. Mostly, the companies involved denied having practiced discrimination, but in every case the committee found evidence sustaining the charges.

The extent of the evil was seen in Legislatures finding necessity to pass penalizing acts. The New York Legislature enacted a law, signed by Governor Lehman, on April 14, 1942, making a misdemeanor of the refusal of employment in any capacity in defence industries because of race, color or creed. And then to make the law's effectiveness more sweeping, the same Legislature passed further measures, which became laws by Governor Lehman's approval, on May 7, 1942, extending the power of State officials to investigate and prevent any such discriminations. A bill providing penalties for the same offence was adopted by the New Jersey Legislature and, on May 9, 1942, was signed by Governor Edison.

The urgent, vital need of such laws was betokened by a mandate, on May 26, 1942, of the President's Committee on Fair Employment Practice. Acting upon evidence brought forth at prior public hearings, it ordered eight industrial concerns, all holding large war contracts, in the New York and New Jersey sections, to desist from discrimination against Jews and Negroes, and often against Catholics. The openness with which such establishments showed their prejudice was manifested in their advertisements. These had specified that eligibles must be "white" or "Protestant" or "Gentile." Other employers were under investigation; Chairman MacLean said that the committee had "a long list who have hitherto refused or who now refuse employment to persons because of their race, religion or their national background." And he added: "This at a time when we must have unity of brain, brawn and loyalty to defeat our common enemies from without."

Chapter XXXII

WARTIME AND POST-WAR

WORLD WAR II had a generally beneficial effect on the status of equal rights in the United States. Under the strain of wartime emergency, Americans of all races and creeds found themselves working together in a wholly new atmosphere. Many barriers crumbled under the pressure, particularly those in the fields of employment and of specialized training and higher education. The need for defense materials and for trained personnel to fulfill vital military and war production assignments was the order of the day. Most important of all, the shocking example of Nazi Germany's barbarous treatment of the Jews and others caused a genuine revulsion throughout America and the free world. It seemed hypocritical indeed for the American people, locked in a desperate global struggle in which they championed the cause of world freedom, to practice discrimination against the minorities in their own midst. Instances of prejudice were more likely to provoke indignation among large segments of the population which, before the war, had been unconcerned with civil rights. With the exception of one group —the Nisei[1]—the wartime period marked a general lessening of discrimination and a new phase of opportunity for America's minorities.

[1] During 1942, some 100,000 United States residents of Japanese descent were evacuated from California, Washington, and Oregon by U.S. military forces and placed in "relocation centers" under military custody. The great majority of those placed in camps—more than 70,000 of them—were American citizens, and many were second and third generation Americans. Prejudice ran high; a bill to deprive all Nisei of their American citizenship was introduced in the U.S. Senate by Senator Holman of Oregon, and there were even plans to expel them from the country. Following the close of World War II, repentant Americans attempted to redress the injustices done to the Nisei, and in 1948, and 1951, and again 1956, Congress passed legislation to settle their claims of property losses.

Particularly significant was the willingness of the federal government to speak out on behalf of civil rights. President Franklin D. Roosevelt had taken the lead when he established the Fair Employment Practices Committee by Executive Order.[2]

Meanwhile, the United States Supreme Court was moving toward a more vigorous enforcement of constitutional guarantees. In 1944, the Court struck down the "white primary," holding that "It may now be taken as a postulate that the right to vote in . . . a primary . . . without discrimination by the State . . . is a right secured by the Constitution."[3] And, two years later, in 1946, the Supreme Court voided a Virginia statute which had required segregation on interstate as well as intra-state commerce.[4] This was the first time that segregation in the field of transportation had been successfully challenged in the courts.

Late that same year, President Harry S. Truman used his federal authority in a move to strengthen civil rights further; he asserted the role and the responsibility of the federal government in safeguarding individual freedom for all Americans, and by Executive Order,[5] he established the President's Committee on Civil Rights, which he charged with the duty of conducting a nationwide inquiry and of recommending new legislation and other appropriate action to be taken by the federal government.

Almost a year later, on October 29, 1947, the President's Committee issued its report.[6] The Committee found many violations of civil rights, in all parts of the nation, and their report contained twenty-seven recommendations for federal legislative action. When Congress failed to enact the legislation, President Truman moved ahead on his own to establish one recommendation of the Commission which could clearly be established by Executive authority alone. In July of 1948, he issued an Executive Order which directed "equality of treatment and opportunity for all persons in the armed services without regard to race, color, religion, or

[2] Executive Order No. 8802, June 25, 1941.
[3] *Smith v. Allwright*, 321 US 649.
[4] *Morgan v. Virginia*, 328 US 373.
[5] Executive Order No. 9808, December 5, 1946.
[6] *To Secure These Rights*, The Report of the President's Committee on Civil Rights (Simon and Schuster, New York, 1947).

national origin."[7] The major discrimination had been
against Negroes, who had been segregated. The barriers
against them were thus removed, and the armed forces were
ordered integrated.

Some state governments were willing to act on behalf
of equal rights, too. In 1945, the State Commission Against
Discrimination was founded in New York, the first such
governmental agency in any state.[8] That same year, New
Jersey and Wisconsin enacted anti-discrimination legislation,
and by the end of 1947, Massachusetts, Connecticut, and
Indiana had followed suit. Only in the four Eastern states
did the legislation have maximum effectiveness, however, as
the Wisconsin and Indiana legislation lacked effective provisions for enforcement.

Nonetheless, the employment fields which first opened up
during wartime continued to provide a greater range of opportunity than ever before for America's minority groups.
The advance of the Negro was most striking. Along with all
Americans, Negroes were becoming more urbanized. And as
Negroes moved to urban centers in order to take advantage
of employment opportunities, they found they had increased
opportunities for voting as well.

Even in the Deep South, bars against Negro voting were
somewhat relaxed. This was not true throughout the whole
of the South; for instance, in an attempt to circumvent the
Supreme Court decision outlawing the white primary, the
South Carolina legislature repealed all of the state laws controlling primary elections, and relinquished to the political

[7] Executive Order No. 9981, July 26, 1948.

[8] For various reasons, New York's SCAD has been from the very first the
leading anti-discrimination agency on the state level. It is the largest in personnel, and by far the best financed; yet the success of SCAD has not been
due simply to an able staff and adequate funds. The social and political climate of New York is probably the most favorable in the entire nation for vigorous assertion and active defense of the civil rights of members of minority
groups. And New York City is one of the most volatile cities in the world; unlike anti-discrimination organizations in some parts of the country which
work in a comparatively stable social, economic, and ethnic situation, New
York's SCAD is continually confronted with new problems as the patterns of
life in New York City constantly shift and change. The cases handled by this
agency provide a cross-section of the different types of bigotry found in the
industrial East during the forties and fifties. The largest number of cases
handled by SCAD involve discrimination on account of color. The agency also
has handled a substantial number of cases involving discrimination against
Jews, and some cases of anti-Catholic discrimination.

parties all responsibilities for conducting primaries. Consequently, the practical result of this was that Negroes still could not participate in South Carolina Democratic primaries. As a result, a Negro voter, George Elmore, sought a declaratory judgment in federal court against South Carolina Democratic party officials who had barred him from the 1946 primary. On July 12, 1947, the local Federal District Court in South Carolina responded by enjoining Democratic officials "from excluding qualified voters from enrollment and casting ballots by reason of their not being persons of the white race." The opinion was delivered by Judge J. Waties Waring, a native South Carolinian, who said, "It is time for South Carolina to rejoin the union. It is time to fall into step with the other states to adopt the American way of conducting elections."

In 1947, there were less than 600,000 registered Negro voters in the South, about one-fourth of the number of Negroes of voting age. Still, progress was being made, even in the Deep South; and in the Border States, Negroes assumed a new place in political influence.

Meantime, progress was being made on yet another front; by 1947, a total of eighteen states had enacted laws prohibiting discrimination in "public accommodations," one of the most vexing humiliations imposed upon Negroes and others. The Middle Atlantic industrial states of New York, New Jersey, and Pennsylvania, and the New England states of Massachusetts, Connecticut, and Rhode Island, had such legislation. In the West, Colorado, and on the Pacific Coast, California and Washington also had these laws. But in numerical terms, the Midwest led the nation, with a total of ten states having adopted laws against discrimination in public accommodations. This Mid-western group included not only the industrial states of Illinois, Indiana, Ohio, and Michigan, and the traditionally liberal states of Minnesota and Wisconsin, but also the predominantly rural, conservative states of Iowa, Nebraska and Kansas. True enough, these laws often were ignored, whatever the state; but the principle had been established legally, and, more and more, it was respected.

In short, the gains achieved during and just after World War II were retained and even widened in the years that followed. Continuing economic expansion played a major rôle; and just how vital a rôle was demonstrated whenever there was economic dislocation. Some industries, and some sections of the country, suffered recessions of various degrees; and when these took place, the workers who were members of minority groups frequently discovered they were the first to be laid off, and the last to be rehired.

Still, the nation at large had accepted Americans of minority groups in their new posts and occupations. Likewise, the anti-discrimination laws were found to be successful. President Truman's Committee on Civil Rights concluded in 1947 that the work of the anti-discrimination commissions in New York, New Jersey, Connecticut, and Massachusetts had resulted in a major decrease of employment discrimination in these states. In 1949, four more states enacted laws prohibiting discrimination in employment. In the East, Rhode Island joined the four states which already had functioning commissions; and with the passage of legislation and the establishment of commissions in Washington, Oregon and New Mexico, official state governmental activity directed against bias in employment spread to the Far West. In 1951, Colorado enacted anti-discrimination legislation, and Colorado's commission joined the list. But anti-bias measures did not win out in every contest; and, notably, in California the legislature failed to enact the anti-bias legislation recommended by the then chief executive, Governor Earl Warren.

The late 1940s marked another innovation in official state protection for the civil rights of minority groups. Again, New York was the pioneer, which in 1948 adopted a Fair Education Practices Act. The next year, 1949, New Jersey and Massachusetts also enacted such legislation.

The year of 1948 was significant for yet another major breakthrough in civil rights. The U.S. Supreme Court declared that covenants designed to restrict ownership of property or residence according to race could not be legally enforced because such covenants denied the excluded groups their rights under the Fourteenth Amendment.[9]

And in 1949, the first state took action concerning discrimination in housing. Connecticut enacted a law barring discrimination in all housing which received public aid or

9 *Shelly v. Kraemer*, 334 US 1; *Hurd v. Hodge*, 334 US 24.

assistance. This was only the first of many anti-discrimination measures yet to come in the field of housing. Also in 1949, Connecticut and New Jersey enacted the first enforceable state legislation banning discrimination in public accommodations.

Thus it was that, year by year, government on the federal level—and on the state level, too, in some parts of the nation —moved more firmly to declare that constitutional guarantees of individual freedom applied to all Americans, regardless of race, creed or color. The policy of the Executive branch of government, which gradually eradicated discrimination within the vast network of federal agencies, set a strong example for the states and for all citizens. The role of the Judiciary was equally important, for now, more than ever before, when members of minority groups were denied their lawful rights, they were likely to persevere in their cause and seek justice in the courts. New cases in the area of civil rights gave the Judiciary the opportunity to clarify and to establish these rights yet more firmly.

As it was the American Negro who, in greatest numbers, had suffered the most obvious and severe restrictions, it was the progress of the Negro that offered the most dramatic contrast to the pre-war days.[10] True enough, discrimination in housing continued much as before, and in all sections of the country. But, in the fields of education and employment and in the exercise of citizenship rights, the old barriers were

[10] The progress of other groups was dramatic, too; for instance, American Jews no longer faced the type of widespread overt bigotry which had confronted them prior to World War II. But, for generations American Negroes had faced barriers more rigid, more widespread and more formidable than those imposed on any other American minority. Consequently, the Negroes have had more distance to cover than anyone else in order to attain equal rights. Significantly, by the 1950s, key Jewish service agencies found that anti-Semitism had so diminished as a general problem that they could devote a considerable part of their efforts and resources toward aiding the American Negro's struggle for equal rights.

The nationwide character of discrimination against Negroes dictated that the movement for Negro rights would tend to obscure regional discrimination against other groups and the efforts being made to correct these regional situations. Thus, it was that the plight of Spanish-Americans—Mexican-Americans in the Southwest and Far West, and Puerto Ricans in New York City—received less national attention that otherwise might have been the case.

Progress was being made by these Spanish groups, both through direct efforts on their behalf and as a result of the advances made by the Negro. As barriers of discrimination based on race and color first weakened, then fell, Spanish-Americans found that they moved forward alongside the Negro.

fast collapsing everywhere, except in the Deep South. For the first time in American history, it was estimated that three million Negroes voted in the national election of 1952. Not only was this a considerable total of votes, but the concentration in politically strategic states such as New York, Pennsylvania, Illinois, Michigan and California further enhanced the growing national political influence of the Negro. In the South, it was estimated by the Southern Regional Council that in 1952 there were one million Negro voters registered in the eleven states which had comprised the Confederacy. By 1953, only five Southern states—Alabama, Arkansas, Mississippi, Texas and Virginia—still maintained a poll tax.

Hand in hand with increased political activity went increased legal activity to obtain those various rights which were still being withheld. Although some states had barred discrimination in public education legally, states of the Deep South had enacted laws with just the opposite intent, laws which formally required segregation in every school in every part of these states. Still other states, although certainly not requiring segregation, did nonetheless permit it legally under local option arrangements. Thus, it was that even in the early 1950s, as many as twenty-one states had some kind of segregation law and practice in public education.

And overt bigotry, although less common during wartime and the immediate post-war years, did not disappear. For instance, the summer and fall of 1950 were marked by a series of anti-Semitic incidents in the Boston area which culminated in a near-riot. In September of 1950, the walls of Independence Hall in Philadelphia were defaced with anti-Semitic slogans and obscenity. And prior to the elections of November, 1950, the Christian Nationalist Party of Gerald L. K. Smith, having obtained certification as a legal political party in Missouri, took advantage of Federal Communications Commission regulations providing free radio time for candidates and scandalized the citizens of Missouri with hate-mongering broadcasts. As usual, the Christian Nationalist campaign played on the themes of racialism and anti-Semitism.

However, the two incidents of this period which would receive the greatest national and international attention were still to come. In Cicero, Illinois, a suburb of Chicago, anti-Negro feeling exploded in July of 1951. The result was a riot of such proportions that Governor Adlai E. Stevenson dispatched National Guard units to restore order. The situation in Cicero was subsequently resolved when the town president, the town attorney, the police and fire chiefs and several policemen were indicted by a Federal Grand Jury on charges on conspiracy and violation of equal-rights law.

During that same year of 1951, bigotry put its ugly mark on the National Capitol. Mrs. Anna M. Rosenberg of New York was named to the post of Assistant Secretary of Defense. In the course of investigation, it was found that an Anna Rosenberg of New York had been an alleged Communist; and in the resulting uproar and confusion, anti-Semitic bigots had a field day. It was soon proven that there had been a case of mistaken identity. Mrs. Rosenberg was vindicated, and the Senate confirmed her in the new post; but she had undergone a disgraceful campaign of vilification.

However, it can be said that, despite these acts of individual and group hostility, the 1950s were generally a decade of increasing mutual respect and harmony between the various racial and religious components of America.

CHAPTER XXXIII

McCARTHY and McCARTHYISM

ON FEBRUARY 9, 1950, Senator Joseph R. McCarthy of Wisconsin stood before a Republican gathering in Wheeling, West Virginia, and declared:

"While I cannot take the time to name all the men in the State Department who have been named as active members of the Communist Party and members of a spy ring, I have here in my hand a list of 205—a list of names that were made known to the Secretary of State as being members of the Communist Party and who nevertheless are still working and shaping policy in the State Department."[1]

This address set off one of the wildest, most fantastic witch-hunts in the history of the United States. McCarthy himself was to insult and defame Presidents Harry Truman and Dwight D. Eisenhower, Cabinet officers, generals, ambassadors, fellow Senators, and Americans from every walk of life.

Nor was the extent of the witch-hunt restricted merely to the activities of Senator McCarthy. A spirit of fear and dread blanketed the nation, and everywhere "little McCarthys" sprang up to accuse, threaten and terrorize their fellow countrymen. This new spirit of reckless defamation of the innocent was to add a new word to the English language: McCarthyism.

Senator McCarthy achieved international notoriety. A noted Washington correspondent reported in a leading national magazine:

"As it is reflected in Washington, foreign opinion of the Wisconsin Senator can be summed up in two words: amaze-

[1] As reported in *The Wheeling Intelligencer* and recorded by Radio Station WWVA, Wheeling. McCarthy later denied the statement.

ment, fear. Bureaucratic opinion in Washington, as held by officials and senior employes of the Federal Government is similar: resignation, deep fear."[2]

His own Republican colleagues in the United States Senate denounced McCarthy in the strongest terms for "selfish political exploitation of fear, bigotry, ignorance, and intolerance," adding "It is high time that we all stopped being tools and victims of totalitarian technique—techniques that if continued here unchecked, will surely end what we have come to cherish as the American way of life."[3]

Who was Senator McCarthy? What was his background? How had he achieved such power?

Joseph Raymond McCarthy was born on November 14, 1908,[4] on his parents' farm in Outagamie County, in east central Wisconsin. He was the fifth of seven children born to Timothy Thomas and Bridget Tierney McCarthy, and like his brothers and sisters, spent his grade school days in a one-room country schoolhouse. As the name would indicate, the McCarthys were of Irish descent, and were devout Roman Catholics. On Sundays, the family attended Mass in the county seat, Appleton. The rest of the week was devoted to rigorous farm work.

Graduating from the Underhill Country School at the age of fourteen, young Joe did not go ahead to high school, but turned his energies to chicken farming, an enterprise which was to occupy him for the next five years. At the age of nineteen, he left home, moving to the small town of Manawa, Wisconsin, in neighboring Waupaca county. In Manawa, the youthful McCarthy got his first job away from home, and also renewed his formal education. He became manager of the local branch of a grocery chain, and the next year—at twenty—enrolled at Little Wolf High School. Work-

2 William S. White, "Joe McCarthy: The Man With the Power," *Look* Magazine, June 16, 1953, p. 30.

3 "Declaration of Conscience," June 1, 1950, signed by Republican Senators George D. Aiken of Vermont, Robert C. Hendrickson of New Jersey, Irving M. Ives of New York, Wayne Morse of Oregon, Margaret Chase Smith of Maine, Edward J. Thye of Minnesota and Charles W. Tobey of New Hampshire.

4 Senator McCarthy has listed his birth date as November 14, 1909, and it is so printed in *The Congressional Directory* and *Who's Who in America;* however, the official records in Wisconsin certify the date as exactly one year earlier. An explanation of McCarthy's apparent reason for wishing to alter his age is given later in this chapter.

ing first at his grocery job, and then as a movie usher, Joe pursued his studies. A year later, he had his high school diploma. That fall, the fall of 1930, he enrolled in the Engineering College of Marquette University in Milwaukee, intent on an engineering career.

After two years of engineering school, the young McCarthy decided this was not the field for him, and switched to law. More years passed—and he was working at part-time jobs all the while, in order to support himself. In May, 1935, he was graduated from the Law College of Marquette University with the degree of Bachelor of Laws, was thereupon admitted to the Wisconsin Bar, and shortly thereafter returned to Waupaca County to set up his new law practice. At twenty-seven, now a lawyer, Joe was returning home—his new law office at Waupaca, Wisconsin, was ten miles from Manawa, and only forty miles from his birthplace.

McCarthy's law practice in Waupaca lasted a brief ten months; in February of 1936, he accepted the invitation of attorney Mike Eberlein to join the latter in practice at Shawano, Wisconsin, approximately forty miles north of Waupaca. That fall, McCarthy made his first plunge into politics; he was elected President of the Young Democratic Clubs of Wisconsin's Seventh Congressional District, and a month later secured the Democratic nomination for the post of District Attorney of Shawano County. That November, Democrat McCarthy came in second; he lost to the candidate of the La Follette Progressive Party, but outpolled the Republican candidate.

The next three years, McCarthy pursued a double career —he continued his law practice with Mike Eberlein, and he prepared himself for his next political try. In 1939, he announced his candidacy for the post of Circuit Judge of Wisconsin's District Ten, comprising the counties of Outagamie, Shawano and Langlade.

It was in this campaign that McCarthy first introduced the political tactics for which he later became internationally notorious. His employer, political mentor and law partner, Mike Eberlein had cherished an almost lifelong ambition to achieve this judicial post, and he confided to McCarthy that he planned to announce as a candidate. McCarthy said nothing to Eberlein about his own ambitions, but promptly made a public announcement timed to forestall Eberlein's own bid.[5]

McCarthy then turned his full artillery on the incumbent, Judge Edgar V. Werner, who had spent twenty-four years of service on the bench. In McCarthy's campaign speeches, "he carelessly referred to 'my 73-year-old opponent,'"[6] and McCarthy campaign literature stated, "The present Judge, Edgar V. Werner, was born in 1866."[7] And, on occasion, McCarthy even raised Judge Werner's age to eighty-nine.[8] It was a matter of public record that Judge Werner was sixty-six, but McCarthy hammered on the theme of age and implied senility. Furthermore, at the same time that McCarthy was falsifying his opponent's age, he altered his own; by chopping off a year of his own age, he could qualify for the distinction of being the youngest Circuit Court Judge in Wisconsin history. McCarthy scored his area's political upset of the year; he unseated Judge Werner, and then rode out a subsequent two-point legal action brought against him for violating Wisconsin's corrupt-practices law by dishonest campaign tactics and by excessive campaign expenditures.

It was not long until Judge McCarthy ran into another sticky situation; his handling of the so-called Quaker Dairy case caused him to be formally censured by the Wisconsin Supreme Court.[9] In June of 1942, he took a leave from his judicial post and enlisted in the Marine Corps. He was commissioned a First Lieutenant, and later rose to the rank of Captain.

In the fall of 1944, still a Marine and still a Judge, he announced himself a candidate for the Republican nomination as United States Senator. He lost to the incumbent, Alexander Wiley, but made a respectable, even impressive, showing.

But this campaign involved McCarthy in charges of violation of both state and federal law. As a military officer, he

5 Jack Anderson and Ronald W. May, McCarthy: *The Man, The Senator, The "Ism"* (Beacon Press, Boston, 1952), p. 37.

6 Ibid., p. 41.

7 Richard H. Rovere, *Senator Joe McCarthy* (Harcourt, Brace and Co., New York, 1959), p. 88.

8 Ibid.

9 *State ex rel Department of Agriculture, Petitioner v. McCarthy, Circuit Judge, Respondent*, 238 Wis. 258.

was forbidden to discuss political issues, yet he even wore his uniform while campaigning; and as a state judge, he was forbidden by the Wisconsin Constitution to run for another office while still holding his judicial post. Finally, as in his previous campaign, there were accusations that he had violated the state corrupt-practices law by excessive campaign expenditures. Again he rode out all charges.

In 1945, McCarthy resigned from the Marine Corps, moved back to Wisconsin, and won re-election as Circuit Judge. And he fixed his sights on the next contest for United States Senator, coming up the following year.

The Senate seat that McCarthy coveted seemed to be completely beyond his reach. It was occupied with great distinction by Robert M. La Follette, Jr., who in 1945 had held it for twenty-one years—and he had inherited the seat from his father, the famous Robert M. La Follette, Sr., who, in turn, had held it for nineteen years. Indeed, from 1905 onward, the United States Senate had been graced by the membership of a La Follette, and it seemed fantastic that, of all people, the brash young McCarthy could bring this era to an end.

Undaunted, McCarthy plowed ahead. The first big victory was his endorsement for the Senatorial nomination by the Republican Voluntary Committee, which represented the conservative organizational Republicans. Then, on primary day, McCarthy edged out La Follette by the razor-thin margin of 5,396 votes (207,935 to 202,539); he had bagged the Republican Senatorial nomination.

At first, the Wisconsin State Treasurer, John Smith, refused to validate McCarthy's nomination; he declined to sign the certificate of nomination because of the state constitutional prohibition against any state judge running for political office. But he buckled under pressure; and McCarthy also survived a subsequent legal action aimed at knocking his name off the November ballot.

The Democratic candidate, Professor Howard McMurray of the University of Wisconsin, did his best to slow down McCarthy, but it was hopeless. When, in a public debate, McMurray pointed out that the canon of ethics of the American Bar Association barred a judge from running for political office and still retaining his judicial office, McCarthy retorted, "I don't belong to the American Bar Association, and I'm not bound by its code," and added, "[it's] a code of ethics written by a few lawyers . . . without the force of law."[10] And so it went; and in November, McCarthy smashed McMurray by 620,430 to 378,772.

How had McCarthy carried off his victory? The November result was to be expected, in a traditionally Republican state; but how had McCarthy unseated La Follette?

Senator La Follette had operated under several handicaps. In Washington, he had studiously devoted himself to public service, and had failed to keep close touch with his constituency. Perhaps more serious was the fact that, prior to 1946, he had been the nominee of the Progressive Party and this was the first time he had sought the Republican nomination. Many conservative Republicans in Wisconsin harbored a keen distaste for the family name of La Follette; and they specifically disliked "Young Bob's" defense of civil liberties and of the rights of organized labor and his support of the welfare legislation associated with the Roosevelt "New Deal."

There were other factors, too. La Follette's organization had become weakened, and made political blunders. A number of Democrats crossed party lines in the primary, voting for McCarthy as the more vulnerable target for their own candidate in November. Finally, the small but powerful group of Communists in Wisconsin detested La Follette, and threw their support to McCarthy. When asked about Communist backing, McCarthy replied, "Communists have the same right to vote as anyone else, don't they?"[11]

McCarthy was later censured by the Wisconsin Supreme Court for his part in this election, the second time he was rebuked by the highest tribunal of the state. The State Board of Bar Commissioners brought an unprecedented action against him, and the court declared:

"It is difficult to conceive of any conduct upon the part of a presiding judge which would bring judges into greater disrepute and contempt than the conduct of the defendant challenged in this proceeding.

"The defendant, by his conduct, chose to defy the rules of ethical conduct prescribed by the Constitution, the laws

10 As quoted by Anderson and May, p. 117.
11 As quoted by Anderson and May, p. 104, and Rovere, p. 104.

of the State of Wisconsin, and the members of the profession in order to attain a selfish personal advantage."[12]

Yet the most tragic result of that campaign was still to come. Robert M. La Follette, Jr., was a scholarly, cultured, conscientious gentleman of high moral dedication and purpose, whom McCarthy retired from politics a broken man. In later years, La Follette committed suicide—a final, tragic footnote to this chapter in McCarthy's political career.

As a freshman Senator, Joseph R. McCarthy floundered about for an issue on which to make a national reputation. He became involved with a number of questionable lobbyists for special interests; and these evolved into questionable financial practices. But probably the most extraordinary incident of McCarthy's early years in the Senate was his part in the Malmédy Massacre investigation.

In 1946, the year of McCarthy's election to the Senate, some seventy German SS men, members of the infamous "Blowtorch Battalion" of the First SS Panzer Regiment, were tried as war criminals for having massacred American military prisoners and Belgian civilians at Malmédy, Belgium, during the Battle of the Bulge. Forty-three of these SS men received the death sentence. Subsequently, rumors circulated that these SS defendants had been subjected to atrocities by American authorities. The death sentences were stayed, and in April, 1949, a subcommittee of the Senate Armed Services Committee opened special hearings on the matter. The subcommittee was composed of Senator Raymond Baldwin of Connecticut, a Republican, as Chairman, and Senators Lester Hunt of Wyoming and Estes Kefauver of Tennessee, both Democrats.

Senator McCarthy was not a member of the Armed Services Committee, or of the subcommittee; but, from the first, he sat in on the hearings and soon dominated them altogether. Senator McCarthy took the position that the rumors of American atrocities against the convicted Nazis were true, and attempted to sustain his viewpoint by browbeating witnesses and making violent accusations against them. McCarthy's remarks made top news in Germany; the Communist press trumpeted his statements as proof of the brutality of the American army and civilian administrators. The

12 *State of Wisconsin v. Joseph R. McCarthy*, 255 Wis. 234.

subcommittee determined that the charges were false; but all Germany was inflamed, and, to forestall riots and serious long-range consequences, the death sentences were commuted. Later developments proved that Senator McCarthy had been the tool and pawn of international Communism. "At a subsequent hearing of the Armed Services Subcommittee in Germany, a notorious Communist agent, Dr. Rudolph Aschenauer, admitted that he had worked up the whole case in defense of the SS men, that he had manufactured all the charges—and that he was the source of the data on which the Senator based his case."[13]

However, not even a year had elapsed until McCarthy was blasting others as Communists, spies and traitors. The famous Wheeling, West Virginia, address rocked the nation; and in March of 1950, a subcommittee of the Senate Foreign Relations Committee took up McCarthy's charges of Communism in the State Department. The subcommittee was headed by Senator Millard Tydings of Maryland, a conservative Democrat and a long-time opponent of the "New Deal," whom President Roosevelt had attempted to purge from the Senate. The subcommittee also included two other Democrats, Senators Theodore F. Green of Rhode Island and the late Brien McMahon of Connecticut, and two Republicans, Bourke Hickenlooper of Iowa and Henry Cabot Lodge of Massachusetts. That July, the Subcommittee issued a sharply-worded report which dismissed the McCarthy charges as unfounded.

But Senator Tydings had not reckoned with McCarthy's fury and vindictiveness. Tydings was up for re-election that November; and McCarthy forces mounted an amazingly vicious campaign against him, symbolized by the now famous forged photograph which showed Senator Tydings in intimate conversation with American Communist leader Earl Browder. McCarthy helped to accomplish what Roosevelt could not: the Maryland aristocrat was defeated that November.

After the new Congress took office in 1951, the campaign against Senator Tydings became a subject for investigation

---

13 James Rorty and Moshe Decter, *McCarthy and the Communists* (Beacon Press, Boston, 1954), p. 63. This is confirmed by Anderson and May, pp. 162-163, and also by Rovere, p. 112.

by the Subcommittee on Privileges and Elections of the Senate Rules Committee. The subcommittee was headed by Senator Guy M. Gillette of Iowa, a Democrat, and consisted of two other Democrats, Senators A. S. Mike Monroney of Oklahoma and Thomas C. Hennings, Jr., of Missouri, and two Republicans, Senators Robert C. Hendrickson of New Jersey, and Margaret Chase Smith of Maine. That summer, the subcommittee unanimously concluded that the Maryland election "brought into sharp focus certain campaign tactics and practices that can best be characterized as . . . destructive of fundamental American principles." The subcommittee "vigorously denounced" what it termed a "despicable, back-street campaign."

Still, the Senate made no move actually to curb McCarthy. Finally, a lone Senator took it upon himself to stand up on the floor of the Senate and demand that Senator McCarthy be censured. On August 6, 1951, Senator William Benton, Democrat of Connecticut, moved that the Senate authorize a wider investigation of McCarthy's conduct, and, if the evidence warranted it, expel him from the Senate. And on September 28, Senator Benton followed up with a 64-page statement before the Subcommittee on Privileges and Elections, in which he backed up his resolution with ten specific cases against McCarthy.

In Senator Benton's words:

"Case Number One establishes that Senator McCarthy apparently lied under oath to a Senate Foreign Relations subcommittee last year by denying he had said in a speech at Wheeling, W. Va., that 'I have here in my hand a list of 205 names that were made known to the Secretary of State as being members of the Communist Party.' This case further indicates deliberate deception of the Senate by Senator McCarthy in altering the text of that sensational speech when he read it into the Congressional Record.

"Case No. 2 illuminates the lack of character, ethical standards and integrity of Senator McCarthy by detailing his acceptance of $10,000 from the Lustron Corp., a corporation which had had a vital interest in the outcome of the deliberations of a Senate housing committee presided over by Senator McCarthy as acting chairman and vice

chairman, and a corporation dependent on the RFC, which in turn is the concern of the Banking and Currency Committee, of which Senator McCarthy was a member.

"*Case No. 3* highlights Senator McCarthy's efforts to hoax the Senate with the incredible charge that Gen. George Catlett Marshall has been part of a 'conspiracy so immense and an infamy so black as to dwarf any previous such venture in the history of man.'

"*Case No. 4* establishes that Senator McCarthy practiced calculated deceit on the United States Senate and the people of the country by falsely stating on the Senate floor that Senator Tydings had forced him to make public the names of Government officials against whom his unsubstantiated charges of communism were directed.

"*Case No. 5* reviews the fraud and deceit practiced by Senator McCarthy on the Senate, on the people of the United States, and on the people of Maryland through taking major responsibility for what this subcommittee, in its investigation of the Maryland elections, already has branded as 'a despicable, back-street campaign,' and in particular through responsibility for the lies in its campaign tabloid from the Record.

"*Case No. 6* examines an instance of deliberate deception of the Senate by Senator McCarthy in offering to repeat off the floor, away from the umbrella of senatorial immunity, libelous statements which he later refused to repeat off the floor.

"*Case No. 7* shows Senator McCarthy pressing on the Senate a claim to possess a so-called FBI chart consisting of photostats listing Communists in the State Department, when in fact, on the word of J. Edgar Hoover, the FBI 'did not send any such chart to the State Department and, of course, made no evaluation of information as was indicated.***'

"*Case No. 8* illustrates conscious 'and deliberate deception of the Senate in Senator McCarthy's promise to list the names of 81 Communists for any Senate committee—a promise on which he was forced to renege—after implying they were the fruit of his own investigations—because in fact his cases obviously came from a 3-year old list of unnamed cases previously compiled by a House committee.

"*Case No. 9* raises the question whether Senator Mc-Carthy falsely accused Americans and excused convicted Germans involved in the infamous Malmédy massacre, possibly on the say-so of a member of the German underground, and whether Senator McCarthy deliberately lied about the Malmédy affair on the floor of the Senate.

"*Case No. 10* adds to the evidence that Senator Mc-Carthy himself committed perjury the further evidence that he continues to employ a man described by a Senate committee as his administrative assistant who, while in his employ, is charged with committing perjury as well as with other serious misdeeds."

Senator Benton concluded by observing, "I do not suggest that these ten case stories which I have submitted to you by any means exhaust the flood of material that has poured in upon me and my office staff. Quite the contrary. These could be multiplied to an extent I've had no time to determine."

For the next year, the Subcommittee sifted Senator Benton's evidence; and finally, in the last days of the Eighty-Second Congress, it issued a report which neither confirmed nor denied the charges, but posed them once again as a series of unanswered questions. McCarthy termed the report a "new low in dishonesty and smear."

Meanwhile, Benton, unlike McCarthy, was willing to waive Senatorial immunity; he did so, and invited McCarthy to sue him. McCarthy responded with a suit for two million dollars. Benton refused to withdraw his charges, and McCarthy eventually withdrew the suit.

Senators McCarthy and Benton were both up for re-election that fall of 1952; and the McCarthy forces concentrated their fire on Benton. The nationwide political trend, with Dwight D. Eisenhower at the head of the ticket, strongly favored the Republicans. Senator McCarthy was re-elected, although he trailed the Republican ticket in Wisconsin; and Senator Benton was defeated.

In January of 1953, the Republicans took control of Congress, and Senator McCarthy became Chairman of the Senate Committee on Government Operations and also of its Permanent Subcommittee on Investigations. The fact that the Executive branch of the Federal Government was now under the direction of a Republican President and administration did not inhibit McCarthy in the least. No longer was he a lone Senator of the minority party; he now had a committee, and a committee staff, of his own.

McCarthy's first subcommittee investigations shredded the effectiveness and morale of the Voice of America, and severely damaged the operation and prestige of the entire overseas information program. McCarthy also permitted his subcommittee to serve as a forum for the charge of J. B. Matthews that, "The largest single group supporting the Communist apparatus in the United States today is composed of Protestant clergymen . . . The Communist Party has enlisted the support of at least 7,000 Protestant clergymen . . ."

By 1954, McCarthy had focused once again on an old target—the United States Army. This was to prove his undoing. In the late spring, the nation was treated to the spectacle of the televised Army-McCarthy hearings. The hearings ran some thirty-five days, and at some points had a television audience of more than twenty million Americans.[14]

The Army-McCarthy hearings concluded on June 17, and on July 30, Senator Ralph Flanders, Republican of Vermont, followed in the footsteps of former Senator Benton of Connecticut and introduced a resolution to censure McCarthy. On August 2, by a vote of 75 to 12, the Senate authorized a new inquiry into McCarthy's conduct. A special investigating committee was set up, the Select Committee to Study Censure Charges, headed by Senators Arthur V. Watkins, Republican of Utah, as Chairman, and Edwin C. Johnson, Democrat of Colorado, as Vice Chairman. Two Southern Democrats, Senators John C. Stennis of Mississippi and Sam J. Ervin, Jr., of North Carolina, and two Midwestern Republicans, Senators Frank Carlson of Kansas and Francis Case of North Dakota completed the committee.

One of the most interesting features of this new committee was the conservative complexion of its membership. Not one champion of the Roosevelt "New Deal" or the Truman "Fair Deal" was included; the noted liberals of both parties were absent. No one in his right mind could characterize

---

[14] In themselves, the hearings provided drama sufficient for an analytical book by Michael Straight, *Trial by Television* (Beacon Press, Boston, 1954).

any member of the committee as "radical"; as a matter of fact, some of the members were so conservative in their voting records that they could scarcely even qualify as "moderates" or "middle-of-the-roaders." It was a select delegation from the inner circles of the Old Guard conservatives of both parties that fixed a cold, penetrating eye on McCarthy.

On August 21, the committee opened hearings, and on September 17, concluded them. The committee recommended that the Senate censure McCarthy on two counts: his abuse and contempt toward the Senate Subcommittee on Priveleges and Elections while it was investigating Senator Benton's charges in 1951 and 1952, and his abuse and contempt toward the Select Committee itself in 1954. On December 2, 1954, Senator McCarthy was formally condemned by the United States Senate; the vote was 67 to 22.

McCarthy was finished. He still retained his Senate seat and prerogatives; but no one paid any attention to him. He continued his attacks and accusations, and, if anything, became more shrill and incoherent. But the newspapers ceased to treat him as "news"; his rantings were ignored, and he was forced to depend on organizations such as the Christian Nationalist Crusade to publish his material.[15] McCarthyism as a national force had ceased to exist; and, two and one-half years later, McCarthy himself passed into history with his death on May 2, 1957.

[15] Joseph R. McCarthy, *Twenty Years of Treason; Historic Milwaukee Speech Which Radio and Television Refused to Carry* (Christian Nationalist Crusade, Los Angeles).

Chapter XXXIV

THE STRUGGLE FOR INTEGRATION

In 1954, the final year of Senator McCarthy's power, a new struggle of national significance began in another area of human rights—the right of equal public school education for all. On May 17, 1954, Chief Justice Earl Warren, speaking for a unanimous Supreme Court, declared:

"We conclude that in the field of public education the doctrine of 'separate but equal' has no place. Separate educational facilities are inherently unequal. Therefore, we hold that the plaintiffs and others similarly situated for whom the sections have been brought are, by reason of the segregation complained of, deprived of the equal protections of the laws guaranteed by the Fourteenth Amendment."[1]

This affected every state; and, at the same time, the Court also announced its decision on a separate case involving racial segregation in the public schools of Washington, D.C.[2] Since the Fourteenth Amendment applies only to the states, the Court, in striking down public school segregation in the District of Columbia, relied on the due-process guarantee contained in the Fifth Amendment. Again, the decision was written by Chief Justice Warren, and again it represented the unanimous verdict of the Court.

Interestingly enough, the case affecting the states, *Brown v. Board of Education of Topeka,* was not one case, but instead represented four cases which had been heard in the Court's 1952 term. Not unexpectedly, two of these four cases were from the Deep South, from Virginia and South Carolina. Another was from the Border State of Delaware. But,

[1] *Brown v. Board of Education of Topeka,* 347 US 483.
[2] *Bolling v. Sharpe,* 347 US 497.

surprising to many, the fourth case was from Kansas.[3] The Kansas case illustrated the "local option" type of segregation; by authority of a state statute which permitted cities of more than fifteen thousand population to maintain separate schools for Negroes and whites, the City of Topeka, the capital city of the state, required Negro children to attend public elementary school on a segregated basis. The Court grouped the Virginia, South Carolina, Delaware and Kansas cases together under the heading of the Kansas case and ruled on all four simultaneously, along with the District of Columbia case, *Bolling v. Sharpe.*

Recognizing the complexity of abolishing school segregation, the Court, while making clear the desegregation would be universally required through the United States, did not require that immediate action be taken. Instead, the Court announced that decrees implementing the decision would not be handed down until further legal rearguments could be heard. The Justices invited the attorneys general of the states affected to advise the Court by submitting legal briefs setting forth their thinking and by appearing in person before the Court and presenting voluntary testimony. The following year, on May 31, 1955, following the scheduled legal rearguments, the Court delivered its supplementary decision, in which it set forth the manner in which the law was to be applied. In the words of the unanimous decision, written by Chief Justice Warren: ". . . the courts will require that the defendants make a prompt and reasonable start toward full compliance . . . Once such a start has been made, the courts may find that additional time is necessary to carry out the ruling in an effective manner. The burden rests upon the defendants to establish that such time is necessary in the public interest and is consistent with good-faith compliance at the earliest practicable date."[4]

The pattern of the next several years to come was soon apparent following the Supreme Court's supplementary decision in May of 1955. The Border States complied and generally without incident; in fact, some sections in the

[3] There was a certain irony that Kansas, the home of John Brown, a state with a unique abolitionist history and tradition, should be practicing segregation almost a century after the Civil War.

[4] *Brown v. Board of Education of Topeka,* 349 US 294.

Border State areas did not wait for the supplementary decision, but instead went ahead and integrated public schools shortly after the 1954 decision. Integration proceeded most smoothly in West Virginia, in the District of Columbia, and in Missouri, most populous of the Border States. By September, 1955, St. Louis, the eighth largest city in the nation, had a completely integrated public school system. Integration also was to be accomplished in the other Border States —Maryland, Delaware, Oklahoma, and in the most "southern" of the Border States, Kentucky.

Of the eleven states which adhered to the Confederacy, three—Tennessee, Arkansas, and Texas—indicated partial willingness to comply, and in all three, some integration took place.

A second group of three Deep South states showed a slight measure of compromise. North Carolina permitted some token desegregation, while, for the first time, Florida and Louisiana opened their state universities to Negroes. However, Louisiana appeared quite as defiant as the five "hard core" segregationist states—Virginia, South Carolina, Georgia, Alabama, and Mississippi—in asserting that integration would never be permitted in elementary or secondary schools.

In all eleven states of the old Confederacy, the state government responded to the Supreme Court decisions outlawing school segregation by enacting special legislation designed to limit integration or prevent it altogether. Each of these states passed resolutions protesting the Court's ruling, and some went so far as to employ the constitutional arguments of interposition and nullification, declaring the Supreme Court decisions to be "null and void." All but Florida, Tennessee, and Texas changed their compulsory school attendance laws, either modifying them or abolishing them altogether. A great variety of legislation was adopted, each measure aimed at circumventing the Court decisions. Virginia led the way with "massive resistance," the term Virginia political leaders used to describe a plan resting upon a series of hastily enacted state laws. These new laws were so arranged that it was anticipated as and when the Federal Courts struck down each law or group of laws as unconstitutional, the state government could fall back upon the next group, a strategy it was hoped would delay and thwart integration indefinitely.

The National Association for the Advancement of Colored People became a prime target for many Southern legislatures. Investigations were authorized and carried out, and demands were made that state and local NAACP officials turn over all membership lists and lists of contributors.

Most disturbing of all was the tolerant way in which law enforcement officials regarded wanton violations of the legal rights of Negroes. State officials deplored violence, and many were sincere; but when it came to enforcing the law, the responsible officers, especially county sheriffs, often looked the other way when the Negro was the target of segregationists. The nation was shocked to discover that in the 1950s, Negroes could be assaulted, beaten, even murdered in cold blood in some areas of the South, particularly Mississippi and nothing whatever would be done.

The spearhead of the anti-integration movement was the White Citizens Council organization, which began in Mississippi soon after the 1954 Supreme Court decisions, and quickly spread to other Southern states. The movement was aimed at "keeping the Negro in his place," which was to be accomplished by economic pressure of every kind, and, if necessary, by direct physical intimidation. Although the main White Citizens Council organization stopped short of advocating physical violence, there were offshoot groups which were not reluctant to do so. Unlike the Ku Klux Klan of the 1920s, the White Citizens Councils of the 1950s made no secret of their membership. The Klan of old consisted almost exclusively of low-income, poorly-educated Southerners, and was scorned by the respected and influential members of Southern communities. In contrast, the White Citizens Council movement was openly led by prominent Southerners, such as corporation lawyers, industrialists, bankers, and even judges and public officials.

This extremist movement was quite effective in some areas of the South in accomplishing what its leaders considered to be a key goal—the creation of an atmosphere of fear which would preclude any local Negroes from bringing lawsuits either to desegregate schools or to secure the franchise.

Throughout 1955, public school integration continued to be the center of attention in the whole area of intergroup relations. Nonetheless, certain advances were made in other fields, advances which tended to be overlooked because of the school question. Three states—Pennsylvania, Michigan, and Minnesota—enacted legislation barring discrimination in employment, while Colorado strengthened the existing law. And the Interstate Commerce Commission decreed that segregation on interstate travel in trains and buses and also segregation in public waiting rooms in railway and bus terminals must end by January 10, 1956.

In 1955, there occurred the first incidents in a chain of events which would attract new national and international attention to the extent of discrimination imposed on the Southern Negro. Throughout the Deep South, the custom regarding public transit was for whites to enter buses and trolleys by the front door, progressively filling seats from the front toward the back. Negroes were required to do just the opposite, to enter by the back door, and take seats progressively toward the front. If the bus or trolley became crowded enough that white and Negro passengers met in taking seats in the center of the car, the Negroes were expected to defer to the whites, to give up their seats, and to stand in the back of the car. This system has long been resented by Negroes, and in Montgomery, Alabama, a Negro woman refused to give up her seat and stand in the back of the bus when directed to do so by the bus driver. Consequently, she was taken to police court and fined.

This touched off the famous "Montgomery bus boycott." Negroes, whose patronage was important to the bus system, simply refused to ride. The Reverend Martin Luther King, a young Protestant clergyman, became internationally famous for his leadership in the Negro protest movement and for his program of nonviolent resistance to segregation. The Reverend Dr. King and his colleagues underwent harassment of various kinds, and 115 persons active in the boycott movement were indicted under an Alabama law which, strangely enough, had originally been designed to curb violence in labor disputes. Withstanding on one hand the great pressures brought to break the boycott, and on the other the incitements to react with violence, the Negro population

of Montgomery held firm to their policy of passive resistance.
Their patience and dignity won admiration even in the
South itself, as many white Southerners came to recognize
the spiritual force which sustained the movement. Finally,
after several years, a clearcut victory was won; Montgomery
buses were integrated, and without violence.

Probably more than any other single struggle to achieve
integration in a Southern community, the Montgomery story
deeply moved people in many parts of the world. Other integration episodes would attract greater national and international attention, but because of the tension involved, the
threat of violence, the vivid clash between two philosophies
of life. The Montgomery story, because it was a successful
application of religiously motivated passive resistance, was
to stand as an outstanding moral accomplishment in the history of the nation.

But segregationists continued their militancy, and prepared
to put their case to the nation. On May 12, 1956, the famous
"Southern Manifesto" was introduced in Congress, bearing
the signatures of nineteen Senators and 77 Representatives.
This protest against integration characterized the Supreme
Court decisions as "clear abuse of judicial power [which]
climaxes a trend in the Federal judiciary undertaking to
legislate in derogation of the authority of Congress and to
encroach upon the reserved rights of the states and the
people." The extent of strong anti-integration pressure
building up in the South was indicated by the fact that all
the Senators from the eleven Deep South states, save only
three, had signed (those who refused were Senator Lyndon
B. Johnson of Texas, the Senate Majority Leader, and the
two Senators from Tennessee, Estes Kefauver and Albert
Gore) and that most of the Representatives who had declined to sign consequently faced new opposition at home.
Some Southern Congressmen, several with considerable
seniority, failed to win renomination solely because they had
held out against signing the "Manifesto."

As months passed, the year of 1956 continued to present
a grim picture of defiance in the South. In August and
September violence erupted as schools were integrated in
Clay and Sturgis, Kentucky, in Clinton, Tennessee, and in
Mansfield, Texas. The Governors of Kentucky and Ten-

nessee refused to give way to mob rule, and declared that they would uphold the law and the directives of the federal courts. Both Governors, Albert B. Chandler of Kentucky, and Frank Clement of Tennessee, sent state troops to enforce order, fully equipped troops armed even with tanks, a graphic symbol of the power of the state government to uphold law and order. In Texas, however, it was shown that, in cases of violence, the power of the state government would be used to maintain segregation; ardent segregationist Governor Price Daniel sent Texas Rangers into Mansfield to put down violence, and also to prevent school integration there.

At election time of 1956, attention turned toward Louisiana, where Negroes not only failed to make gains in terms of voting registration, but where many Negro voters already on the rolls were disenfranchised. In Ouachita Parish alone, thousands of Negroes were stricken from the voting rolls. Early in 1956, there were some 4,000 qualified, registered Negro voters in that north-central Louisiana county; following the purge, the number had dropped to 654. Other purges, large and small, were executed in other parts of the South.

The intransigent attitude of the South attracted no sympathy in other parts of the nation. No political leader from any other section acted as an apologist. Even conservative industrialists became alarmed at the growing violence, and cancelled plans for new Southern plants. Another sign that the South stood alone was the continued willingness of other states across the nation to enact new enforceable anti-discrimination measures. In 1957, Washington adopted a new law barring discrimination in education; Wisconsin strengthened the existing law barring discrimination in employment; and three states, Colorado, Washington and Oregon, enacted laws barring discrimination in public accommodation.

But the most important advance was to come on the national level. Disregarding the pleas and the threats of its Southern members, Congress enacted the first civil rights bill in the 82 years since Reconstruction.

The new civil rights bill[5] was not as strong as the defenders of civil rights had hoped, but it was still a considerable

[5] 71 Stat. 634, September 9, 1957.

step forward. Principally, the bill did three things: 1) It set up a Division on Civil Rights, under the direction of a U.S. Assistant Attorney General, in the Department of Justice. This elevated the standing and prestige of civil rights activities in the Justice Department, as well as making available more facilities for expanded work in this area. 2) It authorized the creation of a Commission on Civil Rights, the members of which would be appointed by the President with the advice and consent of the Senate. This federal commission, set up on a two-year basis, would investigate allegations concerning denial of equal protection of the law and of voting rights. 3) It authorized the U.S. Attorney General to institute civil actions in the federal courts on behalf of any citizen denied lawful voting rights, and to obtain temporary or permanent injunctions in order to secure and protect these voting rights. Previously, any citizen denied his voting rights had to bring suit himself, a courageous and costly act for any Southern Negro.

The biggest news story concerning equal rights in 1957 was yet to come, however; and it was to come about in the most unexpected manner. As Harry S. Ashmore, Executive Editor of the Arkansas Gazette has said, "Little Rock, by any definition, was perhaps the most unlikely site in the South for a second Fort Sumter. And Orval E. Faubus was certainly the most unlikely candidate for the distinction of being the Southern governor who would attempt to recreate the sounds of the past in the very season when the first earth satellite was circling the autumn skies emitting the unnerving sounds of the future."[6]

Little Rock's schools were scheduled to open on September 3, 1957; and on August 28, the federal court ruled that integration must begin then. Little Rock did not show resistance; for three years, the school board had been working on an integration plan. But, on September 3, when the Negro students went to Little Rock's Central High School, state troops barred their entrance into the school. After a conference with President Eisenhower, Governor Faubus withdrew the state troops on September 22. But by that

---

[6] Harry S. Ashmore, *An Epitaph for Dixie*, (W. W. Norton and Co., New York, 1958), p. 38.

time, the ardent segregationists in the Little Rock area had become so inflamed that they gathered in mobs and prevented the Negro students from entering Central High. The police seemed unwilling or unable to restrain the mobs. President Eisenhower then electrified the nation by ordering into federal service all 10,000 members of the Arkansas National Guard, and by sending 1,000 soldiers of the 101st Airborne Division of the U.S. Army into Little Rock. Order was quickly restored and the Negro students were admitted. The federal troops remained to uphold the law for the entire school year, and were not withdrawn until May 28, 1958.

Great national interest focused on Little Rock, as Americans in all parts of the country realized that federal troops could not be maintained in Little Rock indefinitely, nor could they be used to implement integration throughout the South. What would happen when the troops were withdrawn?

The Little Rock school board hoped to find the way out through legal means, and on February 20, 1958, it petitioned the local federal district court to postpone desegregation. On June 20, the petition was granted, but on August 18, this ruling was reversed by the court of appeals. Meanwhile, in July, Governor Faubus had won renomination for a third term—tantamount to election in Democratic Arkansas—and in August, a special session of the legislature met to give the governor power to close the schools to Arkansas, if necessary, to prevent integration.

On September 12, 1958, the United States Supreme Court, convening in a special term in order to cope with the Little Rock crisis, declared unanimously that integration must proceed as scheduled. Governor Faubus responded by closing all of Little Rock's four high schools. On September 27, a special referendum was held in Little Rock, on the question of accepting immediate integration. Integration was rejected by a vote margin of more than two-to-one.

Virginia found itself in much the same situation, as several Virginia schools were ordered integrated by the federal courts. Governor Almond responded as had Governor Faubus; he closed schools in Norfolk, Front Royal and Charlottesville.

Both Arkansas and Virginia then tried to put in effect "private school systems," and thus to operate the public schools on a segregated basis. Federal courts quickly struck down any legal use of tax funds to implement such a subterfuge.

Feeling ran high; and in October, the building of the integrated Clinton, Tennessee, High School was demolished by dynamite blasts. But, as months passed, public opinion in Southern states showed a significant shift; many Southerners had finally understood that they did not have a choice between segregated schools or integrated schools, but rather the choice was between integrated schools or no schools. At last, the Southern moderates were heard; and they demanded schools, even at the cost of integration.

Significantly, one of the surest signs of change in the South was the new climate of opinion toward law enforcement. For generations, Southern Negroes had been denied the equal protection of the law. Almost automatically, the word of a white person was given more weight than the word of a Negro, and often the Negro who dared to lodge a legal complaint against a white person—no matter how just the complaint—found that the local law enforcement agencies not only ignored the complaint, but sometimes even arrested and jailed the Negro for his audacity in thinking he could bring a legal case against a white man. This style of "legal justice" became even more fashionable following the Supreme Court decisions on school integration and voting; more than ever, it was important from the arch-segregationist point of view to demonstrate to the Southern Negro that he had no real standing, legal or otherwise.

But in 1958 and 1959, Southern moderates came to be increasingly heard in the cause of equal protection of the laws. In some areas of the South, whites with criminal intent found they could no longer abuse Negroes with impunity. There were unprecedented cases of white men being put on trial and convicted for offenses where previously there would not even have been an attempt to arrest them. Great attention was attracted by a trial in the capital of Florida, Tallahassee, where two teen-age youths and two young men in their twenties—all four of them white—were speedily arrested for the rape of a Negro college co-ed, were convicted by an all-white jury, and were sentenced to life imprisonment.

In 1959, attention once again focused on the approaching school year. In order to outflank Governor Faubus and the state legislature, the Little Rock school board advanced school openings from September to August. The Little Rock police were well prepared, and on the first day of school they routed a segregationist mob. Integration went forward in Little Rock's Central High School and Hall High School. And in Virginia, integration was initiated in several communities including the second largest city in the state, Norfolk. Still further progress was reported when another Southern state which had previously resisted any integration whatever in elementary and high school passed over into the column of Southern states with some public school integration; such was the situation in Florida, when Miami put into effect a plan of limited integration.

In other parts of the nation, 1959 also marked progress. Colorado became the first state to enact a law prohibiting discrimination in private housing, and Connecticut, Massachusetts and Oregon passed similar laws later the same year. California and Ohio joined the fourteen other states having effective fair-employment-practice laws with commission-type enforcement procedures, and California also enacted a law prohibiting discrimination in public, publicly-aided, and redevelopment housing.

The autumn of 1959 was notable for yet another accomplishment, this one on the national level. In September, 1959, the Commission on Civil Rights, which had been established by act of Congress in 1957, issued a report summarizing its findings and its recommendations.[7] The most important of these recommendations was that appropriate means and procedures be set up by the federal government so that, whenever local registrars refuse or fail to accept the registration of qualified voters because of race, color, religion, or national origin, thus depriving these voters of their right to vote in federal elections, the President of the United States could appoint a federal registrar empowered to accept the registrations.

[7] *Report of the United States Commission on Civil Rights* (U.S. Government Printing Office, Washington, D.C., 1959).

The value of the Commission's report was not restricted to the significance of the recommendations; the careful, thorough description of discrimination in the United States from the historical and legal perspectives made the report itself an important educational document. Southern members of Congress protested, but, despite their objections, Congress went ahead and renewed the life of the Commission, extending its work for another two years.

In 1960, there were still five states, stretching in a tier across the Deep South—South Carolina, Georgia, Alabama, Mississippi and Louisiana—which declared that segregation would stay, and that there would be no compromises. Yet this "solid front" was not quite as solid as might seem on the surface. In Atlanta and in New Orleans, there was strong sympathy for keeping the public schools open, even at the cost of integration. In Georgia and Louisiana, and in Alabama, there were numerous Southerners with moderate and liberal tendencies, men and women who adhered to the "New South" of industrialism, modern agriculture, TVA, and a comfortable existence complete with the very latest modern conveniences. These Southerners, silent for so long, hardly were prepared to stand idly by and see their public schools closed, their region deprived of new industry, and their lives and the lives of their children blighted by an irrational segregationist last stand which would halt the economic advancement of the South.

Still, integration moved slowly; and this slow pace generated a wave of demonstrations which, like the Montgomery bus boycott several years earlier, effectively conveyed the dignified determination of Southern Negroes, and caught the imagination of many persons of all races throughout the nation and overseas. In February of 1960, a group of young Negroes in Greensboro, North Carolina, defied the Southern custom of excluding Negroes from lunch counters in department and variety stores. This quickly spread to other North Carolina communities, and then to other Southern states. In every case, the Negro action was orderly and dignified. Negroes would sit down at the lunch counters and wait patiently for their orders to be taken; they would ignore any insults and heckling, and, when store officials called in the police, they would peacefully surrender themselves and leave in the custody of the police.

This was the kind of demonstration in which every young Negro could participate; one did not have to be an attorney, or the parent of a schoolchild, or a potential voter denied his franchise. Hence, the sit-ins provided a graphic symbol of the general discontent among young Southern Negroes. At the same time, the sit-ins did result in the integration of department and variety lunch counters in a number of Southern communities. The sit-ins received much national attention, and sympathetic demonstrations were staged in the Northern stores of national chains which practiced segregation in the South.

And, through a series of moves in the national convention of July, 1960, the Democratic party cast aside its hesitations about the traditional prejudices of the South. The convention adopted the strongest civil rights plank[8] in the history of the party, and then went on to nominate Senator John F. Kennedy of Massachusetts, a Roman Catholic, as the Democratic Presidential candidate. Senator Lyndon B. Johnson of Texas, the Senate Majority Leader, received the Vice-Presidential nomination, and gave his unqualified support to the

---

8 The civil rights plank stated, "The time has come to assure equal access for all Americans to all areas of community life, including voting booths, schoolrooms, jobs, housing and public facilities." It then went on to make seven specific proposals: 1) That a new Democratic administration "use the full powers" of the Civil Rights laws to insure Negro voting rights, and pledged that if these powers were inadequate, "further powers will be sought"; 2) That the party support whatever action is necessary to eliminate literacy tests and poll taxes as qualifications for voting; 3) That every school district affected by the Supreme Court's order to desegregate classes "with all deliberate speed" to be required to "submit a plan for at least first-step compliance by 1963"; 4) That the Federal government provide technical and financial aid to help school districts with "special problems of transition"; 5) That the U. S. Attorney General be empowered to file civil injunction suits to prevent denial of any Constitutionally guaranteed rights because of race, creed or color; 6) That a Federal Fair Employment Practices Commission be created to insure equal job opportunities for all races; and 7) That the Civil Rights Commission be made a permanent agency with expanded powers covering implementation of rights in "education, housing, employment, transportation and the administration of justice." Finally, the plank endorsed the sit-ins staged by Negroes at segregated lunch counters throughout the South, adding that these demonstrations "are a signal to all of us to make good at long last the guarantees of our Constitution." Civil rights was also a major issue at the Republican National Convention several weeks later, and it likewise adopted a strong civil rights plank.

civil rights plank and to the entire platform. Not a single Southern delegate bolted the convention.

As the 1960s dawned, integration seemed sure of eventual victory—but it had already been a costly struggle. From January 1, 1955 to January, 1959, six Negroes had been killed; 29 persons, including eleven whites, had been shot and wounded in racial incidents; 44 persons beaten, and five stabbed; 60 homes bombed and another eight burned; four schools bombed and two more burned; seven churches and four Jewish institutions, either temples or community centers, bombed, and another church burned; and so on.[9] And even this chronicle of violence does not give the full picture. Thousands of Americans, both Negro and white, suffered indignities and deprivations. All this happened in the South, in just four years. The South, the whole nation, was affected. Americans of good will joined in the hope that this had been the last major outbreak of organized racial bigotry which would tarnish the history of the United States.

[9] *Intimidation, Reprisal, and Violence in the South's Racial Crisis* (published jointly by the American Friends Service Committee, the Department of Racial and Cultural Relations of the National Council of the Churches of Christ, and the Southern Regional Council, 1959).

CAPRICORN TITLES

25. *Symonds,* THE REVIVAL OF LEARNING. $1.45.
26. *White,* THE BESTIARY. $1.45.
27. *Chesterton,* THE MAN WHO WAS THURSDAY. $1.15.
28. *Dewey,* QUEST FOR CERTAINTY. $1.25.
29. *Wood & Edmonds,* MILITARY HISTORY OF THE CIVIL WAR. $1.35.
30. *Pasternak,* POETRY OF BORIS PASTERNAK. $1.25.
31. *Wish,* ANTE-BELLUM: THREE CLASSIC WRITINGS ON SLAVERY IN THE OLD SOUTH. $1.35 (Hardcover $2.50).
32. *Valency & Levtow,* THE PALACE OF PLEASURE: AN ANTHOLOGY OF THE NOVELLA. $1.45 (Hardcover $2.50).
33. *Adler,* THE PROBLEM CHILD. $1.25 (Hardcover $2.50).
34. *Walter Lord, ed.,* THE FREMANTLE DIARY (THE SOUTH AT WAR). $1.25.
35. *Fowlie,* FOUR MODERN FRENCH COMEDIES. $1.25. (Hardcover $2.50).
37. *Ault,* ELIZABETHAN LYRICS. $1.65.
38. *Symonds,* AGE OF DESPOTS. $1.45.
39. *White,* MISTRESS MASHAM'S REPOSE. $1.25.

CAPRICORN GIANTS

201. *Hauser,* NEW DIET DOES IT. $1.25.
202. *Moscati,* ANCIENT SEMITIC CIVILIZATIONS. $1.65.
203. *Chin P'ing Mei,* HSI MEN AND HIS SIX WIVES. $2.45.
204. *Brockelmann,* HISTORY OF THE ISLAMIC PEOPLES. $1.95.

G. P. PUTNAM'S SONS

210 Madison Avenue · New York 16, N. Y.